POLITICS, POLICY AND PUBLIC ADMINISTRATION IN THEORY AND PRACTICE

ESSAYS IN HONOUR OF PROFESSOR JOHN WANNA

POLITICS, POLICY AND PUBLIC ADMINISTRATION IN THEORY AND PRACTICE

ESSAYS IN HONOUR OF PROFESSOR JOHN WANNA

EDITED BY ANDREW PODGER, MICHAEL DE PERCY AND SAM VINCENT

Australian
National
University

PRESS

ANU PRESS

∧NZ SOG Australia &
New Zealand
School Of
Government

Published by ANU Press
The Australian National University
Acton ACT 2601, Australia
Email: anupress@anu.edu.au

Available to download for free at press.anu.edu.au

ISBN (print): 9781760464363
ISBN (online): 9781760464370

WorldCat (print): 1247151126
WorldCat (online): 1247153553

DOI: 10.22459/PPPATP.2021

Cover design and layout by ANU Press

Contents

Section 3: Public policy and administration

Section 4: Working with practitioners

Preface

Ken Smith
ANZSOG Dean

This festschrift celebrates the extensive contribution John Wanna has made to the research and practice of politics, policy and public administration.

John has had a close association with the Australia and New Zealand School of Government (ANZSOG) since its creation in 2003. In 2004, he was appointed the inaugural Sir John Bunting Professor of Public Administration at The Australian National University (ANU) and ANZSOG's director of research. In this role he has ensured ANZSOG continues to bridge research and practice, guiding our conferences and workshops to address contemporary issues and challenges, drawing on known theoretical frameworks and academic research, while also promoting new research and organising publication of a broad range of material from both academics and practitioners, offering lessons from past and current public administration and policy issues for the future. After 15 years in this role, the ANZSOG series, which John edited for ANU Press, has produced over 50 books that have been downloaded well over 2 million times globally.

John's contribution goes well beyond his work for ANZSOG. He edited the *Australian Journal of Public Administration* (*AJPA*) for nearly 20 years, ensuring the journal was relevant to practitioners while also meeting exacting academic standards. I first met John in Queensland in the early 90s. He played a central role in Griffith University's impressive team of public administration scholars in the 1990s and 2000s under Pat Weller's leadership. And he has built a well-deserved international reputation comparing Australian practice and developments to those in a wide range of other countries.

As is made clear in this volume, John takes great care to engage actively with practitioners. He listens and observes. But he also appreciates the political context; and he draws on his expert understanding of political and administrative theory to question and critique.

This book has been edited by Andrew Podger, Michael de Percy and Sam Vincent. Andrew has worked with John for over 25 years, first through the Institute of Public Administration Australia and the editorial board of *AJPA*, then, since 2005, at ANU. Andrew was also on ANZSOG's foundation board and helped with the establishment of the Sir John Bunting chair at ANU. Michael completed his PhD under John, one of an impressive cohort of postdocs who have learned the importance of linking research and practice – three have chapters in the book. Sam has supported John in editing many of the books in the ANU Press ANZSOG series. A Walkley Award–winning writer, he has assisted again in the editing of this volume, which is a great testament to John's career and contribution.

The chapters in the book are in four sections, with an introduction to each prepared by the editors.

- The first section focuses on budgeting and financial management, the field in which John is best known internationally. It includes several chapters with an international perspective, plus a chapter by a current Australian practitioner updating developments in financial management in Australia.
- The second section addresses politics, both in Queensland and federally, and examines the changing relationship between politics and the public sector.
- The third section focuses on policy and public administration, exploring broad international trends and developments in China (in which John has become very interested over the last 15 years), and revisiting the role and importance of the state.
- The fourth section reviews aspects of the relationship between research and practice, a relationship that John has fostered throughout his career.

John has now retired from ANZSOG and ANU, having earned Academic Fellow status and 'Emeritus professorial' status at each institution, respectively. I have no doubt he will continue to make a major contribution to public administration research and practice, from now on as an elder statesman.

We at ANZSOG wish him all the best and thank him for his wonderful contribution to the public sector and academia.

Foreword

Jim Chalmers
Parliament House, Canberra

This ANU Press book is a most appropriate way to commemorate the contribution John Wanna has made to the understanding of the practice of politics, public policymaking and public administration. It includes not only acknowledgement of John's work by his peers, former students and practitioners, but additional material that builds on his work, provides updates on recent developments or reflects new perspectives on his work.

Throughout the book are glimpses of John's personal style, most notably his respect of practice and practitioners and his determination to understand the world of the practitioner. But there is more to his personality and style than this.

I had the privilege of giving the dinner speech at the festschrift workshop held at The Australian National University (ANU) in September 2018. It was a light-hearted 'roast', not really suitable for publication in an ANU Press book, but behind it was heartfelt gratitude from so many people for his friendship and collegiality as well as his ability to inspire and educate.

John is an outstanding expert on public sector management, public policy and public finance. But these were not his initial interests, which have evolved over time.

I knew John was from Adelaide when Pat Weller appointed him to Griffith University along with Glyn Davis. Both arrived in 1985 and began teaching in 1986. Pat chose wisely, and Griffith became the leading public administration school in Australia.

In Adelaide, John had had a more radical reputation. His first book featured a bright red cover with a clenched fist; it was called *Defence Not Defiance: The Development of Organised Labour in South Australia.*

John had also been a bass player in a punk rock band he joined during his third undergraduate year at Adelaide Uni in the 1970s. It was called Diamond Dice. They played in Brighton, South Australia, and then went to the UK, playing a few gigs in London pubs. They had an old 1950s ambulance for a van in which they could sleep if necessary. The van finally broke down and was cremated by the roadside.

John continued his studies in Adelaide, completing his PhD on industrial relations.

His conversion from Adelaide industrial relations radical punk to respected and respectable public policy expert came with the 1988 publication of *Public Policy in Australia*, co-authored by Glyn Davis, John Warhurst and Pat Weller.

The 1990s were among the most consequential of John's personal and professional life. It was when he met Jenni, and when the twin boys, Aidan and Sean, arrived and joined his daughter, Erinn, in their home in Rainworth, Bardon, in Brisbane. It was also when John established himself as one of a handful of the most prominent and prolific public policy experts in Australia, and beyond; and when he also branched out into public finance and became a pioneer in the field, and dabbled in institutional history for good measure. It was when he built around him a team of impressive young academics and earned a reputation for collaboration and for generously including others in his projects.

I was an undergraduate student of John's in the mid-1990s. All my fellow students I have spoken to have identical recollections – of an outstanding teacher, engaging lecturer, generous with his time, wonderful company. He wanted us to do well, and we wanted to do well for him. We still do.

Because for those of us who arrived uncertain of whether we belonged at uni or not, many of us from the outer suburbs, he made us feel like we did. Not everybody has had that experience with their lecturers.

He was also a bit of a style guru in those days, a cultural icon – Hawaiian shirts, shoulder-length silvering hair. His dress sense remains noteworthy.

He was a cultural ambassador too, welcoming visiting academics from around the world, like Rod Rhodes and others, with barbecues and beers, and thanking keynote speakers at conferences with an unusual array of quirky gifts that now populate pool rooms worldwide. Being in a serious game need not mean we take ourselves too seriously. John's sense of fun was a key reason I was so delighted when he agreed to supervise my honours thesis on One Nation.

But I also remember his blunt feedback on inferior work. Something that prepared me well for work in politics.

I remember his air of cheerful disorganisation. The very casual – not causal – relationship between agreeing to meet at a particular time and the meeting actually going ahead then. I remember the look of surprise when you showed up at his door at the arranged time. And I remember his fierce resistance to diaries and deadlines. I am told that his casual disregard for punctuality survived the move south and even compelled his colleagues to decorate his ANU office with a 'Where's Wanna' sign.

But his lack of time in his office may have been a reflection of the amount of time John spent teaching and mentoring mid-career public servants, and engaging with the decision-makers and decision-shapers in the public service – one of the genuine and recognised strengths of his later scholarship. Or that he was plugging away somewhere on what really is an astonishingly long and influential list of publications, many of them in collaboration with distinguished friends who are contributors to this book.

As with all good academic work, John's publications strengthened not just the academy's understanding of public policy and public finance, but the public service's understanding of itself. I have been reminded of this as John has generously shared with me his ideas and understandings as I have plugged away in the Finance and Treasury portfolios up on the hill, picking his brain on public finance, budgeting and public service reform. It has been terrific to be back in touch with the teacher I learned so much from as a student.

John's kindness is worth dwelling on, not because that kindness is rare from him but because it is common. I remember well a trip to London and Berlin we took together with Pat Weller in 2000, when I was 22 and on my first ever trip overseas. He took charge of translating into German; I was responsible for fetching those enormous beers for him and Pat from the bar. Michael Keating was on that trip too – he was responsible for character assessments for the rest of the travelling party, especially its youngest member.

While we were in London, John took me with him to a hearing of a House of Commons public finance committee examining whether the UK should split Treasury as Australia and Canada had done. Her Majesty's Treasury had claimed that that trend was now in reverse: John asked for evidence noting there was no sign of reversal in Australia or Canada and that the US had four central economic and budget agencies.

I am told that a festschrift celebrates the transition of a distinguished academic into the emeritus stage of a great career. The Japanese call it 'ascending to heaven'. Us Queenslanders just call it moving back to Brissie!

Congratulations, John. And thank you, not just for the words you have written, as important as they've been, or for the research you've undertaken, but the friendships you've forged, the encouragement you've given, the knowledge you've shared cheerfully and selflessly, and the immense fun you've had – and we've had – along the way.

Contributors

Jim Chalmers MP has been the federal Member for Rankin since 2013 and Shadow Treasurer since 2019. Before election to Parliament, he was the executive director of the Chifley Research Centre and prior to that, chief of staff and economic advisor to the deputy prime minister and treasurer. He has a PhD in political science and international relations and a first class honours degree in public policy (supervised by John Wanna).

Hon Chan is a professor at the Department of Public Policy, City University of Hong Kong. His research interests are the human resources system in China (cadre personnel and civil service system), and governance issues in Greater China.

Michael de Percy is Senior Lecturer in Political Science in the School of Politics, Economics and Society at the University of Canberra. He is a graduate of The Australian National University (ANU) (PhD) and the Royal Military College Duntroon, and he is a chartered fellow (FCILT) of the Chartered Institute of Logistics and Transport.

John Halligan is Emeritus Professor of Public Administration and Governance at the Institute for Governance and Policy Analysis, University of Canberra. His latest books are: *Reforming Public Management and Governance: Impacts and Lessons from Anglophone Countries* (Edward Elgar, 2020); and, with Jonathan Craft, *Advising Governments in the Westminster Tradition: Policy Advisory Systems in Australia, Britain, Canada and New Zealand* (Cambridge University Press, 2020).

Paul 't Hart is Professor of public administration at Utrecht University. He was professor of political science at ANU from 2006 to 2010 and is still a core faculty member of the Australia and New Zealand School of Government (ANZSOG). Recent books include *The Pivot of*

Power: Australian Prime Ministers and Political Leadership, 1949–2018 (Melbourne University Press, 2017) and *Successful Public Policy: Lessons From Australia and New Zealand* (ANU Press, 2019).

Lewis Hawke is Lead Governance Specialist, East Asia and Pacific, at the World Bank. Prior to joining the Bank he was a senior executive in the Australian Government Department of Finance and UK Treasury for more than 20 years, where he contributed to leading-edge developments such as accrual and performance budgeting, privatisation, public agency governance, service quality, integrated reporting and public sector accountability. He has academic qualification in economics, accounting and business management.

Stein Helgeby is now the Parliamentary Budget Officer. At the time of writing, he was a deputy secretary in the Australian Department of Finance.

Jim Jose is Professor of Politics in the Newcastle Business School at the University of Newcastle in New South Wales, Australia. He undertakes research in various areas of political theory, contemporary governance issues, public policy and gender politics. He has published numerous articles in these areas. Further details can be found at: www.newcastle.edu.au/profile/jim-jose.

Evert Lindquist is Professor of Public Administration at the School of Public Administration at the University of Victoria, British Columbia, Canada. He is also Editor of the Institute of Public Administration of Canada's scholarly journal, *Canadian Public Administration*.

Andrew Podger AO is Honorary Professor of Public Policy at ANU, working with ANZSOG. Prior to joining ANU in 2005, he was a career public servant, his appointments including secretary of the Department of Health, Housing and Regional Development and of the Department of Administrative Services, and Australian public service commissioner. He has been a principal of the Greater China Australia Dialogue in Public Administration since 2009.

R. A. W. (Rod) Rhodes is Professor of Government (Research) at the University of Southampton, UK; and Director of the Centre for Political Ethnography. He is the author or editor of 40 books including, most recently *The Art and Craft of Comparison* (with J Boswell and J Corbett, Cambridge University Press, 2019); *Networks, Governance and the*

Differentiated Polity: Selected Essays. Volume I (Oxford University Press, 2017), *Interpretive Political Science: Selected Essays. Volume II* (Oxford University Press, 2017). He has also published some 200 articles and chapters in books. He is a fellow of the Academy of the Social Sciences in both Australia and the UK. In 2015, the European Consortium for Political Research awarded him their biennial Lifetime Achievement Award for his 'outstanding contribution to all areas of political science, and the exceptional impact of his work'.

Chris Salisbury is a political historian and a researcher in the University of Queensland's School of Political Science and International Studies. His research focuses mainly on the political and social history of Queensland and on histories of Australian public policy reform.

Allen Schick is Professor Emeritus at University of Maryland and is an acknowledged authority on public budgeting theory and practice. Allen's experience includes senior positions with the Congressional Research Service, the Brookings Institution, the American Enterprise Institute, the Urban Institute, the World Bank, the Organisation for Economic Cooperation and Development, and the International Monetary Fund. Allen's awards include a Guggenheim Fellowship and the American Society for Public Administration Waldo Prize.

Peter Shergold AC is Chancellor of Western Sydney University. After an academic career he joined the Australian Public Service for 20 years, including five years as secretary of the Department of the Prime Minister and Cabinet. Peter now chairs a range of private, public and non-profit boards. He remains active in public policy and has written reports to governments on major project failure, engagement of the community sector, regulation of construction, refugee settlement and reform of secondary education.

Ken Smith has been Chief Executive Officer and Dean of the Australia and New Zealand School of Government since May 2017. He is also Enterprise Professor at the University of Melbourne. He has extensive and diverse senior public sector experience from roles in New South Wales, Tasmania and the Queensland Government.

Marija Taflaga is a lecturer at ANU. Her research examines political careers of elites and their interaction with political institutions such as political parties, parliament and the executive in comparative context.

Isi Unikowski's career in the Australian Public Service spanned work in a range of central and policy departments, Centrelink and the Australian Public Service Commission. He has recently completed a PhD with the Crawford School of Public Policy at ANU, under Professor Wanna's supervision, with a focus on intergovernmental management.

Patrick Weller is Professor Emeritus at the Centre for Governance and Public Policy at Griffith University, where he was professor of politics from 1984 to 2015. Author/editor of over 40 books on Australian and comparative politics and on international organisations, his latest book is *The Prime Ministers' Craft* (Oxford University Press, 2018).

Portrait of a life enthralled in politics and academe

John Wanna

I was born on Thursday 20 May 1954 in the UK in the West Riding of Yorkshire at Huddersfield Royal Infirmary. My parents then lived in a cold, damp terrace house in Lockwood, a southside district in the borough of Huddersfield, a textile town with a fierce streak of independence. Later we moved slightly further out to Crosland Moor, closer to foothills of the Pennines, into a better semi-detached house with a garden and a garage and a lilac tree, my favourite spot. I was the eldest of four boys (and later three when one died as a baby) who spent much of their early childhood in the UK. Growing up, besides schooling and sport, we worked in my father's bakery, selling football programs at home games for Huddersfield Town, and I did some work as a junior clerk on a weighbridge for the new M62 motorway being built nearby, and in a warehouse supplying local supermarkets.

Decades later my daughter Erinn traced our family tree back nearly 300 years – all of whom came from within the immediate West Riding region. They were an odd collection of millworkers, weavers, cotton spinners, agricultural labourers, boiler workers, railway workers and porters, coal-lumpers and horse thieves. My maternal great-grandmother, whose husband had died when relatively young, and whom I spent time with as a boy, spent about 25 years bringing jugs of ale up from a cellar to the front bar in a Netherton public house. This early background was vastly different to my life in Australia.

As far back as I can remember, I always had an abiding interest in politics even from seven or eight years old. From the age of 10, I delivered morning newspapers six days a week for around five years. I routinely delivered around 12 different newspaper mastheads each with party-aligned partisan identities, and each with bewilderingly different accounts of what was happening in politics (much of which would now be called 'fake news', if not propaganda). Many times I tried to reconcile these wildly divergent accounts of politics and events. I remember asking adults how such deeply divergent views could be reconciled and rarely got an answer let alone a sensible answer – which only deepened my interest in the political aspects of societies.

Growing up in a working-class town in the north of England taught those who were ambitious to endeavour to improve their circumstances; it also starkly illustrated that things well organised and administered could massively impact on the quality of life of those around you in the community. Some neighbouring towns or parts of nearby cities were entirely dysfunctional at that time and local residents would have had little to expect from life chances. Other places were well administered and the local authorities took pride in their own public service to the community, championing neighbourhood progress and community development. Also my enthralling fascination with politics and history gradually led me to ask questions about how the 'modern state' was organised. For instance, how did government work, both in its 'external face' for public consumption and internally, in more covert ways to shape agendas? How did bureaucracies operate, including what were their strengths or advantages and what were their deficiencies or shortcomings, with their impersonal and autonomous formats? I always believed in the imperative for social improvement but maintained a sceptical disposition towards many of the proposed schemes and motives of those making the decisions. For me, it was not just about the obligation of 'speaking truth to power' as Aaron Wildavsky once ventured, but a deep-rooted scepticism about whether things would turn out as planned or intended (as Peter Self explored in many of his works).

Like so many English families in the 1960s and 1970s we joined the wave of aspiring migrants sailing to Australia as 'ten-pound Poms' in search of better prospects, better life opportunities and better weather (the so-called 'ideal settlers' in Australian demographer 'Mick' Borrie's terms – they came, they procreated and they worked). Indeed, my parents had gained permission to migrate to Australia when I was around four, but as my younger brother and I at the time were the only grandchildren, they were dissuaded by the three remaining grandparents. Although we left extended family behind, we were particularly glad to be leaving the foggy, wet and bleak textile town where future job prospects for my parents and the boys were definitely uninviting. 'No regrets' was our family's unshakable motto as we transposed to the Antipodes.

In the UK, I attended six different government schools, going through the system because my parents kept moving. I took to school because it combined three passions – learning, reading and sport (football). I eventually finished at one of the new comprehensive schools set up in 1965 by the Wilson Labour Government,[1] Fartown County Secondary School, where students were streamed according to ability. I was in the academic stream and, topping the A class for two years, finished school just turning 15 with five GCE (general certificate of education) 'O' levels and seven CSEs (certificate of secondary education), with seven firsts and one second in metalwork. At a final career advisory session in June 1970, I was told I should do 'A' levels and go to one of the local universities – Leicester, Nottingham or Sheffield was suggested. This confirmed my interest in further study, but because we were emigrating I could not enrol in a polytechnic to undertake my 'A' levels as a few of my friends did. Instead, I finished off my schooling at Brighton High School in Adelaide's southern suburbs, where I was regarded as some strange being who had a Monty Pythonesque Yorkshire accent. I could swim but not ride a surfboard, I could play soccer but not Aussie rules; but I could also play chess and became the school's top player in the chess team on board number one.

In South Australia's matriculation exam I did well in geography (ostensibly coming top in the state), and in modern history, biology and English, but scraped a pass in the faddish so-called 'modern mathematics' (all vectors, algebra and calculus). I was the last year to be encouraged to continue the cursive writing style, thereafter for a while all classes were taught an abrupt style of italics. These results got me into the University of Adelaide in early 1971 (I also had an offer from Flinders University, but in those days very few buses connected the university to surrounding suburbs,

---

1   Prime Minister Harold Wilson was born in Huddersfield (the district of Milnsbridge, which was next door to Crossland Moor) and as a child I was tremendously impressed with him for his achievements, although he was not our local member, as he was elected to the Lancashire seats of Ormskirk and the Merseyside seat of Huyton. I remember visiting many times the little hospital where he was born, and to this day have many of the books he wrote and the colossal biography of him by Ben Pimlott. It was inspirational to me that the prime minister came from our town, which was by no means the epicentre of the UK – it was widely disregarded, as if it did not exist, by folk in the southern counties.

whereas I could easily get to Adelaide University on the train). I attended university before Whitlam introduced free tertiary education (the old days of postwar Commonwealth Scholarships that just met tuition fees but initially provided no subsistence). Nevertheless, from 1974, I did benefit from the government's free university education policy for a couple of years, receiving a very small stipend even though my parents' income remained modest. In those days only a small proportion of school leavers went to university (a 'chosen few') and Australia had only around 15 universities proper.

Being the first in my wider family ever to go to university, the transition to tertiary education was a bit daunting and awe-inspiring. However, I increasingly took to the life, the patterns of studying and its academic rigor. I double majored in politics, with minors in history and some units in philosophy and economics. It was an exciting time to study politics. Lots of new issues of public policy were being addressed and contested. Moreover, Labor governments were such a recent novelty where I lived. In the early 1970s, South Australia had a very progressive reformist Labor Government headed by Premier Don Dunstan (I later reviewed his memoirs, entitled *Felicia: Political Memoirs* in 1982). At the federal level Gough Whitlam was prime minister, heading a paradigm-changing Labor Government but also an increasingly chaotic one. Both governments implemented many measures of lasting benefit, but also were characterised by dubious if not wayward judgements – something that sat with me for many decades.

I still remember Whitlam addressing students in the Adelaide University Union Cinema Theatrette as prime minister in mid-1975. He talked about further plans for tertiary education and the end of the Vietnam War, but was questioned on what was Labor's policy towards the embryonic East Timor independence movement called Fretilin (questions I remember he refused to answer, probably so as not to offend the Indonesians!). What we did not know but suspected was that he had given a personal assurance to the Indonesian president not to oppose the annexation of the former Portuguese colony. With the collapse of the Portuguese junta in 1974, East Timor was declared independent after a period of insurgency by the Fretilin revolutionary front, triggering a bloody Indonesian invasion. Australia, to our shame, did not stand up to the Jakarta regime until 1999.

In 1975 I was invited to undertake fourth-year honours at Adelaide University, a mixture of coursework and thesis, and was required to settle on a 'topic'. I was assigned a supervisor, the local political historian RL (Bob) Reid with whom I had studied as an undergraduate. After some discussion, Bob suggested that I look at a public policy initiative currently underway that involved both incumbent Labor governments, intergovernmental relations and the dispensing of large amounts of public largesse. His suggestion was that I should look at the proposed 'New Murray Town' of Monarto on a greenfield site over the Mount Lofty Ranges, some 63 kilometres to the east of Adelaide. So, I did my honours thesis examining the 'virtual' proposal of Monarto from a political economy perspective. At the time, the federal government was financially supporting the concept of states developing 'new cities' to relieve population pressure on their capital cities and assist regional development. One of Whitlam's ambitions involved creating a Department of Urban and Regional Development (with the unenviable acronym of DURD) to plan these new cities scattered around Australia. Attempting to obtain new money for South Australia, Dunstan proposed to create the new city of Monarto, a project not entirely at the forefront of the Commonwealth's priority lists because Adelaide had low population growth and little congestion.

Monarto seemed a crazy and contentious scheme by the state government to establish an over-planned, futuristic new city on an entirely pristine site. The multifunction polis was supposedly to be an 'alternative' self-contained communal city of 200,000 people, free of cars, reliant on public transport and connected by bike paths and pedestrian footpaths (I still have some of the wild imaginary concept plans and glossy brochures spruiking the scheme). It would have an ornamental lake, golf course and areas for open air eating (surprise, surprise!) but no real industries; instead three large government departments related to land, agriculture and environment would be compulsorily relocated there (which caused a virtual riot in the public service and mass demonstrations by those significantly affected). It was nauseatingly 'nice' but totally impracticable.

The Monarto folly was a wonderfully peculiar prism through which to observe politics at play in the federation. I spoke to federal, state, local bureaucrats, and a bevy of town planners and in the end produced a critique of Labor's pie-in-the-sky planning; but I did come across a number of planners who would later become more significant to me. One was Peter Coaldrake, who was an urban geographer and later professor of public management (and the first to give me a continuing job at Griffith

University), and another was Mike Keating, a labour market economist in DURD and later secretary of Finance and then the Department of the Prime Minister and Cabinet (with whom I collaborated after his retirement from the Australian Public Service [APS]). He was a big fan of my budgeting research, especially the documenting of Australia's reform trajectories.

Anyway, after years of faux 'Kodachrome' planning, not a single sod of earth was ever turned on the greenfield site. The entire money forwarded by the federal government was consumed by the initial land purchase, professional consultants and planners. Money that otherwise could have benefited regional growth in larger country towns like Murray Bridge, Mount Barker or Gawler was effectively wasted. But the Dunstonian pipedream that would eventually become an open park zoo earned me a high Div IIA honours degree. Sadly, my supervisor Bob Reid at Adelaide University died of a heart attack a few weeks after I got my results – I was not only distraught but also left without anyone to provide references, although some other Adelaide politics staff helped out and asked me to do a PhD.

University remained a strange world to the rest of my family. Both of my parents went onto the Adelaide campus only once; my mother to attend my PhD graduation in 1985 – totally puzzled as to why I was sitting on the podium with the professors and senior academic staff of the university. My father came in late 1982 to help me clear out my room in the Arts Faculty's Napier Tower (I was in the last room in the territory claimed by the politics department; the economists resided further down the corridor and on the floor below including Bruce Chapman, Judith Sloane, Geoff Harcourt and Cliff Walsh). My dad took one look at the full bookshelf and said, 'When do we take these back to the library?' 'No', I replied, 'they are mine and need packing up'. He was a curmudgeonly Yorkshireman who believed we only needed two types of books – instruction manuals and map books. When my third book came out (*Public Policy in Australia*) he took one look at it, and in his Yorkshire dialect said: 't'cover looks like toilet door', and then added without opening it 'Haven't you said all you have to say yet?' Even today, after some 50 books and the two extensive collections in the ANZSOG and UNSW Press series, all the chapters and articles published, as well as all the journal editing undertaken – he would be amazed but not necessarily impressed.

After honours, I spent two years living overseas mainly in the Netherlands taking a break, working, but thinking of further study at the University of Groningen in the most northern Dutch province. On inquiring, I was told to my disappointment that I had to take a transition year before I could begin a Master's degree in European politics. Instead, I returned to Australia, and secured a part-time place (but with no scholarship) at Flinders University, shared with a colleague Michael Sullivan, because while I had been away Prime Minister Malcolm Fraser had imposed a strict rationing of postgraduate places in the university sector and any department even with modest numbers of postgrads had to curb places. After an enjoyable couple of years part-time with the Flinders politics department, working with Dean Jaensch, Bill Brugger, Andrew Mack and Geoff Stokes, I transferred back to Adelaide, my *alma mater*, to work with Bob Catley, who had secured me one of the few available postgraduate scholarships. By now in my PhD I was specialising in labour relations and, in particular, state regulation of unions and the industrial relations system more generally. Working with Bob Catley was inspiring, but I also worked closely with Doug McEachern, Greg O'Leary, Brian Abbey, Bruce McFarlane, Carol Johnson and fellow postgrads Jim Jose, Chris Nyland and Greg McCarthy. Tutoring undergraduates, from first- to third-year, I taught some wonderful students such as Peter Backhouse, who became a lecturer at Griffith then went into university administration, and Peter Mares, later a prominent ABC journalist and author. As the staff situation in the politics department was becoming a little dysfunctional at that time, Jim Jose and I organised a separate postgrad seminar series to which fellow students were welcome but staff could only attend if personally invited.

Working on my thesis on the politics of organised labour – mainly unions in the metal and vehicle industries – and ending with the Hawke Government's Accord agreements with the union movement – I spent a year at the University of Canterbury, Christchurch, in New Zealand. It was the hardest year I ever worked in my academic career as they ruthlessly exploited the 'poor bunny' they had appointed to a one-year revolving lectureship. I was teaching convenor of the large first-year intake (a huge administrative job), took six tutorials – each with 20–25 students – all in one day, convened and taught a second-year subject in comparative politics later in the week, and taught a Masters-level course! I woke most days at 4.30 am to spend two to three hours on my thesis so that I made steady progress even under the straining teaching load. The best thing

7

about Christchurch was the students, who were a mixture of local Kiwis and Pacific Island scholarship students, all of whom were keen to learn and a joy to teach. But I still remember an intense disagreement with one class when I said in a lecture that British direct investment in New Zealand counted in the 'foreign investment' category. Almost to a student they shook their heads in disbelief and said 'Oh, No! British investments are *our own* investments, not foreign'. Australia had long recognised and counted British investment as a major source of foreign investment in the regular statistics since the immediate postwar years (and many critically informed commentators had often regarded it as foreign since before the Great Depression).

On returning to Australia I resumed the tutorship, before getting an offer of a continuing appointment as a lecturer in public policy at the relatively new and innovative Griffith University in Brisbane. Pat Weller had just been appointed professor in the new specialisation in public policy and had demanded two lecturing jobs to teach into the combined undergraduate program covering business studies and administration. Peter Coaldrake, the dean of the faculty and a public administration specialist, appointed Glyn Davis and myself to the two posts, and with Pat Weller as professor, we all immediately clicked and began decades of collaborative research. As our student numbers grew and we made research waves, we were fortunate to recruit Ciaran O'Faircheallaigh, then Peter Backhouse, Liz van Acker, Robyn Hollander, John Kane, Haig Patapan and Patrick Bishop. We also had close collegial links with Margaret Gardner, Brian Head, John Forster, Ross Homel, Jenny Fleming, John Warhurst, Peter Graham, Stephen Bell and Anne Tiernan. Much of our research work involved close collaboration with practitioners and public servants interested in explaining reform trajectories, analysing problems of policy and management, and managerial improvement. We also began to build an international network of co-researchers with whom we could collaborate and develop comparative projects – mainly through Pat's connections but then through the wider team's growing interactions. In this way, we began active collaboration with Rod Rhodes, RJ (Bob) Jackson, Peter Aucoin, Herman Bakvis, Lotte Jansen, Jouke de Vries, Rudi Anderweg, Evert Lindquist, Allen Schick, Fred Thompson, Hon Chan, Jun Ma and Tsai-Tsu Su. Also important to the team were the development of close relationships with important publishers such as John Iremonger, Patrick Gallagher, Peter Debus, Sue McGuinn, Jenny Curtis, John Elliot and Edward Elgar.

Three important developments occurred with public policy at Griffith over the next two decades. First, the emerging 'Griffith Mafia' (as we were once called) produced a number of leading teaching texts and case studies in public policy, which provided integrated books aimed at university courses that not only analysed the field but also assessed the most recent transformations and developments in thinking or practice. Textbooks came out almost on a production line basis within the school. Second, a large number of us, led by Pat Weller, were awarded a national priority fund grant from the Hawke Government, which allowed us to establish a national-level, externally funded multidisciplinary research centre called the Centre for Australian Public Sector Management (CAPSM). The centre held top-level biannual research workshops with analytical interaction between academics and practitioners. CAPSM produced around 20 research books through Macmillan and Allen & Unwin, a wide range of research occasional papers, reports to government and submissions. The centre was then expanded into the Key Centre for Law, Ethics, Justice and Governance, bringing in greater law ethics and criminology expertise – and later became the National Institute for Law, Ethics and Public Affairs. These centres helped boost Griffith's social sciences credibility and standing. Third, the editorship of the *Australian Journal of Public Administration* was awarded to Glyn Davis and myself in 1995 (previously, Peter Coaldrake and others at Griffith had bid for the job, but Queensland was perhaps considered a little beyond the pale). This editorial diversification was one of the first times the institute's professional and academic journal had moved away from the Government Department at the University of Sydney (although professors Roger Wettenhall and John Halligan, and briefly Roger Scott, had edited the journal for about seven years out of the University of Canberra until 1995). The editorship of the journal (which I undertook for almost 20 years) gave the CAPSM group an expanded horizon to engage with scholars in the field and with practitioners who were prepared to write about their experiences. We set about revamping the journal as an academic journal of standing that spoke to practitioners, and, perhaps more significantly, with the tremendous assistance of Rose Williams at Wiley, shifted it from a subsidised publication and made it very profitable for the institute within a few years.

My own research interests and collaborative relationships were developing into public management (with Pat Weller, Glyn Davis, Ciaran O'Faircheallaigh, Rod Rhodes and later Mike Keating and Andrew Podger); more particularly public budgeting (with Evert Lindquist, John

Forster, Joanne Kelly, Lotte Jensen, Jouke de Vries, Steve Bartos and Stein Helgeby), and continued interest in Australian politics and parliamentary studies (via Brian Galligan, Andrew Parkin, Stephen Bell, Tracey Arklay, John Uhr and Ian Marsh). To gain practical research knowledge and a much closer experience of the practitioners' coalface, I took a series of sabbaticals and research secondments, first in the Parliament of Queensland in 1995 where I teamed up with Tracey Arklay to write their postwar history at a gradual pace. Then with the Department of Finance and Administration, which accepted me as an academic in residence in 2000, with access to almost all their internal information about expenditure management. Finally, in 2010, I undertook research with the Australian Public Service Commission for a year part-time, working on strategic human resource management. I also did occasional research engagements with individual departments, writing teaching cases, undertaking conceptual work and providing reports and submissions.

Along with a few Griffith colleagues, I was involved from 2001 in the consultations to establish a national school of government, to focus on executive development in the public sector. In the negotiations, among the various jurisdictions to sponsor such a school, New Zealand had indicated a strong desire to be involved in the project. The resulting Australia and New Zealand School of Government (ANZSOG) was formally established in 2002 with five jurisdictions (later it encompassed all nine across Australasia), and commencing its ambitious education programs in 2003. I was appointed to The Australian National University (ANU) in late 2003 and took up the ANZSOG research chair on 1 July 2004, also becoming the national research director for the new school. I was the sole appointee at ANU with one administrative support staff member to help out, but had around 30–40 ANZSOG-related colleagues based mainly in Melbourne as well as in Wellington, Griffith University, the University of New South Wales, and later Sydney, Adelaide and Perth. Andrew Podger, who was APS Commissioner when ANZSOG was established, joined me at ANU in 2005, firstly as an adjunct professor and later as honorary professor of public policy. Andrew was an energetic collaborator and team player in our ANU centre, who together with me and a few of his colleagues made a considerable contribution to ANZSOG's research endeavours over many years.

ANZSOG was a real opportunity to engage with governments, politicians, government departments and individual practitioners. We ran hugely successful conferences for around 12 years, as well as a series of issue-related workshops and roundtables, hosted public lectures in various capital cities, encouraged secondments and collaborations, and took on a handful of PhD students with ANZSOG-related interests. ANZSOG became a game changer, a Rolls Royce set of executive development programs that not only delivered state-of-the-art education programs to our member governments, but also set the standard of executive education in public management across the university sector (see Allen and Wanna 2016). Most importantly, in the ANU Press ANZSOG series of monograph publications we produced well over 50 titles over 14 years, on issues of crucial concern to practitioners and their respective organisations. Titles included: *Improving Implementation* (2007), *Putting Citizens First* (2013), *A Passion for Policy* (2007), *Collaborative Governance* (2008), *Dilemmas of Engagement* (2009), *Delivering Policy Reform* (2011), *Public Sector Governance in Australia* (2012), *Measuring and Promoting Wellbeing* (2014), *Social Cost-Benefit Analysis in Australia and New Zealand* (2016), *Sharpening the Sword of State* (2016), *Managing Under Austerity, Delivering Under Pressure* (2015), *Multi-Level Governance* (2017), *Australian Politics in a Digital Age* (2013), *The Three Sector Solution* (2016), *Value For Money* (2018), *Opening Government* (2018) and *Successful Public Policy* (2019) – to name a few.

Building research capacity across the ANZSOG network was a protracted process, not least because not all university teachers are actively engaged in research, and not all researchers are interested in applied research topics. Not all governments or departments were active in their demands for research and the timelines between the providers of research outputs and those seeking them were markedly dissimilar. Also, ANZSOG, out of necessity, operates from multidisciplinary perspectives that are essentially investigatory and problem-oriented, so it is not beholden to one academic discipline – it draws from public administration, political science, management and organisational theories, law, accounting, economics, psychology and even some business perspectives. Practitioners appreciated this breadth of insights and expertise, but sometimes it was hard to distil these approaches into coherent research projects across the network.

ANZSOG provided a convenient platform from which to explore public administration issues in other countries especially in our Asian region. Along with a group of colleagues, we formed the Greater China–Australia Dialogue on Public Administration in 2011 and have had 10 annual roundtables, with many of the papers presented at these events subsequently published in journals or dedicated monographs. ANZSOG also became involved in training senior public sector officials in advanced leadership skills from Mainland China, Taiwan, India, Indonesia, Singapore and the Pacific Islands.

After a career in academe, I had produced 45 authored or edited books, 91 chapters in books, 89 articles, and 56 biannual political chronicles in the *Australian Journal of Politics and History (AJPA)*. In addition, I supervised 65 higher degree students in the completion of their theses across a very diverse range of topics and theoretical frameworks (see Appendix 2 at the end of this book). I was promoted to a full professorship in 1999 at the age of 45, and was elected to the Academy of Social Sciences of Australia in 2006. The Institute of Public Administration Australia (IPAA) appointed me as a National Fellow in 2011 and awarded me a Meritorious Service Award for editing their journal for nearly 20 years in 2014. Terry Moran, then president of IPAA stated in the letter conferring the award:

> Your commitment to IPAA and the AJPA has been exemplary and your vision has been instrumental in making the AJPA a valuable and respected journal of record for developments in public administration. You have become the Boswell of Australia's Westminster System and thus an indelible influence on how public administrators see themselves and their work.

In 2019 I was appointed emeritus professor at both ANU and Griffith University and hold these positions to this day.

References

Allen, P. and J. Wanna. 2016. 'Developing leadership and building executive capacity in the Australian public services for better governance'. In A. Podger and J. Wanna (eds) *Sharpening the Sword of State: Building Executive Capacities in the Public Services of the Asia-Pacific*. Canberra: ANU Press. doi.org/10.22459/sss.11.2016.02.

SECTION 1: BUDGETING AND FINANCIAL MANAGEMENT

Introduction to Section 1: Public finance, budgeting and financial management

The many challenges of public finance have long been the focus of John Wanna's scholarship.

Typical of his approach has been the extent to which he has engaged with practitioners, drawing on their perspectives on real-world practice to test and extend theories of budgeting and financial management. His 'red book', *Managing Public Expenditure in Australia* (Allen & Unwin, 2000), co-authored with Joanne Kelly and John Forster, drew not only on interviews with a wide range of officials but also on a period where John was embedded in the Australian Department of Finance. His books on budget reforms across a range of (mostly Organisation for Economic Cooperation and Development, or OECD) countries (*Controlling Public Expenditure* (Edward Elgar, 2003); *The Reality of Budgetary Reform in OECD Nations,* co-edited by Lotte Jensen and Jonke de Vries (Edward Elgar, 2010); *New Accountabilities, New Challenges,* co-edited by Jensen, de Vries and Evert Lindquist (ANU Press, 2015); and *The Global Financial Crisis and its Budget Impacts in OECD Nations: Fiscal Responses and Future Challenges,* again co-edited by Jensen, de Vries and Lindquist [Edward Elgar, 2015]), all drew on a series of workshops and interviews with officials in each of the selected countries.

Also typical of Wanna: he was never entirely seduced by the practitioners he spoke to, but acted as the acute observer, sceptical of claims of great advances, listening carefully to the debates among the practitioners, recognising different perspectives and demanding evidence. Influenced himself by the work of Aaron Wildavsky on budgeting and policymaking, John continually reminds readers about earlier literature and the academic debates about the politics of budget processes and the limits to 'rational' administration. He also highlights how different histories and institutional structures and practices shape each country's approach despite common economic or financial challenges.

Importantly, John shows how budgeting and financial management reform is not a series of steps in a coherent, steady direction, but a continuous, messy, reactive and evolutionary process, always the subject of political and bureaucratic debates that might have been settled differently. This is not to deny that, in hindsight, trends can be identified and explained, some of which are common across the countries studied whether through shared challenges or the dissemination of ideas, including through the OECD. But it cautions against simplistic and self-serving narratives. A strength of his work has always been his ability nonetheless to distil key developments, common issues and responses while pointing to important contextual differences.

John Wanna is not just an academic observer and analyst. He is keen to influence practice and practitioners. He led an ANZSOG (Australia and New Zealand School of Government) conference on austerity following the global financial crisis in 2008, he has participated in workshops in Australia and China on financial management reform and he has made submissions to various reviews and inquiries on the legislation governing Australian public sector financial management. Among his concerns are the importance of the role of the auditor-general and the power to 'follow the money', including via transfers to the states and contract arrangements, the failure of performance management arrangements to attract adequate political attention, and the reduced emphasis in recent years on program evaluation. To an extent, his concerns have been picked up in changes to the Auditor-General Act and the new *Public Governance, Performance and Accountability Act 2013* (Cth), but practice has yet to fully address the matters he has raised.

There are also new challenges emerging that no doubt will attract his attention in future. These include the accountability challenges associated with increasingly shared responsibilities, whether across jurisdictions or via 'collaboration' and 'co-production' and 'co-design', and the financial control challenges associated with 'citizens-centred services' where considerable discretion is given to citizens/clients, or local communities, over the government-funded services they are entitled to and from whom they are provided. New public management brought with it a wave of financial management reforms to improve efficiency and better 'results', in doing so involving the private sector more in public sector service delivery. New public governance (NPG) has yet to have a similar impact on financial management though there have been significant moves to reinforce collaboration across and beyond government. But as NPG extends further, as it seems to be doing, to facilitate more 'decentring' and 'bottom-up' approaches, allowing citizens and communities more discretion and choice, it is inevitable that budgeting and financial management processes will need further review.

This section begins with an acknowledgement by Allen Schick, perhaps the most eminent of international experts in public sector financial management, of the contribution John Wanna has made; the chapter includes republication of Schick's review of John's 'red book' back in 2001, highlighting its international relevance.

This is followed by Evert Lindquist's detailed review of John's work on budgeting and financial management both in Australia and internationally, and how Wanna makes sense of a bewildering succession of budget and management reforms taking an institutional history approach. Lindquist notes that John does not test or generate theories; rather, he employs theories to frame his observations and analysis and speculates what theory might do as he digs into real worlds of politics, governance and central budget agencies.

In his chapter, Lewis Hawke presents his recent research on performance budgeting and management in Australia and the Philippines, linking this to John Wanna's research findings particularly around who makes use of performance information and whether it makes a difference.

Stein Helgeby, at the time of writing a senior executive in the Australian Department of Finance with whom John worked in the early 2000s, describes the many and changing roles of a central budget agency, reviewing developments in Australia over the last 40 years including since the enactment of the *Public Governance, Performance and Accountability Act 2013* (Cth). He explores some of the key issues involved and how and why approaches to budget control have changed, and he identifies some of the continuing challenges.

John Halligan's chapter completes the section. He has worked with John Wanna over many years although they have never co-authored publications. Among their common interests is the development of performance budgeting and management since the 1980s. In his chapter, Halligan reflects on what has and has not been achieved, and the lessons learned, from the many years now of performance management not only in Australia but across the OECD and beyond.

1

Reflections on John Wanna's contributions to theory and practice

Allen Schick

Introduction

I first met John Wanna in print by reading *Managing Public Expenditure in Australia* (Allen & Unwin, 2000), a book that taught me much about managing public finance in other countries. The book was published at the dawn of the new millennium, a time of great ferment in public management and budgeting. New public administration was challenging embedded tenets of hierarchical, control-based public administration, and budget reforms were challenging long-established roles and practices in public finance. Australia was at the centre of these fundamental transformations, and John Wanna was at the centre of interpreting and integrating these twin developments. Reading his study of managing public expenditure in Australia, I realised that his work had relevance for a broad swathe of advanced countries. In due course, John broadened his scope to OECD (Organisation of Economic Cooperation and Development) countries but, in so doing, he remained grounded on his homeland.

One of the lessons I learned from John is that budgeting is part of a portfolio of administrative practices, and that government cannot reform the way it allocates money unless it also reforms the ways it manages the civil service and delivers public services. This lesson is well understood today, but it was ignored by the many countries that tried to imitate Australia's innovations by fencing off budget work from other administrative processes.

In dozens of articles and essays, John went a big step further by connecting public management to electoral and cabinet politics, thereby teaching us that there are political fingerprints on seemingly technical changes in administrative and budgetary practices. In John's telling, a political battle over bureaucratic cooperation had a profound impact on the course of reform, by leading to the establishment of a separate department of administration, which gained a foothold in Australian national government by spearheading reforms in expenditure management.

Perhaps the most important lesson I learned from John Wanna is that basic reforms emerge more from practice than theory. What are now known as medium-term expenditure frameworks (MTEFs), John explained, began as confidential forward estimates that never saw the light of day. As fiscal prospects darkened in the 1980s, the government thought it useful to publish these estimates, but to do so it had to improve their reliability. One small step led to another, and then to others, and ultimately to the introduction of MTEFs around the world.

By comprehending that experience is the mother of managerial innovation, John nurtured a generation of public sector managers through his work at ANZSOG (the Australia and New Zealand School of Government) and via numerous publications that rang true to practitioners. His works were appreciated by academics, and practised by those charged with making government work.

Having connected budgeting to management and management to politics, John Wanna then broadened his focus to comparative studies, among Westminster countries and within the OECD community. John led studies of how the global financial crisis that devastated public finance in many countries a decade ago impacted budget practices.

It is to be hoped that in active retirement, John Wanna will continue to contribute to theory by focusing on practice. He has a lot more to teach us.

Book review[1] from the *Australian Journal of Public Administration* 61 (3) (September 2001): 114–15

Managing Public Expenditure in Australia by John Wanna, Joanne Kelly and John Forster (Allen & Unwin, 2000 352pp)

By almost all accounts, Australia leads the international budget reform sweepstakes. During the past two decades, it has pioneered forward estimates, running cost arrangements, accrual accounting and budgeting, output–outcome measures, and other reforms. Its innovations have been copied in dozens of countries, and the medium-term expenditure framework it devised has been actively promoted by international institutions.

This informative and insightful book describes how Australia modernised public expenditure management beginning in the 1960s and continuing until the end of the century. The authors weave budget reform, with two parallel stories — the rise and fall of national governments, and repeated efforts to constrain the growth in expenditure. The stories are told in chronological order from one government or crisis to the next. This timeline makes it easy to follow events but sometimes drains the book of some analytical coherence. Forward estimates are first discussed when they originated in the mid 1960s (p.54); they re-emerge more than 100 pages later when budget reform was in full swing during the 1980s (p.178), and their 1990's form is assessed 50 pages later (p.234). Although the book has splendid analytical chapters at the beginning and end, this reviewer would have preferred a more concept-based treatment of the reforms.

The authors make a convincing case that the political, expenditure control and budget reform stories are largely independent of one another. Budget reform, they conclude, was 'driven far more by technocratic concerns than by political ideology or economic rationalism' (p.13). Technocratic reformers gained stature through a 1976 reorganisation that hived off expenditure management from Treasury and assigned this function to a new Department of Finance. At the time, the split was thought to have weakened central control over expenditures. In fact, however, the opposite

---

1 Republished by kind permission of Wiley Publishing.

occurred, because the new Department of Finance could single-mindedly focus on expenditure management, which had previously been a subsidiary concern. With an infusion of young reformers, Finance led the charge for budget improvement. This well told story serves as a useful lesson of how difficult it is to foresee the ultimate effects of structural change in government.

Although reformers defined the direction budget innovation took, politicians played critical roles in supporting change. An expenditure review committee consisting of six ministers served as an inner cabinet that sifted through spending bids and established government expenditure priorities. ERC disciplined the budget process and facilitated the use of forward estimates in reviewing proposed policy changes.

The budget role of politicians was also expanded by the introduction of portfolio budgeting, an innovation that has been given scant attention in international circles. By organising departments into a relatively small number of broad portfolios, the government encouraged ministers to reallocate resources within their areas of responsibility.

The book demonstrates that not only are budget allocations incremental, but so too is the process of reform. From their genesis as crude, internal projections developed by Treasury for its own use, the forward estimates evolved over two decades into the linchpin of the government's medium-term expenditure framework. This development was neither smooth nor quick, for the authors show that as long as the forward estimates were private they could not be reliable, and as long as they were not reliable, they could not be used. Building the forward estimates into the basis for budget decisions was a gradual process that had as many difficulties as successes.

Incrementalism also meant that some reforms failed. This certainly was the case with program budgeting which was inaugurated in the mid 1980s but never amounted to much more than a means of classification. In my view, the authors are too generous in their appraisal of program budgeting, and fail to see that it was fundamentally incompatible with the Financial Management Improvement Program and other contemporary reforms. Program budgeting may have been useful in consolidating the previously separate itemised appropriations, but to the extent it transcended organisational lines, it diminished rather than enhanced managerial accountability, one of the enduring aims of budget reform in Australia. The fact that program budgeting has failed everywhere should indicate that the fatal flaw is in its design, not in the manner it was implemented.

The authors write off Australia's evaluation strategy as another reform that failed. But here I believe the evidence justifies a more favourable appraisal. The government made a determined, and for a time, successful effort, to feed evaluation findings into budget decisions. Ministers had to prepare portfolio evaluation plans and all major policy proposals had to be accompanied with a statement of how they would be evaluated. Each year during the prime of the evaluation strategy, the Finance Department published a report showing the extent to which that year's budget decisions were influenced by formal evaluations. Over time, evaluation faded away, probably because it gets increasingly harder to evaluate programs that have already been reviewed.

Although the book covers the post-1996 reforms introduced by the Howard government, the analysis of this period is not so insightful. Most of the interviews for the book were conducted in 1996 or earlier, and the authors have less access to primary sources than they had for the pre-1996 reforms. Because many of the latest batch of reforms are new, they rely more on the exaggerated claims of reformers than on actual results. This is especially true with respect to price-based budgeting. The authors do not explore how prices can be set independently of both market competition or actual costs. My own sense is that price is simply the in word these days for cost, and that little has changed but the label. In any event, the authors know from their own research that reforms which seem promising at the outset do not always deliver on their expectations. Rather than rush to judgment on the Howard-era reforms, it would be best to wait and see how they stand the test of time.

But with respect to previous innovations, the book's footing is sound. Its lessons are especially relevant for developing and transitional countries where there is a tendency to embrace the most *avant garde* reforms. Australia teaches us that true reform is gradual, and that basic institutions must be in place before advanced methods are tried. Expenditure managers in these countries would do well to draw from the complexity of Australian experiences chronicled in this book. They will gain a deepened appreciation of the challenges that must be overcome in putting expenditure management on a sound basis. As Australia learned, and this book reminds us, a country can move very far by taking one step at a time.

Allen Schick
The Brookings Institution
Washington DC USA

2

Australian budgeting and beyond: Exploring John Wanna's scholarly surplus

Evert Lindquist

Introduction

When I think of defining encounters with John Wanna, where I developed a measure of him as a scholar and person, he was not 'in the room'. The first involved receiving an email from him because John had been to Ottawa and learned about my work on the Treasury Board of Canada Secretariat in the context of government restructuring and deficit-reduction strategies (Lindquist 1994, 1996). He thought it similar to his 'thick', organisationally and historically informed, and recently published work on Australian budgeting and its Department of Finance (Wanna, Kelly and Forster 2000). Two invitations flowed from this: the first was to contribute a chapter to a comparative collection he was planning on *Controlling Public Expenditure* (Wanna, Jensen and de Vries 2003); and the second, his insistence that, during my first journey to Australia,[1] I take a 24-hour side trip to fly to Brisbane (since 'nothing was happening in

---

1   This was for an intriguing symposium in May 2001 organised by Meredith Edwards and John Langford on 'New Players, Partners and Processes: A Public Sector Without Boundaries?' in early April 2001, which resulted in a book collection (Edwards and Langford 2002).

Canberra on a long weekend' and I would be totally bored at University House at The Australian National University [ANU]) to meet and join him, Jenni and their young twins to drive to Noosa, overnight in their hotel, return on a bus at noon the next day for the Brisbane Airport and return to Canberra. My head still spins when I think of that whirlwind experience, but I gained a colleague and family friendship that last to this day, which greatly enriched my career. It was just one example of how over the years he has reached out to people around the world.

The second encounter was when he relinquished his office for me to use while I was on sabbatical in Brisbane at Griffith University's Nathan campus from January to June 2004. He was on leave and I had the ongoing experience of receiving visits and calls from colleagues, a variety of PhD and other students, government officials and journalists seeking him out. Every late afternoon, his telephone would start ringing with a slew of calls from the media and I could detect rising panic as journalists realised they might have less background and commentary for their 5 pm filing deadlines. Not only did I develop a sense of the range of John's interests and the extent of his engagement with practitioners, I came to know the numerous, often exasperated, people who wanted to reach him. I also learned how to 'model' and 'explain' John Wanna, an entire discipline of its own. The third encounter was recently on my home turf: I am still trying to find books or discovering them in entirely new places after he spent two weeks in my office at the University of Victoria during November 2017, but our staff fondly recall how much they enjoyed him, after he regularly worked the halls. Such patterns are familiar to anyone who has worked with or hosted John: he loves interacting with people, injecting subterfuge about his hosts, and gossips and hoovers up incidental information that, amazingly, he retains even decades later. Through these and other experiences I gained an appreciation of the range of his interests, the many colleagues, graduate students, and practitioners he has worked with, and his huge devotion to his family.

To the extent that my research and service contributions intersect with John's, they are but a drop in the overall bucket of his overall contributions to Australian political science and public administration, and, later, the international literature. Here I have been asked to provide some commentary on the stream of his contributions on budgeting and financial management and accordingly, I will focus on his work on budget systems and how governments and central agencies have initiated reforms and responded to domestic and critical international challenges. To do so,

I will review some of the later work he is best known for: *Managing Public Expenditures in Australia* (2000), *Controlling Public Expenditure* (2003), *The Reality of Budget Reform in OECD Nations* (2010), and *The Global Financial Crisis and its Budget Impacts on OECD Nations* (2015). My goal is to describe how he approached these projects as a scholar in terms of method and analytic posture in several successive book projects, the kind of colleagues he brought together, the audiences he was trying to reach (since that also shapes how he went about furthering this work), and to venture an appraisal, and touch on some work-in-progress we have together.[2]

This chapter is organised as follows. The first part will review his contributions on Australian budgeting, focusing heavily on *Managing Public Expenditures*. Then, the next three parts will provide overviews of three Edward Elgar collections for which he was lead editor, and ancillary research that John and some of his colleagues have published. The fifth and concluding section will reflect on these contributions and reflect on what they tell us about John as a scholar.

Monitoring evolution and innovation in Australian budgeting

John's seminal contribution to the Australian literature on public budgeting and reform – *Managing Public Expenditure in Australia* (2000) with Joanne Kelly and John Forster – was produced while he was a professor at Griffith University. It was a wonderful addition to an impressive output of research from a group of scholars that, led by Pat Weller and including Glyn Davis, John Forster, Ciaran O'Faircheallaigh and a host of graduate students, produced numerous studies through the Centre for Australian Public Sector Management during the 1990s on Australian governance, many still cited to this day. Although Weller had, among his extraordinarily broad output, covered the Treasury, producing a seminal study with one of my former colleagues, Jim Cutt (Weller and Cutt 1976), it was 'dead just after arrival' because Australia's Treasury was divided into two, with the new Department of Finance taking over the

---

2   There are several works with and by current and former graduate students, as well as the author, that John was instrumental in encouraging, along with other studies he co-authored, but that will not be the focus of this chapter (see Gash 2005; Kelly and Lindquist 2003; Good and Lindquist 2010, 2015; Forster and Wanna 1990; Wanna 2011, 2015, 2018, 2021).

responsibilities for expenditure management and later for a succession of budget and management reform initiatives. It fell to John Wanna and his colleagues to chronicle and make sense of a bewildering succession of budget and management reforms. It was informed by earlier work of John Forster as well as Joanne Kelly's dissertation research on Canadian reforms (Kelly 2000), which John was supervising.

Managing Public Expenditure is essentially an institutional history of budgeting in Australia, locating the importance of budgeting as part of the larger democratic, Westminster approach to governance. John and his colleagues showed the breadth of budgeting, from its macro qualities (e.g. politics, national economic trends, priorities of successive governments, broad budget trajectories and international developments, etc.), to meso characteristics (the budget function, budget cycle and key agencies involved), and to more micro relationships with departments, agencies and other key stakeholders, such as commissions, boards, reviews, consultants or parliamentary committees. The book reviewed the essentials of budgetary politics and the budgetary cycle, such as budgets as a matter of confidence and the secrecy surrounding their development and presentation in Westminster systems. Relying heavily on primary documents and many interviews with budget officials, it provided a chronicle of reform eras, various initiatives as well as their implementation, superseding of initiatives, tensions among central agencies and departments, reviews and results. It reviewed the changes in the budget system in the 1960s and early 1970s as a precursor for the more detailed account and analysis of the major machinery shifts of the late 1970s and process reforms of the 1980s, part of the larger reorientation of public management during this time (Weller, Forster and Davis 1993). The book was also an effort to modernise the analytic perspectives on Australian budgeting, engaging the sensibilities of Wildavsky (1964) about the politics and organisational aspects associated with budgeting but, of course, located in the Australian Westminster context. However, it seems that Australian research was more advanced than that of its British counterparts, in part because Wanna, Kelly and Forster did not hesitate to interview and interact with budget practitioners, and also because they closely followed Canadian, New Zealand and US developments and literature on budgeting. Indeed, John's collaborator and PhD student, Joanne Kelly, would complete her dissertation and move to Canada to take up an appointment with the Treasury Board of Canada, further enriching these connections.

The book tracked the evolution of Treasury up until the Royal Commission on Australian Government Administration, which reported in 1976, followed by the split of Treasury later that year. It chronicled innovations like the Expenditure Review Committee, experimentation with expenditure limits and savings targets. It further chronicled the developments of the 1980s, as British-style managerialism came to Australia: the advent of the Financial Management Improvement Program (FMIP) (1984 or so), a running costs system, the adoption of value-for-money principles, and, later in the 1980s, when overall expenditures continued to rise, the push towards reducing spending growth with *ex ante* efficiency dividends and investing in evaluation to review programs. Such budget-related reforms were soon caught up against the Hawke and Keating struggles, followed by the ascension of Keating as prime minister and an era of major deficits in the early 1990s (225–228). In this context, the book reviews additional innovations such as multi-year expenditure planning (234), portfolio budgeting to accompany larger ministerial portfolios, growing interest in accrual and output budgeting by the mid-1990s, and the ascendancy of purchaser/provider split thinking as Prime Minister Howard and his Coalition took power. With the adoption of the *Charter of Budget Honesty*, Mid-Year Economic and Fiscal Outlook (MYEFO) planning, and accrual 'output-based' budgeting, the result was a significant shift in the core capabilities of the Department of Finance and Administration's (DOFA) expenditure group, with analysts sporting accounting backgrounds as opposed to program-based knowledge. All of these initiatives expanded DOFA's role beyond a traditional expenditure budget office towards more of a management board. All of these developments were noteworthy by international standards, though not without controversy, and *Managing Public Expenditure in Australia* was a primary means of conveying this succession of intersecting initiatives to interested practitioners and scholars around the world, aside from the usual Organisation for Economic Cooperation and Development (OECD) channels. It articulated a different model to the New Zealand approach, being more pragmatic and experimental, but every bit as dynamic.

How the book drew on theory was interesting. Wanna and his colleagues used Wildavsky's (1964) work early on to motivate the study and describe what constitutes the domain of budgeting, but relied heavily on Schick (1997) and background developments in the US along with New Zealand and Canada as comparators. Most of the book was very descriptive in terms of the take-up of ideas and reform initiatives in

Australia and, though drawing on the literature to explain the sources of these approaches, it was not focused on testing or generating theory. In part this was because, unlike New Zealand, Australian reform was not theory-driven or dogmatic, but rather, pragmatic and what design theorists would now call iterative and experimental (Wanna, Kelly and Forster 2000, 311). It concluded, however, by speculating about what theory might do, given what the book covered. It suggested that scholars ought to take an information-based view on the dynamics of DOFA as an organisation, factor in competing cycles or trajectories in the medium and longer term affecting budgeting (e.g. election cycles, business and growth cycles, new governments, government popularity, etc.) and:

> provide explanations for budget systems and frameworks, patterns of resource management, policy preferences and the strategic capacities to pursue goals, the performance of management and the outcomes of decisions, and the forms of accountability for spending collective resources through government. (314)

Wanna and his colleagues also suggested that budget changes may have lagged impacts, only taking root and having an impact in the longer term (313). They also noted the huge importance of political *and* bureaucratic will in driving reform, noting that while reform in Australia was largely public servant–designed, it still needed support from key ministers as reform champions.

Budgeting and the evolving roles of central agencies

The *Controlling Public Expenditure* (Wanna, Jensen and de Vries 2003) project was a natural outgrowth of *Managing Public Expenditure in Australia*, moving from a substantial domestic case study to a more systematic comparative analysis going beyond comparisons with New Zealand, Canada, the UK and the US, to include a range of continental European nations and China. One can easily see that the questions animating a comparative collection of case studies arose from the Wanna, Kelly and Forster Australian case study: to what extent were the pressures on central budget agencies (CBAs), the changing political and governance environment in which they working, the new strategies and capabilities of CBAs, and whether they were the initiators or objects of reform at play, relevant in other jurisdictions? Kelly and Wanna had been sharing research findings in international journals (Kelly and Wanna 1999, 2000) but such questions called for a comparative approach. The project proceeded in the slipstream of the deficit-reduction strategies of many jurisdictions in the late 1990s and early 2000s.

The driving force behind the project was John Wanna, who assembled a mix of scholars, practitioners, and 'pracademics' of different kinds and sought to engage central budget officials where possible. Ten countries with different governance systems were identified, as well as six US states: the more often explored cases of Australia, New Zealand, the UK, the US (national) and Canada; and, as a contrast to these cases, Sweden, the Netherlands, Denmark, Germany and China. Interestingly, when the case study guidelines and overarching questions were circulated, John's message to contributors was essentially not to let answering the questions get in the way of a good story. John wrote the introduction, which provided an engaging canvas of the context, issues and tensions around the evolving roles of CBAs (this, by the way, became his *modus operandi* for the ANU Press series and for the design and proceedings of the Australia and New Zealand School of Government (ANZSOG) conferences). For example, he contrasted the pre-eminence of treasuries in Westminster systems versus the more narrow roles of CBAs in continental European countries, while noting that, due to increasing budget pressures and more political interest in budgets, prime ministers and ministers of finance were taking more of a role in budget-making (Wanna, Jensen and de Vries 2003, xxiv–xxvi). Likewise, he noted that historically Treasury departments as central agencies had been more focused on macro-economic and fiscal policy and far less interested in expenditure budgets, but since the 1980s, as fiscal policy foundered and deficits increased, increasingly more attention was directed to the budgeting, management and effectiveness of programs.

This led to other questions about how CBAs had been changing: were they getting changed by reform, or were they driving the changes? Indeed, some treasuries or finance ministries had hived off the divisions responsible for managing expenditure budgets, creating new departments for this purpose (Australia, Canada). In this connection, John invoked Heclo and Wildavsky's (1974) concept of the 'budgetary village' with its own culture based on trust and shared understandings guiding budget games and decisions, and Schick (1997, 1998) on the pressures on expenditure forcing CBAs to change how they behaved and operated, moving from less controlling guardian entities to more flexible, monitoring and strategic entities with varying degrees of cooperation and oversight of departments and agencies (Wanna, Jensen and de Vries 2003, xxxiv). The goals of the book were to ascertain if CBAs were taking up new roles and responsibilities, if they had new roles in broader decision-making processes, whether they were the objects or initiators and agents of reform, and were new 'village cultures' emerging accompanying the reform changes? The book also addressed future prospects facing CBAs, the challenges they would encounter and the strategic directions they could advance (xxxvi–xxxvii).

Although the experience of every jurisdiction was unique, in aggregate the cases confirmed that the challenging economic and fiscal conditions of the previous decade or so had meant that CBAs had grown in importance but were under stress, typically moving into rounds of repetitive budgeting and tinkering around the edges, with governments reluctant to tackle core programs. As governments and their CBAs (with various portfolios of responsibilities) sought to impose fiscal discipline in different ways, action was taken sometimes as a result of economic and fiscal crisis, sometimes by government political leadership and sometimes by CBAs themselves stepping in to assert change, often in combination and not necessarily in this order. The deficit and debt problems of the 1980s and early 1990s, along with growing public interest in seeking 'value for money' of programs, served to increase the power of CBAs and led governments to develop management and performance frameworks, though differing across institutional and political contexts. As budget surpluses emerged in Australia, New Zealand, Canada, Norway, Denmark, Sweden and the UK due to economic growth and budgetary restraint, new challenges emerged for CBAs that could not rely on expenditure-cutting to anchor their authority. Thus CBAs began a search for new roles and budget procedures, including articulation of top-down frameworks; reduced *ex ante* scrutiny (which provided flexibility to departments and agencies); concentrating advice and oversight on larger or more politically important initiatives; focusing on tracking implementation (with 'delivery' repertoires and using IT to better deliver outputs, more monitoring of spending against formal targets and with more updates and roll-ups); and encouraging, sponsoring or requiring evaluation and other forms of better reporting – including, in the UK, comprehensive spending reviews. In some jurisdictions, particularly with respect to fiscal plans and aggregates, new conventions and legislation emerged to focus on fiscal rules and targets, new responsibilities and more transparency, but an important question was whether these were effective tools or created more constraints or shackles for central agencies and the entities they monitored (263–264). Although the extent of such shifts varied across jurisdictions, the nature of CBA work was evolving: from budgeting to encouraging better management to performance reporting and even to providing strategic advice on budget 'investments', which required new skills and repertoires (265–268); moving from 'bean counters' to analysis, which required new practices and skills to work within broader budget policy frameworks; and moving to a more rapid turnover of new generations of staff, which meant that the old 'village cultures' could no longer be maintained (268–270).

This repositioning of CBAs and their tools and repertoires during the late 1980s and 1990s seemed particularly pronounced in the UK, Australia and Canada, but were apparent in other jurisdictions covered by the book's cases. However, on reading all of the case chapters in the collection, one cannot help but be impressed by the diversity of experiences across jurisdictions and different pathways, contexts, responsibilities and capabilities of different CBAs. As with all of the collections, the objects of comparison (CBAs and larger budget systems and processes) resisted easy and definitive categorisation.

Public sector budgeting, reform trajectories and progress

John's next comparative collection – *The Reality of Budgetary Reform in OECD Nations: Trajectories and Consequences* (2010) – sought to explore the question of whether reforms to CBAs and broader budget systems and processes identified in *Controlling Public Expenditure* had made a difference over the last 20 or 30 years. Interestingly, the workshop that brought together contributors and the first drafts of their papers took place in 2008, just before the advent of the global financial crisis, which meant that, no matter what progress had been made in terms of budgetary results, institutions and processes, they would be severely tested.

John again invited authors to contribute case studies on expenditure budgeting reforms in Australia, Canada, New Zealand, the US, the UK, the Netherlands, Sweden and Denmark, but also invited contributors from Spain, Italy, Japan and Korea (11 countries in total). This ensured considerable variation across distinctly different regions and attracted new cases. His introduction outlined different kinds and elements of reform, which could take shape as: transformative, system-wide reforms; reform of selected components of budget systems; cross-government restraint exercises; review and reallocation initiatives; changes to internal procedures and informal rules; taking up of new technical and specialised knowledge; and cultural and attitudinal changes. This essentially provided a checklist of possibilities of what combinations of reform and pacing might emerge in different countries and provided a basis for tentative generalisations across them. Added to this was the goal of exploring narratives of reform (often touted as transformational) versus the reality of practice in each country, such as when governments might emphasise managerial reforms when budget efficiencies were the real focus. More specifically, the collection sought to identify the catalysts and trajectories of reform, if they were episodic or sustained, and if they were selective or more comprehensive in nature. Once again, the conceptualisation of the study was informed by the work of Allen Schick (2004) who had reflected on 20 years of budget reform.

The findings from the case chapters were, again, quite diverse and it was difficult for the editors to generalise across them. Distinctions needed to made, separating out the experience of wholesale changes in public sector structure and budget systems associated with new public management (NPM) exemplars like New Zealand and the UK during the 1980s, and typically more limited, incremental and episodic reforms to budget systems in other jurisdictions during that era and since. Reaching back in time, some countries – such as Japan, Canada, New Zealand and the UK – had relied on external events as catalysts for reform, while others such as Spain, Denmark, Korea, and Italy were far less responsive to these external catalysts, and others – such as the US and to some extent Italy – seemed not to care. Every country had its own needs and cornerstones guiding reforms and, accordingly, different selective initiatives that it felt prudent pursuing – that said, CBAs were watching and learning from each other, courtesy of organisations like the OECD and other international agencies and experts, but without leading to conformity across jurisdictions. One of the more interesting findings was that some countries and their CBAs seemed to focus on either instituting managerial and performance reforms or on fiscal control, while other countries vacillated between these competing emphases (e.g. Spain and Canada) or tried to tackle both simultaneously (e.g. Australia and New Zealand) but found this difficult to sustain. In contrast to the NPM-related exemplar reforming countries of the late 1970s and 1980s, the case chapters suggest few, if any, major institutional reconfigurations of budget systems and frameworks have occurred in more recent years, though discernibly closer relationships between finance ministers and prime ministers have emerged as the budget cycle became more integrated with the overall management of government mandates. As a result, John and his colleagues suggested that more recent budget-related reforms were not comprehensive, but better described as 'punctuated stability' (288).

Providing stability in many jurisdictions was the articulation of top-down policy and budget frameworks by CBAs, along with multi-year budgeting and integration with government priority setting, which not only generated rules and guidelines but also provided flexibility to departments and agencies. These were complemented by results frameworks and episodic reviews and/or efficiency dividends, or budget clawbacks from programs by CBAs.[3] Such frameworks and approaches sought to guide more sustainable budgeting in an era of surpluses, a constraining influence given that memory of deficits and mounting debts had not been erased. The countries with weaker fiscal and budget performance, and CBAs with less capacity or clout, experienced more involvement from the World Bank, International Monetary Fund and the OECD. Generally, all CBAs had been steadily introducing better procedures and new information technologies for budget booking and monitoring systems, which allow for closer monitoring and control. Such evolutionary and selective changes were not as glamorous as bigger reforms but might be more important in the longer run. However, as the global financial crisis would soon prove, governments were still presumed to be the backstops for the private sector and for citizen investments in financial markets, as insurers of last resort.

Budgeting systems and the global financial crisis

When the workshop was held for the first drafts of papers for *The Reality of Budgetary Reform in OECD Nations* (Wanna, Jensen and de Vries 2010) in June 2008, the world was experiencing the widening global financial crisis. Its effects moved across the world as the collection moved

3   Indeed, Kelly and Wanna (2004) focused in more detail on the Australian experience with efficiency dividends and accrual accounting reforms.

through revisions. Even before the book's publication in 2010, there was no question that the next collection should focus on how governments, CBAs and budget systems in different countries handled the near-global shock and developed strategies for moving forward, and whether the crisis precipitated transformation of budget systems, having severely tested them. Indeed, in many ways we had something tantamount to a 'natural experiment', though, as we indicate below, this had to be qualified because there were many different financial crises experienced across jurisdictions. The result was the third Edward Elgar collection, *The Global Financial Crisis and its Budget Impacts in OECD Nations: Fiscal Reponses and Future Challenges* (Wanna, Lindquist and de Vries 2015).

Positioning the collection required a nuanced approach: rather than chronicle the spread of the financial crisis per se, we sought to encourage authors to establish how the crisis appeared in their jurisdictions and how well-prepared governments and CBAs were to recognise and react to such shocks, and whether any central agencies anticipated that shocks like this could happen to them. We wanted the contributors to provide perspective on the short-term responses to the initial crisis, and to give a sense of the political and governance environment in which the crises were manifested, the effects of the crises and initial responses on political and budget systems, and whether confidence in governments and central budget systems were shaken. To the extent that the crises that materialised in different jurisdictions were comprehensive in nature, we encouraged authors to explore whether ministers of finance and budget agencies had to rely on a broader set of instruments, political support and other institutions in order to respond. Finally, we asked contributors to indicate whether budget systems needed to be strengthened or reformed, and what the medium-to-long-term strategies were for regaining confidence in economies and possibly budget balance. Once again we found it useful to use OECD discussion papers by Schick (2010a) as points of departure. In particular, his distinction between normal and 'crisis budgeting' to capture non-incremental responses – which could involve shortcuts and prime ministers, and not just central agencies working in routine mode – and ask whether the crisis served to dampen or exacerbate internal conflict, and his prediction that, once the crisis had passed, budget systems would stabilise and revert back to previous paths and balances (Schick 2010b). We wondered if there might be a possibility that weaker budget systems and central agencies might undergo reform and threshold improvements.

To guide contributions, a 'readiness–response–resilience' analytic framework was developed to outline the financial crisis response cycle (which itself is complicated), to identify different kinds of crises (e.g. the collapse of financial institutions, credit squeezes, negative economic growth, debt crises, political crises, housing or property bubbles) and whether they occurred in some combination, and to explicate the different variables that might be at play at different phases (readiness for crisis, handling the crisis and setting a new course, and readiness for new challenges) of the crisis constellation experienced in different jurisdictions. These variables included fiscal and financial health, stability and strength of governments, capability and readiness of budget offices, budget system maturity, the readiness and speed of initial government responses, whether initial stabilising responses succeeded, the process and policies for medium-term budget trajectories, whether governments built reputations or suffered consequences, and whether the systems seemed precarious or ready for the next round of challenges (Wanna, Lindquist and de Vries 2015, Chapter 1). Using an approach similar to the first two collections, a diverse range of OECD cases were commissioned: the US, Canada, Australia and New Zealand, Japan, the Netherlands, Denmark and Sweden, Spain, Portugal, Greece, and Ireland. In particular, including Spain, Portugal, Greece and Ireland allowed consideration of jurisdictions with weak or exposed economies and public finances, their attenuated initial responses contrasting with those with more robust budget agencies and capacities.

Given the diversity in jurisdictions, that each country's trajectory was unique came as no surprise, but there were interesting patterns and findings. The treasuries of a handful of countries (Australia, Canada and New Zealand) anticipated the crisis, with Australia having imagined crisis scenarios similar to what happened; some were fast responders, including Australia, the Netherlands, New Zealand, Sweden and the US. Some countries experienced very different crises (i.e. various combinations of declines in financial markets and failures of financial institutions, bursting of housing bubbles, weak public finances and unstable coalitions), which presented unique challenges to their governments, particularly on top of the structural deficits in Spain, Portugal, Ireland and the US. Some governments were comprised of coalitions of parties and had more fragmented budget systems (Sweden, the Netherlands and Denmark), with mixed views on how to respond; others were simply resistant to the notion of intervening in markets and fiscal stimulus (Canada, New Zealand, Sweden), and still others were already in precarious fiscal and budgetary situations.

Interestingly, the governments in Australia and the US, which reacted the most quickly, were not rewarded at the ballot box, a form of public indifference if anything (perhaps suggesting that balanced budgets were an expectation not an achievement), whereas other countries found themselves enmeshed in political crisis (Canada, Germany, Spain, Ireland and Japan). Slower responses came from Canada, Japan and Ireland, although the Harper Government in Canada, under extreme political pressure, was able to buy time by using questionable legislative tactics, undertaking an amazing policy backflip and introducing a stimulus budget, ultimately getting rewarded with a majority government. We found that the countries with weak public finances and budget systems (such as Spain, Portugal and Greece) relied heavily on interventions from the European Union and other international banks, but the crisis strained the ability of the supra-national institutions to deal simultaneously with them. Aside from Greece, we were struck by the limited amount of political unrest. Given the extraordinary nature of the crisis, treasurers and ministers of finance had to work in tandem not only with prime ministers and other departments and agencies, but also with the private sector, other countries and international institutions. Despite some jurisdictions discovering a lack of repertoires, tools and capacities in their CBAs (particularly Ireland), wholesale reform did not follow (unlike the reforms of the 1980s and early 1990s in many OECD countries) – at least, not in the sense of inventing new budget systems – but there were different degrees of strengthening of procedures, capacities and regulations within existing systems, with broader strengthening in Ireland, Portugal and Spain. Many nations simply adopted 'battening down' strategies, waiting for things to improve.

Returning to Schick (2009, 2010a) and his predictions, we concluded that there were few instances of treasuries and finance departments getting overwhelmed, despite varying degrees of readiness, and a need to work with prime ministers and leaders to respond in more comprehensive ways to crises. We saw that the very notion of 'budget system' expanded considerably from what was considered in *The Reality of Budget Reform* collection in order to respond to the challenges posed by the global financial crisis. Existing processes and authorities were effectively levered and, despite some symbolic or procedural tactics, the core features of budget systems served their governments well. Despite a reversion of sorts to existing budget processes and procedures, we felt that a 'new normal' emerged in terms of scrutinising and monitoring progress with budget expenditures. All of the case studies pointed to tentative and difficult paths forward, given the challenges of lower revenue streams, tighter fiscal policy, more budget discipline, the need to deal with underlying structural problems in economies and public finances, controlling real estate speculation, lowering debt and reducing exposure to pension and other social program liabilities, and dealing with the considerable labour market dislocation caused by the global financial crisis. This suggested that national banks and treasurers or ministers of finance would have difficult balancing acts in the years to come, and needed a lot of patience as investments, trust and growth had to be nurtured over longer time horizons.

Looking back and beyond: Appraising John's contributions on budgeting

This chapter has looked at only one domain of John's scholarly contributions, focusing exclusively on his contributions since the late 1990s to the Australian and international literature on budgeting, along with his teaching and research supervision in that area. These contributions alone deserve celebration and would constitute a productive career by any standard. But it does not broach his many other contributions beyond budgeting: his work on Australian politics, governance and public administration, and on Queensland politics and public administration; his histories of legislatures and other agents of parliament; and the numerous doctoral dissertations he supervised to completion. Beyond his regular scholarly duties there have been the many professional development events he led or contributed to, his editorship of close to 20 years of the *Australian Journal of Public Administration*, and his regular media (newspaper, radio, television) commentary on Queensland and national elections. His contributions to ANZSOG also stand out: not only did he edit the ANZSOG ANU Press series (50+ publications), he was extensively involved in almost all of the annual ANZSOG conferences, helping to conceive overarching themes and topics as part of the program committee, identifying speakers, volunteering to draft the animating discussion paper for speakers to consider, chairing or serving as discussant for several sessions and working with Sam Vincent and others to produce proceedings.

John's research on budgeting has been theoretically informed, but he cannot be seen as a theorist; rather, he prefers to dig into the real worlds of politics, governance and CBAs and explore the diversity of experiences across jurisdictions. That said, John has always employed theory and concepts to identify challenges, set out the issues and explore the idiosyncratic experience of different jurisdictions and eras. He provides or invites fulsome accounts and analyses of the history and dynamics of budget actors, institutions and processes, ones that have verisimilitude for practitioners and scholars alike. For John, as a researcher and project leader, nuance and accessibility are both important in the research he has undertaken and commissioned, hearkening back to an earlier time when he dreamed of being a journalist. I suppose another way to think of the gap John has filled with his work is to think of typical OECD events on topics like budgeting exploring particular themes, animated by a discussion paper and followed by PowerPoint presentations and brief papers offered by country representatives: the productive discussions and information exchanges take place in roundtables behind closed doors and over dinners, where trials, tribulations and minor successes are shared and reminders of previous reforms – not just the ones promulgated for public discussion – get discussed and the real learning occurs. Those lessons never get captured in publications but the lessons from various country cases developed and corralled by John do: they show how reform proceeds in fits and starts, how they get superseded or tweaked by later reforms and never quite disappear, how culture changes gradually because of new technology and repertoires (and not just crises and changes of government, but those too), and how remarkably different the experience of CBAs and strategies can be, despite dealing with similar challenges. His accounts lead readers to appreciate that budgeting and reform are more continuous, evolutionary and dialectic in nature (Benson 1977) than stepwise, locked-in and transformative reforms.

John has always been an engaged scholar, in the fullest sense of the term. His range of interests is truly enormous, so his willingness to read and comment on anyone's work is remarkable. When he does get around to reviewing a manuscript (and many have had to wait quite a while), the speed, intensity and quality of his commentary and editing is extraordinary, as his many students and colleagues know, and likewise, he is unafraid to take on his own work. John's editing style complements his writing ethic: given his broad interests, responsibilities and prodigious output on so many fronts, there has always been a backlog of projects but once he gets to a project he works intensively, with great focus, and loves to collaborate. He is one of those scholars who can craft fully formed paragraphs while reviewing source material (whether secondary literature, memoirs, legislative records, or the interviews with practitioners he loves to conduct), happily using only four or five fingers. Along with this engagement comes his generosity in sharing authorship with others who could not possibly have put in nearly as much work as he did; in encouraging and moving along someone else's work from behind the scenes; or in supporting staff on contract with ambitions entirely outside the scholarly world but whose creative spark and contributions John appreciated, not to mention their ability to roll with his work style. He has encouraged and supported many scholars at critical times in their careers. For those who know about John's earlier years, his disposition and experience working in care facilities, and his interest in moving beyond narrow academic considerations, have been revealed in a very different professional context.

What will life be like for John Wanna after holding the ANZSOG–ANU Sir John Bunting Chair in Public Administration? It is hard to imagine such an engaged and dynamic scholar throwing away his pen or turning off his computer (he has at least one significant project we are working on together on budget theory and budgeting while he continues his association with ANZSOG through Griffith University), but over the years, just like the different reform trajectories he has so ably described in his three comparative collections, I have been struck by the diverse retirement trajectories of even the most productive scholars. Many of John's professional colleagues are unaware of his many other interests, including cooking, encouraging Jenni in her career, coaching the twins' football teams, futsal, gardening and raising chooks in the backyard, and his unnatural fidelity to the music of a once well-known progressive rock band, Yes. John and his family gravitated back and settled into their beloved Brisbane, and he seems determined to move into a more complete retirement as a gentleman farmer (*á la* the 'Diggers' movement) and perhaps some contract work for ANZSOG, but I would counsel him: 'don't slam the door …'[4] There will be only so many times

---

4   Advice he repeatedly gave to our second daughter, Sarah, in 2010, when he and the boys would pick her up in a new car and ferry her to Canberra High School.

he can listen through all of Yes's albums, and many of us will miss him roaming the halls and offices of universities, governments and ANZSOG headquarters, brightening up the days of staff and colleagues with his tweaks and humour.

References

Benson, J. K. 1977. 'Organizations: A dialectical view'. *Administrative Science Quarterly* 22(1): 1–21.

Edwards, M. and J. Langford (eds). 2002. *New Players, Partners and Processes: A Public Sector Without Boundaries?* Canberra and Victoria: National Institute on Governance and University of Victoria Centre for Public Sector Studies.

Forster, J. and J. Wanna (eds). 1990. *Budgetary Management and Control: The Public Sector in Australasia.* Melbourne: Macmillan.

Gash, A. 2005. 'Anticipatory budgeting: A long-term analysis of old age pensions in Australia, Canada and Sweden'. PhD thesis. Brisbane: Griffith University.

Good, D. A. and E. A. Lindquist. 2010. 'Discerning the consequences and integrity of Canada's budget reforms: A story of remnants and resilience'. In J. Wanna, L. Jensen and J. de Vries (eds) *The Reality of Budgetary Reform in OECD Nations: Trajectories and Consequences.* London: Edward Elgar. doi.org/10.4337/9781849805636.00011.

Good, D. A. and E. A. Lindquist. 2015. 'Canada's reactive budget response to the global financial crisis – from resilience and brinkmanship to agility and innovation'. In J. Wanna, E. Lindquist and J. de Vries (eds) *The Global Financial Crisis and its Budget Impacts in OECD Nations – Fiscal Responses and Future Challenges.* Cheltenham, UK: Edward Elgar. doi.org/10.4337/9781784718961.00009.

Heclo, H. and A. Wildavsky. 1974. *The Private Government of Public Money: Community and Policy Inside British Politics.* London: Macmillan.

Kelly, J. 2000. 'Managing the politics of expenditure control'. PhD thesis. Brisbane: Griffith University.

Kelly, J. and E. A. Lindquist. 2003. 'Metamorphosis in Kafka's castle: The changing balance of power among central budget agencies in Canada'. In J. Wanna, L. Jensen and J. de Vries (eds) *Controlling Public Expenditure: The Changing Roles of Central Budget Agencies – Better Guardians?* Cheltenham, UK: Edward Elgar.

Kelly, J. and J. Wanna. 1999. 'Once more into surplus: Reforming expenditure management in Australia and Canada'. *International Public Management Journal* 2(1): 127–146. doi.org/10.1016/s1096-7494(00)87435-8.

Kelly, J. and J. Wanna. 2000. 'New public management and the politics of government budgeting'. *International Public Management Review* 1(1): 33–55.

Kelly, J. and J. Wanna. 2004. 'Crashing through with accrual-output price budgeting in Australia: Technical adjustment or a new way of doing business?' *American Review of Public Administration* 34(1): 94–111. doi.org/10.1177/0275074003253315.

Lindquist, E. A. 1994. 'Citizens, experts and budgets: Assessing Ottawa's emerging budget process'. In S. D. Phillips (ed.) *How Ottawa Spends, 1994–95: Making Change.* Ottawa: Carleton University Press.

Lindquist, E. A. 1996. 'On the cutting edge: Program review, government restructuring, and the Treasury Board of Canada'. In G. Swimmer (ed.) *How Ottawa Spends 1996–97: Living Under the Knife.* Ottawa: Carleton University Press.

Schick, A. 1997. *The Changing Role of the Central Budget Office.* Discussion Paper (OECD/GD 97/109). Paris: Organization for Economic Cooperation and Development.

Schick, A. 1998. *A Contemporary Approach to Public Expenditure Management.* Washington: World Bank, International Bank for Reconstruction and Development.

Schick, A. 2004. 'Twenty-five years of budgeting reform'. *OECD Journal on Budgeting* 4(1): 81–102. doi.org/10.1787/budget-v4-art4-en.

Schick, A. 2010a. 'Crisis budgeting'. *OECD Journal on Budgeting* 9(3): 119–132. doi.org/10.1787/budget-9-5kmhhk9qf2zn.

Schick, A. 2010b. 'Post-crisis fiscal rules: Stabilising public finance while responding to economic aftershocks'. *OECD Journal on Budgeting* 10(2): 35–51. doi.org/10.1787/budget-10-5km7rqpkqts1.

Wanna, J. 2011. 'Treasury and economic policy: Beyond the dismal science'. *Australian Journal of Public Administration* 70(4): 347–364. doi.org/10.1111/j.1467-8500.2011.00747.x.

Wanna, J. 2015. 'Through a glass darkly: The vicissitudes of budgetary reform in Australia'. In J. Wanna, E. Lindquist and P. Marshall (eds) *New Accountabilities, New Challenges.* Canberra: ANU Press. doi.org/10.22459/nanc.04.2015.05.

Wanna, J. 2018. 'Government budgeting and the quest for value-for-money outcomes in Australia'. In T. Su, J. Wanna, A. Podger, S. U. Chan and M. Niu (eds) *Value for Money Budget and Financial Management Reform in the People's Republic of China, Taiwan, and Australia*. Canberra: ANU Press. doi.org/10.22459/vm.01.2018.02.

Wanna, J. 2021. 'Conformity and diversity in budgetary systems: Aspirations, routines, and recalibration'. In B. Hildreth, G. Miller and E. A. Lindquist (eds) *Handbook of Public Administration*. 4th edition. Cheltenham, UK: Edward Elgar.

Wanna, J., L. Jensen and J. de Vries (eds). 2003. *Controlling Public Expenditure: The Changing Roles of Central Budget Agencies – Better Guardians?* Cheltenham, UK: Edward Elgar.

Wanna, J., L. Jensen and J. de Vries (eds). 2010. *The Reality of Budgetary Reform in OECD Nations: Trajectories and Consequences*. Cheltenham, UK: Edward Elgar. doi.org/10.4337/9781849805636.

Wanna, J., J. Kelly and J. Forster. 2000. *Managing Public Expenditure in Australia*. Sydney: Allen & Unwin.

Wanna, J., E. Lindquist and J. de Vries (eds). 2015. *The Global Financial Crisis and its Budget Impacts in OECD Nations – Fiscal Responses and Future Challenges*. Cheltenham, UK: Edward Elgar. doi.org/10.4337/9781784718961.00007.

Weller, P. and J. Cutt. 1976. *Treasury Control in Australia: A Study in Bureaucratic Politics*. Sydney: Ian Novak.

Weller, P., J. Forster and G. Davis (eds). 1993. *Reforming the Public Service: Lessons from Recent Experience*. Brisbane: Centre for Australian Public Management, Griffith University.

Wildavsky. A. 1964. *The Politics of Budgetary Process*. Boston: Little Brown.

3

Performance management for success: Public sector organisations in Australia and the Philippines

Lewis Hawke

Introduction

I knew of John long before I met him. His 1992 book with Weller and O'Faircheallaigh was one of the first academic texts I had in my library on public sector reform. I had been inducted into public sector reform during a secondment in the UK with Her Majesty's Treasury in the mid-1990s, where I was involved in managing and implementing some of the most innovative public management reforms at the time. When I returned to Australia, John had become well established as a gifted and insightful academic and commentator on the public sector, then based in Canberra. He seemed to be a regular fixture on television and was a very engaging speaker, able to present ideas and observations in a way both incisive and accessible to a diverse audience. By then, his works with Forster and Kelly (2000), and Jensen and de Vries (2003) has also become well established references for me.

I met John shortly after I had been involved in designing and implementing the accrual, outcomes and outputs budget framework for the Australian Government. His voracious interest and infectious enthusiasm for knowledge about the initiative was a rare and welcome experience. Until I met John, I had found it uncommon for academics to take such a strong interest in every aspect of public policy, including the arcane technical and operational elements. He helped to broaden my perspective on the multiple dimensions of public policy, from the mostly technical and theoretical aspects that I had previously focused on, to the political, historical and sociological. During the process of preparing our joint contribution to the volume *The Reality of Budgetary Reform in OECD Nations: Trajectories and Consequences* (2010), I developed a great respect for his incredible productive output. His ability to orchestrate the work from discussion of the micro-level details of our chapter to the macro-level themes and content of the whole book with Jensen, de Vries and other contributors was most impressive. His insights on the significance of politics, history, public policy and management and how they shaped public finance and economic outcomes has guided my approach to public sector reform since then.

My most enduring memory of meetings with John was a dinner we had with John Halligan and Allen Schick at my home in Canberra. My wife, Carol Kiernan, had done the hard work of putting together a menu that met everyone's needs, while I had the delight of sharing ideas on public sector reform with three of the most experienced and celebrated brains in the business. At the time I had just started thinking about my PhD on public sector performance under the sage guidance of John Halligan, so the ideas forming the germ of the paper below were high on my agenda for discussion. I have no doubt that the influences of all who attended that dinner have shaped my subsequent research. John Wanna's encouragement and his vibrant approach to enquiry and analysis continues to guide and motivate my work in this field.

Context

The use of public sector performance management and budgeting has expanded from a small group of early adopters in the 1960s and 1970s to a wide range of countries across all continents and income groups (Moynihan and Beazley 2016). Some valuable early work on performance management in Australia emerged from Griffith University (Wanna, O'Faircheallaigh and Weller 1999; Wanna, Forster and Kelly 2003). Ironically, much of the literature on public sector performance practices documents the underachievement of the approach and the various attempts to modify and address the symptoms of unrealised goals. This paper takes an optimistic perspective to public sector performance, seeking to determine common success factors for the practice that would offer a pathway to better outcomes for all users.

The research for this paper draws from the growing body of literature to establish a broadly applicable framework for systematically analysing and addressing the common, fundamental challenges and success factors for public sector performance management. This paper focuses on the organisational level rather than the system-wide approach prevalent in the literature. There are two main reasons for concentrating on organisations. Firstly, the literature indicates that the organisational level is where public sector performance management is likely to have the greatest impact and potential value (Moynihan and Pandey 2010). Secondly, experience within and across countries demonstrates that the organisational level is characterised by considerable diversity in the results achieved from adopting performance-based arrangements (De Waal 2010; Taylor 2011). These observations suggest that analysis of the opportunities for improving performance management may be more fertile at the organisational level than by tinkering with the broader system settings (Hawke and Wanna 2010; Hawke 2012).

The first step on the path to establishing an analytical framework is to develop a basic hypothesis and apply it to real-world practices to test its relevance. The paper firstly explains how the core influences on public sector performance management have been distilled from the literature. The methodology for testing the framework is then outlined, along with an explanation of the approach to data collection. The results of the survey are summarised in the third section of the paper, focusing on whether there is support for the hypotheses underpinning the framework. Finally, the limitations, implications, conclusions and directions for further work are discussed.

The data used in this study were obtained using a survey of central government organisations in Australia and the Philippines. Both countries were among the early adopter group for performance management around four decades ago and therefore have considerable experience in the application and adaptation of the practices (Hawke and Wanna 2010; Venner 2019).

Despite similarity in the extensive gestation period for performance management in both countries, the two countries selected are quite different in their economic and social circumstances, institutional and political arrangements, cultural heritage and many other important respects. These differences offer the opportunity to test the accuracy and relevance of the hypothesis across national as well as organisational boundaries. They also provide a basis for identifying characteristics that may have a greater or smaller influence on success in performance management for individual organisations in both countries.

Theoretical framework and hypothesis

In preparing for the literature review for this study, it was essential to set boundaries to limit the scope to a manageable range. One aspect of boundary-setting involved defining the key elements. The main elements that warrant definition are captured in the title of this paper, specifically: 'performance management', 'public sector', 'organisation' and 'success'.

This study adopts Australia's Management Advisory Committee's (MAC 2001, 14) definition of performance management as, 'interrelated strategies and activities to improve performance of individuals, teams and organisations. Its purpose is to enhance the achievements of agency goals and outcomes for government'. The public sector refers to the International Monetary Fund's Government Finance Statistics Manual definition, as that which contains all units controlled directly or indirectly by government (IMF 2014). Organisation is used as an umbrella term in this study to refer to a body with an explicit form, responsibility and authority bestowed on it by government. Organisations can include bodies described as ministries, departments, agencies, corporations, cooperatives, entities, service delivery units, associations and authorities, among other terms used in government. Success is defined as the achievement of some or all of the goals and objectives set for performance management practices. The goals and objectives that are considered important for this study are whether performance management contributes to better quality performance information, if performance information is used by public sector stakeholders, and whether it causes or contributes to positive changes within the organisation or the matters for which it has authority and responsibility.

The literature search was structured using the defined terms, focusing primarily on research with the highest relevance and citation frequency during the last two decades. Where possible, existing literature review articles were used to limit the search (Talbot 2010; Hawke 2012; Gao 2015; Kroll 2015a, 2015b; among others).

One important aspect missing from many academic studies is an examination of the practitioner literature that has emerged from governments and international institutions during the period under review. This was a feature of John Wanna's body of work on public financial management, which was particularly notable for his pairing of academics and practitioners in the international comparative volumes, for example, *Controlling Public Expenditure* (Wanna, Jensen and de Vries 2003) and *The Reality of Budgetary Reform in OECD Nations* (Wanna, Jensen and de Vries 2010). The practitioner literature is important because it provides details on a more extensive range of applications and the lessons learned by the institutions and governments involved. Other published and unpublished works outside the conventional realm of public management literature and the time period for the main review have been examined where they have demonstrated high relevance and are empirically robust.

The literature review performed for this study has identified six broad categories of factors influencing public sector performance management. These factors are: external, institutional and structural, leadership and management, technical capability, organisational culture and behavioural. Other factors have been considered by researchers but generally found to have minimal or inconsistent direct influence on success, such as the size and type of organisation. While those factors have sometimes been linked to one or more of the six core factors, for example through issues such as span of control and complexity (Bohte and Meier 2001), they have not been found to be important per se for the success of performance management. The precise definitions and boundaries of the six groups of influences can be debated, but at this stage of development, it is considered more important to recognise the nature and significance of their individual and joint influences than develop a detailed taxonomy. There will be ample opportunity for refinement when, or if, their importance is confirmed and when systematic research on their influence becomes more prevalent.

(a) External influences

These influences are, by definition, actions or events that are exerted from outside organisations. They can come from elsewhere in the public sector, from other parts of the jurisdiction or from foreign sources. External influences can be positive, negative, transformative or reinforcing. A prominent external influence identified in the literature comes from the political sphere, sometimes through embedded political appointments in organisations, and more broadly through policies and practices that the organisations are obliged to implement. The potential significant effects of political economy on the efficient and effective functioning of government has been a feature of practitioner literature for at least a decade (Fritz, Verhoeven and Avenia 2017). In some instances, shifts in political power have resulted in major changes to the performance management arrangements (Hood 2006) while, in others, they have maintained and reinforced the basic approach applied by predecessors (Hawke 2012; Venner 2019).

Economic and social change have been identified as another subgroup of external influences on performance management. Strong economic downturns with contractionary fiscal consequences have been shown to displace evidence-based policy refinements and reallocations with arbitrary sectoral or across-the-board expenditure cuts (Schick 2014). The displacement of performance-based approaches by subjective cuts is often a temporary feature to deal with urgent, short-term macro-fiscal concerns and reverts to the previous approach once the latter concerns have been addressed.

External pressures have been identified as providing a catalyst or tipping point for the introduction or substantial change in performance management arrangements (Moynihan and Beazley 2016). In newer adopters of performance management methods, this can be isomorphic, in an attempt to achieve benefits claimed by other adopters (Mussari et al. 2016) or in response to weaknesses identified by critics of existing models within countries.

The separate and complementary roles of parliament and state audit has been examined in many studies. Key findings include the observation that, where either or both institutions are actively and positively engaged in performance monitoring and review, the results are significantly better than in those where little or no interest is shown in efficiency and effectiveness issues. Results are also weaker where the institutions are not well connected in their oversight (Santiso 2015).

Many authors have noted the importance of a strong central finance organisation in establishing and maintaining effective performance management arrangements (e.g. Wanna, Forster and Kelly 2000; Wanna, Jensen and de Vries 2003). Central organisations are seen to have an important role in setting and policing the procedures that must be followed, as well as providing guidance and capacity building needed by other organisations. It is common for central organisations to exert an accountability or challenge role to ensure rigorous and reliable use of performance information within the government system.

The role of public participation and citizen engagement has been seen as an area of external influence that is increasing in significance as trust in government has receded. It has not been identified as having a major influence on performance management for individual organisations or at the system level to date, except where local community interest is strong and their views are effectively channelled into the policymaking process (Moreno and Garza 2015).

(b) Institutional and structural influences

This group of influences includes the legal and regulatory framework in which organisations are established and the formal public sector environment in which they operate. The roles and responsibilities, organisational composition and interrelationships with other organisations all serve to fix an organisation within a symbiotic organism of government. Each organisation has its place in the organism and is affected by other parts to a greater or lesser extent. The structures within this group of influences may be internal or external to the legal boundaries of the organisation but still part of its operations, for example in relation to other organisations within a sector or policy grouping, subsidiary entities or regional bodies.

Institutional and structural influences are distinguished from external and managerial influences because they involve actions directly affecting the organisation as a result of institutions exerting powers that they have attained, either by law or convention, within the organism of government. This includes the extent to which organisations have autonomy to perform the functions and responsibilities expected of them, and the degree of control and rigidity imposed on the organisation from the other parts of the government organism.

Structure within organisations is an important part of this group of influences. Nicholl (2006) highlighted the stark difference in governance and performance outcomes between the well-structured central bank and other government structures within the newly established state of Bosnia–Herzegovina. Bohte and Meier (2001) identified significant differences between performance outcomes as a result of differences in span of control among educational organisations in Texas, where the roles and functions of the organisations were otherwise quite similar. Structure can be a negative or complicating influence on performance where the organisation's operations are not effectively aligned with performance goals, and vice versa. It increases transaction costs required to achieve joint responsibilities, allows for confusion or dilution of accountability and reduces efficiency.

(c) Leadership and management influences

Leadership and management influences are the most reported and analysed of all six groups within the academic literature. The linkage between new public management and performance measurement in the 1990s and 2000s was a strong theme in the literature. More recently, the focus has moved from principal agent issues to the role of leaders and managers in setting the performance agenda and driving better results either directly or indirectly through their actions, engagement and encouragement (Moynihan and Pandey 2010; Dull 2008). Leaders are seen as those within organisations who initiate or catalyse change and transformation, while managers are considered to be instrumental in implementing change and maintaining direction and momentum.

Leadership and management can have positive and negative influences, as is true for all six groups. The absence of performance-supportive leadership and management has been shown to be a major impediment to effective change, through various techniques such as passive resistance at one end of the scale, or active gaming at the other. Some writers have identified important subtleties in the use of leadership and management to facilitate change. Engagement in routine dialogue on performance and change with staff has been shown as a positive influence (Moynihan and Pandey 2010), while more heavy-handed monitoring and control has been shown to have a detrimental effect (Rasul, Rogger and Williams 2018).

(d) Technical influences

Technical influences encompass the rules, procedures, requirements, specifications and limitations on performance management arrangements. This group also includes the systems, practices, skills, resources and capabilities for implementation, management and maintenance of the schemes. It occupies the largest seam of literature among practitioners – from system design, best practices and refinements, to lessons learned and comparative analysis (Wanna, Jensen and de Vries 2010; OECD 2018, 2019).

Within this theme there is an ongoing tension between those who see performance information as a tool for allocating budgets, and those who see it as an input for informing budget and policy decisions. Others see it as separate from budgeting, as a vehicle for improving services, accountability for achieving targets or alignment with policies and strategic objectives. Behn (2003) identified eight different purposes for performance information: to evaluate, control, budget, motivate, promote, celebrate, learn and improve. His advice was to be clear about the purpose(s), which would then help to design the architecture to go with it. While the advice appears clear and simple, the technical application has proved to be more challenging.

One reason for the relatively large share of practitioner literature devoted to technical issues is that they have proved to be very difficult, if not intractable (Wanna et al. 2010). Measurement of performance has been a challenge for practitioners for more than 40 years in some countries, particularly in relation to the identification, measurement and attribution of outcomes. Complexity has been another challenge, where getting the right balance of the number and importance of performance measures, and methods of performance assessment, appears to be more of an art than a science. There has been a general trend among longer-serving practitioners to reduce the number of performance indicators that are regularly reported. It is not clear whether this has contributed significantly to better results from performance management (OECD 2019; Moynihan and Beazley 2016).

Monitoring of performance management practices by state audit agencies has demonstrated that there are substantial differences between the success of organisations in the application and use of arrangements in their respective national and subnational governments. This is often attributed to inadequate compliance, weak internal processes and procedures, low implementation capacity or other technical aspects, as evident in published performance audit reports by state audit institutions in the UK, Canada, Australia, New Zealand, the US and elsewhere.

Countries that have changed their performance management arrangements, often multiple times over the decades of implementation, have sought to resolve technical weaknesses with varying degrees of success (Moynihan and Beazley 2016; Curristine and Flynn 2013).

(e) Cultural influences

Cultural influences encompass norms, modes of operation, communications, understandings and tacit routines. Woolcock (2014, 16) describes them as the 'use of symbols, frames and narratives connecting structure and agency'. Reformers in government seek to embed a 'performance culture' in which all agents see the importance of performance information and use it to enhance organisational achievements. Schick (2014) noted that there is a dark side of culture as well. He referred to culture as 'obdurate' and able to withstand waves of reform pressure.

Organisational culture provides a subliminal means for navigating the unknown, unfamiliar or uncomfortable in the company of others who share it. Where it is aligned with performance objectives, it can be effective in overcoming the challenges of disappointing results or inconvenient outcomes. Where culture is not aligned with performance objectives, it can be a source of resistance, opposition and ultimately failure of systems altogether.

Moynihan and Pandey (2010) and others have postulated a link between leadership and culture, through which leaders can steer culture to a more benign or positive association with new approaches. It can be a fickle link, however, if those being led are not convinced by the leaders' apparent commitment (Dull 2008).

People who work in the public sector are considered to have a more supportive attitude to their organisations and stronger commitment to its goals, rather than the more utilitarian and contractual association attributed to private sector organisations. Some researchers have observed that where systems or organisations have taken a more contractual and incentive-based approach to public services, the responses of staff have changed the organisation in ways that are less communal and more individualistic (Rasul, Rogger and Williams 2018).

(f) Behavioural influences

Performance management, and more often performance budgeting, has been found to have a strong interrelationship with behaviour. A common justification for introducing performance management practices has been to provide stronger incentives and signals to organisations and their staff about the expectations on their behaviour, productivity and satisfaction (Department of Finance 2016; Department of Budget and Management 2016). It is argued that clear goals and targets will focus the minds of staff and managers on what is important and improve the efficiency and effectiveness with which it is achieved.

Paradoxically, it has been shown that where goals and targets are tightly prescribed, and incentives or sanctions are strong, performance-based initiatives can have perverse effects through gaming, cheating or misinformation. The literature abounds with examples of perverse behaviours resulting from poorly implemented performance management arrangements (Radin 2006; Hood 2012). Short of corrupt or fraudulent practices, it is also argued that the perverse effects can be ameliorated or eliminated by more effective oversight, increased dialogue and building trust with organisations to address the source of behavioural dissonance.

(g) Denouement

The six groups of influences outlined above are strongly represented in the literature, either individually or in various combinations. The interrelationship between them, and even potential overlap, is evident such as at the boundary of external and institutional influence, or the interaction between leadership, culture and behaviour. More important for this study is that the main strands of performance management literature do not identify any other significant influences on performance management outside one or more of those groups. Thus the central hypothesis to be tested by this study is whether the six elements identified above are the only influences on performance management in public sector organisations. The remainder of this paper seeks to put this hypothesis to the test and to assess how those or other influences are manifest in the Australian and Philippine central government organisations.

Methodology

In the absence of suitable existing data on this topic, it was necessary to collect sufficient new data to allow for reasonable assessments to be made about the influences on performance management and how they affect the quality and use of performance information. The study sought to obtain the maximum number of observations on public sector entities within the two countries chosen using an ethically appropriate methodology. The study was initially discussed with central budget departments in both countries, which are responsible for performance management arrangements, to seek their agreement for the study to be performed, though not necessarily seeking their endorsement of it.

In both countries the central budget departments made first contact with potential participants to inform them about the study. They requested that any organisation willing to participate should respond to them, and only then would their contact details be provided to the researcher. One reason for seeking clearance for data collection with policy departments was to reassure participants that the process was neutral in relation to existing policies of government and responsible agencies. This aimed to avoid reticence or defensive behaviour in responding to the survey, which might otherwise be expected from public sector organisations responding to requests from an un-vetted external analyst. Self-nominating organisations were contacted by the researcher if they responded positively to the central agencies.

The survey adopted a structured approach involving a carefully designed questionnaire combined with follow-up interviews to confirm responses and obtain supplementary information on each organisation. The questionnaire and interviews were targeted to the person and position in each organisation with primary responsibility for administration and oversight of the performance management arrangements.

The questionnaire was designed using mainly multiple-choice questions, applying various response techniques to solicit accurate and unbiased responses but primarily using adaptations of the Likert five-point scale. Many questions included an 'other' option to avoid unduly limiting the scope for answers. This was considered to be particularly important in relation to the main research questions where the existence and significance of other influences on performance management was crucial to the study. It was also important in areas where a comprehensive list of possible options was not practical or realistic, for example, results achieved, challenges experienced and procedures adopted.

The length and complexity of the questionnaire sought to balance the desire for as much information as possible from the maximum number of respondents with the need to achieve the maximum number of fully completed questionnaires. The intended result appears to have been successful because more than 90 per cent of people who volunteered to undertake the survey completed all questions. Most of those who completed the questionnaire were also willing to be contacted for face-to-face interviews, indicating that they were not deterred from further participation by the content, length or complexity of the questionnaire.

The questionnaire sought to obtain data that were relevant to the essential research questions in addition to other useful information gathered in previous surveys on performance management by other researchers. This broader focus allowed the study to obtain useful contextual data and provide an additional test of the credibility and reliability of results, to the extent they were consistent with the findings of other studies, while also taking account of important differences. The sources of relevant work on countrywide practices included the International Monetary Fund (Robinson and Brumby 2005) survey of performance budgeting and management in 16 developing countries and the Organisation for Economic Cooperation and Development's (OECD) Government at a Glance (2011 to 2017) survey, which covered aspects of structural, institutional and technical matters. Moynihan and Pandey's (2010) survey of individual managers gathered data on other relevant issues, including incentives, behaviour and organisational culture, but adopted a more quantitative approach that was not completely suited to the current study.

The format for the questionnaire included identification of defining characteristics of the organisation and the characteristics of performance management arrangements. Approximately 75 per cent of the questionnaire examined the six influences on design, implementation, utilisation and impact of performance management. The questionnaire ended with three open questions seeking general impressions on the strengths and weaknesses of performance management and suggestions for improvement. The questions were mostly the same for both countries except where terminology, policy and institutional differences warranted some adaptation. Interview candidates were selected after the questionnaires closed based on their willingness, their accessibility and the desire to achieve a balance in the characteristics of organisations and their performance management experiences.

In Australia, two phases of the survey were performed: one in 2012 and the second in 2019. One reason for undertaking two surveys was to consider potential differences over time. It was also of interest to examine whether the major change of performance management policies and practices after the survey in 2012 had a material impact on the significance of different influences.

The main change in performance management policy and practice in Australia between the two phases of the survey was the enactment of the *Public Governance, Performance and Accountability Act 2013* (Cth) (PGPA Act). This legislation combined the coverage of previous public entity laws and established for the first time legal obligations to prepare performance plans and report performance results. The PGPA covered all national government entities and was accompanied by extensive guidance from the Department of Finance (DOF) and scrutiny by the Australian National Audit Office.

Only one phase of the survey is being conducted in the Philippines, in 2019, coinciding with the timing of the second Australian phase.

Main findings

The questionnaires in both countries garnered responses from approximately 20 per cent of the total number of organisations subject to performance management practices. The responses contained a suitable cross-section of sizes, types and functions of organisations within each country, as summarised in Figures 3.1 and 3.2.

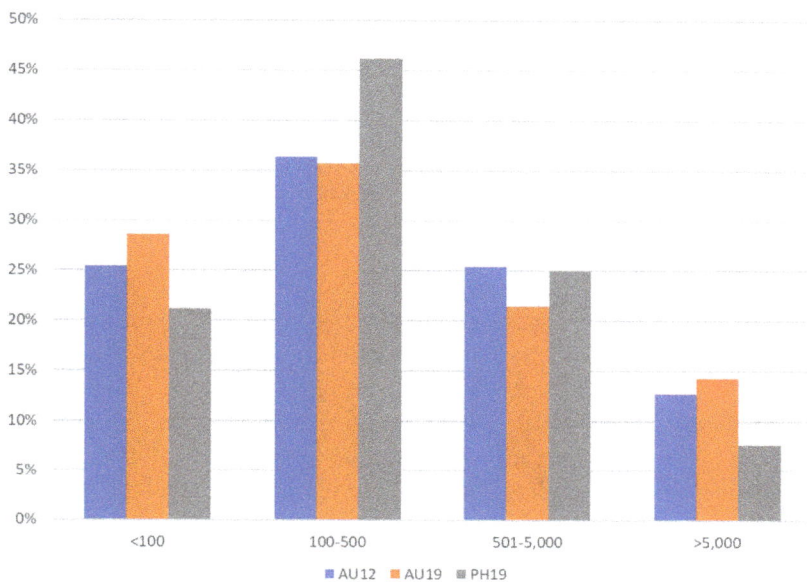

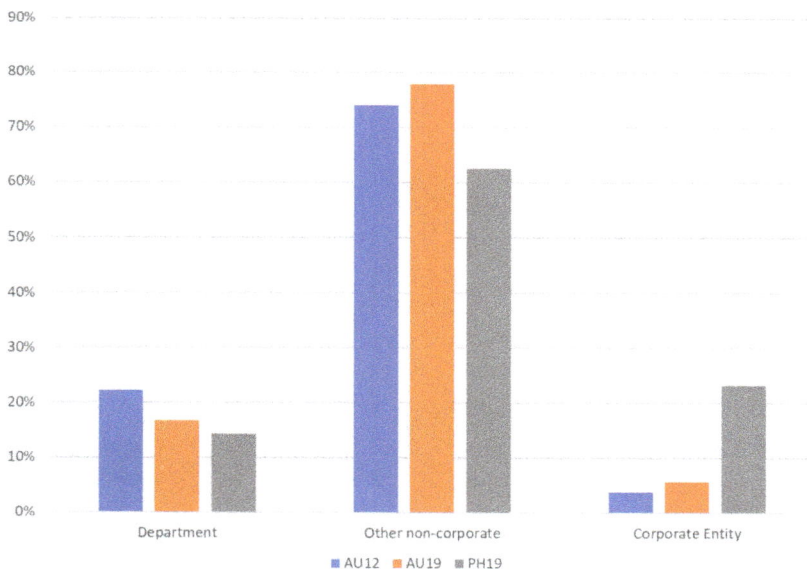

Figures 3.1 and 3.2. Organisation size and types (% of respondents).

Source: Author's summary of study results.

The first phase of the Australian study (AU12) obtained completed survey responses from 49 organisations. The second Australian phase (AU19) has produced 16 completed responses to date, but more are anticipated from a second round of invitations. Even though the number of respondents to the second phase so far is smaller than the first phase, it includes a sound cross-section of organisations, most of which are the same or include functions performed by participants in the first phase.

The proportion of organisation types and sizes that have participated in the survey reflect a similar pattern to the sizes and types across the total population of organisations in both Australia and the Philippines. The remainder of this paper draws on results from one or both phases of the Australian study to illustrate various characteristics in the simplest and clearest way. Both sets of results are presented where there are significantly different findings between the two phases.

The Philippine survey (PH19) yielded completed responses from 57 organisations. The coverage included government departments, public enterprises, educational institutions, service delivery agencies and regulatory bodies of various sizes. The areas of responsibility covered most sectors of public responsibility including finance, budget, education, transportation, law enforcement, environment and regional administration.

Both countries have applied performance management in the public sector for more than three decades, so the arrangements in place incorporate many of the common features used in other countries, as reported by the OECD (2019). Figure 3.3 shows that performance information is collected at multiple levels within organisations, primarily at the whole organisation level. Both countries produce published performance reports incorporating performance indicators and evaluation findings. Most organisations link their performance information to organisational strategy and goals, particularly in the Philippines. Both countries require regular review and audit of performance information.

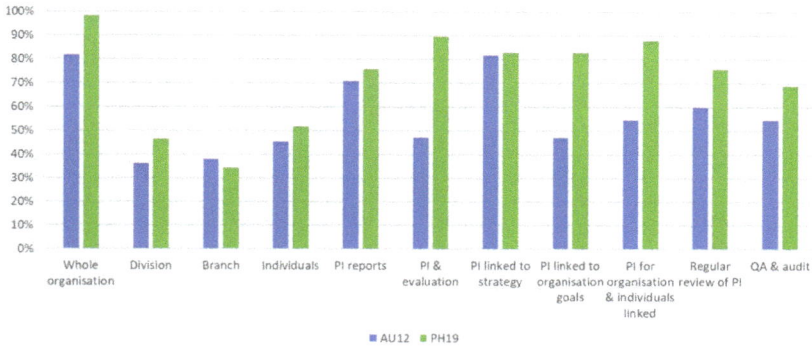

Figure 3.3. Organisational performance management attributes.
Source: Author's summary of study results.

The pervasiveness of performance management attributes in both countries offers benefits and challenges for this study. The benefits are that they provide positive examples of countries where performance is embedded in organisational management and operations so they are most likely to exhibit robust findings on performance management practices. The challenge arises from the same attribute, which means that weaknesses and major differences in performance measurement are less likely to be apparent than between countries with more diverse performance management trajectories.

The headline result of the study is that both countries have identified all six elements presented in the hypothesis as important influences on the success of performance management, as measured by quality and use of performance information. Figure 3.4 summarises the responses from both countries, including the two phases of the Australian study.

The results indicate that the Philippine organisations consider all six elements to be strong influences, with slightly more important influences provided by institutional and structural factors and leadership and management than the other four elements. Australian organisations considered that leadership and management was the most important influence in both phases of the survey. Cultural and technical aspects were considered the next most important in both phases and both of those elements appeared to be more important in the recent Australian phase than in the earlier phase.

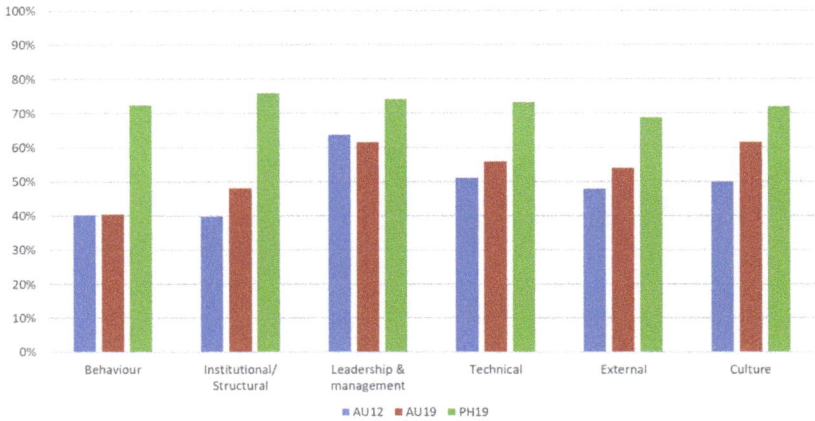

Figure 3.4. Identified influences on performance management (0 = weak, 100 = strong).

Source: Author's summary of study results.

Figure 3.4 does not include information on other influences because no organisation in either country considered that any other factors were important, despite specific questions in the questionnaire and interviews prompting suggestions for other influences. This may be because the six specific influences identified can be interpreted quite broadly, but even so, it provides an encouraging endorsement of the hypothesis. The remainder of this paper seeks to explain and discuss how the six elements have contributed to performance management success within public sector organisations in both countries.

Discussion

Before examining the contributions of individual influences, it is important to provide a foundation and context for the analysis in terms of whether performance management achieved any success at the organisational level in either or both countries covered by the research. The survey included several specific questions relating to the quality of performance information, the challenges faced in achieving good quality performance, the use of performance information, the effects of performance information and their impact on aspects of performance commonly claimed by proponents to be directly related to performance management.

(a) Quality of performance information

Quality of performance information was assessed in this study using a commonly adopted checklist referred to as 'SMART': specific, measurable, achievable, relevant and timed. Although the criteria used in the acronym may vary among countries the intent is generally the same. The countries using this acronymic model consider that performance information that rates highly on all of the criteria is more useful and robust than that which do not. Respondents to the Australian and Philippine questionnaires scored themselves above the mid-range against all of the SMART criteria, though 'measurability' was considered to be more of a challenge to the 2012 Australia respondents and 'timed' indicators were more challenging for 2019 Australian respondents. The Philippine respondents scored themselves higher on all attributes than Australians, possibly reflecting an 'optimism bias' for each criterion, but the differences between criteria are notable. They considered that they were particularly strong on the 'relevance' and 'specificity' of their information. 'Measurability' was the weakest for Philippine organisations, but still averaged more than 70 per cent of the maximum score, as shown in Figure 3.5.

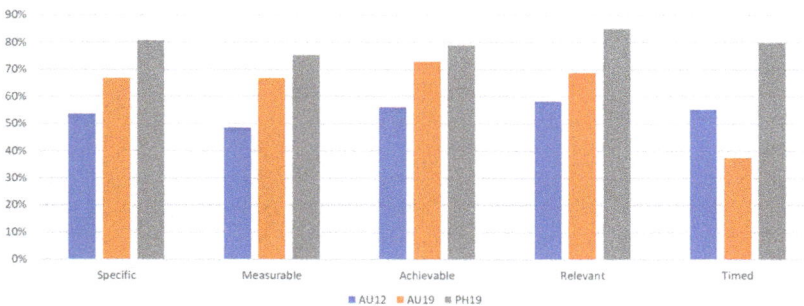

Figure 3.5. Quality of performance information (0 = weak, 100 = strong).
Source: Author's summary of study results.

(b) Use of performance information

Philippine questionnaire respondents identified substantial usage of performance information by organisational management, as shown in Figure 3.6. This included politically appointed secretaries and chief executives of public sector organisations who are responsible for the management and operations in those bodies. Politically appointed ministers in Australia were identified as only moderate users of performance information and other elected officials reportedly showed little interest. In Australia, operational unit managers and senior management were the main users of performance information but both groups of managers showed less interest than their Philippine counterparts. This is consistent with research and analysis on Australia by Wanna and others (Wanna and Podger 2017). This may reflect an important difference between Australia and the Philippines in how performance information is used. The Philippines Government provides financial incentives at organisational and individual levels for excellent performance, sometimes more than 15 per cent of salary, so there is a stronger personal motivation for internal management to focus on organisational performance.

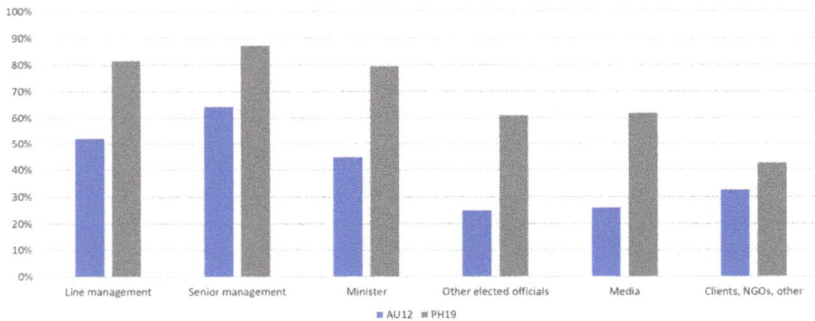

Figure 3.6. Users of performance information (0 = not at all, 100 = extensively).

Source: Author's summary of study results.

The greater interest in performance information in the Philippines appears to have translated into greater use of the data, as shown in Figure 3.7. According to respondents, the use of performance information directly contributed to refinement of processes, improvement of service design and quality, and development of budgets and policy. The Philippines' use of performance information was reportedly more extensive in all areas than Australia. The relatively low use of performance information in policy development and design in both countries compared with its use for other activities suggests a strong emphasis on annual performance indicators and less use of broad program and policy evaluation, which is more often associated with policy development and advice (Wanna, O'Faircheallaigh and Weller 1999).

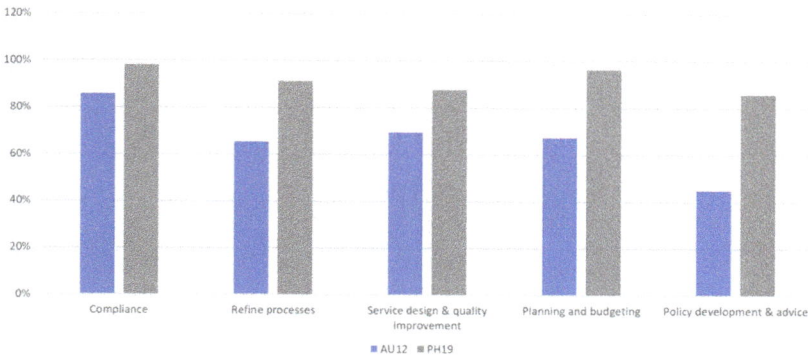

Figure 3.7. Uses of performance information (0 = not used, 100 = extensive use).
Source: Author's summary of study results.

Even in Australia, however, there was a high positive correlation between the level of use and the application of performance information for operational improvements. For example, the correlation coefficient between operational management use of performance information and process refinement was 0.67. The correlation coefficient between operational management and service quality improvement was 0.75 and with planning and budgeting it was 0.64. Similar correlation was found with operational improvements and senior management use of performance information. While the accuracy of correlation-using ratings data can be unreliable from a strict statistical perspective, it provides an indication that the relationships are at least consistent with expectations.

(c) Effects and impact of performance information

Australian and Philippine respondents reported that the use of performance information also resulted in systemic organisational benefits, as summarised in Figure 3.8. The most significant impacts in both countries were greater employee focus on results, more accountability, improvement in service quality, improved information for decisions and better budget allocation. Smaller impacts were reported in relation to efficiency improvements, communications and external relationships in both countries. In all categories of impact, Philippine organisations reported more extensive use than Australia, which could indicate an optimism bias in their self-reported achievements, as mentioned previously. This will be scrutinised carefully in completing the interview process to see if the actual changes reported are stronger or simply interpreted differently by the respondents.

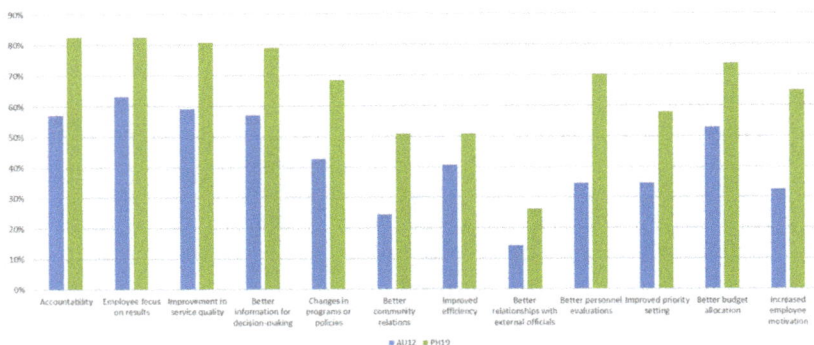

Figure 3.8. Effects and impact of performance management (0 = no effect/impact, 100 = extensive effect/impact).
Source: Author's summary of study results.

In summary, respondents in both countries reported strong performance in terms of quality, use and impact of performance management. Even allowing for a generous margin of optimism bias that can be expected from self-reported results, the overall conclusion of respondents in both countries is that performance management has achieved significant benefits. The question of what has influenced the achievement of such positive results is addressed in the remainder of this section.

(d) External influences

Survey participants were asked about seven external influences commonly noted in the literature. These included political, economic and customer-related factors in addition to economic and fiscal conditions, comparison with other organisations, and actions by other public sector bodies that had implications for their performance. As illustrated in Figure 3.9, Australian respondents identified political and client-related factors as the main external influences with economic and fiscal conditions and other public sector bodies as important factors. Australian respondents were less concerned about the media and comparisons with other organisations.

The aggregated responses from Philippine organisations rated clients and media as most important. This was partly due to the importance of those groups to many of the state universities and colleges, which made up about one-quarter of the Philippine respondents. Other Philippine respondents identified political factors, especially from parliament, other public sector bodies and economic and fiscal conditions as major external influences. Philippine respondents also reported little influence from comparisons with other organisations domestically or internationally.

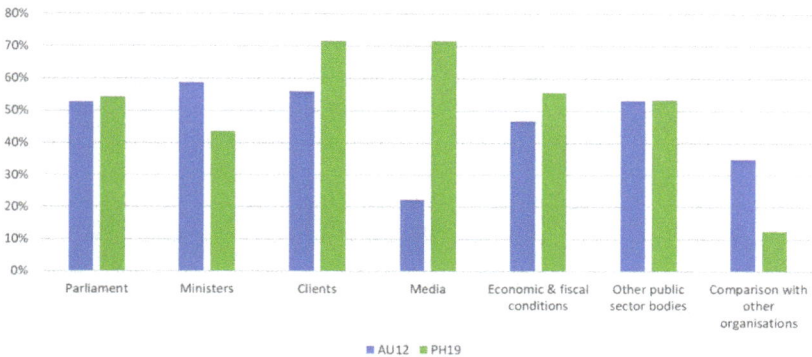

Figure 3.9. External influences on organisational performance management.
Source: Author's summary of study results.

The other public sector bodies referred to by respondents are primarily the central budget departments and state audit institutions in each country. The central budget departments are responsible for public sector performance policy development and implementation. Both countries have powerful central budget departments that closely supervise the implementation of budget policy, primarily through the annual budget process, but also through issuance of circulars requiring action by budget-dependent organisations. The state audit institutions in both countries have wide remits covering the financial and non-financial practices and performance by central government organisations.

(e) Institutional and structural influences

Institutional and structural factors control the form, scope and framework in which performance management operates. They have a direct effect, through determination of what is required from organisations, such as the form, content and frequency of reporting on performance. They also have an indirect effect by excluding or limiting what is not permitted, or what is more difficult because it requires management across structural boundaries where accountability and responsibility become blurred or more complex. Survey respondents identified five institutional and structural aspects that were important influences on performance management, as summarised in Figure 3.10.

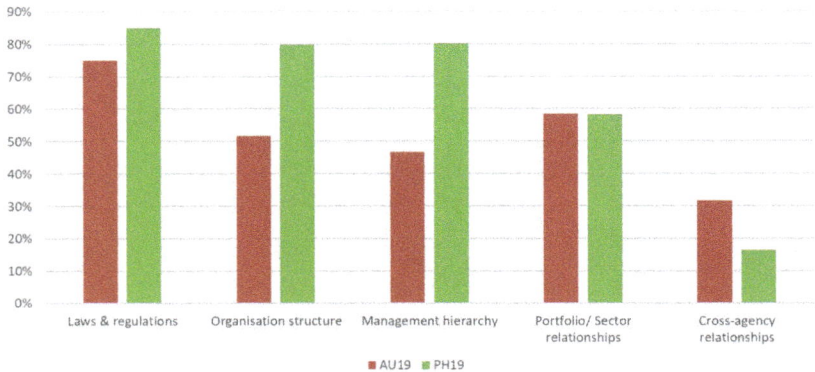

Figure 3.10. Institutional and structural influences on organisational performance management.

Source: Author's summary of study results.

The most important institutional and structural aspects in both countries were laws and regulations. In Australia, the next most important aspect was portfolio and sector relationships. The Australian public sector at the national level is organised by portfolio under the supervision of ministers and department heads. The departments within portfolios have oversight and coordination responsibilities for other organisations assigned to them. The non-departmental organisations are not strictly subsidiaries of the departments of state, but they are required to comply with portfolio regulations and directions, which include coordinated budget planning and reporting. Survey respondents indicated that this has an important influence on their performance management.

The Philippine survey respondents identified organisational structure and management hierarchy as very important influences on performance management, much more important to them than to their Australian counterparts. One reason for this is that staff structures and budgets are more tightly controlled in the Philippines. It is much more difficult to reallocate staff and budgets between organisational units in the Philippines than Australia. This constraint means organisations have to pay more attention to the boundaries of operations because they impose a hard limit on how and where money can be spent and what activities can be performed. The limits on organisational structures and budgets are not necessarily related to the outcomes that organisations are trying to achieve. This is one of the major differences between Australian and Philippine public administration.

Institutional and structural influence was the highest rated among the six success influences in the Philippines but was the lowest for Australia in the first phase of the study and second lowest for the second phase. It is not clear from this study whether those differences had an impact on the relative effectiveness of performance management. This may be an area for closer examination in future research.

(f) Leadership and management influences

The importance of effective leadership and management has been a recurring theme in public and private sector management literature. Its importance to the public sector has been given more attention since the emergence and spread of new public management practices in the 1980s. Evidence from the performance management literature (Wright, Moynihan and Pandey 2012) supports the significance of leadership and management and the current study offers further support. Leadership and management was the main influence on performance management identified by Australian respondents and a close second to institutional and structural influence in the Philippine survey.

The survey identified several ways in which leadership and management affected performance management. Chief executive officers (CEOs) and departmental secretaries (who are also ministers in the Philippines) were considered to be the most influential on organisational performance management in both countries, followed by senior executives, ministers and management boards, as shown in Figure 3.11. Government and other external entities ranked lower on the scale of influence in both countries. Middle management and team or unit managers were more important in the Philippines than Australia.

The role of CEOs and secretaries was most evident to respondents through their roles in monitoring results and ensuring that performance information was current and consistent with organisational plans and strategy. They played a less important, though still significant, role in the selection of indicators and targets and provision of feedback on results. Senior management was the most substantial user of performance information in both countries, followed by operational managers. Internal management received more frequent performance reports, usually on a quarterly basis, but sometimes more frequently.

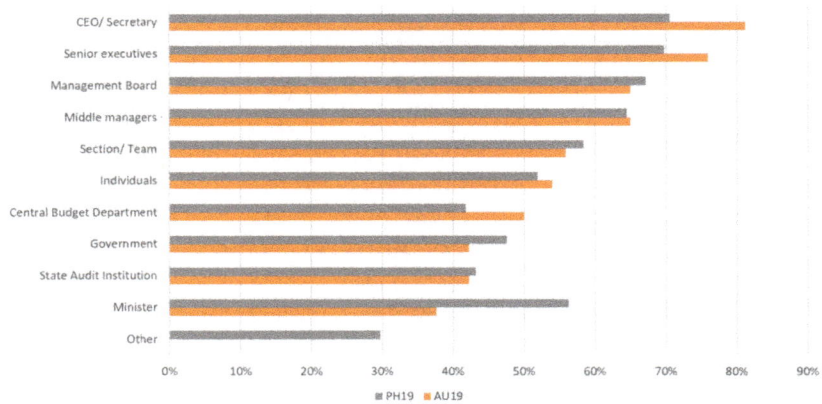

Figure 3.11. Influential people in performance management (0 = low, 100 = high).

Source: Author's summary of study results.

Leadership and management was also strongly related to the other five success factors identified in this study, particularly organisational culture and behaviour. In common with other studies, leadership was identified more in a facilitative role, providing direction and encouragement for performance management, rather than in an implementing role. The changes attributed to performance management were often more closely associated with technical, cultural and behavioural influences. Leadership and management were considered to have played important roles in performance-related budget allocation, program revision and priority setting.

(g) Technical influences

Previous studies, particularly in the professional literature (Schick 2003; World Bank 2005; OECD 2018; Ho, De Jong and Zhao 2019), have noted that a common cause of weaknesses in the quality of performance management is the use of overly complex performance information requirements. Complexity produces challenges for measurement, cost, reporting, interpretation and use of performance information. Countries such as the UK, France, Korea, Netherlands, the US and Canada have all learned the lessons of establishing overly complex performance information arrangements early in the life of their broad-based arrangements. Each of those countries, and others, have refined their systems over time, resulting in fewer, more focused indicators and measures. There is no consensus in the literature on what constitutes the best level of complexity for performance information but there is wide acceptance of the view that more is not necessarily better.

In Australia and the Philippines there is considerable variation across organisations but no strong correlation between the size or type of organisation and the complexity of performance data. Figure 3.12 shows that most organisations consider that a set of key performance indicators (KPIs) of between 11 and 50 offers a reasonable balance between the desire for more information and the challenges of maintaining it. The Australian results suggest that, between the two phases of this study, a higher proportion of organisations have concluded that the middle range of complexity examined in this study is appropriate. Figure 3.12 shows that there are around 20 per cent fewer organisations with more than 50 KPIs and 3 per cent fewer organisations with less than 10 KPIs in 2019 compared with 2012.

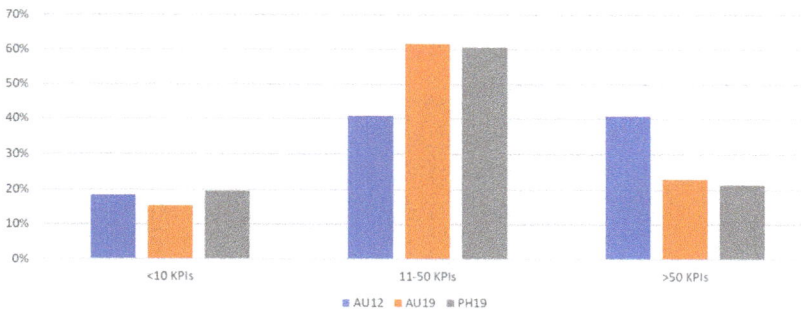

Figure 3.12. Complexity of KPIs.
Source: Author's summary of study results.

It is not clear that complexity is a major distinguishing feature between Australia and the Philippines, and so this would not be expected to be a significant explanation for differences in the quality and use of performance information. This conclusion is supported by attitudes of respondents to the major challenges they are facing in managing performance, as summarised in Figure 3.13. For example, both the Philippine and Australian respondents considered that they only faced moderate challenges in managing performance, which would not have been expected if the level of complexity was problematic. Both countries' respondents identified inconsistent quality, skills, data quality and cost of maintaining the currency of information as among the most significant challenges. Australian respondents found budget rigidity to be less of a problem than their Philippine colleagues, which may be related to the more flexible basis for budget appropriations in Australia.

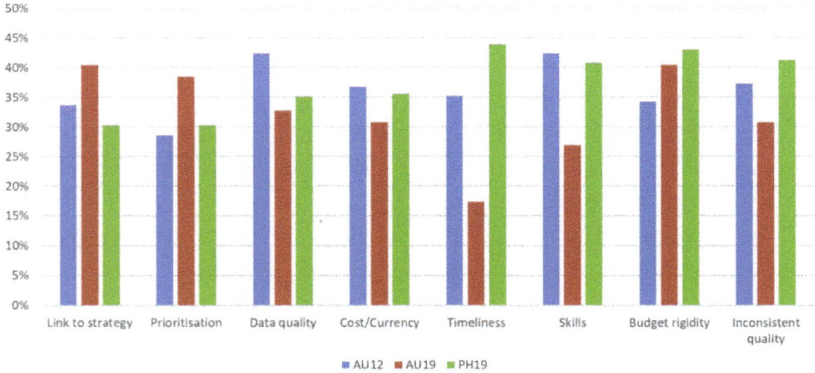

Figure 3.13. Challenges for performance management (0 = no challenge, 100 = extremely challenging).
Source: Author's summary of study results.

The Philippine organisations identified timeliness of performance information as its most challenging feature, in contrast to the most recent phase of the Australian study which reported it as least challenging. This could be associated with more frequent reliance on manual recording systems for performance information in the Philippines and less frequent use of special systems or general electronic information systems than Australia, as reported in the survey.

The challenge of skills and capability to produce consistent quality through performance management has been addressed differently in the two countries. In 2012, Australian respondents relied to a greater extent on internal guidance and less on support from central finance and audit institutions. This was different for respondents to the 2019 Australian questionnaire, where central finance and audit institutions were more important than internal sources. This may have been related to the increase in guidance and support provided by DOF following implementation of the PGPA Act in 2013. Philippine respondents relied most heavily on the Department of Budget and Management (DBM) while still drawing on guidance from state audit (COA) and internal sources.

The importance of performance dialogue and analysis of results is evident in the use of data collection and reporting at multiple levels within organisations in both countries. Philippine organisations use management and planning units within organisations more extensively and Australia has relied more on central finance and budgeting units. Both have also collected data at service delivery level and neither have relied on external contractors to collect and manage performance data to a significant extent.

Both countries produce performance reports for different groups of stakeholders, more frequently (monthly or quarterly) for internal stakeholders within operating units and senior management, and less frequently (often yearly) for external stakeholders. The Philippine respondents provided more frequent reports to elected or politically appointed officials than Australia. This could reflect the more extensive involvement of elected or politically appointed officials in the operations of organisations in the Philippine system than the Westminster-style separation between elected and career officials in the Australian administration.

(h) Cultural influences

Understanding and interpreting organisational culture is a challenging undertaking. Identifying its influence on performance management adds another level of complexity, but one that is increasingly being seen as important for public sector organisations (Ginevičius and Vaitkūnaite 2006; Woolcock 2014). The Australian Public Service Commission placed strong emphasis on organisational culture in its recent report on performance management (APSC 2019).

Respondents in both countries identified organisational culture as one of the most important influences on their performance management. The first aspect of culture examined by this study was the overall attitude of organisations to performance management. Respondents were asked to identify what they thought people in their organisations considered to be the main purpose(s) of performance management. In both countries compliance with government requirements and improving organisational processes were identified as the top two purposes. Improvement of results and providing a better understanding of organisational performance were considered to be less important purposes but still significant, as shown in Figure 3.14.

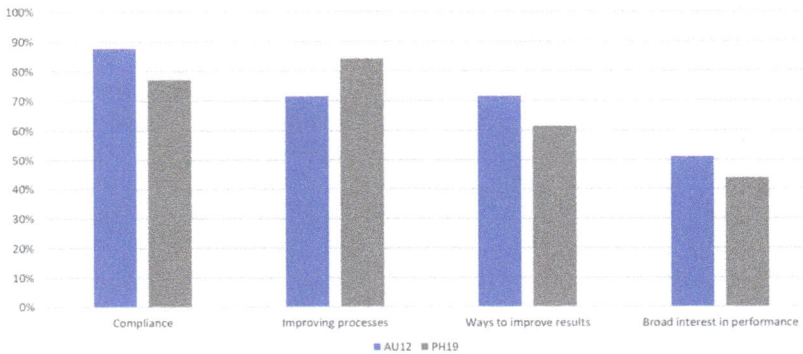

Figure 3.14. Purpose of performance management practices (% of respondents).

Source: Author's summary of study results.

Figure 3.14 suggests that respondents have a more functional view of performance management: that it is intended to address immediate needs and operational efficiency, rather than more fundamental considerations of effectiveness and impact. This is consistent with findings on Australian government organisations by Wanna and Podger (2017). This may have been influenced by the positions held by respondents to the survey, most of whom were in central areas of their organisations rather than service or program delivery areas. It could be examined in future work by obtaining multiple responses from within organisations from people with different perspectives and responsibilities.

The second aspect of culture examined by this study was to identify the ways in which organisations operated, along the lines of work by Hofstede, Hofstede and Minkov (2010). Participants were asked about the features of culture in their organisation, aimed at identifying the extent to which they demonstrated qualities such as dynamism, adaptability, flexibility, loyalty and commitment, and being hierarchical or open to new ideas and ways of working. The survey results, summarised in Figure 3.15, indicate that loyalty to the organisation is a major factor for staff in both countries. This is consistent with other studies that have found public service workers to be highly motivated by public service ideals, goals and objectives rather than individualistic or financial goals (Taylor 2013; Rasul, Rogger and Williams 2018).

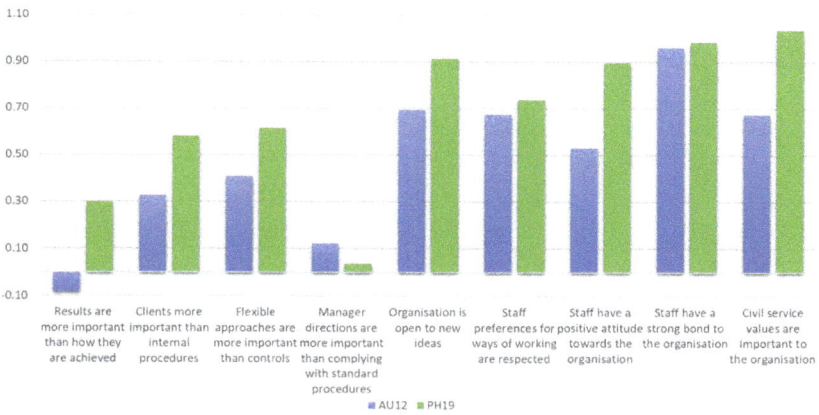

Figure 3.15. Attributes of organisational culture (2 = strongly agree, 0 = neutral, –2 = strongly disagree).
Source: Author's summary of study results.

The study found that staff in both countries tended to place significant emphasis on procedures, processes and controls, which moderated their preparedness to be flexible and results-driven. This is also consistent with other studies and the conventional Weberian concepts of public administration, which emphasise the importance of orderly, well-defined practices and procedures as a foundation for effective operations.

The pattern of results relating to organisational culture was similar for both countries, although the Philippine organisations scored more positively on all aspects, particularly in relation to loyalty to civil service values, their organisation and its leadership.

(i) Behavioural influences

The work of Smith (1995), Bevan and Hood (2005), Radin (2006) and others has provided convincing evidence of the strong, often disastrous, behavioural responses to performance targets in the public sector. When incentives, either positive or negative, are sufficient to influence behaviour, individuals and organisations will respond with attempts to meet the requirements, including through gaming, narrowing their focus to what is measured or, in extreme cases, falsifying reports.

The analysis of behaviour in this study focused more on the consequences of behaviour for organisational performance rather than the behaviour per se. On the positive side, it identified the incentives and encouragement to improve performance by individuals and organisations. On the negative side, it examined the sensitivity of organisations to criticism of performance as an incentive to avoid disappointing or controversial results. Comparing those responses with the effects and impacts of performance management was expected to provide an indication of whether behaviour was positively or negatively affecting success, and the strength of its influence.

This is one aspect where Australia and the Philippines have significantly different practices in relation to performance management, as illustrated in Figure 3.16. The Philippines Government provides annual financial incentives to organisations and their staff for meeting agreed targets. The financial rewards for individuals amounted to over 15 per cent of annual salary for more than half of the Philippine respondents. In 2012 some Australian organisations provided financial rewards for outstanding performance but were usually less than 5 per cent of salary and were not available to all staff. In 2019, none of the Australian respondents reported offering financial rewards for performance.

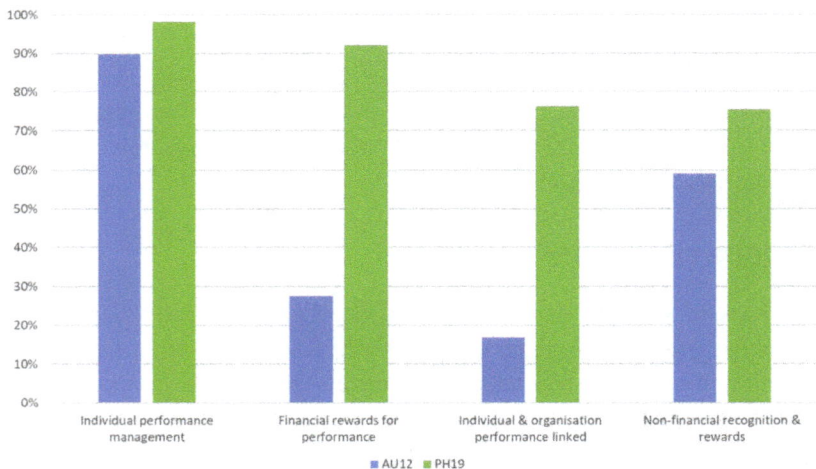

Figure 3.16. Performance incentives.

Source: Author's summary of study results.

Individual performance management practices were applied in both countries and both offered non-financial rewards and recognition for good performance. In the Philippines, the most widely used scheme mentioned by respondents was the Program on Awards and Incentives for Service Excellence (PRAISE). Australian organisations mentioned a variety of awards, including organisation-specific schemes and Australia Day awards used across the public service.

The survey results did not indicate a strong and systematic relationship between performance improvement and provision of financial rewards linked to organisational performance in the Philippines. The correlation between financial and non-financial rewards and performance improvements was close to zero for both countries. The correlation was even slightly negative between financial rewards and staff motivation and personnel evaluation results. The relationship was more positive between financial rewards and the quality of performance measures. The significance of these relationships should be treated with caution, however, considering the broad rating categories used for this study. More precise analysis would need to be performed to achieve a better understanding of the relationships.

Examination of the response to criticism focused on the main external influences on organisations, as shown in Figure 3.17. Philippine respondents were most responsive to DBM and COA while Australian respondents were more responsive to criticism by their minister and parliament. The Philippine results may have been affected by the financial performance scheme because both DBM and COA have important roles to play in deciding on whether organisations satisfy the requirements for rewards. The monitoring of organisational performance by the Australian DOF is less intensive, and oversight of performance by the Australian National Audit Office is limited to performance audits and assessment of organisational performance management arrangements.

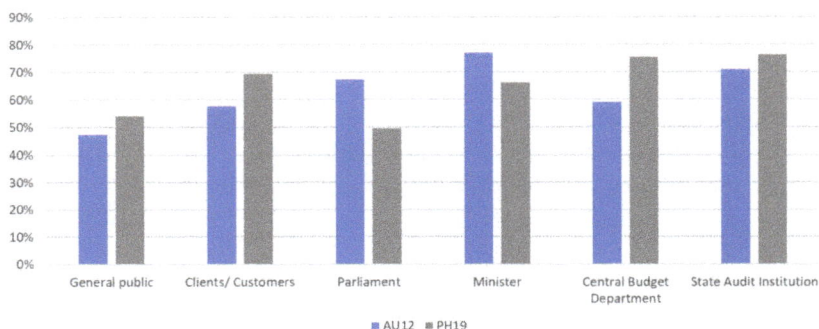

Figure 3.17. Response to criticism (0= no response, 100 = strong response).
Source: Author's summary of study results.

The response to criticism was only weakly related to performance improvements but, as with positive incentives, it was more closely related to the quality of performance information. Sensitivity to criticism from central budget departments and state audit institutions was most strongly related to quality improvements. The stronger influence of central agency criticism on quality is understandable because they are more likely to include technical matters in any comments about performance than other stakeholders.

(j) Individual organisation results

Much of the emphasis in this paper has been on the aggregate or average results in both countries. It would be too time- and space-consuming to report findings in relation to each of the organisations, so the discussion has been limited to higher-level attributes. In fact, the variation of results within each of the countries was greater than the differences between aggregated country scores. One question that was important for this research was whether the aggregate findings were consistent at the individual organisation level. The study undertook an in-depth sample analysis of 20 per cent of highest and lowest scores on the six influences referred to in the central hypothesis. Their scores on quality, use and impact were reviewed in detail along with other survey data to determine whether there was consistency in results across all aspects.

The sample analysis showed that each organisation that achieved low scores on a majority of the six influences also had low scores on quality, use and impact questions. It also showed that organisations with high scores on most of the six influences had high scores on quality, use and impact. The impact scores were less consistently related to the six influences than quality and use. This is not surprising considering that many other factors affect an organisation's impact, many of which are outside their control. This would alter the extent to which performance management alone could achieve an impact.

One strong feature of the sample analysis that warrants specific mention is the strong correlation between performance information use by management and ministers and the effects (coefficient = 0.74) and impacts achieved (coefficient = 0.67). This finding reinforces a key theme within the literature that use of performance information is crucial to the value of performance management arrangements (Moynihan 2008). Simply producing high-quality information is not sufficient; it has to be used to achieve any benefit. Culture and behaviour, followed by leadership and management, were the most important success factors associated with use of performance information in the detailed sample analysis.

Conclusions

The study presented in this paper sought to identify the main influences on success of performance management in public sector organisations. It found strong support for the proposition that there are six main influences encompassing external, institutional and structural, leadership and management, technical, cultural and behavioural factors. Organisations responding to the survey from the Philippines and Australia considered that all six influences were important, and no other influences were identified.

The importance of the six influences was supported by indications that the improvements directly attributable to performance management showed strong relationships with the extent of improvements. When the influences were stronger, performance improvement was stronger. When the influences were weak, very little performance improvement was identified by respondents. The most important influence on performance management in the Philippines was institutional and structural aspects. These included laws, regulations and organisational structure as the most important elements. Leadership and management was also very important in the Philippines and was most important for Australian respondents. The main characteristics of leadership and management that were noted by survey respondents were the involvement of senior management in monitoring performance and ensuring it was up to date and aligned with organisational strategy.

The study found that senior management was the main user of performance reports in both countries. The survey showed that stronger usage by senior management and ministers was correlated with higher levels of performance improvement across a variety of attributes including staff focus on results, internal processes, service delivery, program improvement and budget allocation. The six influences were strongly correlated with the quality and use of performance information, especially culture, behaviour, leadership and management. The six influences were less closely related to improvements and impacts of performance management, but the study did not filter out the effects of other influences on results, some of which would be outside of each organisation's control.

There are strong parallels between the findings of this study and previous works. In relation to this volume, it is particularly relevant to highlight the parallels with John Wanna's oeuvre. John has consistently identified the importance of performance management at the organisational level and shown how it has influenced the quality of performance information and performance results (Wanna, O'Faircheallaigh and Weller 1999; Hawke and Wanna 2010; Podger et al. 2018). He has highlighted the potential for performance information to be a political tool and has noted the differential ways in which it has been used across governments and in different periods and contexts (Wanna, Jensen and de Vries 2010). An important feature of John's work has been to identify the complexity of incentives and influences on performance management for the various groups of stakeholders, including politicians, ministers, central finance agencies, service delivery organisations and other government bodies. He has also emphasised the important roles of different technologies and processes, and the potential for citizens to actively participate in design, implementation and monitoring of public services (Lindquist, Vincent and Wanna 2013).

There are limitations of the approach taken in this study which should be considered when interpreting the findings. The main limitations relate to the selection of two countries with long experience in performance management and the data collection method. The results may be stronger for Australia and the Philippines because they have a long tradition of including performance information in their planning and management.

The results may not be so clearly positive in countries with less experience or less positive experiences with performance management. The use of a single respondent for each organisation places heavy reliance on that individual having a sound knowledge of performance management and how it affects the organisation. A wider sample of individuals within organisations may have provided a more varied picture. Self-reported performance without robust validation should be treated with caution. It is more likely to be subject to optimism bias, particularly where it reflects on the quality or performance of the respondents or their organisations, as is the case for this study.

In consideration of these limitations, the researcher has sought to mitigate the risks by including two countries to provide some measure of cross-reference. The individuals selected for responses to the survey were carefully chosen as the most knowledgeable about the arrangements in each organisation, with assistance from the central budget department in each country (though the departments were not involved in distributing, collecting or analysing the questionnaires and were not involved in interviews). Interviews were undertaken to confirm and validate responses from a large, targeted sample of respondents. Ultimately the robustness of the analysis will be strengthened by additional work in the two countries covered by the study and other countries using the same, or improved, methodology. Those options will be considered at the end of this study and may be taken up by other researchers as well.

The results of this study are encouraging, as they have supported the basic hypothesis and have supported findings from previous research and confirmed six influences on success of performance management in public sector organisations, and only six. This provides a firmer foundation for further research within and between those six areas to strengthen and deepen understanding of how they influence and how they can be used to improve performance management.

References

Australian Public Service Commission (APSC). 2019. *Performance Management in the APS*. Canberra: Commonwealth of Australia.

Behn, R. D. 2003. 'Why measure performance? Different purposes require different measures'. *Public Administration Review* 63(5): 586–606. doi.org/10.1111/1540-6210.00322.

Bevan, C. and C. Hood. 2005. *What's Measured is What Matters: Targets and Gaming in the English Public Health Care System*. Discussion paper no. 501. Public Services Programme, Economic and Social Research Council, UK.

Bohte, J. and K. Meier. 2001. 'Structure and the performance of public organizations: Task difficulty and span of control'. *Public Organization Review* 1 (September): 341–354.

Curristine, T. and S. Flynn. 2013. 'In search of results: Strengthening public sector performance'. In M. Cangiano, T. Curristine and M. Lazare (eds) *Public Financial Management and its Emerging Architecture*. Washington DC: International Monetary Fund.

De Waal, A. A. 2010. 'Performance-driven behavior as the key to improved organizational performance'. *Measuring Business Excellence* 14(1): 79–95. doi.org/10.1108/13683041011027472.

Department of Budget and Management (Philippines). 2016. *Program Expenditure Classification: The Next Phase of the Performance-Informed Budget*. Manila: Government of the Philippines.

Department of Finance (Australia). 2016. *Overview of the Enhanced Commonwealth Performance Framework*. Resource Management Guide no. 130. Canberra: Commonwealth of Australia.

Dull, M. 2008. 'Results-model reform leadership: Questions of credible commitment'. *Journal of Public Administration Research and Theory* 19(2): 255–284. doi.org/10.1093/jopart/mum043.

Fritz, V., M. Verhoeven and A. Avenia. 2017. *Political Economy of Public Financial Management Reforms: Experiences and Implications for Dialogue and Operational Engagement*. Washington DC: World Bank.

Gao, J. 2015. 'Performance measurement and management in the public sector: Some lessons from research evidence'. *Public Administration and Development* 35: 86–95. doi.org/10.1002/pad.1704.

Ginevičius, R. and V. Vaitkūnaite. 2006. 'Analysis of organizational culture dimensions impacting performance'. *Journal of Business Economics and Management* 7(4): 201–211. doi.org/10.3846/16111699.2006.9636141.

Hawke, L. R. 2012. 'Australian public sector performance management: Success or stagnation?' *International Journal of Productivity and Performance Management* 61(3): 310–328. doi.org/10.1108/17410401211205669.

Hawke, L. R. and J. Wanna. 2010. 'Australia after budgetary reform: A lapsed pioneer or decorative architect?' In J. Wanna, L. Jensen and J. de Vries (eds) *The Reality of Budgetary Reform in OECD Nations: Trajectories and Consequences*. Cheltenham, UK: Edward Elgar. doi.org/10.4337/9781849805636.00010.

Ho, A. T., M. De Jong and Z. Zhao. 2019. *Performance Budgeting Reforms: Theories and International Practices*. New York: Routledge.

Hofstede, G., G. J. Hofstede and M. Minkov. 2010. *Cultures and Organizations: Software of the Mind*. 3rd edition. McGraw Hill.

Hood, C. 2006. 'Gaming in targetworld: The targets approach to managing British public services'. *Public Administration Review* 66(4): 515–521. doi.org/10.1111/j.1540-6210.2006.00612.x.

Hood, C. 2012. 'Public management by numbers as a performance-enhancing drug: Two hypotheses'. *Public Administration Review* 72(1): S85–S92. doi.org/10.1111/j.1540-6210.2012.02634.x.

International Monetary Fund (IMF). 2014. *Government Finance Statistics Manual 2014*. Washington DC: International Monetary Fund.

Kroll, A. 2015a. 'Drivers of performance information use: Systematic literature review and directions for future research'. *Public Performance & Management Review* 38(3): 459–486. doi.org/10.1080/15309576.2015.1006469.

Kroll, A. 2015b. 'Exploring the link between performance information use and organizational performance: A contingency approach'. *Public Performance & Management Review* 39(1): 7–32. doi.org/10.1080/15309576.2016.1071159.

Lindquist, E., S. Vincent and J. Wanna (eds). 2013. *Putting Citizens First: Engagement in Policy and Service Delivery for the 21st Century*. Canberra: ANU E Press. doi.org/10.22459/PCF.08.2013.

Management Advisory Committee (MAC). 2001. *Performance Management in the Australian Public Service: A Strategic Framework*. Canberra: Commonwealth of Australia.

Moreno, R. and M. Garza. 2015. *Public Participation and Change: Three Cases where CSOs used Public Participation to Advance Fiscal Transparency in Mexico*. Global Initiative for Fiscal Transparency. Available at: www.fiscaltransparency.net/resourcesfiles/files/20151015135.pdf.

Moynihan, D. P. 2008. *The Dynamics of Performance Management: Constructing Information and Reform*. Washington DC: Georgetown University Press.

Moynihan, D. P. and I. Beazley. 2016. *Towards Next-Generation Performance Budgeting: Lessons from the Experience of Seven Reforming Countries.* Washington DC: World Bank. doi.org/10.1596/978-1-4648-0954-5.

Moynihan, D. P. and S. K. Pandey. 2010. 'The big question for performance management: Why do managers use performance information?' *Journal of Public Administration Research and Theory* 20(March): 849–866. doi.org/10.1093/jopart/muq004.

Mussari, R., A. E. Tranfaglia, C. Reichard, H. Bjorna, V. Nakarosis and S. Bankauskaite-Grigaliuniene. 2016. 'Design, trajectories of reform and implementation of performance budgeting in local governments: A comparative study of Germany, Italy, Lithuania and Norway'. In S. Kuhlmann and G. Bouckaert (eds) Local Public Sector Reforms in Times of Crisis. London: Palgrave Macmillan. doi.org/10.1057/978-1-137-52548-2_6.

Nicholl, P. 2006. 'Organisational structures do matter for good governance and good performance'. *Comparative Economic Studies* 48: 214–228. doi.org/10.1057/palgrave.ces.8100166.

Organisation for Economic Cooperation and Development (OECD). 2018. *OECD Best Practices for Performance Budgeting.* GOV/PGC/SBO(2018)7. OECD Public Governance Directorate, Public Governance Committee.

Organisation for Economic Cooperation and Development (OECD). 2019. *Budgeting and Public Expenditures in OECD Countries 2019.* Paris: OECD Publishing. doi.org/10.1787/8b33361e-en.

Podger, A., T. Su, J. Wanna, H. S. Chan and M. Niu (eds). 2018. *Value For Money: Budget and Financial Management Reform in the People's Republic of China, Taiwan and Australia.* Canberra: ANU Press. doi.org/10.22459/vm.01.2018.

Radin, B. A. 2006. *Challenging the Performance Movement: Accountability, Complexity, and Democratic Values.* Washington DC: Georgetown University Press.

Rasul, I., D. Rogger and M. Williams. 2018. *Management and Bureaucratic Effectiveness.* Policy research working paper 8595. Washington DC: World Bank.

Robinson, M. and J. Brumby. 2005. *Does Performance Budgeting Work? An Analytical Review of the Empirical Literature.* IMF Working Paper WP/05/210. International Monetary Fund. doi.org/10.5089/9781451862294.001.

Santiso, C. 2015. 'Why budget accountability fails? The elusive link between parliaments and audit agencies in the oversight of the budget'. *Brazilian Journal of Political Economy* 35(3): 601–621. doi.org/10.1590/0101-31572015 v35n03a12.

Schick, A. 2003. 'The performing state: Reflection on an idea whose time has come but whose implementation has not'. *OECD Journal on Budgeting* 3(1): 71–103. doi.org/10.1787/budget-v3-art10-en.

Schick, A. 2014. 'The metamorphoses of performance budgeting'. *OECD Journal on Budgeting* 13(2): 49–79. doi.org/10.1787/budget-13-5jz2jw9szgs8.

Smith, P. 1995. 'On the unintended consequences of publishing performance data in the public sector'. *International Journal of Public Administration* 18: 277–310. doi.org/10.1080/01900699508525011.

Talbot, C. 2010. *Theories of Performance: Organizational and Service Improvement in the Public Domain.* Oxford: Oxford University Press.

Taylor, J. 2011. 'Factors influencing the use of performance information for decision making in Australian state agencies'. *Public Administration* 89(4): 1316–1334. doi.org/10.1111/j.1467-9299.2011.02008.x.

Taylor, J. 2013. 'Goal setting in the Australian Public Service: Effects on psychological empowerment and organizational citizenship behavior'. *Public Administration Review* 73(3): 453–464. doi.org/10.1111/puar.12040.

Venner, M. 2019. 'The long history of performance budgeting in the Philippines'. In A. T. Ho, M. De Jong and Z. Zhao (eds) *Performance Budgeting Reforms: Theories and International Practices.* New York: Routledge. doi.org/10.4324/9781351055307-8.

Wanna, J., J. Forster and J. Kelly. (2000) 2003. *Managing Public Expenditure in Australia.* St Leonards: Allen & Unwin.

Wanna, J., L. Jensen and J. de Vries. 2003. *Controlling Public Expenditure: The Changing Roles of Central Budget Agencies – Better Guardians?* Cheltenham, UK: Edward Elgar.

Wanna, J., L. Jensen and J. de Vries. 2010. *The Reality of Budgetary Reform in OECD Nations: Trajectories and Consequences.* Cheltenham, UK: Edward Elgar. doi.org/10.4337/9781849805636.

Wanna, J., C. O'Faircheallaigh and P. M. Weller. (1992) 1999. *Public Sector Management in Australia.* South Melbourne: Macmillan.

Wanna, J. and A. Podger. 2017. 'Submission to the independent review of the PGPA Act'. Canberra: Parliament of Australia.

Woolcock, M. 2014. *Culture, Politics and Development*. World Bank Policy Research Working Paper No. 6939. Washington DC: World Bank.

World Bank. 2005. *Public Financial Management Performance Measurement Framework*. Public Expenditure and Financial Accountability Secretariat, Washington DC: World Bank.

Wright, B. E., D. P. Moynihan and S. K. Pandey. 2012. 'Pulling the levers: Transformational leadership, public service motivation and mission valence'. *Public Administration Review* 72: 206–215. doi.org/10.1111/j.1540-6210. 2011.02496.x.

4

A system in adjustment: Australia's evolving public budget management system

Stein Helgeby[1]

I met John in the 1990s, first at a conference at Griffith University, and then a bit later, when he asked for, and was granted, access to the Department of Finance, and to Finance people, to conduct some research. I was assigned to help him. To 'help' a researcher doing field work in a department might sound like a euphemism for 'minding' him – making sure he didn't do anything he shouldn't, and otherwise keeping an eye on him. It soon became obvious, though, that no minding was required. John wasn't interested in numbers, or policy proposals or state secrets of any kind. Instead, he was interested in things that people spent their time working on and with, but not as much time thinking about – the rules, practices and relationships at work in a central budget agency when it conducts its part of public financial management. Far from being a risk, this unusual interest could actually be a good thing, if it led to better formulated ideas and more intelligent practice. So, helping John was easy.

1   The views in this paper are my own and are not to be taken to represent those of the Department of Finance. I would like to thank John Wanna and Andrew Podger for their comments and Lembit Suur, Gareth Hall and Tracey Carroll for their advice on earlier drafts.

The multiple and changing roles of a central budget agency

There has rarely been much theorising undertaken in the Commonwealth to articulate what a central budget agency should be and what approaches should be applied to its work. The Department of Finance was created in a pragmatic political move in the 1970s, and it had at its core some very un-theoretical-sounding functions – 'supply divisions' and 'financial management' roles, carved out of Treasury. The very names of these roles should keep theorising at bay. But the department was also emerging in its own right as an important voice in the decision-making processes of government, which was the original intention. It was benefiting from the standing of its ministers, two important white papers of the early 1980s and the intellectual capacity of its senior people to innovate and drive change in a broader field – to see itself as an important contributor to public management, and to reshape what that meant, and to contribute to policy solutions.

If you wanted theory, you looked at New Zealand, which had implemented perhaps the most conceptually coherent approach to public sector management at the time, showing how to fit financial management within a broader system. They had imbibed public choice theory, but their emphasis on theory also seemed to reflect the fact that they needed to do something more drastic than we did, to meet their very serious economic and fiscal challenges. We could breathe a bit easier, seeing New Zealand as something to learn from without having to turn ourselves inside out as they had to do. The New Zealand approach also seemed to be relevant to the Victorians, who also had more of an interest in theory than the Commonwealth.

Pragmatism was no barrier to innovation, and John's interest in practice sat comfortably with both. Instead of having to work everything through from first principles, you could conceptualise the Commonwealth practice as operating at multiple levels. Public management, and public financial management in particular, interacts simultaneously, but in different ways, with macro-economic policy, micro-economic policy, organisational and service delivery design, institutional behaviour and incentives, and the management of the various levers of change in the public sector – rules, people, resources and technological possibilities. A central budget agency in the Finance mould is not one thing (e.g. a financial controller), nor is it even one thing, then another thing (e.g. a financial controller, then an enabler). Instead, it is many things simultaneously, in a perpetual process of renegotiation. The systems with which it concerns itself are not standalone, they are linked, and theory has only limited value in informing the process of articulating intentions, accommodating practice to circumstance and reflecting on experience as part of re-articulating intentions. Description, history and the stimulation provided by peers and exemplars are exactly the sorts of things that a department like Finance can best use. The open question is always, 'where do we need to work next?'

The open and shifting view I am putting forward sits uncomfortably with some well-known views. In 1997, for example, the Organisation for Economic Cooperation and Development (OECD) published a paper, written by Allen Schick, under the title *The Changing Role of the Central Budget Office* (OECD 1997). The opening to that work says:

> The traditional role of the central budget office is incompatible with the management reforms enfolding in various member countries. The traditional role of the budget office has been to function as a central command and control post … This role cannot coexist with the discretion accorded managers in the new public management. (1)

It goes on to say that the new roles of the central budget office, concerning institutions, integrating budgeting and management processes, and seeking to improve performance and evaluation, together with pursuing broader reforms of accountability and improved information technology, are 'likely to be a transitional phenomenon'. In the long run, the argument went, innovation needed to be undertaken by managers, not central policymakers. In the long run, too, the budgetary control role would be diminished by this new focus (OECD 1997, 4).[2]

In the long run, perhaps this argument will be right. But at least we should say that the transition is taking a long time. I would go a bit further, too: the transition isn't going to end any time soon. I think this is because Allen Schick's traditional characterisation of the budget task under three headings – aggregate fiscal discipline, allocative efficiency and technical efficiency – is reinforced by the depth of understanding of the public

---

2   Schick's recent views on such issues appear to have changed from this position, as shown in his contribution to this festschrift. Andrew Podger has noted that such criticisms were made at the time, but also more recently.

sector as a set of connected systems that active engagement in public management can bring. Indeed, Schick envisaged this, but nevertheless drew a different conclusion.

I draw the opposite conclusion to Schick, for two reasons. Firstly, the control model of a central budget office involves incentives that entrench information asymmetry; engagement does not eliminate it, but it does mitigate it. Secondly, at least in Australia, the innovation that Schick thought should come from managers is only possible with the active engagement of central institutions. This is because innovation is made possible or, alternatively, frustrated, by the systems of accountability and risk that operate across the public service. Innovation is enabled, or not, by the resource framework and by the practical arrangements that are put in place to support it.

Balancing 'devolution' and central control

At the same time as our own central budget office was changing its role, there was a strong emphasis on what was called at the time 'devolution', to be contrasted with 'central control'. In fact, devolution was always the wrong word for it, because (as a number of key players kept emphasising at the time) devolution is primarily about the exercise of authority. What took place, instead, was a type of localised responsibility for administration, under the banner of devolution.

What we ended up with was a system that often placed authority for decision-making closer to the point of delivery, but also produced fragmented sets of administrative arrangements. The varying resources and circumstances of individual agencies could produce inconsistency, duplication and inefficiency across the sector, built on systems and processes that may themselves have lost their original rationale. As resources have tightened in recent years, the ability to sustain or improve these arrangements has itself come into question.

For the past decade, in the Commonwealth at least, we have been slowly, and often uncomfortably, unpicking this patchwork and seeking to put in place centralised or more standardised arrangements where this makes sense. There is no theory to say what the sweet spot is for the balance between the centre and individual agencies in the sector, but across areas such as procurement, human resources, planning, accountability and process design, the centre is being built again, in the interests of allocative and technical efficiency, scale and innovation. What hasn't been done yet is to re-articulate a modern account of devolution, which puts the emphasis back on authority, and drops the idea that this is the same as localised administration.

Only a few years after Schick's paper, John Wanna co-edited a volume with a similar title: *Controlling Public Expenditure: The Changing Roles of Central Budget Agencies – Better Guardians?* (Wanna, Jensen and de Vries 2003). In that volume, he identified a list of 13 possible functions for a central budget agency, including Allen Schick's three, but explicitly excluding some functions then, and subsequently, delivered by the Australian Department of Finance (Wanna 2003). Finance was described as having undertaken four main roles since 1901, including when certain functions were part of Treasury: bookkeeper, expenditure controller, budget resource manager and policy analyst, and strategic adviser on investment and related matters (Wanna and Bartos 2003). While these were represented as distinct phases, not just roles, I think it would be better to characterise them as elements that are present to varying degrees at different points in time, but perhaps never entirely absent.

When Finance took on more of an investment orientation in the late 1990s, it didn't lose the other functions; it did them in a different context, and with a change of relevant impetus. Today, we are all of those things that John identified, but we also see our role as a leading contributor to achieving a modern and adaptable public service, which operates as efficiently as possible. We see ourselves as a leading partner within the broader context of the public sector, alongside other organisations. If you want a label, let's label it the 'strategic partner' model: the system offers more than its parts. We share the challenge of building Australians' trust in their institutions and the capacity of governments to meet the needs of citizens in a rapidly changing international and economic environment.

Custodian and steward of government systems

Governments exist to meet non-financial purposes, whether these are economic, social, environmental or security-related, in varying emphases and combinations over time, as governments themselves interpret and respond to community circumstances and aspirations. A central budget agency, however it is constituted, is part of reconciling these changing (and sometimes contradictory) interests at a point in time, but also over time, between generations. The systems that enable this to occur need to have a permissive or enabling character, as well as a directional or translation aspect (e.g. from high-level aspiration to local impact). They also need aspects of control and accountability, at aggregate and lower levels, particularly given that there are public resources and public interests at stake.

A central budget agency is a custodian and steward of these systems, seeking to adjust them from time to time. It isn't alone, however. One of the most important inputs to the system in the past decade has been the High Court. In the two *Williams* cases, notionally about whether the Commonwealth could pay for school chaplains, and in the more recent *Australian Marriage Law Postal Survey* cases, the court has exerted significant influence. In the *Williams* cases (*Williams v Commonwealth of Australia* and *Williams v Commonwealth (no. 2)*, respectively [2012] HCA 23 and [2014] HCA 23), the court overturned the Commonwealth's 110-year-old understanding of the place of appropriations in the system of financial management. It held that the making of a constitutionally valid appropriation is not in itself enough to support a spending activity. Instead, spending activities need to be referrable to a head of power in the Constitution, and there has to be parliamentary authority for the activity, in addition to an appropriation. That reading has important implications for how parliament and the executive operate, and for how financial management has to be undertaken in the Commonwealth.

In the *Australian Marriage Law Postal Survey* cases (*Wilkie v Commonwealth; Australian Marriage Equality v Minister for Finance*, [2017] HCA 40), the court supported the Commonwealth's view and clarified an issue about which there had been speculation over several decades. It held that the Advance to the Minister for Finance in the annual appropriation acts is an authority within the appropriation acts for the minister for finance to vary certain appropriations, if he is satisfied that certain criteria are met. This is important, because it makes clear that the issue with the advance is not one, as some have thought, about the use of an amount of money seemingly appropriated to the minister for finance without further constraint, but about the criteria under which the flexibility that exists within the system of appropriations is used.

Performance management and budgeting systems

In my mind, the High Court's decisions not only deal with these specific questions, but they ought to put an end to another long-running debate – about whether the appropriations framework can or should drive public sector performance in some other way. This is the argument that, if appropriations are constructed on a particular basis, they would provide an incentive to manage on that basis. There is some merit to this argument, seen from the negative. A system of appropriations that works at a detailed level, such as the postage and phone call level that prevailed up until the reforms of the 1980s, will clearly put constraints on management. A system that appropriates at a more generic level, as has existed from the late 1980s onwards, particularly for the ordinary annual services of government, better handles changing choices of input type in pursuit of a consistent outcome. The benefits of trying to tie the appropriation basis tightly to a performance framework are, however, marginal. This is because appropriations have a basis in the Constitution and are laws made by parliament, classified into different types (e.g. annual or special), with particular constraints and requirements applied to them, whereas performance frameworks need to range across the types. The alignment of appropriations to 'outcomes' in the Commonwealth's appropriation acts is clear only in relation to the annual appropriation acts. To understand the impact of government activity on an outcome in the sense of its social, economic or environmental impact, however, it is necessary to look at multiple appropriations and diverse sources of funds and how they work together. The appropriation framework can never, therefore, fully align with the needs of the performance framework. It can assist, but not drive. The appropriation framework has to be oriented to its primary job – authorising the flow of resources, under the Constitution, against a head of power and subject to other legislative requirements.

A performance framework, then, needs to have other underpinnings. Governments undertake activities primarily for policy purposes, rather than for financial purposes. Financial objectives are supportive of, and constraints to, broader policy purposes. From that perspective, the framework used to articulate policy objectives, and performance against those objectives is just as important as the financial framework. In practice, though, performance frameworks are a relatively recent creation, beginning with the Financial Management Improvement Program in the 1980s, and going through a number of iterations to the present day. In one sense, the technical aspects of each of these frameworks are simply variations on a central theme. That theme is that governments pursue policy agendas, that those agendas are about achieving something for the community, which can be articulated, whether it is social, economic, environmental or something else, and that the impacts of those policies can and should be assessed in forming views about whether to continue them, amend them, replace them or abandon them. Everything else is just technicalities, whether the articulation is through budget papers, corporate plans or both, or whether assessment is by formal evaluation, reporting against performance criteria, impressionistic or measurable. The judgements made on the back of those assessments ought to meet a number of purposes – public accountability, resource allocation from lower-impact to higher-impact initiatives, ongoing improvement of programs and implementation, and ensuring strong governance.

In practice, the simple idea of a sound performance framework, meeting multiple needs, has been achieved only in part, and that level of achievement has been variable over time, depending on individuals, organisational cultures and the interest or lack of interest of key stakeholders, including the parliament. The interesting question is why the achievements have been only partial. It used to be said that this is because it is hard – the public sector does not have simple objectives like the private sector does, the impact of policy is difficult to entangle from other factors, and so on. These arguments have some force in a performance framework that only permits metrics. It is much less forceful in a performance framework that puts the question differently – not, 'how do you measure it?', but 'what evidence do you take into account when you form the view whether things are working well, or not?'

I think we need to look for other reasons for the partial success of the various performance frameworks. These go partly to culture, and partly to use. The cultural issue is that Commonwealth bodies with corporate structures have typically been more attuned to themes such as performance and risk management. They have boards, with directors drawn from a variety of fields and with a mix of skills and expertise to apply to questions of governance and risk. The organisations themselves have developed skills and expectations in these areas, and in governance more broadly, which reflect the relative autonomy they exercise and the clear remits within which they operate. In non-corporate bodies, the situation has been relatively less stable. There are frequent changes of function and role, through machinery of government or policy means, and the role of any one organisation is often redefined relative to that of others. This makes it hard to achieve meaningful and consistent approaches to purpose and performance that hold over several years. There may be information relevant at a point in time, but that point in time might pass relatively quickly. The investment, personal and organisational, that is needed to develop a robust approach to performance may therefore deliver lower returns in the short run than an approach that simply focuses on activity and deliverables.

The second issue is that of use. Organisations and managers respond to the signals they get about what is valued and what is of use. Again, where a board is the primary user of information, a robust approach to performance will develop. Where ministers or parliaments are the primary intended users, there can be both inconsistent levels of interest and conflicting interests at play. Information about performance can be used out of context, or to make some point, rather than to improve a program or illuminate potential future decisions. Parliamentary scrutiny can be a strong driver of improved performance, but it can also focus primarily on individual activities or topical issues. Finally, and increasingly significantly, decision-making in government needs to be timely and respond to changing circumstances, whereas formal performance assessments can be slow processes, and the information difficult to relate in a timely manner to upcoming decisions. There can therefore be a disconnect that reduces the potential impact of information about performance on the workings of government. This disconnect is exacerbated when decision-making takes place at a significantly different level of detail and disaggregation than the level at which performance information is focused.

The most recent iteration of a performance framework for the Commonwealth tries to make inroads on both culture and use. Under the *Public Governance, Performance and Accountability Act 2013* (Cth) (PGPA), there has been a conscious move to strengthen the emphasis on performance, by embedding relevant duties and obligations in legislation governing all of the public sector, other than a very small number of institutions. Underpinning that, the performance framework itself allows for the temporal dimensions of government activity, rather than being focused purely on the near term, and welcomes evidence of performance in whatever form it comes, rather than being limited to metrics. An explicit role has been created for audit committees to take a continuing interest in the way individual organisations approach their planning and performance. The development of an institutional user outside the direct line of responsibility and accountability ought, over time, to allow other potential and more intermittent users to have confidence in the performance material and in its relevance to the goals articulated in forward-looking documents such as *Portfolio Budget Statements* and *Corporate Plans*. By itself, this approach will not, though, address all the relevant questions of immediacy.

Information systems for timely decision-making

Currency and immediate relevance is particularly important in decision-making processes, rather than for the purposes of accountability or authoritative record. At any one time, public management, and financial management in particular, can be seen from a political, communications, macro, micro or sector management perspective. The information requirements for decisions at each of these levels is quite different. For example, the aggregate level of transfers in the economy, and the level of targeting of those transfers, is clearly an important macro consideration, although not one that changes rapidly from year to year. Judgements about such matters need a different information base compared to micro-level decisions about incentive effects and policy interactions.[3] Financial and budget decision-making typically operate at this lower level, and financial frameworks are typically framed to address these lower levels.

An important test for the health of a public management system is how well information and thinking about different time periods are integrated. In better practice models, there is a close link between a thorough understanding of actuals and what is driving them, and the construction and updating of forward estimates.[4] Over longer time horizons, trade-offs that might need to be made in relation to international risks, for example,

---

3   There is a continuing trade-off between the use of financial means to achieve policy objectives, compared to the use of regulation. One means by which these trade-offs can be made more explicit, at least conceptually, is the development of regulatory budgets. There does not seem to have been, at least in Australia, much practical interest in this field, and in how regulatory budgets and financial budgets might interact.

4   There is an apparent corollary of this: the discount applied to advice from Treasury/Finance departments is a function of the size of the gap between prognostications about the future (positive or negative) and actual revenue collections/spending.

will appear differently if our focus is the short term, or 10 years out, or 30 years out. A strong decision-making framework needs ways to think concurrently about how risks differ over these time frames, based on very different information – solid information about past performance, robust modelling of the short-to-medium term and scenario-based analysis of the longer term.

'Bottom-up' and 'top-down' budget control: The role of the forward estimates

Viewed on a comparative basis, Australian approaches to decision-making, particularly around budgets, tend to involve relatively high levels of bidding or 'bottom-up' proposals, generally exceeding capacity many times over when seen against a set of budgetary aspirations or aggregate targets. They are not usually shaped 'top-down', against a set of specific policy or sectoral goals and financial parameters that have been established outside the budget process itself. Rather, priorities are shaped by and emerge in the decision-making process; 'themes' are more likely to be settled at the end.

In any budget process, bidding can have the effect of keeping unrelenting pressure on financial aggregates, in the absence of significant improvements to the financial position arising from economic or other circumstances. There is an upwards bias, even as economic circumstances vary, because future needs and costs are imperfectly understood; when they emerge, they clamour for attention. Over time, what was discretionary in earlier years becomes more non-discretionary because it is part of a set of expectations. Decisions taken in one year often have consequences that require further decisions to be taken in subsequent years; decisions about savings sometimes lead to later arguments that new spending is needed to offset their effects.[5]

Against this background, a strong and well-developed forward estimates system (now linked in the Commonwealth to corporate planning and the performance framework) is clearly important in managing a government's financial position and sustainability. It provides a baseline and a system of

---

5   The use of portfolios as the default organising principle for budget framing and decision-making, for saving as much as for spending, raises the question of how best to manage cross-portfolio and whole-of-government issues. Multi-agency ideas and big shifts of emphasis across sectors can be more difficult to achieve when the focus is at portfolio level.

accountability for changes to that baseline, whether these arise from policy decisions or from changes in other parameters. Commentary often focuses on the policy variations and 'measures' that a government introduces from time to time, but these are usually only a very small percentage of spending and revenue. They are almost always outweighed by 'parameter and other variations'. One way to think about these is that movements of this type represent the implications of decisions made in prior years. Commentary, however, very rarely asks interesting questions about these items, questions like: 'How well are the implications of previous policy settings understood? Are the implications accepted or not? To what degree do the policy decisions that a government makes from time to time vary the drivers, and not just the dollar value, of a program or policy setting?'

It is important to remember that forward estimates, in the way we understand them today, as part of a system of management, only date to the 1980s. The origin of forward estimates was as a source of discipline, even if some of the later uses reshaped announcements on spending to add across multiple years. They originated on the 'outlays' side of the budget and only later developed into a full set of estimates covering revenue and the balance sheet. In fact, Tasmania, rather than the Commonwealth, takes the credit for being the first to produce a full set of forward estimates (Challen 2011, 55–60; see also Wanna, Kelly and Forster 2000, especially 177–180, 319–322).

At the time they were introduced, forward estimates made a significant contribution to bringing predictability and aggregate management into what had been largely year-to-year processes that started from ambit claims.[6] New initiatives take time to set up, and time to reach maturity, particularly in terms of their full cost. In the absence of forward estimates, the implications of government policy settings in their mature operation would not be visible. In short, before forward estimates there was a 'year one' problem – what issues lurked beyond the budget year? For over three decades we have had four-year forward estimates, which means the system has a 'year five' problem – what happens in year five? In a 10-year forward estimates system, in addition to the inherent uncertainty of projecting over a longer time frame, there is a 'year eleven' problem, and so on. Whatever the time frame of the forward estimates, there is the risk of significant gaps, if low costs in the forward estimates period mask rapidly

---

6   During discussion at the festschrift, Andrew Podger recalled that the introduction of forward estimates at the Commonwealth level was initially proposed by Finance, but opposed by Treasury.

growing costs beyond it. Similarly, small contributions today can seem to make too insignificant an impact in the short term, leading to calls for interventions on top of interventions, without the first set of impacts having yet been felt.

Other approaches to address temporal issues: The role of accrual accounting

To address these limitations, a number of governments have introduced a range of longer-term projections. For example, the Commonwealth's periodic *Intergenerational Report* goes out 40 years. That is a way to deal with the time frame issue, and to draw attention to underlying trends; it doesn't, though, provide a planning or management framework. In addition, new institutions such as the various parliamentary budget offices often have remits that allow them to undertake analyses on an ad hoc basis, not constrained to any particular time frame.

Since the late 1990s, the problem of how to reflect and to analyse the impacts of decisions and policy settings has been given new dimension through the widespread adoption of accrual accounting. This has enriched the information available, although it has also multiplied the challenge of understanding and communicating that position. Victoria was the first to publish an accrual budget.

In the accrual world, a clear understanding of a government's financial situation and commitments does not come from focusing on a single set of numbers (surplus/deficit, however defined) across a particular time horizon. Rather, since financial management is a 'repeat game', it is like seeing a movie twice. The first time you see the movie you might be focused on the stars and the main events in the plot. The second time, you might pay more attention to the fine ensemble cast that has been put together, and the way they frame the whole production. By all means, look at the surplus or deficit, but then, turn your mind to the ensemble cast. For example: 'What is happening to debt, in terms of ratios as well as absolute values? What are the trajectories of particular components of the financial position over time? What items are expressed as present values on the balance sheet? What scenario modelling has been provided or made possible by new data and new ways of making it available? How well do the system of targets that a government has set support each other

– do they cover recurrent as well as capital, liabilities as well as assets, taxing as well as spending, the size of government as well as the functions or services of government?'

Before, when there were only cash numbers, there weren't as many things to track, or as many angles through which you could understand a decision. The label 'cash' even sounds comforting, like something to which every household can relate. That was always a bit of an illusion, however – for example, the term 'underlying cash' looks much more complicated when you talk about what it actually is trying to measure (the cash investment–saving balance) or how it is measured.[7] In fact, modern households work all the time with accrual tools like credit cards, and have a concept of wealth that looks at their assets and liabilities (e.g. a home and a mortgage). They would be surprised to think that their economic activity should be measured principally when they transfer cash to meet their obligations. Yet, that is often the lens through which Commonwealth activity is seen. By contrast to the Commonwealth, states and territories have the conceptual advantage that they run significant physical assets, which depreciate over time, and consequently need to maintain a clear focus on a capital program as distinct from operating commitments alone.

An alternative way to solve the problem of understanding the implications of government decisions is not to seek an ideal time frame for the forward estimates, but to bring present value to bear in the analysis. That is, long-term implications appear immediately in the financial position of the year in which the decisions are made. The development of forward estimates systems was the product of a cash world, and, at least initially, simply a spending world. The shift to accrual accounting, something where Australian jurisdictions were among the early movers, came a decade or more later. We can now see that this has given a much richer perspective on a government's financial position, by including a perspective on

---

7   At the time of the festschrift, the definition was: net cash flows from operating activities *plus* net cash flows from investments in non-financial assets *equals* ABS GFS (Australian Bureau of Statistics Government Finance Statistics) cash surplus/deficit *less* net acquisitions of assets acquired under finance leases and similar arrangements, *less* net Future Fund cash earnings (but only until 1 July 2020) *equals* underlying cash balance. (See, for example, Budget Paper Number 1, 2018–19, Statement 10, 10-38.) Since December 2019, following the introduction of revised accounting standards for leases (AASB 16), the '*less* net acquisitions …' line is now '*plus* Net cash flows from financing activities for leases' (AASB 2016). (See, for example, Budget Paper Number 1, 2019–20, Statement 9, 9-38–39.) This approach preserves the consistency of the time series. The point I am making is not about the definition, but simply that the term 'cash' makes things sound less complex than they are.

revenue and expenses, not just spending, and by developing a balance sheet covering assets and liabilities that were barely visible in the cash-only world. This has made possible a system of constraints, rather than a reliance on a single set of numbers to provide that constraint.

Australian jurisdictions are much more sophisticated now in relation to how they manage physical assets, particularly at the state and territory level. They often have asset replacement and investment programs that cover a decade or more, increasingly take a life-cycle view and sometimes budget for capital in a way that disentangles investment needs from recurrent commitments. All Australian jurisdictions now clearly identify their financial liabilities, such as their defined benefit superannuation schemes. The move, over the past two decades, to replace defined benefit schemes with accumulation schemes makes much less sense in a cash world, but is very important in an accrual world. From a cash perspective, replacing a defined benefit with an accumulation scheme can have a negative cash impact in the early years, and the real benefits only emerge decades later. From an accrual perspective, the positive impact on the balance sheet is, however, immediate, because the balance sheet shows the present value of obligations as at a particular point in time, and closing a defined benefit scheme significantly reduces this. Interestingly, though, the accounting world has in some senses struggled with government issues – a case in point is the issue of the discount rate used to value long-term liabilities. Accounting standards have landed on the spot-rate at a point in time. When this is applied to a forward estimates model, it creates considerable volatility between budget and actuals.[8]

In other respects, big issues that were initially seen as limitations when accruals were first introduced in government may come, over time, to seem within reach of a sensible outcome. The key example here is obligations arising from the welfare system, whether in the form of pensions or other supplements. These have long seemed out of scope from the perspective of bringing them to book on the government's balance sheet (and regardless of whether or not revenue can be treated in an equivalent way). Nevertheless, the topic remains under active professional consideration by standard setters and practitioners throughout the world. The recent interest in taking an actuarial approach to social welfare, such as in New Zealand, offers considerable prospects over the long term. Looking at this

---

8   The alternative, to use an actuarially determined rate, is not currently accepted.

issue from a very high level, welfare obligations ought to be expressible in present value terms – we know the population at a certain point in time, its relevant characteristics and life expectancies. We know what the policies are at any given time, and can assess longer-term economic conditions, and apply appropriate discount rates. Variations to that present value over time ought also to be expressible as arising from policy or other parameters.

Future challenges and directions

I stated earlier that the open question for a central budget agency is: 'where do we need to work next?' Public financial management is changed both by waves, such as the introduction of accruals, and by iteration, such as the focus on performance. The next changes might be more like waves than iterations, although they may be many years in the making. Data and real-time analysis of options will help to close the gaps between reliable information and immediacy. They will meet both accountability and decision-making needs. They will open up the potential for better integrating scenario analysis, and therefore the longer term, into decisions taken in the here and now. We need also to consider how well the traditional focus on linear decision-making and on a major event known as the budget will meet the expectations of governments and the community into the longer term.[9] To meet rapidly changing needs, we might be better served by greater clarity on overall financial parameters to set the constraint within which trade-offs can be made, while allowing decisions to be made in a more timely and responsive manner. This might over time mean slightly less focus on major set-piece accountability documents and more room for a continuous disclosure approach, with key thresholds driving the disclosures. The Australian Securities Exchange listing rules, with their emphasis on materiality and a reasonable person test, would provide an interesting starting point for such thinking.[10] Where might such ideas take the public sector?

---

9   John Wanna has drawn my attention to similar arguments made about budgets in the US – see Smith and Thompson (2012, 53–66), which argues, among other things, that budgets do not do what they are supposed to do.

10   See, for example, the relevant guidance note: www.asx.com.au/documents/rules/gn08_continuous _disclosure.pdf (ASX 2020).

At the start of this chapter, I mentioned two attempts at a taxonomy of what central budget agencies do – one by Allen Schick, and the other by John Wanna. In talking about developments over the past few decades, I have started out from the assumption that understanding the role of central budget agencies should involve understanding systems in their continual process of adjustment. It is a matter of contexts and relationships. The pragmatic approach to understanding central budget agencies and their roles, with which John has been so closely associated, has enriched discussion because it has paid attention to possibilities and actualities, not taxonomy narrowly defined.

References

Australian Accounting Standards Board (AASB). 2016. *Australian Accounting Standard AASB 16: Leases*. Australian Accounting Standards Boards Standard 16. Available at: www.aasb.gov.au/admin/file/content105/c9/AASB16_02-16.pdf.

Australian Government. 2018. *Budget Paper Number 1, 2018–19: Budget Strategy and Outlook*. Canberra: Commonwealth of Australia. Available at: archive. budget.gov.au/2018-19/bp1/bp1.pdf.

Australian Government. 2019. *Budget Paper Number 1, 2019–20: Budget Strategy and Outlook*. Canberra: Commonwealth of Australia. Available at: budget. gov.au/2019-20/content/bp1/download/bp1.pdf.

Australian Securities Exchange (ASX). 2020. *Continuous Disclosure: Listing Rules 3.1–3.1B*. ASX Listing Rules Guidance Note 8. Available at: www.asx.com. au/documents/rules/gn08_continuous_disclosure.pdf.

Challen, D. 2011. 'Quarter century in financial accountability: Scrutiny through transparency'. *Public Administration Today* 26(April–June): 55–60.

Organisation for Economic Cooperation and Development (OECD). 1997. *The Changing Role of the Central Budget Office*. OECD/GD(97)109. Paris: OECD Publishing.

Smith, K. and F. Thompson. 2012. 'Budgets? We don't need no stinkin' budgets: Ten things we think we know about budgeting and performance'. *Yearbook of Swiss Administrative Sciences* 3(1): 53–66. doi.org/10.5334/ssas.39.

Wanna, J. 2003. 'Introduction: The Changing Role of Central Budget Agencies'. In J. Wanna, L. Jensen and J. de Vries (eds) *Controlling Public Expenditure: The Changing Roles of Central Budget Agencies – Better Guardians?* Cheltenham, UK: Edward Elgar.

Wanna, J. and S. Bartos. 2003. '"Good practice: Does it work in theory?" Australia's quest for better outcomes'. In J. Wanna, L. Jensen and J. de Vries (eds) *Controlling Public Expenditure: The Changing Roles of Central Budget Agencies – Better Guardians?* Cheltenham, UK: Edward Elgar.

Wanna, J., L. Jensen and J. de Vries (eds). 2003. *Controlling Public Expenditure: The Changing Roles of Central Budget Agencies – Better Guardians?* Cheltenham, UK: Edward Elgar.

Wanna, J., J. Kelly and J. Forster. 2000. *Managing Public Expenditure in Australia.* St Leonards: Allen & Unwin.

5

Contradictions in implementing performance management

John Halligan

Performance has been a leitmotif of the reform era and the centrepiece of managerialism in Anglophone countries. Its pervasive influence has dictated the operations of government departments (Bouckaert and Halligan 2008; Radin 2006). It is impossible to envisage public management without regard to results, targets and performance measurement. However, a paradox of performance has been that the information generated for management frameworks has been often unused. The tension between the managerial and the political purposes of performance management has been a continuing dynamic of the reform era, which is one reason why the design of performance systems remained unresolved (Halligan 2020).

The performance movement shifted the focus from inputs and processes to outputs and outcomes, or more generally results. The underlying proposition was deceptively simple: to establish a process for advancing objectives with the promise of measurement and accountability, and then reporting results against indicators. There were, however, complications, for purposes were not always clear and often competing, their relevance varied with stakeholders (Behn 2003) and different logics were in play (Pollitt 2013; Gill 2011b). The practice was also demanding, as it entailed the intricacies of performance measurement and reporting, leading to complex interactions with politicians about the results. Given the pitfalls, it was not unexpected that the efficacy of performance management was mixed.

The Anglophone countries (Australia, Canada, New Zealand and the United Kingdom) were more committed at an early stage in the reform era to performance management and measurement than most Organisation for Economic Cooperation and Development (OECD) countries (OECD 1995; Bouckaert and Halligan 2008). This level of commitment has continued for over three decades, during which the countries have reworked their measurement and performance frameworks and expanded the range of performance instruments. There were variations in approaches to the common arrangement for all departments – the whole-of-government performance framework – and the use of specific performance instruments for measuring efficiency or tracking progress against targets. The countries' distinctive pathways allow comparisons of approaches to managing performance systems, the clusters of instruments used and lessons from the constant redesign of frameworks. Questions are raised as to whether progressive development has occurred with the core framework and the performance system and reported limitations of a performance approach have been addressed.

The purposes and instruments of performance

Several purposes have been differentiated for performance information (Van Dooren, Bouckaert and Halligan 2015), but essentially there are five: public accountability, central control, management improvement and learning, business planning and strategy, and results or priorities. The last three have assumed greater centrality for several countries. It can be argued that the standard purpose has always been about performance and therefore results, but these are subject to different interpretations and practice.

Performance measures can be used for multiple purposes (Behn 2003; Gill and Schmidt 2011; Van Dooren, Bouckaert and Halligan 2015), but the extent to which more than one (or two) can be appropriately achieved simultaneously through measuring information can be problematic. Much depends on the degree of clarity and understanding of the accountabilities, the handling of multiple stakeholders and the complexities of attending to several purposes. The primary purpose of a performance instrument has been first and foremost about reporting, of putting on the record what has been done; in other words, accounting against intentions. Or is it about attaining progress on an activity, which is then documented through measurable results? If the first, it leans towards accountability, and at worst becomes a matter of compliance and retrospectivity. If the latter, it may be primarily focused on achieving a government agenda. Of course, it may purport to be about both, and have other purposes.

The solution under the standard logic model has been that outcomes will provide the effects or results. Outcomes are however subject to two primary difficulties that often seem insurmountable: first, articulation and application (credible measurement), a constant problem being consistency in applying an outcomes approach; the second is about accounting for achievements where there are factors that cannot be controlled for. This has led to a focus on intermediate outcomes in the language of results. There are well-established understandings about the weaknesses of performance management (Radin 2006), and major issues have also arisen with the unintended consequences of performance assessment at the delivery level.

Performance is multifaceted and extensive. The focus here on the organisational and systemic performance of the central government raises two considerations. First, in demarcating the performance system, much performance activity is excluded: the macro or whole-of-government level is central, as is the meso level (performance of joint activity) and to some extent the micro level (the department). An understanding of cases (Gill 2011a), and factors affecting performance at this level, form one basis for generalisations. Secondly, different instruments have been used for judging performance, ranging from the general framework for departments to specific and highly focused tools.

The generic performance management framework is conceived in different ways depending on what is expected of it (e.g. a strategic framework: NAO 2016), but the core element is the parliamentary estimates (or plan) and annual reporting. While the focus is on the overarching performance framework, other specialised instruments of performance have been recognised, and six are identified here: implementation in furtherance of government priorities, chief executive assessment, organisational capabilities, efficiency, corporate planning and program evaluations. These may be either ad hoc or ongoing, published or unpublished (the latter not being of demonstrable public significance), or hybrids (either largely unpublished or opaque to the public and of questionable value). Departmental head reviews are private, although the integrity of the system depends on the clarity of the assessment criteria and the process. Results can be either integrated with the performance management framework or form an 'overlay' of government objectives.

In order to consider the focus and role of the country frameworks, five dimensions are derived from the literature and official documents (Table 5.1). The first is the degree of focus or spread of the purposes (ranging from the basics to a comprehensive 'road map'). The significance of planning and whether it has been used internally by departments is relevant here. Also important is the political executive's role and the centrality of its priorities (which are also related to ownership of the framework, either by one or two central agencies). A corollary of these last two is the question of the range and relative importance of stakeholders (Talbot 2008). Third is the question of whether the framework has been stable and durable across governments (NAO 2016). The cross-cutting component is the fourth element. Finally is the question of whether evaluation is built into performance management (Talbot 2010).

Performance management frameworks: How have countries handled them?

The core of the performance system has been the performance management framework for departments and agencies. The four countries detailed below have had a fully-fledged model that fitted within the 'performance management' ideal type differentiated by Bouckaert and Halligan (2008). The official model has usually been based on an outputs and outcomes framework that covered organisational dimensions and their management interrelationships. Their frameworks have been pursued in some form since the 1980s and have provided the longest records of most OECD countries – an exception being the US – in wrestling with how to make performance management work.

Australia: Path dependence

The Australian agenda since the mid-1980s has involved three phases, each initiated by a new performance framework: the first dating from the inauguration of a new system (1986); the second from its reformulation (1997–99); and the third implemented in 2014–16. The first two frameworks reflected two reform phases: managerialism and the new public management variant (Halligan 2007a). In the first, the elements of performance management were developed through the Financial Management Improvement Program. The focus on results, outcomes and performance-oriented management dates from this time (Wanna, Kelly and Forster 2000). The core was program budgeting and management, which was to assist managers' assessments of program development and implementation relative to objectives. All programs had to be reviewed every five years and departmental evaluation plans produced annually for the Department of Finance (Campbell and Halligan 1992; Keating and Holmes 1990; TFMI 1993). In this phase, the elements of performance management were developed within a centralised approach. The strengths were institutionalised performance management and the experience of formal evaluations by the centre. The weaknesses were the quality of objectives for, and performance information on, programs.

The second formulation was based on an outcomes/outputs framework, devolution, principles instead of formal requirements and an emphasis on performance information. Departments and agencies were required to identify explicit outcomes, outputs and performance measures, and their heads were assigned responsibility and accountability for performance. However, problems with the design and implementation became apparent, and a succession of piecemeal interventions occurred, which failed to prevent a continuing critique. Departmental programs were reincorporated because ministers argued they lacked the information required for making decisions. Even where a principle-based approach was used, controls were reimposed in the form of inputs and 'front-end processes'. The framework became more compliance-focused and less about performance and achieving results (DFD 2012, 34). A succession of studies by the audit office and a ministerial review, Operation Sunlight, raised serious questions about the efficacy of aspects of the framework and the need for renewal (e.g. Tanner 2008; ANAO 2011; Hawke 2012). There were strengths, such as strong ownership for departments. Weaknesses included insufficient information for parliamentary needs and sound management (Mackay 2004), weak support for evaluation and problems arising from combining a centralised budgetary process with devolved departments.

After 30 years, Australia still lacked an effective system (ANAO 2011, 2013; Halligan 2007b; Hawke and Wanna 2010; Mackay 2011; Tanner 2008). The framework was the subject of a multi-year review by Finance (DFD 2012; DoF 2014). Under the *Public Governance, Performance and Accountability Act 2013* (Cth), a new framework was implemented with outcomes and programs retained. It was intended to resolve limitations, to report more effectively and to integrate departmental planning and performance management, using corporate plans, plus other aspirations, such as improved risk management. An initial survey reported that notable challenges remained, including overcoming risk aversion and improving performance (DoF 2015; Podger 2015). The third framework was a progressive development (Hawke 2016), but the quality of reporting on performance information still required improvement. In key areas – such as management of risk and cross-government cooperation – little had changed (Alexander and Thodey 2018).

Canada: Confronting conundrums

Canada's pathway is notable for an early succession of trials and acknowledged failures, followed by a gestation period before a fully-fledged and durable performance management framework was installed in the 2000s. This was then somewhat overtaken by the 'results and delivery' agenda in the late 2010s.

The shift from structuring the main estimates as a traditional program budget occurred after 1995 with the introduction of the Planning, Reporting and Accountability Structure (PRAS). Departments and agencies reported on their plans and priorities in the main estimates to inform parliament about the outputs and outcomes they wanted to achieve. There were issues with the quality and coverage of financial and performance data and the lack of outcomes focus. Assessments of departmental performance reports showed a limited focus on outcomes (Bouckaert and Halligan 2008).

By the mid-2000s, these issues had been responded to, if not convincingly addressed in practice. The Management Accountability Framework (MAF), was introduced in 2003, and the Management, Resources and

Results Structure (MRRS) replaced PRAS as the basis for departmental reporting. A standardised approach was used to incorporate performance information in management and policy cycles. The MRRS established the link between results and programs connected with departmental management and structure. The requirements for departments were codified and integrated through reports on plans and priorities and departmental performance, which were designed to indicate the links between plans, performance and achievements. There was a shortage of independent analysis, and scepticism existed about performance management and the mandatory federal agenda (Clark and Swain 2005; Thomas 2004). The approach was heavily top-down, featuring central agencies, particularly the government's 'management board', the Treasury Board Secretariat. Nevertheless, by the mid-2000s, Canada had a developed performance management framework, which continued to evolve and be refined, and readily fitted within the 'performance management model' (Bouckaert and Halligan 2008). The MAF created a broader framework to anchor the performance focus by providing deputy ministers with tools to assess and improve management practices.

The Policy on Results supplanted MRRS in 2016 with the purpose of improving the attainment of results. Departments were expected to be clear about objectives and the measurement of success, and to measure and evaluate performance and use the information for managing and improving programs (Lindquist 2017).

New Zealand: Escaping the constraints of the original model

A key feature of the financial management reforms of the late 1980s was the distinction between outputs and outcomes, and their assignment respectively to chief executives and ministers. Under New Zealand's Public Finance Act, departments acquired responsibility for financial management from the Treasury. Chief executives managed inputs to produce outputs that ministers purchased. The focus was on chief executives and their responsibilities for managing departments under contract, as specified through performance and purchase agreements, and the annual assessment of their performance by the State Services Commission (Boston et al. 1996; Scott 2001).

New Zealand was slow to tackle weaknesses of the model in the areas of accountability, performance measurement and strategic management. Two limitations were the emphasis of the output orientation on managerial accountability at the expense of public and parliamentary accountability, and gaps in the system's capacity to learn from experience. The link between outputs and desired outcomes was variable because of how the political executive engaged: ministers were expected to utilise the connection and set performance targets (Boston et al. 1996; Schick 1996; Scott 1997; Kibblewhite and Ussher 2002). To address long-term strategic thinking, managing for outcomes was implemented through statements of intent (SOIs). Incremental improvements occurred in the quality of departmental planning, but most SOIs did not show much improvement (CAG 2006), and there was a need to refine output and outcome indicators and improve the links between them. The focus on performance was also applied to a broad agenda for better overall performance of the state services and development goals.

The focus on outputs and chief executive responsibility for delivering goods and services produced distortions, while ministers let their purchaser role override their responsibility for outcomes (Schick 2001). The system addressed outcomes conceptually but had problems integrating them into public management because of difficulties both in specification and in measurement (Kibblewhite and Ussher 2002). Performance information was not used much in the budget process, and the effectiveness of annual budgeting for assessing public performance was questioned (Shand and Norman 2005). Changes were difficult, because removing the output focus 'would strip the system of its magnificent conceptual architecture' (Schick 2001, 2).

The Public Finance Act 1989 was amended in 2013 to require agencies to address meaningful and useful performance measures for reporting externally. Agencies must still describe and evaluate performance, but Treasury prescriptions are more flexible and allow agencies to specify how performance is to be assessed. A turning point was the report of the Better Public Services Advisory Group, which stipulated improved performance by the state services by 'securing the outcomes that matter most to New Zealanders' wellbeing'. The system's strength, service delivery (outputs), was insufficient because, performance was not 'gaining traction on the big outcomes that matter' (BPSAG 2011, 14, 15). The report led to extensive activity centred on 10 result areas, and government prioritising ensured progress on targets (Morrison 2014; Scott and Boyd 2017). The 2019 budget has been produced on a wellbeing basis (James 2019), and the 2019 reform process is intended to support higher performance.

United Kingdom: System churn – governing without a framework?

The Financial Management Initiative was designed to focus on objectives and measure outputs and performance but was only partly successful. Outputs and service delivery became important from the late 1980s, and outcomes in the late 1990s (Bouckaert and Halligan 2008). The last decade has been notable for a succession of frameworks.

The political executive's drive for performance, delivery and results was relentless and reflected in instruments for aligning government priorities with progress in implementation. A turning point was when the performance framework, Output and Performance Analysis (OPAs), introduced in the mid-1990s, was replaced by Public Service Agreements (PSAs). The OPAs provided continuity with previous systems but were unaligned with key election pledges and omitted targets for measuring improvements (Panchamia and Thomas 2014). The PSAs were linked to spending reviews, which examined resources for each field of expenditure and the related service delivery in order to integrate a multi-year policy perspective with a budgetary process. Further spending reviews occurred mainly at two- or three-year intervals. Each department had a PSA, a two-yearly agreement with Treasury consisting of an aim, objectives, performance targets, value-for-money targets and a responsibility statement. They were operationalised through plans for reaching targets with reporting to the Cabinet Office and Treasury on implementation. The PSA was a novel instrument for bringing central government under a performance framework, but limitations included frequent changes to targets, unclear objectives and weak incentive effects on priorities (James 2004). Treasury made limited use of departments' performance reports (Talbot 2010). The PSA evolved, and was simplified (fewer PSAs and targets), enhanced (joint targets), and linked to spending reviews.

Departmental business plans (DBPs) were introduced by the Cameron Coalition to provide democratic accountability and to hold departments centrally accountable for implementing the reform program. Each plan addressed the coalition's priorities and program for the department, focusing on areas that the government could control in contrast to 'aspirational outcomes' (Stephen, Martin and Atkinson 2011). Issues about usability were apparent, including ambiguity with the data, format inconsistencies, and difficulties with accuracy, analysis and comparability (Institute for Government 2011). There was no evidence that plans were being used by the Cabinet Office or ministers (Institute for Government 2012). For many departments, the business plans were unserviceable for measuring performance (Bull et al. 2013).

The DBPs were replaced in 2015 by a new business planning and performance management system, Single Departmental Plans (SDPs), that were designed for reporting on key priorities, crosscutting goals spanning departments and departmental day-to-day business. Oversight bodies observed the lack of a 'cross-government approach to business planning, no clear set of objectives, no coherent set of performance measures and serious concerns about the quality of data that was available' (NAO 2016, 12; CPA 2016). The government claimed nonetheless that these processes added up to a management system. The contrary position was that the 'collection of processes does not amount to the coherent strategic framework for planning and managing public sector activity' (NAO 2016, 7). The SDPs were judged to be potentially a step forward, but their effectiveness remained untested, and they needed further development (CPA 2016). Priorities of departments were 'vague statements of intent or platitudinous aspirations' (PACAC 2018, 16), the link between priorities and resources was tenuous and there remained 'weak incentives to prioritise, make realistic plans and consider long-term value' (NAO 2018, 12).

Other performance instruments

In addition to the generic performance management framework, each country developed specialised ongoing and ad hoc whole-of-government instruments for pursuing performance. Many efficiency reviews, however, are not subject to public reporting and do not qualify here.[1]

---

1   Economy exercises may have performance implications. Australian functional reviews were concerned inter alia with the identification of barriers to performance (Cormann 2015).

Implementation/delivery and monitoring

Results and government priorities agendas are sometimes reflected in implementation/delivery units (e.g. the UK's Prime Minister's Delivery Unit), and minister-led cross-departmental priorities (such as those resulting from New Zealand's Better Public Services report [BPSAG 2011], and potentially from the UK's cabinet taskforces).

Executive performance

The development of secretary performance assessment has been an element in the panoply of performance instruments. All Anglophone systems have some form of performance assessment for department heads. Of the four described in this chapter, the Australian arrangement appears to have been less publicly developed. There has been also a possible underlying sanction entailing career prospects other than short-term rewards (Podger 2007).

Canada has had formalised guidelines for deputy ministers in some form since at least the early 2000s. The Privy Council Office's (2018) performance guidelines read prima facie as a compensation plan that includes performance pay. Performance agreements are made between the PCO clerk and the deputy minister for commitments in the results areas of policy and program, management (as specified by MAF), leadership and corporate. New Zealand redefined the relationship between ministers and departmental chief executives appointed on performance agreements. The State Services Commission has been responsible for their performance agreements as a cornerstone of performance management. The commissioner has appointed, employed and reviewed chief executive performance, including the achievement of results and investment in organisational capability (SSC 2006; Scott 2016). Permanent secretary objectives have been used in the United Kingdom for performance management. The objectives of each secretary are agreed with ministers and the prime minister and have been publicly available since 2012. They are reviewed annually by the civil service head. The objectives have covered priorities such as strategic, business, diversity, leadership and capability, and generic responsibilities: contributing to the corporate leadership of the civil service and supporting civil service reform (Freeguard et al. 2017).

Organisational capabilities

A focus on management capability addresses the organisational attributes (e.g. human capital, systems, relationships) required for the performance expected. Capability reviews have been used in Australia and the United Kingdom, and Performance Improvement Frameworks (PIFs) in New Zealand. The Canadian MAF has a capability element. Capability reviews were discontinued in Australia and the United Kingdom; self-assessments have been used in both countries and critiqued in the UK as a poor variant. New Zealand continued to make use of its adapted version, PIFs, which have also had a more explicit performance aspect (School of Government 2017).

Program evaluation

The use of evaluation has been highly variable in the Anglophone systems, which have not been responsive to renewed international interest in a central role, with one exception. For Australia, evaluation was a crucial element in the 1980s managing for results because it linked policy development and program implementation (Keating and Holmes 1990; Halligan and Power 1992; Di Francesco 1998). Following an experiment with mandatory program evaluation there were over two decades of indifference except for a few departments. The lack of departmental agreement meant nothing emerged, although an independent review supported greater use (Alexander and Thodey 2018). In New Zealand, evaluation has also been essentially a departmental responsibility, and several have had evaluation capacities (Scott 2016). Although, an outcomes approach requires measurement based on evaluation (Hughes and Smart 2012), the use of evaluation for policy advice processes was limited compared to other countries (Scott, Faulkner and Duignan 2010). UK evaluation was at a low ebb prior to 1997 (Talbot 2010). Since then 'some progress' occurred, although doubts existed about whether it produced meaningful learning, and the obstacles to quality evaluation were substantial (Hallsworth, Parker and Rutter 2011; NAO 2010). The exception has been Canada, which has a long history of mandatory evaluation through the Treasury Board Secretariat (Shepherd 2016). All programs were to be reviewed every five years and departments were expected to maintain 'a robust, neutral evaluation function' (TBS 2016). The record with program evaluation was mixed, depicted as being about 'turning a crank that's not attached to anything' (Savoie 2014, 149; Savoie 2011).

Management Accountability Framework (MAF)

Canada is unusual in relying on the MAF as an omnibus approach for over two decades. The MAF has entailed a top-down system of monitoring and compliance by the Treasury Board Secretariat. Despite a performance element to the framework, MAF was 'more audit and process-based' (Dean 2009, 31). It has been used to comprehensively assess departmental performance for 10 areas, guided by a framework, 'a high-level model of the attributes of a "well-performing" public sector organisation, but MAF increasingly has the look and feel of a quality assurance and risk management assessment system' (Lindquist 2009, 49, 56). The value of MAF has continued to be hazy (and debated) given the transaction costs. It has provided an instrument for monitoring departmental performance, and MAF results do feed into deputy ministers' assessments (Lindquist 2017), but the regulatory compliance aspect lingers despite modifications over time. MAF is part of an extensive oversight system of instruments, which, according to the auditor general, existed to prevent the Phoenix fiasco but did not (SSCNF 2018).

Corporate performance assessment

New Zealand has used the annual Administrative and Support Services Benchmarking (BASS) since 2010 for systematising information about corporate services. It has provided agencies with performance information on expenditure on back office services, consistent performance data across agencies and an 'evidence base' for performance assessment.[2] It was pitched as a benchmarking analysis to assist agencies with achieving efficiencies by using targets. Initial improvements were not sustained, suggesting that the instrument was not driving performance improvement. System-level impacts were modest, and the degree of comparability was unclear (Bonner 2014).

---

2   For more information, see: www.treasury.govt.nz/statesector/performance/bass.

Crosscutting program performance

New Zealand's Better Public Services is arguably the best documented exercise at the subsystem level (Scott and Boyd 2017). The concept of a leadership superstructure overlaying several departments in pursuit of defined objectives is not new (although like other international experiments has not been durable: Peters 2015).

The performance system consists of the core framework and specialised instruments. These performance instruments can be represented as being part of a system. Performance instruments can be designed for distinctive purposes (e.g. accountability to parliament or implementing priorities). However, there is a question as to what extent the centre operates corporately in using levers for modulating and strengthening systemic performance (and there are issues in steering performance systems: Talbot 2008). New Zealand has had a conscious approach to using a range of performance instruments, although the elements in its system of performance were not linked effectively (Allen and Eppel 2017).

Performance frameworks in flux?

An ever-growing catalogue of weaknesses in performance management was evident by the third decade of the reform era, which have not been resolved by framework development (Bouckaert and Halligan 2008; Radin 2006). These need not be reproduced here beyond noting the most salient and intractable issues. Practice generally fell short of aspirations, and significant questions remained about the quality and use of performance information in the budget process and for internal decision-making; questions also remained about the relevance of performance information for external reporting and its political relevance, and about the variable engagement of departments and agencies. The limitations of country approaches included questions about the effectiveness of their frameworks, particularly the tendency towards a compliance emphasis focused on external reporting rather than other objectives. Performance management systems were regularly modified to improve operability, but their effectiveness was undermined by tardiness and reluctance in modifying the framework, and by churn (in the case of the United Kingdom). Common features were disconnects between outputs and outcomes and between internal planning and reporting, and reconciling demand and supply of performance information (i.e. what politicians want) (Bouckaert and Halligan 2008; Gill 2011a; Talbot 2010; Edwards et al. 2012; NAO 2016).

Outcomes and outputs

All management frameworks have featured outputs and outcomes in some form. Both Australia and New Zealand were talking outcomes in the 1980s, but the paths diverged. New Zealand identified outcomes with ministers and outputs with chief executives, with a performance agreement between them. This was perceived in Australia as institutionalising the separation of policy and delivery, a perennial issue in public administration. In contrast, Australia wished to bring them together, but ambiguity, even blurring, remained as to responsibilities (Holmes 1989). In the long term, neither approach was sustained. The outcomes side remained underdeveloped or unresolved, eventually being either assigned to politicians or overshadowed by an output focus. New Zealand's 'managing for outcomes' approach was discontinued because performance measures lacked the rigour of those for outputs (Hughes and Smart 2012). The inclination in New Zealand was to reject outcomes in favour of some form of results, although by the end of the 2010s they were back in favour. Australia eventually opted for outcomes and programs instead of outputs for the 2009–10 budget. Performance management capability in the United Kingdom has been poor with respect to performance measurement for developing 'outcome-based and longer-term indicators' (NAO 2016, 35). UK Treasury has acknowledged the challenge of moving from inputs to outputs to outcomes, and inputs have continued to be a focus reflecting the central agency's role in public spending and because manifestos have focused on levels of expenditure (CPA 2018, Q23).

Quality of performance information

Issues with performance information have long been raised by auditor generals in all four countries with two recent examples being noted here. UK oversight agencies, like counterparts elsewhere, have long had issues with the quality of performance information. Insufficient information was provided 'to hold departments to account for all costs, outcomes and value for money on both the coalition agreement and across all of a department's work' (NAO 2016, 24; CPA 2011). The Committee of Public Accounts found no improvements, concluding that accountability officers lacked the cost and performance data required for undertaking effective oversight. This was regarded as a long-standing problem, as the National Audit Office had previously reported that 'variation in the scope and completeness of information currently available limited its ability to inform public choice and accountability' (NAO 2016, 24). The Canada Revenue Agency misrepresented its performance in dealing with taxpayers: 'Too often ... performance measures do not reflect the actual performance' (SSCNF 2018; OAG 2017).

Decoupling of functions

The decoupling of functions – outcomes and outputs – from operational practice (Dormer and Gill 2010) was a commonplace response to central performance management systems. The frontline may be either disengaged from the senior management's preoccupation with outputs and outcomes that was expected at the whole-of-government level, or reflective of departmental operating principles.

Australian departments went through the routine of producing the material for reporting purposes but were inclined to rely on their own internal planning for operational matters under the second model, while the third framework sought to integrate performance and internal corporate reports. One dimension was organisational incentives. The performance framework did not require departments to integrate their own internal planning processes, with the performance process, which was an external imposition. Consequently, the two processes were run in parallel. Priority was given to external reporting, while performance information was not generally made use of for internal purposes. Since the incentives didn't exist for departments to apply the framework for their own purposes, there was insufficient attention given to organisational culture, and the embedding of performance. The inclination of departments to deviate from performance management frameworks has been long argued by the Australian National Audit Office (Bouckaert and Halligan 2008; McPhee 2005).

Targetism

The use of targets has been commonplace but pursued with particular zeal in the UK. The fixation on targetism under Blair extended from the composition of PSAs with departments, mainly defined in terms of outputs and outcomes, to delivery organisations operating under tough sanctions for missing targets, such as threats of job loss, agency termination and publicity on results (Flynn 2007). In New Zealand, achieving results through targets became simply another control function (Gill 2011a).

Performance in Canada became:

> the product of many hands, from the political level down to the most junior front-line worker. There was no incentive for public servants to draw attention to problems, to explain what has gone wrong, or to suggest why performance targets may not be realistic. (Savoie 2011, 160)

Savoie quotes Michael Warnick (then deputy minister and later a clerk of the PCO) who reported that departments dealt with central agency demands by producing 'fake stuff', which is 'the stuff you pretend to do that you feed to the central agencies to get them off your back' (Savoie 2011, 160).

Use of information

Who uses performance information and why is it not used (Van Dooren, Bouckaert and Halligan 2015)? A range of factors have contributed to the mixed use of performance information (e.g. the standard problems with devising indicators for outcomes), the organisational-level performance gaps derived in the first instance from the design and implementation of the framework, and the inability of political and public service leadership to respond to the weaknesses. This situation can be argued to be a consequence of a combination of a new public management–type solution and a political nexus that is diffident about the role of central leadership in performance management.

Pollitt (2006) pointed out that research has rarely focused on the 'end users' of performance information in the traditional model of representative democracy – that is, ministers, parliamentarians and citizens – and that if they used performance information it would, 'constitute the definitive justification for the practices of evaluation, performance management and performance audit as components of a *democratic* polity, rather than as merely an artefact of technocratic administration' (38).

More generally, the use of performance information to underpin budgeting has long been an unfulfilled objective, although it may inform aspects (Cangiano et al. 2013).

Renewal through planning and priorities?

The four systems described have followed different pathways within a performance management framework. Their early implementation styles differed in terms of conceptions of the relationship between outputs and outcomes, the responsibilities given to chief executives, and the roles of the central personnel agency in handling performance oversight. There continue to be differences in approach and with the treatment of outcomes and outputs. Several generations of performance management provided extensive experience of potential limitations. The management discipline, efficiencies and accountabilities achieved under these frameworks sustain commitment and the quest for system improvements in managing performance.

Three of the frameworks have undergone recent transformations: Australia's third framework formally incorporates business planning and Canada's two-level results focus combines the revised performance management framework of the TBS with a political overlay for driving the focus through the PCO. The UK approach has had the most discontinuity and its poor public articulation has been ambitious and multipurpose. In the case of New Zealand, the inability to move from an entrenched focus on output accountability, which served the system well for efficiency purposes, left the framework otherwise unserviceable (Morrison 2014; NAO 2016; Gold 2017). For some time, results replaced the language of outcomes, and were 'effectively bite-sized pieces of an outcome (similar to what were previously called intermediate outcomes)'. The government wanted 'tangible progress towards its larger objectives, which in effect was a renaming of outcome indicators' (Morrison 2014, 47). A switch back to outcomes has occurred under the Arden Government.

The dissatisfaction with obtaining results through outputs and outcomes had not led to a focus on results instead of outcomes. The knitting together of performance with planning and/or priorities caters for different purposes. The expansion of purposes means that distinctions could be made between keeping to the basics and more comprehensive schemes.

The later part of the 2010s has been a time of evolution and experiments with frameworks in all four countries, with the level of change and other details not necessarily yet publicly available. With that caveat in mind, several dimensions are distinguished in Table 5.1. In terms of purposes, all systems provide for formal accountability, and usually some measure of internal department planning, with the level of central control variable. Results are more formally recognised in two countries for the whole-of-government framework.

Table 5.1. Dimensions of frameworks

	Australia	Canada	New Zealand	United Kingdom
1.Purposes	Focused	Multiple	Focused	Comprehensive
Accountability*	Formal	Formal	Formal	Formal
Planning	Yes	Yes	Yes	Yes
Priorities	In development	Evolving	In selected areas	Still evolving
2. Stakeholders	Focused	Focused	Focused	Broad in concept
3.Stability	Yes, but evolving	Yes, overlay effects unclear	Yes, but evolving	Changeable in 2010s
Continuity across governments	Yes	Yes, but augmented	Yes	No
4. Cross-government	Available, unused	Unclear	Recent experience	Unfulfilled in latest iteration
5. Evaluation	Left to departments	Central role	Left to departments	Left to departments

* Relatively unused in practice.

Source: Author's summary.

Framework stability and continuity across governments have been apparent in three cases, the exception being the United Kingdom. Attention to fundamentals for planning, managing and changing priorities has been lacking in the UK's SDP framework:

> Government needs a proper framework for planning to the medium term and beyond, that will allow it to make achievable plans, and to understand what it needs to know to stay on track. This framework should be stable and enduring, existing independent of political priorities. (NAO 2016, 6)

The stakeholder approach was generally focused, but the United Kingdom's aspirations were more broadly conceived. The SDP framework was designed by the Cabinet Office and Treasury:

> to cover a large number of different stakeholders' needs, by capturing for the first time the whole range of departments' aims and objectives including departmental commitments, cross-department goals, day-to-day service delivery, business transformation programmes and efficiency improvements. (NAO 2016, 14)

It was subsequently judged to require a range of changes, without which 'government will continue to be trapped in a cycle of short-termism, over-optimism and silo decision-making, which creates real risks to value for money' (NAO 2018, 13).

The interest of political executives in results and priorities has varied between countries. It has also been underpinned by the strong role of the prime minister's department in performance management in two jurisdictions (e.g. the Canadian Privy Council Office and the UK Cabinet Office). The others are active in cross-government activity. Evaluation was mainly a matter for departments.

Conclusion

Bearing in mind the introductory questions, how has this uneven record been worked through? Performance management frameworks have neither gelled nor become durable as multipurpose fixtures. The 2010s have been a decade of experimentation with instruments for performance improvement. What form of performance is appropriate is not amenable to a consistent answer beyond the basic requirement of satisfying a public accounting for results against objectives. In responding to multiple objectives and stakeholder expectations, two polar options are to rely either on an omnibus document (more like the UK) or several instruments (New Zealand). The purposes of performance management remain unresolved, particularly where it is subject to turnover with governments.

The place of 'results' in the overall scheme of things remains a conundrum. Performance has become more focused on achieving political agendas. The framework is likely these days to be skewed in that direction rather than serving the needs of either departments or the public, although the former is catered for if the renewed emphasis on business planning works. However, inflexibilities are still present, and the cross-departmental aspect problematic.

Have the four countries discussed in this chapter devised stable performance instruments to provide the information expected by stakeholders? One has persisted with progressive iterations of a core framework (Australia). Two have worked around limitations with the framework overlaying a results reporting facility (Canada and the United Kingdom) while New Zealand now accords centrality to its wellbeing budget (New Zealand).

The United Kingdom has opted for regularly replacing the framework, and while its ambitious 'road map' remains unrealised, if successful, it will potentially provide a new model. To what extent a performance system exists is dependent on design questions and the attention given by a corporate centre to systemic questions and impacts of performance.

There have been long-term difficulties with engaging effectively with a performance approach. Frameworks take time to develop and implement and perennial issues continue to resurface. All systems are working through new arrangements, the results of which remain unclear. What is apparent is that the performance story is still in progress after over three decades and, without resolution of chronic issues, will remain a contested area.

References

Alexander, E. and D. Thodey. 2018. *Independent Review into the Operation of the* Public Governance, Performance and Accountability Act 2013 *and Rule*. Canberra: Commonwealth of Australia.

Allen, B. and E. Eppel. 2017. 'The New Zealand performance improvement framework – Strategic conversation, organisational learning or compliance tool?' Paper presented at IRSPM Conference, Budapest, 19–21 April.

Australian National Audit Office (ANAO). 2011. *Development and Implementation of Key Performance Indicators to Support the Outcomes and Programs Framework*. Auditor-General Report No. 5 of 2011–12. Canberra: Commonwealth of Australia.

Australian National Audit Office (ANAO). 2013. *The Australian Government Performance Measurement and Reporting Framework: Pilot Project to Audit Key Performance Indicators*. Auditor-General Report No. 28 of 2012–13. Canberra: Commonwealth of Australia.

Behn, R. D. 2003. 'Why measure performance? Different purposes require different measures'. *Public Administration Review* 63(5): 586–606. doi.org/10.1111/1540-6210.00322.

Better Public Services Advisory Group NZ (BPSAG). 2011. *Better Public Services: Advisory Group Report*. Wellington: New Zealand Government. doi.org/10.26686/pq.v8i3.4422.

Bonner, S. 2014. 'Performance management in the New Zealand public sector'. Business research project for MBA. Wellington: Victoria University of Wellington.

Boston, J., J. Martin, J. Pallot and P. Walsh. 1996. *Public Management: The New Zealand Model*. Auckland: Oxford University Press.

Bouckaert, G. and J. Halligan. 2008. *Managing Performance: International Comparisons*. London: Routledge.

Bull, D., J. Stephen, P. Bouchal and G. Freeguard. 2013. *Whitehall Monitor: No. 41: How Departments Measure their Performance*. London: Institute for Government.

Campbell, C. and J. Halligan. 1992. *Political Leadership in an Age of Constraint: The Experience of Australia*. Sydney: Allen & Unwin and Pittsburgh: University of Pittsburgh Press.

Cangiano, M., T. Curristine and M. Lazare (eds). 2013. *Public Financial Management and Its Emerging Architecture*. Washington DC: International Monetary Fund.

Clark, I. D. and H. Swain. 2005. 'Distinguishing the Real from the Surreal in Management Reform: Suggestions for Beleaguered Administrators in the Government of Canada'. *Canadian Public Administration* 48(4): 453–477. doi.org/10.1111/j.1754-7121.2005.tb01198.x.

Committee of Public Accounts UK (CPA). 2011. *Accountability for Public Money*. 28th report of session 2010–11. HC 740. London: House of Commons.

Committee of Public Accounts UK (CPA). 2016. *Managing Government Spending and Expenditure*. 27th report of session 2016–17. HC 710. London: House of Commons.

Committee of Public Accounts UK (CPA). 2018. *Driving Value in Public Spending: Oral Evidence*. 78th report of session 2017–19. HC 1596. London: House of Commons.

Controller and Auditor-General (CAG) 2006. *Central Government Results of the 2004–2005 Audits*. Parliamentary Paper. Wellington: Office of the Auditor General.

Cormann, M. 2015. *Smaller and More Rational Government 2014–15*. Ministerial Paper. Canberra: Commonwealth of Australia.

Dean, T. 2009. *UK Public Service Reforms: A Canadian Perspective*. Toronto: Institute of Public Administration of Canada.

Department of Finance (DoF). 2014. *Enhanced Commonwealth Performance Framework: Discussion Paper*. Canberra: Commonwealth of Australia.

Department of Finance (DoF). 2015. *Findings Report on the July PGPA Benefits Realisation Survey*. Canberra: Commonwealth of Australia.

Department of Finance and Deregulation (DFD). 2012. *Sharpening the Focus: A Framework for Improving Commonwealth Performance*. Canberra: Commonwealth of Australia.

Di Francesco, M. 1998. 'The measure of policy? Evaluating the evaluation strategy as an instrument for budgetary control'. *Australian Journal of Public Administration* 57(1): 33–48. doi.org/10.1111/j.1467-8500.1998.tb01362.x.

Dormer, R. and D. Gill. 2010. 'Managing for performance in New Zealand's public service – A loosely coupled framework?' *Measuring Business Excellence* 14(1): 43–59. doi.org/10.1108/13683041011027445.

Edwards, M., J. Halligan, B. Horrigan and G. Nicoll. 2012. *Public Sector Governance in Australia*. Canberra: ANU Press. doi.org/10.22459/psga.07.2012.

Flynn, N. 2007. *Public Sector Management*. 6th edition. London: Sage.

Freeguard, G., R. Adam, E. Andrews and A. Boon. 2017. *Whitehall Monitor 2017: The Civil Service as it Faces Brexit*. London: Institute for Government.

Gill, D. (ed.). 2011a. *The Iron Cage Recreated: The Performance Management of State Organisations in New Zealand*. Wellington: Institute of Policy Studies.

Gill, D. 2011b. 'Introduction'. In D. Gill (ed.) *The Iron Cage Recreated: The Performance Management of State Organisations in New Zealand*. Wellington: Institute of Policy Studies.

Gill, D. and T. Schmidt. 2011. 'Organisational performance management: Concepts and themes'. In D. Gill (ed.) *The Iron Cage Recreated: The Performance Management of State Organisations in New Zealand*. Wellington: Institute of Policy Studies.

Gold, J. 2017. *Tracking Delivery: Global Trends and Warning Signs in Delivery Units*. London: Institute for Government.

Halligan, J. 2007a. 'Reintegrating government in third generation reforms of Australia and New Zealand'. *Public Policy and Administration* 22(2): 217–238. doi.org/10.1177/0952076707075899.

Halligan, J. 2007b. 'Performance management and budgeting in Australia and New Zealand'. In P. de Lancer Julnes, F. Berry, M. Aristigueta and K. Yang (eds) *International Handbook of Practice-Based Performance Management*. Thousand Oaks, California: Sage. doi.org/10.4135/9781412982719.n17.

Halligan, J. 2020. *Reforming Public Management and Governance: Impacts and Lessons from Anglophone Countries*. Cheltenham, UK: Edward Elgar.

Halligan, J. and J. Power. 1992. *Political Management in the 1990s*. Melbourne: Oxford University Press.

Hallsworth, M., S. Parker and J. Rutter. 2011. *Policymaking in the Real World: Evidence and Analysis*. London: Institute for Government.

Hawke, L. 2012. 'Australian public sector performance management: Success or stagnation?' *International Journal of Productivity and Performance Management* 61(3): 310–328. doi.org/10.1108/17410401211205669.

Hawke, L. 2016. 'Australia'. In D. Moynihan and I. Beazley (eds) *Towards Next-Generation Performance Budgeting: Lessons from the Experience of Seven Reforming Countries*. Washington DC: The World Bank. doi.org/10.1596/978-1-4648-0954-5_ch5.

Hawke, L. and J. Wanna. 2010. 'Australia after budgetary reform: A lapsed pioneer or decorative architect?' In J. Wanna, L. Jensen and J. de Vires (eds) *The Reality of Budgetary Reform in OECD Countries: Trajectories and Consequences*. Cheltenham, UK: Edward Elgar. doi.org/10.4337/9781849805636.00010.

Holmes, M. 1989. 'Corporate management: A view from the centre'. In G. Davis, P. Weller and C. Lewis (eds) *Corporate Management in Australian Government*. Melbourne: Macmillan.

Hughes, P. and J. Smart. 2012. 'You say you want a revolution … The next stage of public sector reform in New Zealand'. *Policy Quarterly* 8(1): 3–16. doi.org/10.26686/pq.v8i1.4408.

Institute for Government UK. 2011. 'Business plans: A long way to go'. Press release. 11 July. Available at: www.instituteforgovernment.org.uk/news/latest/business-plans-long-way-go.

Institute for Government UK. 2012. 'Government business plans fail to live up to expectations'. Press release. 20 November. Available at: www.instituteforgovernment.org.uk/news/latest/government-business-plans-fail-live-expectations.

James, C. 2019. '"Wellbeing" facet points to different way of governing'. *Otago Daily Times*, 31 May, 8.

James, O. 2004. 'The UK core executive's use of public service agreements as a tool of governance'. *Public Administration* 82(2): 397–419. doi.org/10.1111/j.0033-3298.2004.00400.x.

Keating, M. and M. Holmes. 1990. 'Australia's budgetary and financial management reforms'. *Governance* 3(2): 168–185. doi.org/10.1111/j.1468-0491.1990. tb00113.x.

Kibblewhite, A. and C. Ussher. 2002. 'Outcome-focused management in New Zealand'. *Journal of Budgeting* 1(4): 85–109. doi.org/10.1787/budget-v1-art23-en.

Lindquist, E. 2009. 'How Ottawa assesses department/agency performance: Treasury Board's management accountability framework'. In A. M. Maslove (ed.) *How Ottawa Spends 2009–2010: Economic Upheaval and Political Dysfunction.* Montreal and Kingston: McGill-Queen's University Press.

Lindquist, E. 2017. 'Rethinking the management accountability framework for the open government era'. In K. Graham and A. Maslove (eds) *How Ottawa Spends 2017–2018: Canada @150.* Ottawa: School of Public Policy and Administration, Carleton University.

Mackay, K. 2004. *Two Generations of Performance Evaluation and Management Systems in Australia.* ECD Working Paper Series 11. Washington DC: World Bank.

Mackay, K. 2011. 'The performance framework of the Australian Government, 1987 to 2011'. *OECD Journal on Budgeting* 11(3): 75–122.

McPhee, I. 2005. 'Outcomes and outputs: Are we managing better as a result?' Paper presented at CPA National Public Sector Convention, Melbourne, 20 May.

Morrison, A. 2014. 'Picking up the pace in public services'. *Policy Quarterly* 10(2): 43–48.

National Audit Office UK (NAO). 2010. *Evaluation in Government.* London: National Audit Office.

National Audit Office UK (NAO). 2016. *Government's Management of its Performance: Progress with Single Department Plans.* HC 872. Session 2016–17. London: National Audit Office.

National Audit Office UK (NAO). 2018. *Improving Government's Planning and Spending Framework.* HC 1679. Session 2017–19. London: National Audit Office.

Office of the Auditor General of Canada (OAG). 2017. *Report 1 – Phoenix Pay Problems.* 2017 Fall Reports: Report 1. Ottawa: Auditor General of Canada.

Organisation for Economic Cooperation and Development (OECD). 1995. *Governance in Transition: Public Management Reforms in OECD Countries.* Paris: OECD Publishing.

Panchamia, N. and P. Thomas. 2014. *Civil Service Reform in the Real World: Patterns of Success in UK Civil Service Reform.* London: Institute for Government.

Peters, B.G. 2015. *Pursuing Horizontal Coordination: The Politics of Public Sector Coordination.* Lawrence: University of Kansas Press.

Podger, A. 2007. 'What really happens: Departmental secretary appointments, contracts and performance pay in the Australian Public Service'. *Australian Journal of Public Administration* 66(2): 131–147.

Podger, A. 2015. 'Further development of Australia's performance management system: Emphasising "how" and "why" as well as "what"'. Paper presented at 2015 AGPA Conference, Seoul, September.

Pollitt, C. 2006. 'Performance information for democracy: The missing link?' *Evaluation* 12(1): 38–55.

Pollitt, C. 2013. 'The logics of performance management'. *Evaluation* 19(4): 346–363.

Privy Council Office of Canada. 2018. 'Performance management program for deputy ministers, associate deputy ministers and individuals paid in the GX range'. *Government of Canada.* Available at: www.canada.ca/en/ privy-council/programs/appointments/governor-council-appointments/ performance-management/senior-public-servants.html.

Public Administration and Constitutional Affairs Committee, House of Commons UK (PACAC). 2018. *The Minister and the Official: The Fulcrum of Whitehall Effectiveness.* 5th report of session 2017–19. HC 497. London: House of Commons.

Radin, B. 2006. *Challenging the Performance Movement: Accountability, Complexity, and Democratic Values.* Washington, DC: Georgetown University Press.

Savoie, D. J. 2011. 'Steering from the centre: The Canadian way'. In K. Dahlström, B. G. Peters and J. Pierre (eds) *Steering from the Centre: Strengthening Political Control in Western Democracies.* Toronto: University of Toronto Press. doi.org/ 10.3138/9781442687066-009.

Savoie, D. J. 2014. *Whatever Happened to the Music Teacher? How Government Decides and Why.* Montreal and Kingston: McGill-Queen's University Press.

Schick, A. 1996. *The Spirit of Reform: Managing the New Zealand State Sector in a Time of Change*. Report prepared for the State Services Commission and the Treasury. Wellington: New Zealand Public Service Commission.

Schick, A. 2001. *Reflections on the New Zealand Model*. Based on a lecture at New Zealand Treasury, August.

School of Government. 2017. *Independent Review of the Performance Management Framework*. Wellington: School of Government, Victoria University of Wellington.

Scott, G. 1997. 'Continuity and change in public management: Second generation issues in roles, responsibilities and relationships'. In State Services Commission, *Future Issues in Public Management*. Wellington: State Services Commission.

Scott, G. 2001. *Public Management in New Zealand: Lessons and Challenges*. Wellington: New Zealand Business Roundtable.

Scott, G., P. Faulkner and P. Duignan. 2010. *Improving the Quality and Value of Policy Advice*. Review of expenditure on policy advice. Wellington: Government of New Zealand. Available at: treasury.govt.nz/sites/default/files/2011-04/report-repa-dec10.pdf.

Scott, R. 2016. *Theoretical Foundations of Department Chief Executive Performance Appraisals*. Working Paper 2016-4. Wellington: State Sector Performance Hub.

Scott, R. and R. Boyd. 2017. *Interagency Performance Targets: A Case Study of New Zealand's Results Programme*. Washington, DC: IBM Centre for the Business of Government.

Shand, D. and R. Norman. 2005. 'Performance budgeting in New Zealand'. Paper prepared for IMF Fiscal Affairs Department Seminar on Performance Budgeting, Washington DC, 5–7 December.

Shepherd, R. P. 2016. 'The program evaluation function: Uncertain governance and effects'. In T. Klassen, D. Cepiku and T. J. Lah (eds) *The Routledge Handbook of Global Public Policy and Administration*. New York: Routledge.

Standing Senate Committee on National Finance (SSCNF). 2018. *Proceedings of the Standing Senate Committee on National Finance: Issue No. 70, Evidence*. Ottawa, 12 June.

State Services Commission (SSC). 2006. 'The Role of the State Services Commissioner'. *Public Service Commission*. Available at: www.publicservice.govt.nz/about-us/sscer.

Stephen, J., R. Martin and D. Atkinson. 2011. *See-Through Whitehall: Departmental Business Plans One Year On*. London: Institute for Government.

Talbot, C. 2008. 'Performance regimes – The institutional context of performance policies'. *International Journal of Public Administration* 31(14): 1569–1591. doi.org/10.1080/01900690802199437.

Talbot, C. 2010. *Performance in Government: The Evolving System of Performance and Evaluation Measurement, Monitoring, and Management in the United Kingdom*. ECD Working Paper Series No. 24. Washington DC: World Bank.

Tanner, L. 2008. *Operation Sunlight: Enhancing Budget Transparency*. Canberra: Australian Government.

Task Force on Management Improvement (TFMI). 1993. *The Australian Public Service Reformed: An Evaluation of a Decade of Management Reform*. Canberra: Commonwealth of Australia.

Thomas, P. 2004. *Performance Measurement, Reporting and Accountability: Recent Trends and Future Directions*, Public Policy Paper 23. Regina: The Saskatchewan Institute of Public Policy.

Treasury of Canada Board Secretariat, Internal Audit and Evaluation Bureau (TBS). 2016. 'Evaluation of the management accountability framework'. 16 December. Available at: www.canada.ca/en/treasury-board-secretariat/corporate/reports/evaluation-management-accountability-framework.html.

Van Dooren, W., G. Bouckaert and J. Halligan. 2015. *Performance Management in the Public Sector*. Second edition. London: Routledge. doi.org/10.4324/9781315817590.

Wanna, J., J. Kelly and J. Forster. 2000. *Managing Public Expenditure in Australia*. Sydney: Allen & Unwin.

SECTION 2: POLITICS

Introduction to Section 2: Queensland and Australian politics

Increasingly, academic reward systems have pushed scholars to specialise in narrow fields and to publish their research only in high-ranking journals in order to advance university rankings. For all John Wanna's specialisation in budgeting and finance, he has resisted these pressures, retaining interest in a wide range of public policy and administration, bridging theory and practice, and also being a significant player in Queensland politics in particular and in Australian politics more generally. Much of his mark has been outside of traditional academic work, often participating in the political sphere as one of the 'talking heads' on television.

In a major textbook for policy scholars, Davis, Wanna, Warhurst and Weller (1993, 15) defined public policy as 'the interaction of values, interests and resources guided through institutions and mediated through politics'. The impact of politics on policy and administration is not lost on John and his knowledge has been a game-changer in the political realm on many important occasions.

John has not been shy to venture into the political fray. Most famously, the 'smoking gun' document (Comitatus 2009) was a short paper based on a consultancy for the Queensland Labor Party. The only debate of the 2009 election campaign between Lawrence Springborg, leader of the newly merged Liberal National Party (LNP), and Labor premier Anna Bligh focused on Springborg's plan to make a 3 per cent across-the-board budget cut. During the debate, Bligh produced a report written by John

(Wanna 2009) stating that the budget cuts would result in a reduction in frontline services in Queensland. This effectively ended the debate and Springborg lost the election.

Few people know, however, of John's earlier contact with Springborg, which sowed the seed that brought about the LNP. Over coffee with Springborg one day in 2002, John mentioned that the tenuous National–Liberal Coalition in Queensland could be resolved through a merger based on the Conservative Party of Canada. Years later, Springborg went on a study tour to Canada and in 2012 the LNP went on to win the Queensland election.

Pat Weller[1] picks up on the theme of John's eclectic contribution using Isaiah Berlin's metaphor of the hedgehog and the fox: hedgehogs know one big thing; foxes know many things. John is the latter. Weller, a long-time collaborator with John, outlines the process of cabinet government as an adaptive process where the 'political, economic and administrative perspectives intersect'. To comprehend cabinet government, scholars of politics have to be foxes. Like cabinet governments, they have to manage the trade-offs of balancing the theoretical with the practical, the technical with the political. Weller agrees with John's approach to politics: 'to understand how and why the system works and explain it in terms that practitioners understand' rather than reinventing language that makes political science theories 'exclusive'.

Chris Salisbury[2] covers the trajectory of academic analysis of Queensland politics, noting with some concern the decline in such analysis in recent years notwithstanding John Wanna's contributions (both scholarly and as an active media commentator) after he moved to Queensland in the mid-1980s (where he again lives today). Queensland politics has been a source of influence on Australian politics more generally, with colourful characters and stories such as Joh Bjelke-Petersen's breaking of the convention on appointing a party-nominated senator following a senator's death, ultimately assisting the dismissal of Gough Whitlam, the 'Joh for PM' campaign and the infamous gerrymander, the Fitzgerald Inquiry, and the rise of alternative political parties such as Pauline Hanson's One

---

1   Pat Weller recruited John Wanna to Griffith University in the late 1980s.
2   John Wanna marked Chris Salisbury's PhD thesis.

Nation and Clive Palmer's Palmer United Party influencing politics on the national stage. Salisbury, through a historical lens, brings to light some of Queensland's unique political culture.

Salisbury's conclusion about the decline of scholarly analysis of Queensland politics, caused in part by financial pressures on universities and reliance on international students seeking courses and research activity that places more emphasis on national, international and transnational politics and history, has far broader resonance. Academic reward systems favour publication in high-ranking journals that tend to be international and not to favour research of limited interest to their international audiences. This is adversely affecting not only research into Queensland politics, but all social science research focused on Australia or parts of Australia. It is a serious issue that undermines research that is directly relevant to Australian public policy and administration practitioners, the sort of research John Wanna spent years trying to encourage.

Marija Taflaga[3] examines how political parties in Westminster systems reshape and exercise power in the executive and legislative arms of government. Combining John's interest in the political side of policymaking in Westminster systems (Patapan, Wanna and Weller 2005; Rhodes, Wanna and Weller 2009), Taflaga's analysis suggests that much policy discussion downplays the role of 'capital P' politics in policymaking in Westminster government. 'Capital P' politics is also bringing about changes in the institutional framework of policy advisory systems as the delineation between political and professional careers is becoming increasingly blurred.

Michael de Percy[4] finishes the section by bringing together several key themes covered by John during his career – government–business relations, comparative politics and industry policy – through a comparison of industry policy in the telecommunications industry, the automotive manufacturing industry, trade policy and reducing carbon emissions. De Percy's examination of ideological preferences versus pragmatism during short terms in office was based on a conversation that began in John's festschrift podcast (de Percy 2019). This chapter also addresses one of John's early interests and the focus of his 1984 PhD thesis: industry policy in the automotive manufacturing industry.

---

3   John Wanna was Marija Taflaga's PhD supervisor.
4   John Wanna was Michael de Percy's PhD supervisor.

The four chapters cover some of the breadth of John Wanna's interest in politics and its impact on public policy and administration. The range of authors also represents the 'passing of the baton' of the sage experience of the mentor to the emerging skill of the student. John's legacy, from breaking the mould to resisting the pressures of current university financial and career reward arrangements, has hopefully become a legitimate scholarly pursuit for the next generation of Australian political scientists.

References

Comitatus, P. 2009. 'Wanna document: Smoking gun?' *Crikey*, 13 March. Available at: blogs.crikey.com.au/electioncentral/2009/03/13/wanna-document -smoking-gun/.

Davis G., J. Wanna, J. Warhurst and P. Weller. 1993. *Public Policy in Australia*. St Leonards: Allen & Unwin.

de Percy, M. A. (producer). 2019. 'Special edition: Interview with Professor John Wanna: Career reflections'. *Le Flâneur Politique*. Podcast. Available at: soundcloud.com/madepercy/special-edition-professor-john-wanna-career-reflections.

Patapan, H., J. Wanna and P. Weller (eds). 2005. *Westminster Legacies: Democracy and Responsible Government in Asia and the Pacific*. Sydney: UNSW Press.

Rhodes, R. A. W., J. Wanna and P. Weller. 2009. *Comparing Westminster*. Oxford: Oxford University Press. doi.org/10.1093/acprof:oso/9780199563494.001. 0001.

Wanna, J. 2009. *Briefing Note Regarding the Claim by Mr Springborg to Cut $1 Billion P.A. from Queensland Government Expenses over the Next Three Years*. Available at: blogs.crikey.com.au/electioncentral/files/2009/03/wannareport.pdf.

6

Cabinet government: The least bad system of government?[1]

Patrick Weller

Isaiah Berlin (1953) once classified people as either hedgehogs or foxes. The hedgehogs knew one big thing; the foxes knew many things. The categories led to innumerable games as people were classified. How best to describe the ideas and interests that people had, and the way that they developed their cases and arguments. Festschrifts provide the excuse to indulge, look back on a person's body of work and try to decide whether to identify a single thread or to acknowledge the diversity of their contribution.

John Wanna must surely justify the fox title. We first met in Christchurch in 1983 when I visited the university to talk to Professor Keith Jackson, one of the established figures in New Zealand politics, about Kiwi prime ministers. Keith gathered a few of his colleagues for lunch before we headed off to the ski fields, discussing politics on the chair lifts on the way up each time. John was one of those at the lunch and recalls better than I do the conversation we had. He claims I asked him what he was doing there; I can't believe I was so tactless. We then recruited him to

---

1   For a later development of these themes, see Patrick Weller, Dennis Grube and R. A. W. Rhodes (forthcoming).

Griffith; he had a book on trade union politics and came to Griffith to develop a strand on government–business relations. That was more than 33 years ago, so we have known each other a long time.

Since then he has ranged widely and fruitfully. He has books on public policy, public sector management and, most impressively, on budgeting. The last became his tour de force. What other academic chose to spend a sabbatical in the Department of Finance? And what other political scientist would the Department of Finance be prepared to host, providing a room and support for John and his research assistant, Charles Broughton, (one of John's bright graduates that the department then recruited)? John also developed connections with the budget gurus elsewhere, adding a comparative component to his work. He started in Europe and now includes comparative work with China.

He wrote constantly for the press and talked on the radio, one of the talking heads whom journalists approach to provide an aura of authenticity to their passing impressions. John had the advantage that he always seemed to know what he was talking about.

I suppose I could be regarded as somewhat biased in any assessment. John and I have combined in writing four textbooks as well as *Comparing Westminster* (Rhodes, Wanna and Weller 2009). In our texts on *Public Policy in Australia* (Davis et al. 1988, second edition 1993), he was the resident Marxist writing on the role of the state. We have edited a number of volumes together and participated in numerous volumes, both jointly and separately. He was a stalwart of the Centre for Australian Public Sector Management and the Key Centre for Ethics, Law, Justice and Governance at Griffith University for more than a decade. So he has been a good colleague to work with; he always delivers (… eventually) and it always is illuminating and interesting to read. A fox indeed.

That is an easy segue to my broader subjects that provides variations on the fox theme: the cabinet system in Australia and elsewhere. My title is of course a misuse of Churchill's faint praise for democracy. My purpose is to suggest that, for all its failings, which are so enthusiastically and persuasively documented, cabinet government remains a more viable form of government in a parliamentary democracy than any of the alternatives. The reason is because cabinet government is the ultimate fox (if we can reify the institution for the moment). It has multiple competing functions; it may not be particularly good at any one of them but at its best it can cover the range of analytically distinct activities in a way that is adequate. It is in the drawing together of these different perspectives that cabinet government gains its advantages and to which it can attribute its longevity; its flexibility and lack of rigid rules allow it to metamorphose as circumstances demand. Like jazz, it is predicated on extemporisation. We should not overstate the case; at its worst, cabinet processes can be as dysfunctional as any other form of government.

Practitioners consistently stress that they practice cabinet government. The critiques, often but not exclusively from academics, seek to reconceptualise the mode of government with new phrases that may become established among observers but obtain little traction among the politicians, public servants and advisers who have to make the system work. I would agree with John Wanna that our role is to understand how and why the system works and explain it in terms that practitioners understand and with which they can debate. If we go too far in reinventing language and concepts that become unique to academe, the debates become self-referential; if political science becomes exclusive in its theories, its language and its interests, we screen out all but the cognoscenti; if we become obsessed with theory and methodology to the exclusion of tackling real problems of politics, and if we become more interested in what we as academics do than what they as practitioners do, then we both court irrelevance and sever our links with those who actually do what we nominally choose to observe. Political scientists find it hard enough to be taken seriously as it is. Unlike economists we cannot deliver predictions enveloped in maths and models. I agree with Susan Strange's opinion:

> Hard empirical work is needed in every aspect. There is no substitute for it. Only in doing so is it possible to acquire confidence to test for oneself the theoretical explanations put forward by others and to develop explanatory theories that are more than mere word-plays and metaphorical analogies. (Strange 1985, 22)

If our language and interests become arcane, unrelated to the common usage, no one else will care what we do. The loss is ours, not theirs.

We need too to beware the temptation to develop cute managerial solutions that can be presented as a way to make cabinet government work 'better'. We invariably do so in a way that denies cabinet government vulpine characteristics, the requirement that it simultaneously fulfils several functions. The challenge is not to identify better ways of doing one or other of its functions; that is comparatively easy but opens itself up to the potential consequence that such a process will lead to a decline in other activities. Rather, the challenge for its critics must be to devise a system that can integrate all the activities of the cabinet government in a way that leads to an overall improvement of governance. That is the challenge I seek to tease out in this tribute to John in the confident assumption that he probably agrees with its main direction, even if not the details.

Explaining cabinet government

First, we need to avoid the trap of narrowly defining cabinet government in such a way that the definition restricts or pre-empts any analysis. If we say that 'cabinet has decided', what do we mean? It can be any one of many interpretations. It can refer to a *meeting* of the 'full' cabinet, a *group* of cabinet ministers or a cabinet committee. It can draw attention to a written cabinet *decision* (or minute, depending on local terminology). A cabinet decision could derive from an occasion where the prime minister suddenly decided to record the outcome of a meeting with a few ministers in the Prime Minister's Office (PMO) as a formal decision, or even record a formal decision as a result of a series of phone calls to ministers without meeting them at all. The term *cabinet* can thus refer to a meeting, to a group of ministers, to a decision or a system of government. It is so ambiguous a term that we should try to avoid using it on its own.

There is a danger in seeking to limit the term to outcomes of particular meetings: a full cabinet in Britain or Canada, the Ministerial Council in the Netherlands, for example. In Britain the 'full' cabinet is a selection of senior ministers, about 25 per cent of the total. Some ministers will be given cabinet status, others will not but will be constant attendees. In Canada, all ministers are in cabinet; there is no 'inner' or 'full' cabinet. However, the numbers are so large that key discussions take place in priorities and planning committees. In the Netherlands the weekly Ministerial Council endorses decisions worked out in a series of committees and party meetings in the previous week; the Council is not expected to reopen discussion but to legitimise and authorise. In Australia, cabinet ministers include two-thirds of the ministers, but often are not involved in the work of expenditure committees. Prime ministers have established smaller coordination committees (Fraser) or strategic priorities and budget committees (Rudd) to consider key issues. To argue in any of these cases that discussions only constitute cabinet discussions if they take place in only one forum is not tenable.

The concept of 'cabinet government' is inevitably debated and contested, and it must be accepted as fluid. Who actually governs? In 1962 John Macintosh argued:

> The country is governed by the Prime Minister who leads, coordinates and maintains a series of Ministers, all of whom are advised and backed by the Civil Service. Some decisions are taken by the Prime Minister alone, some in consultation between him and Senior Ministers, while others are left to heads of departments, the Cabinet, Cabinet Committees, or the permanent officials … There is no simple catch-phrase that can describe this form of government, but it may be pictured as a cone. The Prime Minister stands at the apex, supported by and giving power to a widening series of rings of senior ministers, the Cabinet, its Committees, Non-Cabinet ministers, and departments. (1962, 451–452)

Macintosh's conclusions are worth repeating because they are so much subtler than the caricature that later emerged from Richard Crossman's search for a catchy headline. Macintosh did *not* argue that the prime minister made *all* the decisions, but that the decisions might be made in a wide variety of forums that included ministers, committees and permanent officials. The prime minister sat at the apex of the cone. Crossman, looking for that 'simple catch-phrase', came up with a proposition that the evidence did not justify when he translated Macintosh's findings to the claim that 'Cabinet government has been transformed into prime ministerial government' (1963, 51).

Cabinet government is therefore best described as an adaptive process: continuing, often ambiguous, always potent. Practitioners appreciate the ambiguity because they know it is the only way the system can be made to work. Their concern is far more with *how* than with *whom*. They are not interested in limiting definitions but in actual practice. Take two definitions from experienced practitioners:

- Cabinet government is a shorthand term for the process by which government determines its policy and ensures the political will to implement it
- Cabinet has two main functions: policy coherence and political support.

The first is from a cabinet secretary in Britain, the second from a secretary of the Department of the Prime Minister and Cabinet in Australia (cited in Weller 2003). Both stress the need for decisions on policy and the assurance of political support, the two essentials for successful *outcomes*. Both were neutral about how and where the issues should be debated and determined. They wanted a process that achieved those ends. The brilliant, but recently deceased, secretary to the British cabinet, Jeremy Heywood, was asked whether cabinet government still existed in Britain. He asserted the same concept but as a set of principles:

> It partly depends on whether you mean cabinet government as a meeting once a week or cabinet government as a set of principles ... *It just manifests itself in different ways.* Every single decision coming through one meeting a week at which there are 20–25 people is not a test of whether cabinet government is dead. (Heywood 2010, 158, emphasis added)

There is nothing new here. In one of his antipodean excursions to observe his beloved Australian politics, David Butler wrote of cabinet:

> One trouble about discussion of cabinet power is the ambiguity of the word cabinet. Does it refer to the formal weekly or bi-weekly discussion of the twelve or sixteen or twenty-three or twenty-seven men [sic] sitting round the table? Or does it refer to the total cabinet system, with the routine circulation of papers and the opportunities for ministers to raise their doubts about impending policy decisions informally with their colleagues or with the Prime Minister's Department (in Britain the cabinet secretariat ...) or with the Prime Minister himself? (Butler 1973, 59)

If cabinet government is the process through which collective purpose is developed and maintained by the central members of the core executive, analysts should identify activities by what they seek to achieve, by what they do. There can be no simple assumption that some people have legitimacy in the process and others do not, but with one caveat. Whoever is involved in developing a proposal, and the numbers are likely to include a range of people within the core executive, in the end ministers must have a say, however nominal. They have the authority that is required to legitimise and finalise a process that other participants cannot wield. The label under which a meeting is held is less significant than what the participants decide. There can be a wide range of forums, and constellations of supports, where discussion can take place.

For illustrative purposes, here is a spectrum of the range of forums in which cabinet government can be delivered.

Spectrum of 'cabinet government' decision forums and likely attendees

1. The entire ministry: meetings of all ministers including ministerial retreats.

2. Full cabinet meetings as exclusively a ministers' forum: ministers and supporting officials from Cabinet Office only.

3. Full cabinet meetings: ministers, officials as above plus advisers (public servants and/or political advisers) as observers.

4. Cabinet committee as preparatory forum with recommendations (sometimes pro forma) to full cabinet meetings: ministers, officials and advisers.

5. Cabinet committees with decision-making powers such as National Security Council, Expenditure Review Committee, war cabinets: ministers, officials and advisers.

6. Inner cabinet: officially recognised committee of ministers with officials and advisers: Strategic Budget and Priority Committee, coordination committee, Danish Prime Minister's Strategic Committee.

7. Inner cabinet, unofficial: senior ministers with officials and advisers, taking final decisions: sometimes kitchen cabinets, David Cameron's coalition 'Quad'.

8. Inner cabinet, unofficial without officials: prime minister getting commitment and support from ministerial colleagues; ministers and advisers without officials reporting decisions: aka kitchen cabinets.

9. Meetings of prime minister, ministers and advisers to debate specific issues: Blair's 'sofa governments'.

10. Meetings of ministers from the same party (in coalition governments) to plan cabinet tactics: ministers and parliamentary leaders (where distinct).

11. Bilaterals: prime minister and ministers with officials on policy issues in portfolio; stocktakes.

12. Leaders' group: senior ministers, parliamentary leaders, top party officials to discuss political strategy for government.

13. Core bilateral: prime minister and deputy prime minister and/or chancellor/treasurer.

14. Prime minister and PMO staff meeting including some ministers: Cameron and Osborne plus chief whip.

15. Prime minister and PMO staff meeting without other ministers.

This list makes no pretensions to be complete. It is not intended to represent the full range of meetings in any one country. Rather, it is an amalgam of sites identified across a range of countries. It seeks to move from the meeting with the widest representation to the most limited, but even that task is open to ambiguity. Cabinet processes are always the consequences of choices of who should be involved and to what degree. Should all ministers be members of the 'full' cabinet? If not, then a simple full cabinet meeting is itself a limited selection of ministers, as is a cabinet committee, an inner cabinet (whether official or not) and a meeting of ministers in the PMO.

The calculations may be administratively expedient (keep the number of attendees down to allow discussion), strategic (we want the key ministers and advisers only), political (they will leak), efficient (get decisions made by senior ministers, so the rest will fall into line), or sheer reality (we can get them together quickly). Some arrangements will combine several of those objectives. An inner cabinet, whether formal or informal, can bring political weight, effective decision-making and security, albeit at the cost of representativeness and a wider array of opinion. Many gatherings may serve a number of simultaneous functions. We can assert that cabinet government is not only what happens in cabinet meetings but in positive terms – there is no simple description – just an acknowledgement of the value of collective government and debate.

Again, note the common component: ministers. Meetings of senior officials may screen the documents to ensure they are ready for consideration. They may act as gatekeepers. They may exclude some propositions at an early stage. They may recommend preferred options. They will be massively influential in determining the agenda and the strategy. However, in the last resort they need ministerial approval, however limited the role ministers may play in the actual process. Ministers, even passive and dull ones, play an authorising role in cabinet processes.

This array of sites also identifies the range of levers that can be applied and by whom and some of the ways in which leaders may seek to bring different groups and opinions together. Some leaders may be able to determine the attendance (who is invited), the rules that will be applied (the process), the terms in which the particular problem is defined, the urgency of the issues (whether politically or externally driven), and who has the political weight to be involved. These powers accrue in particular to prime ministers in Westminster systems where power is concentrated. That is far from the norm globally. In many countries, leaders have their powers circumscribed by coalition arrangements. Positions and policies may be part of the agreement and the freedom to change these may be restricted to leadership groups, not prime ministers alone. Ministers protected by such agreements may be freer to argue a case in the government's forums and the need to maintain the coalition becomes a central calculation. In the Netherlands there is an agreement that a policy will not be pursued if a coalition party, rather than an individual minster, is opposed. The cabinet process becomes one means for alleviating coalition tensions. The power of patronage may not be as effective in these cases. Those ministers who are appointed by another party do not owe their jobs to the prime minister; they cannot be so readily fired or reshuffled as a negotiation is required.

The cabinet processes in these cases reflect some of the complications. All the power does not rest with one position; others have resources and assets that they can apply. Coalition partners or party heavyweights have levers that they too can pull in debates on maintaining collective governments, where the leader is dependent on them. There is always the option of a resignation or defection where the impact is disproportionate to the sheer numbers. In situations where the government does not hold a clear majority in Westminster systems the parliamentary numbers may have to be constantly calculated. Where party discipline has collapsed, it just gets harder. In other proportional representative systems, that again is just the normal circumstances, where legislation has to be negotiated before it can be passed. Neustadt's proposition that the power of the president is the power to persuade has resonance in parliamentary systems where leaders must constantly use the available levers to ensure they rule, at least in part, by consent.

Can we be more precise about the nature or existence of cabinet government? Only with difficulty as there is a danger that the definition precludes more substantive discussion. The New Zealand Government, for instance, defines a cabinet meeting as an occasion when ministers discuss issues, with officials there to take notes of conclusions. Its Cabinet Office states that, if there are no officials, it is not a cabinet meeting, just a meeting of ministers. That might work in the small NZ system where all ministers have offices in the Beehive, the administrative building attached to Parliament House. However, as other systems have a practice of officials frequently taking notes at ministers' meetings whatever their standing, the NZ definition does not translate readily to elsewhere.

We need to see cabinet government as a continuing process in which key players manage issues and people in a kaleidoscope of meetings and discussions to ensure that collective government is developed and continued. What matters is what is being achieved, not whatever formal title a meeting may attract. As Macintosh foreshadowed, decisions can be made in a multiplicity of places as a means of settling disputes, consolidating support and determining mutually acceptable outcomes.

The dilemmas of cabinet

Why is there such a need? Because cabinets must multitask and often are not in control of their own agenda; rather, they must react to events and circumstances thrust upon them. All the time they are required to balance often incompatible objectives and provide a result that has an air of certainty, confidence and precision. Lists of the functions that the cabinet process must fulfil can be readily identified. They include: clearing house, information exchange, arbiter between ministers, political decision-maker, coordinator, guardian of the strategy. Add to that crisis manager, and potentially a host of other functions. Some issues may be routine, requiring authorisation rather than debate. Often the issues are contested between ministers or their departments, between central agencies and spending departments, with state implications or political consequences. Issues come to cabinet because they are hard and cannot be determined at an official level or by individual minsters. The results will be 'on balance' decisions, seldom clear cut and never certain of success in their application. Ambiguity may infest actual cabinet debates, but the conclusions have to be presented as though they are the only feasible outcome. Expressing doubt can be politically corrosive. That is the nature of their position.

Those conclusions can be restated as a series of dilemmas with which all leaders and participants must grapple, dilemmas that need to sit at the heart of any analysis of cabinet government. They all require choices. They all hold the potential for catastrophe.

- The *process* dilemma. How best to run a government? Prime ministers must balance the representative legitimacy of the broad membership and the need for tight and effective decision-making. The dilemma is that they need both, but the two may work against each other. They must also determine in what forums decisions are made, by whom and through what procedures; these are the routines through which predictable decision-making can occur.

- The *policy* dilemma is to determine the best outcome or mix and match between the available criteria and options. It requires not only balancing good politics and good policy, but also puzzling over difficult issues where there is no right answer and where even the formulation of the problem is debated.

- The *political* dilemma is how to balance the political forces that might split the government. The ambitions of parties, putative successors, coalition partners and parliamentary rebels are always a calculation; the essence of political life is contest, values and disagreement.

- The *accountability* dilemma is how to keep the support and confidence of the party, the parliament and the electorate when tough, and potentially unpopular, decisions must be made.

- Finally, the *leadership* dilemma is what levers are available for a prime minister to lead; assuming that political leadership is based on the power to persuade, how and where that can occur.

Consider the consequences if any or all of the above are not adequately taken into account.

The routines of cabinet allow a process by which a broad range of activities can be managed through the systematic consideration of priorities, the presentation of data and the preparation of agreed positions at the official level. The idea is that cabinet forums are dedicated to those issues that only ministers can determine. What can be settled before the meeting should be. When the systems break down, when cabinet cannot manage the agenda, then there is likely to be gridlock. Nothing significant happens. Even though much of the management can be delegated to officials, there is still the need for the formal imprimatur of ministers as authorising agents. There is much to be said for the opinion of a Canadian official who reflected on the value of routines and due process:

> I don't care if ministers actually read the memorandum or not. I care that the system has subjected it to the discipline of critique and comment and improvement and that our thinking has improved as a result. That doesn't necessarily mean sitting round a table in a meeting room. (quoted in Weller 2018, 154)

Solving problems is what is meant to drive cabinet. The sentiment that 'good policy is good politics' sounds encouraging, even if seldom actually applied. Shortage of time, inadequate information and divided positions can make solutions difficult. Bad policy, even if seen as a temporary placebo, may create problems in later years. Who determines what good policy is, and for what purpose it may be introduced, will always be contested. Buying votes with policies that contain devastating delayed long-term grenades for future governments may be common: are such policies good or bad?

Who cares about longer-term impacts? There are always issues about the immediate consequences in terms of political support. Malcolm Fraser argued that, if a fair proportion of his cabinet was unhappy with a proposal, then a similar proportion of the party was likely to be concerned too. And they were all meant to be on the same side. At a national level the opposition of aroused groups would be so much greater. So good policy has to be seen through the prism of political support. The decisions have to consider parliamentary and party support too. As long as governments are accountable, even the best policy needs to balance the good sense of the decision against the prejudgements, even prejudices, of those who will be required to vote on the measures.

The politics is of course a given. Cabinet processes are where political, economic and administrative perspectives intersect. Australian prime ministers have become even more sensitive to immediate stimuli. That is understandable, given the mortality rate. They know that rivals are sitting round the cabinet table, looking for signs of weakness and assuring themselves about their own ability to do so much better. Cabinet rooms, more than most meeting rooms, are havens of hubris.

Who implements cabinet decisions? In Australia it is seldom the federal government alone, but even if it is there is a need for policies to be practicable, or sufficiently flexible. More often there is a requirement to work with state governments and other organisations. And so the story can be ever expanded.

There may be better ways of developing the routines, so cabinet decisions are only made when all the information is available and analysed. There may be better polices, given more time, better research and a constructive debate dedicated to the single problem. At times it can happen, but rarely does. There may be a variety of tactical steps that can be taken to ensure the political support. In summary, it may be possible to do any one of these functions better if they were to be considered in isolation; indeed, it would generally be hard not to.

That is not an option that cabinets have. They may sometimes be too political or too technical. They may be so intent on getting the policies right that they give too little attention to the raw politics. All these positions can lead to problems. There can be no one correct stand or approach, no one ideal way of managing policy development or responding to a crisis. We need to accept that cabinet ministers need to balance these demands, and to judge issues on the effectiveness of the balance rather than focusing only on a particular aspect.

The rotating prime ministership over the past decade is taken as a sign that the process is broken. The primacy of internal party division and personal revenge has trumped the needs for policy development. Policies were always likely to be compromises, if not between governing factions, then between different conceptions of what the country needs: financial restraint or program delivery, equity against development. And so on.

Prime ministers, like jugglers, must balance these interests with the available tools: agenda setting, ministerial selection, public communication, developing narratives, corralling support. Their vulnerability to internal revolt, a function of party rules and circumscribed electorates, makes the constant (self-imposed) obsession with polls self-reinforcing. Coups against prime ministers, it is worth remembering, are a consequence of the unique set of rules developed in Australia; they are not universal. In other systems prime ministers may be less vulnerable to internal revolt. They have other pressures: maintaining coalitions, balancing their own party interest against the national needs for policy. Among the dilemmas they face, the need for support will be continuous, with its stress on the short term. There have in the past, with the same rules and nominal circumstances, been times when prime ministers can push their own barrow against majority cabinet opinion. When there is something they want, cabinet ministers would acquiesce, even when they disagreed. But not all the time.

The poverty of the metaphor

Writers cannot resist a good metaphor. They seldom work because metaphors tend to simplify what is, as I have suggested, a complex, multifaceted process. Cabinets have been described as sounding boards, as focus groups, as charades, as 'sofa government', as part of a system of court government. They may be all those things at different times, but they are never exclusively one or the other. In each case one characteristic is identified as emblematic and then the argument is run that that single activity symbolises the way that cabinet government works. Sometimes they fall into the rather silly assumption that cabinet government is what exclusively takes place in a formal cabinet meeting, which, as I suggested, underplays the kaleidoscopic rush and bustle of central government. Too often metaphors evoke a commonly used image that takes the reader perhaps further than the author would like.

So 'court politics' wants to draw attention to the internal politics of the executive centre and to the different beliefs and interest of the actors there but, by evoking the court, it evokes the monarch (even if it never describes the prime ministers as monarchs). The metaphor can then get out of hand. Courtiers depend utterly for their continued influence in the good favours of the monarch; even the great servants of the crown like Thomas Cromwell, Bismarck and Metternich lost office when they lost royal favour. There is simply no comparison to the relationship between courtiers and monarchs, and between ministers and prime ministers. Ministers have resources and ambitions that are just so different. That may be why, when they talk of the centre of government, actors at the centre of government often talk of cliques, of kitchen cabinets, of factions and of conspiracies, but in the 40 years I have been interviewing never of courts. They appreciate the fundamental difference between court politics and executive politics.

Metaphors can confuse, oversimplify or mislead. Cabinet processes are complicated enough as it stands. We do better by using the clear, mutually understandable language of practitioners and then demystifying the process that they pursue.

Cabinet as collective

There is a dictum attributed to Ben Chifley: 'One man and a dozen fools are likely to govern better than one man alone'. Given the uneven quality of his ministers, he was well positioned to judge. Prime ministers cannot constantly dictate (unless they have already built up a strong position); they need to work *through* cabinet to ensure support and balance all the competing interests. After an early setback Fraser could not recall a time he was overruled by cabinet because he made sure that he had support for his position before issues came to cabinet, or sometimes went on and on till he could generate acquiescence. John Howard stated:

> I was very keen on running an orthodox Westminster system; I rarely ambushed the cabinet except when it was an acceptable ambush such as declaring in Washington on 12 September that we'd stand beside the Americans. (Weller 2018, 153)

Their skills were managing those multiple dilemmas in ways that gave defensible policy and political support most of the time until their almost inevitable electoral loss. Both Fraser and Howard wanted the support of their cabinets, not only because they saw the benefits of a common voice. It was not a coincidence that they were the last two prime ministers who won government from opposition and maintained their leadership for the duration of their party's term of office for seven and 11 years, respectively. They balanced those multiple dilemmas effectively. Hawke was a skilled chair of cabinet, insisting on unity and common policies, wherever they came from. Notably these cabinets appear far more united most of the time than their successors. Hence collective responsibility could be achieved. These prime ministers were able to make cabinet government work most of the time.

Richard Neustadt asserted that presidents wear many hats but do not distinguish when they act; he argued that the scholar needs to see the world through the president's eyes, 'from over the President's shoulder' (1960, xxi). Prime ministers must blend their multiple dilemmas to provide a coherent decision that combines political support, administrative feasibility and programmatic sense. The balance will slip from one to another, but they ignore any one of them to their peril. The benefit of well-managed cabinet government is that it is flexible enough to manage the trade-offs. At its best that is why it survives; that is why it must be and must appear as the fox in politics.

References

Berlin, I. 1953. *The Hedgehog and the Fox*. London: Weidenfeld and Nicolson.

Butler, D. 1973. *The Canberra Model*. Melbourne: Cheshire.

Crossman, R. H. S. 1963. 'Introduction'. In W. Bagehot, *The English Constitution*. London: Fontana.

Davis, G., J. Wanna, J. Warhurst and P. Weller. (1988) 1993. *Public Policy in Australia*. Second edition. Sydney: Allen & Unwin.

Heywood, J. 2010. Evidence to House of Lords Select Committee on the Constitution. In *The Cabinet Office and the Centre of Government: Report with Evidence*. HL Paper 30. London: House of Lords.

Macintosh, J. 1962. *The British Cabinet*. London: Stevens and Sons.

Neustadt, R. 1960. *Presidential Power*. New York: Wiley.

Rhodes, R. A. W., J. Wanna and P. Weller. 2009. *Comparing Westminster*. Oxford: Oxford University Press. doi.org/10.1093/acprof:oso/97801995 63494.001.0001.

Strange, S. 1985. 'International political economy'. In W. Hollist and F. Tullis (eds) *An International Political Economy*. Boulder: Westview.

Weller, P. 2003. 'Cabinet government: An elusive ideal?' *Public Administration* 81(4): 701–722. doi.org/10.1111/j.0033-3298.2003.00368.x.

Weller, P. 2018. *The Prime Ministers' Craft*. Oxford: Oxford University Press.

Weller, P., D. Grube and R. A. W. Rhodes. Forthcoming *Comparing Cabinets: Dilemmas of Collective Government,* Oxford: Oxford University Press.

7

'A long revolution': The historical coverage of Queensland politics and government

Chris Salisbury

Queensland is still a place that is much talked about but little understood. We have a history that is exciting, complex, surprising, nuanced and more than a little shocking. It does not lend itself easily to simplification. It still dances like a shimmering heat-haze at the edge of our present perceptions.[1]

– Raymond Evans, quoted in Burns (2013, 5)

Introduction: The decline in academic analysis of Queensland politics

Owing to a recent decline in state-focused academic analysis and publication, the body of literature covering Queensland's political history is not as substantial nor as current as was once the case. Contextual accounts are somewhat threadbare, being comprised largely of standard (and some now dated) texts in the field of Australian political history as

---

1   This series has historians offering contemporary analyses on, particularly, northern Queensland. For an earlier standout regional study, see Bolton (1963).

well as contemporary journalistic coverage. Despite Queensland boasting a proud record of expertise in this field – names such as Colin Hughes, Denis Murphy and Ross Fitzgerald come readily to mind – specifically state-based historical analysis of politics and government has lately suffered from a dearth of scholarly attention, not unlike other formerly prominent fields within the humanities and social sciences. Indeed, after something of a surge of publications on state political history during the middle to latter parts of the twentieth century – appearing, perhaps not coincidentally, at around the same time as the incumbency of Queensland's longest-serving premier, Sir Joh Bjelke-Petersen – interest and activity in state-based political analysis has since waned to an unsettling degree (Macintyre 2009, 87–90; Manwaring 2020). It seems that, as online media and television news coverage of local politics has steadily overwhelmed academic discussion around the field, and according to some even surpassed the state opposition in the role of chief scrutineer (Chamberlain 2011; see also Green 2017), public attention has increasingly been drawn to political happenings at the supposedly more compelling national level – especially when many news services are run from distant national offices interstate, exacerbating the decline or demise of state-produced current affairs programs (Young 2008; see also Williams 2020).

This preponderance of media reportage over scholarly discourse could possibly be an unintended consequence of Phil Dickie's skilful investigative journalism for the *Courier-Mail* (and Chris Masters's for the ABC's *Four Corners*) in the late 1980s helping to bring about the 'Fitzgerald Inquiry' in Queensland. The inquiry's public hearings provided a constant stream of lewd and scandalous news headlines, dished up daily by local media outlets to an incredulous but voracious public audience.[2] Since, it has fallen as much to the media, almost by dint of public expectation, to provide a level of scrutiny and analysis of the state's political figures and events that once was largely the domain of academic observers and only the most senior print journalists, such as the influential and nationally circulated Hugh Lunn in *The Australian* and Tony Koch in the *Courier-Mail* (later of *The Australian*).[3] Bearing all of the above in mind, there is

2   See Dickie (1989) for the journalist's account of events surrounding and in the aftermath of the Fitzgerald Inquiry into official corruption, as portrayed in his and others' print media columns of that time; and Masters (2008). See also Hede, Prasser and Neylan (1992) and Prasser, Wear and Nethercote (1990). For concise, more contemporary retrospectives on this turbulent period, see Beattie (2007) and Salisbury (2019).

3   See Koch's comments regarding decreasing interest in state government affairs and 'the media's role', in ASPG (2000, 16). See also Lunn (1987) and Miller and Koch (1983).

an apparent diminution in long-form academic analysis of Queensland's more recent political history, particularly in the contemporary 'modern Labor' era (not to ignore some recent scholarly journal attempts to redress this 'imbalance': see Williams 2011; Bowden 2013).

Past academic study of Queensland politics

As diminished as this scholarly field of enquiry might have become recently, there is a long and robust track record of critical academic analysis surrounding Queensland's history, and in particular its political history. From the media-based and largely internet-driven scrutiny of more recent times to past scholarly analysis and serialised reportage of the state's and the nation's political heritage, Queensland's historical background and seemingly distinct political culture have encouraged several eminent local observers to pen a long line of esteemed works in this field. John Wanna, at The Australian National University and now again at Griffith University, a long-time keen observer of Queensland politics, depicted this considerable output in positive terms as 'a long revolution' of recorded historiography (Wanna 1990).[4] This tradition stretches back as far as the earliest chroniclers of the colony's foundation in 1859, from which time there began to appear serialised publications such as *Pugh's Almanac* and *The Queenslander* – the latter of which in December 1899 broke news of the world's first Labour Government in Queensland with the 'measured' headline, 'POLITICAL CRISIS' (*The Queenslander* 1899; Fitzgerald 1999). Following later in the nineteenth century came monthly journals representing sectional, and increasingly politically active, interests within Queensland's developing colonial society – *The Shearer's Record* and *The Worker* being prime examples – and then early in the twentieth century appeared Queensland's longest established serial, the *Journal of the Royal Historical Society of Queensland*. This august publication's somewhat conservative editorial perspective has evolved over time – and with it a change of name in 2008 to the *Queensland History Journal* – extending beyond heroic pioneering accounts of 'taming the

---

4   For broad coverage of generalised through to more specialised historiography relating to Queensland's post-colonisation development, including some of the earliest monographs in this field, see Johnston and Zerner (1985), Thorpe (1987) and Metcalf (2010).

land' to include the broader social and political context of Queensland's postcolonial development (see 'Editorial' 1963; Rechner 1994; see also Bernays 1920; Megarrity 2004).[5]

The 1950s and 1960s

Critical scholarly treatment of local historical and political themes increased noticeably between the mid-1950s and early 1960s, probably stimulated by the government-endorsed hoopla surrounding Queensland's 1959 centenary of separation from New South Wales – an event worth celebrating 'triumphantly', according to the book commissioned to mark the occasion (Cilento and Lack 1959; Lack 1959; Lack 1962). The earlier founding of the University of Queensland Press (UQP) in 1948 also contributed to this increase in locally focused, scholarly publications. Additionally, one cannot dismiss the impact that a change in government – a relatively infrequent occurrence in Queensland's past – has had upon the production of political commentary and analysis; this was observed around the time of the Labor Party's split and the Country Party's ascendancy in 1957, and then the National Party's demise 32 years later, as well as either side of the one-term Newman Liberal–National Party Government from 2012 to 2015 (Wanna 1990, 139; see Higgins 1960; Yarrow 2015; Coaldrake 1990a; Reynolds 1990; Whip and Hughes 1991; Salisbury 2020; Prasser 2012; Williams 2018b).[6]

From 1955, extensive coverage and analysis of important events and significant issues of the day appeared in new journals such as the then UQP-published *Australian Journal of Politics and History* (*AJPH*), including its excellent biannual series of 'Political Chronicles' providing expert summation of recently transpired happenings in the state and federal spheres (a disclaimer: I am now an associate editor for the *AJPH*, responsible for editing 'Political Chronicles' entries). In 1964 came *Queensland Heritage*, later renamed the *John Oxley Journal* and produced by the State Library of Queensland. The most substantial and arguably influential of the mid-century monographs emerged in 1960 when Solomon Davis, a Reader in Political Science at the University

---

5   For digitised copies of these and other early print publications detailing Queensland history and events, see Centre for the Government of Queensland, *Text Queensland*, available at: www.text queensland.com.au.

6   As a rule, elections of course provide regular opportunity for political and (sometimes) historically contextual analysis; see, for instance, Scott (2016), Salisbury (2018) and Williams (2018a, 2018c).

of Queensland (UQ), edited a collection of fine scholarly essays about government in each of the Australian states (Davis 1960). From that time, the field of politically themed historical enquiry generated significant interest and a growing following. In Australia, the *AJPH* represents the best sustained intellectual interaction between historians and political scientists; apart from this forum, these disciplines have in recent times gone their separate ways in terms of publication avenues. In the decades since the publication of Davis's edited book, taking up this line of state-based enquiry – and applying it especially to Queensland's example – have been some of this state's and the nation's most eminent scholars and prolific historical writers of succeeding generations.

In 1968 Colin Hughes, who took up residence as a leading academic in UQ's School of Government, co-produced the first issue of his much-utilised, ongoing series analysing the governments, politics and elections of the state and national jurisdictions, spanning events from before federation up to the mid-1960s (Hughes and Graham 1968: see also updated editions produced in 1977, 1986 and 2002). Subsequent volumes cover periods of a decade or longer until, by the time of the final instalment in 2002, the minutiae of the nation's electoral and political history throughout the twentieth century had been compiled and studied in impressive detail. Hughes followed this earlier effort with one of his finest works on Queensland politics, and indeed one of the first comprehensive election studies in Australia, expertly analysing successive state elections in the mid-1960s (see Hughes's [1969] work, in which he argued persuasively that politics in Queensland was largely 'bluster and noise' but with little change evident at election time when results were calculated). Among other works, Hughes also added one of the most definitive assessments of governance and parliamentary representation in Queensland's political past, standing equal amid a conclusive series, of which he was the general editor, analysing the governments of each Australian state and territory (Hughes 1980). This theme of 'state by state' examination was adopted and given further impetus by academic writers in other corners of the nation, such as John Rorke at the University of Sydney and Brian Galligan, a Queenslander by birth and education, at La Trobe University (Galligan 1986; Rorke 1970; see also Eccleston 2009;

Joyce 1977).[7] Hughes's efforts are still standouts, though, and retain the perceptive insights of works written close at hand to events; for this, and more, they are of enduring value.

Moving on to the 1980s and 1990s

Perhaps inspired by Hughes's example, the field of political history in Queensland was bolstered subsequently by the works of other eminent scholarly observers – including Margaret Cribb, Roger Joyce, Denis Murphy, Peter Coaldrake, Paul Reynolds, Rae Wear, Ray Evans and Ross Fitzgerald – all having held senior academic posts at UQ and other Queensland universities over the past 40 years or more. Indeed, the last two historians mentioned above made significant contributions to the field in recent years, the latter with two diligent co-authors, both publishing accomplished works broadly analysing Queensland's political, social and cultural make-up.[8] While Fitzgerald, Megarrity and Symons's effort drew mixed reactions from some, this concerned more the circumstances in which the book had been commissioned by Peter Beattie's Premier's Department, to mark the sesquicentenary of responsible government in Queensland. In any event, the work – including the efforts of Fitzgerald's co-authors – stands as a well-researched and smartly presented examination of Queensland's history and prehistory, albeit one that delves a little less deeply into critical reflection than Evans's work.[9] This latter text is thoroughly researched and engagingly written, and is in many regards the standout work on Queensland's history – social, political and otherwise – from the last two decades.

---

7   For a standout account of the coal-driven political economy of 1960s–70s Queensland, see Galligan (1989). For a selection of astute analyses of industrial relations, political activism, racial exploitation and wartime state intervention in Queensland's economy, see Bowden et al. (2009), Brennan (1992), Cameron (1997), Evans (1988), Evans and Ferrier (2004), Evans, Saunders and Cronin (1993), Gough et al. (1964), Harris (1984), Lewis (1973), May (1994), Megarrity (2018), Menghetti (1981), Munro (1995), Murphy (1968), Murphy (1983), Ørsted-Jensen (2011), which makes the convincing argument that Queensland's colonial era history and politics needs revisiting and renewed scholarly scrutiny, Piccini (2010), Richards (2008), Saunders (1993, 2011b), Svensen (1989) and Thorpe (1996).

8   For complementary and almost coinciding accounts of Queensland's history, see Evans (2007) and Fitzgerald, Megarrity and Symons (2009).

9   In this respect Fitzgerald's book, building upon the combined premises of two of his earlier works, does not quite match the focus or acclaim of its predecessors: see Fitzgerald (1985, 1986). For further discussion of Fitzgerald, Megarrity and Symons's (2009) commissioned history, see Saunders (2011a).

Over time, this esteemed cohort mentioned above, and their contemporaries, provided specialist analysis of all points of Queensland's political spectrum. Cribb was a noteworthy chronicler of the development of the Country Party (later National Party) and conservative political trends in Queensland, improving on the partisan writings of some of those before her such as Ulrich Ellis (Ellis 1963; Cribb and Boyce 1980; see also Wear 2009; Hunt 2009; Cockfield 2020; Scott and Ford 2014). Murphy was a renowned labour historian and academic who, in practical terms, notably helped reform the Queensland branch of the Australian Labor Party (ALP), then represented it briefly in the state's parliament prior to his untimely death in 1984 (Costar 1988; see also Saunders and Costar 2006; Bongiorno 2006). Earlier, Murphy and colleagues published an influential collection of vignettes on Queensland's premiers, providing engaging characterisations of the state's prominent and sometimes idiosyncratic leaders, revised and updated twice after Murphy's death (and the deaths of co-editors Cribb and Joyce) (Murphy, Joyce and Cribb 2003).[10] Fitzgerald also added his impressions of the ALP's place in Queensland's political landscape, co-writing a noted study of a century of the state's Labor Party history, released just prior to the Goss Labor Government taking office in 1989 (Fitzgerald and Thornton 1989; see Murphy 1975; Murphy and Cross 1985; Murphy, Joyce and Hughes 1970; Murphy, Joyce and Hughes 1980). Yet, in spite of their expertise, many of these otherwise respected scholars and their peers in the 'commentariat' were often regarded with suspicion and derision in certain quarters of the political arena, let alone by an at times unappreciative or uninterested public. Politicians' scorn and their shying from critical attention long kept academic analysis of the state's political milieu largely confined to the halls of its universities. Despite this, the practice of local scholarly political analysis did not expire.

More recent decades

Added to it since are the works of other notable contributors and long-time UQ academics of recent decades, including Ross Johnston, whose standout edited collection of significant documentary sources from Queensland's

---

10   See also Kerr (2001), Murphy and Joyce (1978), including portraits of colonial-era Queensland premiers, less of whom feature in Murphy, Joyce and Cribb's later (2003) revised collection; and Cribb's and Murphy's several biographical entries on, respectively, conservative and Labor politicians in the National Centre of Biography's *Australian Dictionary of Biography*, Australian National University, available at: adb.anu.edu.au.

past continues to be a signpost for researchers today (Johnston 1988);[11] and Rae Wear (2002), whose deft political biography of Joh Bjelke-Petersen, alongside Reynolds's (2002) similarly fine work on Mike Ahern, rate among the recent best of their kind in a genre that has sometimes focused more on the off-beat dimensions of the state's political leaders (Bastian 2009; Beanland 2013; Fitzgerald 1994, 1997; Joyce 1984; Megarrity 2017; Murphy 1990; Walker 1995; Weller 2014; Young 1971).[12] In a similar style, albeit a genre that it pays to approach with a degree of circumspection, is the relatively recent preponderance (in this country) of the political memoir or autobiography. Queensland's political leaders and even influential senior bureaucrats have not been immune to this exercise in (usually, though not in every case) post-career self-reflection; it might not surprise to learn that the notable local examples begin with Bjelke-Petersen's aptly titled contribution (Bjelke-Petersen 1990; Beattie 1990, 2005; Bligh 2015; Hielscher 2014; Rudd 2017; see also Button 2006). On a related tack, Paul Davey, a former journalist and senior National Party officeholder at state and federal levels, recently published his insider's memoir of the politically disruptive 'Joh for PM' campaign of 1987 and the ill-judged attempt to install Bjelke-Petersen as federal Nationals leader (Davey 2015).[13] Other observers from outside Queensland, such as Swinburne University's Brian Costar, have also provided interesting and enlightened commentary on the more distinctive elements of the state's political culture (Costar 2006; Brett 2019; Megalogenis 2010).[14] In the last two decades, this of course has incorporated several scholarly and journalistic attempts to fathom the appearance – and then later 'unlikely' revival – of the modern Queensland political phenomenon that is Pauline Hanson and the One Nation Party (Manne 1998; Leach, Stokes and Ward 2000; Kingston 2001; Salisbury 2010b; Broinowski 2017; Scott 2017; see also Grant, Moore and Lynch 2019). As such, there undoubtedly exists a significant and reputable body of scholarly and other literature on the longer political history of Queensland.

---

11   For a 'landmark' environmental study of the land's influence upon Queensland's post-colonisation history, see Johnston (1982).

12   For biographies and studies in the 'larger than life' (or sometimes hagiographic) style, see: Cameron (1998), King (2015), Parnell (2013) and Townsend (1983). See also Brett (2003), Bolton (2006) and Walter (2009).

13   While offering some interesting correlations with Clive Palmer's cash-heavy foray into federal politics in recent years, Davey's account does not reveal much in the way of new insights beyond a generally sympathetic view of Bjelke-Petersen's federal ambitions.

14   The reader can find several references to Queensland's past political figures, episodes and details in Davison, Hirst and Macintyre (2001), Galligan and Roberts (2008), and Macintyre (1991).

In fact, respected analysts and commentators such as John Wanna and, more recently, Griffith University's Paul Williams, have extended this important work by contributing to the contemporary coverage of state and national political affairs in the *AJPH*'s biannual 'Political Chronicles' series, as well as in other forums (Wanna 2004; Williams 2012; see also Wanna 2000, 2017; Mickel and Wanna 2020; Wanna and Williams 2005; Williams 2007, 2009, 2019). Wanna recently supplemented these efforts with a remarkably detailed and voluble monograph, co-written with Griffith University colleague Tracey Arklay, focusing on Queensland's parliamentary history during the long period of conservative governments from the 1950s to 1980s (Wanna and Arklay 2010). This work provides a unique insight into the workings – and sometimes the failings – of Queensland's unicameral parliamentary system as it operated under the leadership of National Party premiers. But it stops short of placing subsequent Labor administrations under a similar focus, leaving open the question of whether the state's parliament and governance functions operated any differently or even better in later years. So this valuable scholarly output focused on government performance and political activity, as already mentioned, can still do with further addition. With more critical accounts from observers of Queensland's governance machinery and distinctive politics in the modern era providing some foundations – notable works by Peter Charlton (1987), Peter Coaldrake (1989) and Evan Whitton (1993), among others, readily come to mind (Caulfield and Wanna 1995; Cork 2006; Davis 1995; Stevens and Wanna 1993) – there is a body of pertinent, informative background material from the last few decades to draw upon and contrast with the relatively fewer recent scholarly observations in this field.

It is worth recognising that some of these earlier monographs are positioned firmly within a framework that depicts Queensland as different to the rest of the nation, particularly in its political culture and the way that it is governed – Charlton's work obviously fits this billing, if in a somewhat superficial, almost cartoonish way, complete with caricatures by noted cartoonist Alan Moir. While there are certainly aspects of difference to Queensland, much as there are to the other states, the argument that Queensland's difference has somehow seen it develop a peculiarly aberrant culture compared to its fellow states has been debated often and refuted by many observers, including some not born as Queenslanders (Morrison 1960; Murphy 1978; see also Fitzgerald 1985, 250–252; Harrison 2006; Head 1986; Hughes 1973; Reynolds 1986; Scott et al. 1986; Schultz

2008; Spearritt 2010; Wear 2010). It pays to recall that many works subscribing to the 'difference' treatise emerged either during the time of the Bjelke-Petersen Government's excesses and the Fitzgerald Inquiry that exposed them (Lunn 1980; Metcalf 1984; Smith 1985; Wells 1979; see also Coaldrake 1990b; Coaldrake and Wanna 1988; McQueen 1979), or in the reformist period of Wayne Goss's government immediately following. Little since then has so obviously followed this line, although a very recent compilation of local recollections of the Bjelke-Petersen era could revive the theme (Shaw 2019).[15] Subsequent additions, from political science exponents predominantly (although not exclusively), focus more on broader themes of governance, reform, political leadership or policymaking (Ahamed and Davis 2009; Bell and Hindmoor 2009; Coaldrake and Nethercote 1989; Coaldrake, Davis and Shand 1992; Colley 2006; Davis 2002; Davis and Weller 2001; Gibney, Copeland and Murie 2009; Head, Wanna and Williams 2005; Kefford and McDonnell 2016; Madison and Dennis 2009; Orr and Levy 2009; Walter 2010; Weller 2005). These works complement the Queensland-specific literature and extend analysis of the state government's performance in such areas.

Government publications, retrospectives and digitised content

Such works are supplemented by the ever-increasing output of the state government itself, which in recent times has become nearly as prolific as the academic fraternity in publishing its own reports and accounts ('objective', naturally) of major policy initiatives and programs in any given year. While this might be viewed by some as emblematic of modern government's – and allegedly Labor's – obsession with 'spin-doctoring' and 'style over substance', the practice has precedents from earlier administrations. The Bjelke-Petersen Government pioneered in Queensland the brash self-promotion so readily associated with today's professional administrative operations, engaging former ABC journalist Allen Callaghan as press secretary in the early 1970s to assist the premier 'glad-handle' the media. To the consternation of a perpetually underfunded opposition, Bjelke-Petersen's government even procured with taxpayer

---

15   For an alternative – if highly personalised and, occasionally, debatable – account to the 'difference' theme, which posits instead that the rest of the Australian polity is becoming more like Queensland (which, thus, is no longer so different), see Bahnisch (2015).

funds its own promotional television slot – titled 'Queensland Unlimited' – which aired on Sunday evenings five minutes before 6pm news bulletins, beaming the premier's face into lounge rooms in little more than a public relations exercise. Bjelke-Petersen's government duly established its own media units and photographic teams (as other jurisdictions were doing, to be fair), and seconded public servants to author documents that were often little more than party promotional material or marketing merchandise; some proposed publications, sadly perhaps for later scholars, never made it past the planning stage.[16]

Some of the more recent administrative documentation, published and slickly packaged by well-resourced 'corporate information' offices within government departments – and a till recently state-owned printing facility – can at least be cross-checked against a recent work of scholarly critique that draws heavily on departmental records, ministerial notes and private papers. Appealingly turned out by UQP, the weighty *Engine Room of Government* by the University of the Sunshine Coast's Joanne Scott and colleagues is a considered attempt to bring to light the past undertakings and centralised workings of Queensland's Premier's Department over the period of the state's self-administration (Scott et al. 2001).[17] Like Fitzgerald's later collaborative work mentioned previously, the book received government funding as a Centenary of Federation project and features a foreword by premier Beattie; it is, regardless, a valuable resource of anecdotal and recorded source data. However, even a tome such as this cannot entirely do justice to, or hope to compete with, the extent of government material that has been generated over recent decades. Among these materials, none are more telling than the strategic policy documents emanating from the Premier's Department; although not neglecting the numerous publications from other Queensland or Commonwealth agencies, as well as the valuable – and now digitised – transcripts of parliamentary debates recorded in 'Hansard' (Queensland Government 2002, 2005; see also Australian Government 2001; Queensland Government 2004; Queensland Parliament 2020). Considered examination of this extensive stockpile of published administrative records can add considerably to the

---

16   One proposal that never saw publication was a piece to be titled 'Queensland: Australia's Superstate', originally commissioned by the Premier's Department and receiving cabinet approval in late 1979. It aimed to build a 'corporate image' for the state government and afford Queensland a 'newly acquired prestige'. See Salisbury (2010a).

17   An interesting, if not exactly scholarly, recent addition to this retrospective theme can be found in Office of the Queensland Governor (2016); see also Queensland Parliament (2018).

understanding of coordinated policy platforms and political agendas, especially as witnessed recently in Queensland (Sullivan Mort and Roan 2003; Bowden 2011; Salisbury 2011).

In further terms of 'non-standard' resources of political and historical analysis or data, it will have escaped nobody's attention that, increasingly, such source material can be found online and in digitised format. A leading example is the large assemblage of novel research material contained in the testimonies of past political and bureaucratic leaders, recorded in interviews for the 'Queensland Speaks' oral history project. These annotated recordings address issues of governance, policymaking and political decision-making in Queensland over the last half century; they are publicly accessible through a website produced by UQ's now defunct Centre for the Government of Queensland (a disclaimer: I was a member of this project's research and interviewing team).[18] It should not be overlooked, however, that much worthy source material can still be gleaned from the printed word, including texts situated outside strictly 'political history' confines but also comprising works of social and cultural history. Thankfully, there are very recent and leading examples of these sources as well.

Related popular history

Starting with *Three Crooked Kings*, journalist and author Matthew Condon's best-selling trilogy on corruption in Queensland in the postwar decades tells in stark detail how closely government and law enforcement in this state became entwined (Condon 2013, 2014, 2015; see also Dillon 2016). Containing some stunning revelations previously unaired outside select 'insider' circles, Condon's works exposed for many the tawdry extent of dishonest policing and politics in pre-Fitzgerald Queensland, albeit in sometimes journalistic, almost lurid style. Andrew Stafford's rightly popular and evocative *Pig City* resonates especially with many who were resident in Queensland during the years of the Bjelke-Petersen Government. His account records the development of Brisbane's 'subterranean' popular

---

18 See Centre for the Government of Queensland, *Queensland Speaks*, University of Queensland, www.queenslandspeaks.com.au, last updated April 2015. See also Centre for the Government of Queensland, *Queensland Historical Atlas*, University of Queensland, www.qhatlas.com.au, last updated April 2015, for thematic and typically map-based historical analyses of Queensland's (often political) past.

culture – in the guise of its prolific and brash music scene – which thrived despite, or perhaps partly in response to, the authoritarian bent of the local constabulary (Stafford 2014; see also Walker 2005). In a comparable vein, Jackie Ryan's award-winning and similarly evocative account of 1988's World Expo in Brisbane reveals the behind-the-scenes political dealings of Queensland gaining the event's hosting rights. The book fondly recalls the months-long festival that many Queenslanders consider transformed their capital to a modern metropolis – all while the Fitzgerald Inquiry aired its damning revelations of government corruption and police vice (Ryan 2018; see also Carroll 1991). These recent, acclaimed accounts attest to Ray Evans's assertion cited previously that Queensland's political history is indeed 'exciting, complex, surprising, nuanced and more than a little shocking'.

Conclusion

As is evident above, there has been considerable output over some time – what John Wanna called 'a long revolution' – of academic analysis of Queensland's politics. Current scholars and readers outside the academy alike are blessed with a rich and diverse body of literature that, from varying perspectives, is being added to still. Yet, this robust record of past analysis notwithstanding, it is disappointingly clear that there is now a comparative lack of more recent scholarly attention to Queensland's political history. Besides the valuable contributions of eminent scholars such as Wanna, as well as his peers and predecessors, those lately devoting attention and outputs of their own to this field are fewer in number and finding their 'impact' somewhat crowded out by other, more in-demand areas of inquiry. This scholarly decline relates particularly to study of the contemporary period of Queensland's politics, although also it can be argued to newer studies of earlier periods of state and colonial administration.

The reasons for this are many, and too complex to expand upon here. Certainly, though, a key factor in recent years is our universities' budgetary reliance on a growing cohort of international students, with humanities faculties and schools giving more credence (and prominence in the curriculum) to courses of study and research activity in national, international and transnational politics and history. Accordingly, academic focus on state-based political analysis and historical contextualising has waned noticeably in the last two decades. However, this development has not gone unnoticed or unlamented; as a very recent *AJPH* special issue highlighted, there is need for and interest in 'fresh examination of [this] rather neglected aspect of Australian politics' (Manwaring 2020). As long as Queensland remains, in Evans's words, 'much talked about but little understood' – and recent reaction to high-profile political and electoral events would seem to reinforce that impression (Blaine 2019) – there will be room and reason for new scholarly additions to this esteemed body of literature.

References

Ahamed, S. and G. Davis. 2009. 'Public policy and administration'. In R. A. W. Rhodes (ed.) *The Australian Study of Politics*. Basingstoke, UK: Palgrave Macmillan. doi.org/10.1057/9780230296848_16.

Australasian Study of Parliament Group (ASPG). 2000. 'Forum on love/hate relationship between media and parliamentarians'. ASPG Forum series. Brisbane: ASPG Queensland Chapter.

Australian Government. 2001. *Backing Australia's Ability: An Innovation Action Plan for the Future*. Canberra: Australian Commonwealth Department of Industry, Science and Resources.

Bahnisch, M. 2015. *Queensland: Everything You Ever Wanted to Know, but were Afraid to Ask*. Sydney: NewSouth Books.

Bastian, P. 2009. *Andrew Fisher: An Underestimated Man*. Sydney: UNSW Press.

Beanland, D. 2013. *The Queensland Caesar: Sir Thomas McIlwraith*. Salisbury: Boolarong Press.

Beattie, P. 1990. *In the Arena: Memories of an A.L.P. State Secretary in Queensland*. Bowen Hills: Boolarong Publications.

Beattie, P. 2005. *Making a Difference: Reflections on Life, Leadership and Politics*. With A. Loukakis. Pymble: HarperCollins.

Beattie, P. 2007. 'A line through Queensland history: Reflections on the 20th anniversary of the Fitzgerald Inquiry'. *The Proctor* 27(5): 25.

Bell, S. and A. Hindmoor. 2009. *Rethinking Governance: The Centrality of the State in Modern Society*. Port Melbourne: Cambridge University Press. doi.org/10.1017/CBO9780511814617.

Bernays, C. 1920. *Queensland Politics During Sixty (1859–1919) Years.* Brisbane: A.J. Cumming, Government Printer.

Bjelke-Petersen, J. 1990. *Don't You Worry About That! The Joh Bjelke-Petersen Memoirs.* Sydney: Angus & Robertson.

Blaine, L. 2019. 'How good is Queensland?' *The Monthly*, November. Available at: www.themonthly.com.au/issue/2019/november/1572526800/lech-blaine/how-good-queensland#mtr.

Bligh, A. 2015. *Through the Wall: Reflections on Leadership, Love and Survival.* Pymble: HarperCollins.

Bolton, G. 1963. *A Thousand Miles Away: A History of North Queensland to 1920.* Canberra: Australian National University Press.

Bolton, G. 2006. 'The art of Australian political biography'. In T. Arklay, J. Nethercote and J. Wanna (eds) *Australian Political Lives: Chronicling Political Careers and Administrative Histories.* Canberra: ANU E Press. doi.org/10.22459/APL.10.2006.01.

Bongiorno, F. 2006. 'The importance of being practical: D. J. Murphy and Australian labour history'. In 'Tropical Transformations: Denis Murphy in Queensland History', special issue. *Journal of the Royal Historical Society of Queensland* 19(9): 31–53.

Bowden, B. 2011. 'How smart now? The Bligh Government and the unravelling of the "Smart State" vision, 2007–11'. In 'Labor in Queensland, 1989–2011', special issue. *Queensland Review* 18(2): 134–144. doi.org/10.1375/qr.18.2.134.

Bowden, B. 2013. 'Modern Labor in Queensland: Its rise and failings, 1978–98'. *Labour History* 105(November): 1–26. doi.org/10.5263/labourhistory.105.0001.

Bowden, B., S. Blackwood, C. Rafferty and C. Allan (eds). 2009. *Work and Strife in Paradise: The History of Labour Relations in Queensland 1859–2009.* Annandale: Federation Press.

Brennan, F. 1992. *Land Rights Queensland Style: The Struggle for Aboriginal Self-Management.* St Lucia: University of Queensland Press.

Brett, J. 2003. 'The tasks of political biography'. In J. Damousi and R. Reynolds (eds) *History on the Couch: Essays in History and Psychoanalysis.* Carlton: Melbourne University Press.

Brett, J. 2019. 'Queensland makes it compulsory'. In *From Secret Ballot to Democracy Sausage: How Australia got Compulsory Voting.* Melbourne: Text Publishing.

Broinowski, A. 2017. *Please Explain: The Rise, Fall and Rise Again of Pauline Hanson*. Docklands: Penguin Random House Australia.

Burns, A. (ed.) 2013. *Selected Lectures on Queensland History from the Lectures in Queensland History Series, 30 November 2009 – 27 February 2012*. Townsville: Townsville City Council.

Button, J. 2006. 'Writing political autobiographies'. In T. Arklay, J. Nethercote and J. Wanna (eds) *Australian Political Lives: Chronicling Political Careers and Administrative Histories*. Canberra: ANU E Press. doi.org/10.22459/APL.10. 2006.16.

Cameron, D. 1997. 'Queensland, the state of development: The state and economic development in early twentieth century Queensland'. *Queensland Review* 4(1): 39–48. doi.org/10.1017/S1321816600001306.

Cameron, H. 1998. *Feeding the Chooks: A Selection of Well-Known Sayings of Former Queensland Premier, Sir Joh Bjelke-Petersen, in his Career of Almost 41 Years as a Politician – Farmyard Politics*. Kingaroy: self-published.

Carroll, P. 1991. 'Organising for Expo 88: The intergovernmental dimension'. *Australian Journal of Public Administration* 50(1): 74–83. doi.org/10.1111/ j.1467-8500.1991.tb02457.x.

Caulfield, J. and J. Wanna (eds). 1995. *Power and Politics in the City: Brisbane in Transition*. South Melbourne: Macmillan Education Australia.

Chamberlin, G. 2011. 'Media: An uneasy relationship'. In 'Labor in Queensland, 1989–2011', special issue. *Queensland Review* 18, (2): 105–111. doi.org/ 10.1375/qr.18.2.105.

Charlton, P. 1987. *State of Mind: Why Queensland is Different*. Revised edition. North Ryde: Methuen Haynes.

Cilento, R. and C. Lack (eds). 1959. *Triumph in the Tropics: An Historical Sketch of Queensland*. Brisbane: Smith & Patterson.

Coaldrake, P. 1989. *Working the System: Government in Queensland*. St Lucia: University of Queensland Press.

Coaldrake, P. 1990a. 'Labor to power in Queensland'. *Current Affairs Bulletin* 66(8): 16–21.

Coaldrake, P. 1990b. 'Reforming the system of government: Overview'. In S. Prasser, R. Wear and J. Nethercote (eds) *Corruption and Reform: The Fitzgerald Vision*. St Lucia: University of Queensland Press.

Coaldrake, P., G. Davis and D. Shand. 1992. 'Public sector reform in Queensland'. In J. Nethercote, B. Galligan and C. Walsh (eds) *Decision Making in Queensland Government*. Canberra: Federalism Research Centre with Queensland Public Sector Management Commission.

Coaldrake, P. and J. Nethercote (eds). 1989. *What Should Government Do?* Sydney: Hale & Iremonger.

Coaldrake, P. and J. Wanna, 1988. '"Not like the good old days": The political impact of the Fitzgerald Inquiry into police corruption in Queensland'. *Australian Quarterly* 60(4): 404–414. doi.org/10.2307/20635502.

Cockfield, G. 2020. 'The formation of the Queensland Liberal National Party: Origins, prospects and implications for Australian political systems'. *Australian Journal of Politics and History* 66(1): 78–93. doi.org/10.1111/ajph.12636.

Colley, L. 2006. 'Approaches to the merit principle in Queensland Public Service recruitment 1859–2000: From rich and dumb to gender discrimination to politicisation?' *Australian Journal of Public Administration* 65(1): 46–60. doi.org/10.1111/j.1467-8500.2006.00471a.x.

Condon, M. 2013. *Three Crooked Kings*. St Lucia: University of Queensland Press.

Condon, M. 2014. *Jacks and Jokers*. St Lucia: University of Queensland Press.

Condon, M. 2015. *All Fall Down*. St Lucia: University of Queensland Press.

Cork, J. 2006. 'The Queensland public sector: Assessing the Goss government reforms'. MPhil thesis. Brisbane: University of Queensland.

Costar, B. 1988. 'Denis Murphy: Labor activist, labour historian'. *Australian Journal of Politics and History* 34(1): 93–99. doi.org/10.1111/j.1467-8497.1988.tb00797.x.

Costar, B. 2006. 'Political leadership and Queensland nationalism'. *Journal of the Royal Historical Society of Queensland* 19(9): 65–82.

Cribb, M. B. and P. J. Boyce (eds). 1980. *Politics in Queensland: 1977 and Beyond*. St Lucia: University of Queensland Press.

Davey, P. 2015. *Joh for PM: The Inside Story of an Extraordinary Political Drama*. Sydney: NewSouth Books.

Davis, G. 1995. *A Government of Routines: Executive Coordination in an Australian State*. South Melbourne: Macmillan Education Australia.

Davis, G. 2002. 'A little learning? Public policy and Australian universities'. Professorial lecture. Nathan: Griffith University.

Davis, G. and P. Weller (eds). 2001. *Are You Being Served? State, Citizens and Governance*. Crows Nest: Allen & Unwin.

Davis, S. R. (ed.). 1960. *The Government of the Australian States*. Melbourne: Longmans.

Davison, G., J. Hirst and S. Macintyre (eds). 2001. *The Oxford Companion to Australian History*. Revised edition. South Melbourne: Oxford University Press. doi.org/10.1093/acref/9780195515039.001.0001.

Dickie, P. 1989. *The Road to Fitzgerald and Beyond*. Revised edition. St Lucia: University of Queensland Press.

Dillon, C. 2016. *Code of Silence: How One Honest Police Officer Took On Australia's Most Corrupt Police Force*. With Tom Gilling. Crows Nest: Allen & Unwin.

Eccleston, R. 2009. 'Political economy'. In R. A. W. Rhodes (ed.) *The Australian Study of Politics*. Basingstoke, UK: Palgrave Macmillan. doi.org/10.1057/9780230296848_17.

'Editorial: Australia's land of tomorrow'. 1963. *Journal of the Royal Historical Society of Queensland* 7(1): 201.

Ellis, U. 1963. *A History of the Australian Country Party*. Carlton: Melbourne University Press.

Evans, R. 1988. *The Red Flag Riots: A Study of Intolerance*. St Lucia: University of Queensland Press.

Evans, R. 2007. *A History of Queensland*. New York: Cambridge University Press.

Evans, R. and C. Ferrier (eds). 2004. *Radical Brisbane: An Unruly History*. Carlton North: Vulgar Press.

Evans, R., K. Saunders and K. Cronin. 1993. *Race Relations in Colonial Queensland: A History of Exclusion, Exploitation and Extermination*. St Lucia: University of Queensland Press.

Fitzgerald, R. 1985. *A History of Queensland: From 1915 to the 1980s*. Revised edition. St Lucia: University of Queensland.

Fitzgerald, R. 1986. *A History of Queensland: From the Dreaming to 1915*. Revised edition. St Lucia: University of Queensland Press.

Fitzgerald, R. 1994. *Red Ted: The Life of E. G. Theodore*. St Lucia: University of Queensland Press.

Fitzgerald, R. 1997. *The People's Champion, Fred Paterson: Australia's Only Communist Party Member of Parliament*. St Lucia: University of Queensland Press.

Fitzgerald, R. 1999. *Seven Days to Remember: The World's First Labor Government – Queensland, 1–7 December 1899.* St Lucia: University of Queensland Press.

Fitzgerald, R., L. Megarrity and D. Symons. 2009. *Made in Queensland: A New History.* St Lucia: University of Queensland Press.

Fitzgerald, R. and H. Thornton. 1989. *Labor in Queensland: From the 1880s to 1988.* St Lucia: University of Queensland Press.

Galligan, B. J. (ed.). 1986. *Australian State Politics.* Melbourne: Longman Cheshire.

Galligan, B. J. 1989. *Utah and Queensland Coal: A Study in the Micro Political Economy of Modern Capitalism and the State.* St Lucia: University of Queensland Press.

Galligan, B. J. and W. Roberts (eds). 2008. *The Oxford Companion to Australian Politics.* South Melbourne: Oxford University Press. doi.org/10.1093/acref/9780195555431.001.0001.

Gibney, J., S. Copeland and A. Murie. 2009. 'Toward a "new" strategic leadership of place for the knowledge-based economy'. *Leadership* 5(1): 5–23. doi.org/10.1177/1742715008098307.

Gough, M., H. Hughes, B. J. McFarlane and G. R. Palmer. 1964. *Queensland: Industrial Enigma – Manufacturing in the Economic Development of Queensland.* Carlton: Melbourne University Press.

Grant, B., T. Moore and T. Lynch (eds). 2019. *The Rise of Right-Populism: Pauline Hanson's One Nation and Australian Politics.* Singapore: Springer Nature. doi.org/10.1007/978-981-13-2670-7.

Green, A. 2017. 'Lessons from the 1998 Queensland election on preference dealing with One Nation'. *ABC News,* 13 February. Available at: www.abc.net.au/news/2017-02-13/lessons-from-the-1998-queensland-election-on-preference-dealing-/9388866.

Harris, C. 1984. *Regional Economic Development in Queensland 1859 to 1981, With Particular Emphasis on North Queensland.* Canberra: Centre for Research on Federal Financial Relations with The Australian National University.

Harrison, J. 2006. *Joh Bjelke-Petersen: Pietism and the Political Culture of Queensland.* Auchenflower: Hydrotherapy Services Australasia.

Head, B. 1986. 'The Queensland Difference.' *Politics* 21(1): 118–122. doi.org/10.1080/00323268608401986.

Head, B., J. Wanna and P. D. Williams. 2005. 'Leaders and the leadership challenge'. In J. Wanna and P. D. Williams (eds) *Yes, Premier: Labor Leadership in Australia's States and Territories*. Sydney: UNSW Press.

Hede, A., S. Prasser and M. Neylan (eds). 1992. *Keeping Them Honest: Democratic Reform in Queensland*. St Lucia: University of Queensland Press.

Hielscher, L. 2014. *Sir Leo Hielscher: Queensland Made*. With J. Holliman. St Lucia: University of Queensland Press.

Higgins, E. M. 1960. 'Queensland Labor: Trade unionists versus premiers'. *Historical Studies: Australia and New Zealand* 9(34): 140–155. doi.org/10.1080/10314616008595162.

Hughes, C. A. 1969. *Images and Issues: The Queensland State Elections of 1963 and 1966*. Canberra: Australian National University Press.

Hughes, C. A. 1973. 'Political culture'. In H. Nelson and H. Mayer (eds) *Australian Politics: A Third Reader*. Melbourne: Cheshire.

Hughes, C. A. 1980. *The Government of Queensland*. St Lucia: University of Queensland Press.

Hughes, C. A. and B. D. Graham (eds). 1968. *A Handbook of Australian Government and Politics 1890–1964*. Updated editions produced in 1977, 1986 and 2002. Canberra: Australian National University Press.

Hunt, D. 2009. 'Writing political history: Joh Bjelke-Petersen and the 1970 leadership challenge'. *Queensland History Journal* 20(10): 470–494.

Johnston, W. R. 1982. *The Call of the Land: A History of Queensland to the Present Day*. Milton: Jacaranda Press.

Johnston, W. R. 1988. *A Documentary History of Queensland*. St Lucia: University of Queensland Press.

Johnston, W. R. and M. Zerner. 1985. *A Guide to the History of Queensland: A Bibliographic Survey of Selected Resources in Queensland History*. Brisbane: Library Board of Queensland.

Joyce, R. 1977. 'Queensland'. In P. Loveday, A. W. Martin and R. S. Parker (eds) *The Emergence of the Australian party System*. Marrickville: Hale & Iremonger.

Joyce, R. 1984. *Samuel Walker Griffith*. St Lucia: University of Queensland Press.

Kefford, G. and D. McDonnell. 2016. 'Ballots and billions: Clive Palmer's personal party'. *Australian Journal of Political Science* 51(2): 183–197. doi.org/10.1080/10361146.2015.1133800.

Kerr, R. 2001. 'Queensland political personalities'. *Journal of Australian Studies* 25(69): 23–28. doi.org/10.1080/14443050109387684.

King, G. 2015. *Can Do: Campbell Newman and the Challenge of Reform.* Ballarat: Connor Court Publishing.

Kingston, M. 2001. *Off the Rails: The Pauline Hanson Trip.* Crows Nest: Allen & Unwin.

Lack, C. (ed.). 1959. *Queensland, Daughter of the Sun: A Record of a Century of Responsible Government.* Brisbane: Jacaranda Press.

Lack, C. (ed.). 1962. *Three Decades of Queensland Political History, 1929–1960.* Brisbane: Government Printer.

Leach, M., G. Stokes and I. Ward (eds). 2000. *The Rise and Fall of One Nation.* St Lucia: University of Queensland Press.

Lewis, G. 1973. *A History of the Ports of Queensland: A Study in Economic Nationalism.* St Lucia: University of Queensland Press.

Lunn, H. 1980. *Behind the Banana Curtain.* St Lucia: University of Queensland Press.

Lunn, H. 1987. *Joh: The Life and Political Adventures of Sir Johannes Bjelke-Petersen.* Revised edition. St Lucia: University of Queensland Press.

Macintyre, C. 1991. *Political Australia: A Handbook of Facts.* South Melbourne: Oxford University Press.

Macintyre, S. 2009. 'Political history,' In R. A. W. Rhodes (ed.) *The Australian Study of Politics.* Basingstoke, UK: Palgrave Macmillan. doi.org/10.1057/9780230296848_6.

Maddison, S. and R. Dennis. 2009. *An Introduction to Australian Public Policy: Theory and Practice.* Port Melbourne: Cambridge University Press. doi.org/10.1017/CBO9781139168656.

Manne, R. (ed.). 1998. *Two Nations: The Causes and Effects of the Rise of the One Nation Party in Australia.* Melbourne: Bookman Press.

Manwaring, R. 2020. 'Introduction: Labor in the Australian states'. In 'Labor in the Australian states', special issue. *Australian Journal of Politics and History* 66(1): 1–2. doi.org/10.1111/ajph.12664.

Masters, C. 2008. 'Moonlight reflections'. In 'Hidden Queensland', special issue. *Griffith Review* 21: 83–89.

May, D. 1994. *Aboriginal Labour and the Cattle Industry: Queensland from White Settlement to the Present*. Melbourne: Cambridge University Press.

McQueen, H. 1979. 'Queensland: A state of mind.' *Meanjin* 38(1): 41–51.

Megalogenis, G. 2010. 'A tale of two elections: One Nation and political protest'. *Queensland Historical Atlas 2009–10*. Available at: www.qhatlas.com.au/content/tale-two-elections-%E2%80%93-one-nation-and-political-protest.

Megarrity, L. 2004. 'The 1900s: A forgotten turning point in Queensland history'. *Queensland Review* 11(1): 65–81. doi.org/10.1017/S1321816600003561.

Megarrity, L. 2017. 'The life and times of Sir Robert Philp'. *Queensland History Journal* 23(1): 328–343.

Megarrity, L. 2018. *Northern Dreams: The Politics of Northern Development in Australia*. North Melbourne: Australian Scholarly Publishing.

Menghetti, D. 1981. *The Red North: The Popular Front in North Queensland*. Studies in North Queensland History No. 3. Townsville: James Cook University History Department.

Metcalf, A. 1984. *In their Own Right*. St Lucia: University of Queensland Press.

Metcalf, B. 2010. 'Histories of Queensland: A bibliographic survey'. *Queensland History Journal* 21(3): 162–180.

Mickel, J. and J. Wanna. 2020. 'The Longman by-election of 2018: An ordinary result with extraordinary consequences'. *Queensland Review* 27(1): 83–99. doi.org/10.1017/qre.2020.6.

Miller, I. and T. Koch. 1983. *Joh's K.O.* Bowen Hills: Boolarong Publications.

Morrison, A. A. 1960. 'Queensland: A study in distance and isolation'. *Melbourne Studies in Education* 4(1): 191–203. doi.org/10.1080/17508486009555933.

Munro, D. 1995. 'The labor trade in Melanesians to Queensland: An historiographic essay'. *Journal of Social History* 28(3): 609–627. doi.org/10.1353/jsh/28.3.609.

Murphy, D. 1968. 'The establishment of state enterprises in Queensland, 1915–18'. *Labour History* 14(May): 13–22. doi.org/10.2307/27507888.

Murphy, D. 1975. 'Queensland'. In D. Murphy (ed.) *Labor in Politics: The State Labor Parties in Australia 1880–1920*. St Lucia: University of Queensland Press.

Murphy, D. 1978. 'Queensland's image and Australian nationalism'. *Australian Quarterly* 50(2): 77–91. doi.org/10.2307/20634955.

Murphy, D. (ed.). 1983. *The Big Strikes: Queensland 1889–1965.* St Lucia: University of Queensland Press.

Murphy, D. 1990. *T. J. Ryan: A Political Biography.* Second edition. St Lucia: University of Queensland Press.

Murphy, D. and M. Cross (eds). 1985. *The Australian Labor Party and its Leaders.* 3rd edition. Alderley: Gem Press.

Murphy, D. and R. Joyce (eds). 1978. *Queensland Political Portraits, 1859–1952.* St Lucia: University of Queensland Press.

Murphy, D., R. Joyce and M. Cribb (eds). 2003. *The Premiers of Queensland.* 3rd edition. St Lucia: University of Queensland Press.

Murphy, D., R. Joyce and C. A. Hughes (eds). 1970. *Prelude to Power: The Rise of the Labour Party in Queensland 1885–1915.* Milton: Jacaranda Press.

Murphy, D., R. Joyce and C. A. Hughes (eds). 1980. *Labor in Power: The Labor Party and Governments in Queensland, 1915–57.* St Lucia: University of Queensland Press.

Office of the Queensland Governor. 2016. *A Portrait of a Governor.* Brisbane: State of Queensland.

Orr, G. and R. Levy. 2009. 'Electoral malapportionment: Partisanship, rhetoric and reform in the shadow of the agrarian strong-man'. *Griffith Law Review* 18(2009): 638–665. doi.org/10.1080/10854659.2009.10854659.

Ørsted-Jensen, R. 2011. *Frontier History Revisited: Colonial Queensland and the 'History War'.* Coorparoo: Lux Mundi Publishing.

Parnell, S. 2013. *Clive: The story of Clive Palmer.* Pymble: HarperCollins.

Piccini, J. 2010. 'Changing landscape of radicalism'. *Queensland Historical Atlas.* Available at: www.qhatlas.com.au/content/changing-landscape-radicalism.

Prasser, S. 2012. 'What went wrong? The Queensland election'. *Viewpoint* 9(June): 29–33.

Prasser, S., R. Wear and J. Nethercote (eds). 1990. *Corruption and Reform: The Fitzgerald Vision.* St Lucia: University of Queensland Press.

Queensland Government. 2002. *Queensland the Smart State: Education and Training Reforms for the Future.* Brisbane: State of Queensland Department of the Premier and Cabinet.

Queensland Government. 2004. *Achieving a Smart State Economy by Driving the Economic Development of Queensland.* Brisbane: State of Queensland Department of State Development and Innovation.

Queensland Government. 2005. *Smart Queensland: Smart State Strategy 2005– 2015.* Brisbane: State of Queensland Department of the Premier and Cabinet.

Queensland Parliament. 2018. *The People's House: Queensland's Parliament House in Pictures.* Salisbury: Boolarong Press.

Queensland Parliament. 2020. *Record of Proceedings (Hansard).* Last updated July 2020. State of Queensland. Available at: www.parliament.qld.gov.au/work-of-assembly/hansard.

The Queenslander. 1899. 'POLITICAL CRISIS'. 2 December, 1083.

Rechner, J. 1994. 'The Queensland workers' dwelling, 1910–1940'. *Journal of the Royal Historical Society of Queensland* 15(6): 265–278.

Reynolds, P. 1986. 'Queensland politics: The rise and rise of populism'. *Social Alternatives* 5(3): 50–53.

Reynolds, P. 1990. 'The 1989 Queensland state election: The end of an era'. *Australian Journal of Politics and History* 36(1): 94–103. doi.org/10.1111/ j.1467-8497.1990.tb00647.x.

Reynolds, P. 2002. *Lock, Stock and Barrel: A Political Biography of Mike Ahern.* St Lucia: University of Queensland Press.

Richards, J. 2008. *The Secret War: A True History of Queensland's Native Police.* St Lucia: University of Queensland Press.

Rorke, J. (ed.). 1970. *Politics at the State Level: Australia.* Sydney: University of Sydney Press.

Rudd, K. 2017. *Not for the Faint-Hearted: A Personal Reflection on Life, Politics and Purpose.* Sydney: Pan Macmillan Australia.

Ryan, J. 2018. *We'll Show the World: Expo 88.* St Lucia: University of Queensland Press.

Salisbury, C. 2010a. '1979 Cabinet minutes: Selected highlights'. Queensland State Archives. State of Queensland, 1 January. Available at: publications.qld.gov.au/ dataset/cabinet-minutes/resource/a19422e5-76f5-4532-879c-fd09be3c56de.

Salisbury, C. 2010b. 'Dividing Queensland – Pauline Hanson's One Nation Party'. *Queensland Historical Atlas.* Available at: www.qhatlas.com.au/content/ dividing-queensland-pauline-hanson's-one-nation-party.

Salisbury, C. 2011. 'Farm and quarry or Smart State? Queensland's economy since 1989'. In 'Labor in Queensland, 1989-2011', special issue. *Queensland Review* 18(2): 145–151. doi.org/10.1375/qr.18.2.145.

Salisbury, C. 2018. 'A tale of two parties: Contrasting performances of Annastacia Palaszczuk's Labor and the post-Newman LNP in Queensland'. *Queensland Review* 25(1): 50–61. doi.org/10.1017/qre.2018.6.

Salisbury, C. 2019. 'Thirty years on, the Fitzgerald Inquiry still looms large over Queensland politics'. *The Conversation*, 1 July. Available at: theconversation. com/thirty-years-on-the-fitzgerald-inquiry-still-looms-large-over-queensland-politics-119167.

Salisbury, C. 2020. '"It was 'year one'" – Insiders' reflections on Wayne Goss and the 1989 Queensland election'. *Queensland Review* 27(1): 73–82. doi.org/10.1017/qre.2020.5.

Saunders, K. 1993. *War on the Homefront: State Intervention in Queensland 1938–1948*. St Lucia: University of Queensland Press.

Saunders, K. 2011a.'"The restless energies of freedom": Revisiting the celebration of Queensland history'. *Queensland History Journal* 21(7): 447–455.

Saunders, K. 2011b. *Workers in Bondage: The Origins and Bases of Unfree Labour in Queensland, 1824–1916*. Revised edition. St Lucia: University of Queensland Press.

Saunders, K. and B. Costar. 2006. 'Introduction'. In 'Tropical transformations: Denis Murphy in Queensland History', special issue. *Journal of the Royal Historical Society of Queensland* 19(9): 11–13.

Schultz, J. 2008. 'Disruptive influences'. In 'Hidden Queensland', special issue. *Griffith Review* 21(2008): 9–41.

Scott, A. (ed.). 2016. *The Newman Years: Rise, Decline and Fall*. Brisbane: TJ Ryan Foundation.

Scott, J., R. Laurie, B. Stevens and P. Weller. 2001. *The Engine Room of Government: The Queensland Premier's Department 1859–2001*. St Lucia: University of Queensland Press.

Scott, R. 2017. *Phoenix? Pauline Hanson and Queensland Politics*. With Ann Scott. Brisbane: TJ Ryan Foundation.

Scott, R., P. Coaldrake, B. Head and P. Reynolds. 1986. 'Queensland'. In Brian J Galligan (ed.) *Australian State Politics*. Melbourne: Longman Cheshire.

Scott, R. and J. Ford. 2014. *Queensland Parties: The Right in Turmoil 1987–2007.* St Lucia: Centre for the Government of Queensland.

Shaw, E. (ed.). 2019. *Bjelke Blues: Stories of Repression and Resistance in Joh Bjelke-Petersen's Queensland 1968–1987.* Brisbane: AndAlso Books.

Smith, P. 1985. 'Queensland's political culture'. In A. Patience (ed.) *The Bjelke-Petersen Premiership 1968–1983: Issues in Public Policy.* Melbourne: Longman Cheshire.

Spearritt, P. 2010. 'Distinctiveness: How Queensland is a distinctive landscape and culture'. *Queensland Historical Atlas.* Available at: www.qhatlas.com.au/essay/distinctiveness-how-queensland-distinctive-landscape-and-culture.

Stafford, A. 2014. *Pig City: From The Saints to Savage Garden.* Revised edition. St Lucia: University of Queensland Press.

Stevens, B. and J. Wanna (eds). 1993. *The Goss Government: Promise and Performance of Labor in Queensland.* South Melbourne: Macmillan Education Australia.

Sullivan Mort, G. and A. Roan. 2003. 'Smart State: Queensland in the knowledge economy'. In 'Queensland: The Smart State', special issue. *Queensland Review* 10(1): 11–28. doi.org/10.1017/S132181660000249X.

Svensen, S. 1989. *The Shearers' War: The Story of the 1891 Shearers' Strike.* St Lucia: University of Queensland Press.

Thorpe, B. 1987. 'Class and politics in recent Queensland historiography: A Marxist critique'. *Australian Journal of Politics and History* 33(1): 19–29. doi.org/10.1111/j.1467-8497.1987.tb00356.x.

Thorpe, B. 1996. *Colonial Queensland: Perspectives on a Frontier Society.* St Lucia: University of Queensland Press.

Townsend, D. 1983. *Jigsaw: The Biography of Johannes Bjelke-Petersen – Statesman, Not Politician.* Brisbane: Sneyd & Morley.

Walker, C. (ed.). 2005. *Inner City Sound.* Revised edition. Portland, OR: Verse Chorus.

Walker, J. 1995. *Goss: A Political Biography.* St Lucia: University of Queensland Press.

Walter, J. A. 2009. 'Political biography'. In R. A. W. Rhodes (ed.) *The Australian Study of Politics.* Basingstoke, UK: Palgrave Macmillan. doi.org/10.1057/9780230296848_7.

Walter, J. A. 2010. 'Political leadership'. In D. Woodward, A. Parkin and J. Summers (eds) *Government, Politics, Power and Policy in Australia*. 9th edition. Frenchs Forest: Pearson Australia.

Wanna, J. 1990. 'A long revolution: Writing the political history of Queensland regimes'. *Australian Journal of Political Science* 25(1): 139–143. doi.org/10.1080/00323269008402112.

Wanna, J. 2000. 'Queensland: Consociational factionalism or ignoble cabal?' In J. Warhurst and A. Parkin (eds) *The Machine: Labor Confronts the Future*. St Leonards: Allen & Unwin.

Wanna, J. 2004. 'Political chronicles: Queensland, January to June 2004'. *Australian Journal of Politics and History* 50(4): 605–612.

Wanna, J. 2017. 'Why is One Nation so keen on a "pre-nup" in Queensland?' *Machinery of Government*, 3 November. Available at: medium.com/the-machinery-of-government/why-is-one-nation-so-keen-on-a-pre-nup-in-queensland-697492f6ca28.

Wanna, J. and T. Arklay. 2010. *The Ayes Have It: The History of the Queensland Parliament, 1957–1989*. Canberra: ANU E Press. doi.org/10.22459/AH.07.2010.

Wanna, J. and P. D. Williams. 2005. 'Peter Beattie: The "boy from Atherton" made good'. In J. Wanna and P. D. Williams (eds) *Yes, Premier: Labor Leadership in Australia's States and Territories*. Sydney: UNSW Press.

Wear, R. 2002. *Johannes Bjelke-Petersen: The Lord's Premier*. St Lucia: University of Queensland Press.

Wear, R. 2009. 'Countrymindedness and the Nationals'. In L. Botterill and G. Cockfield (eds) *The National Party: Prospects for the Great Survivors*. Crows Nest: Allen & Unwin.

Wear, R. 2010. 'Johannes Bjelke-Petersen: Straddling a barbed wire fence'. *Queensland Historical Atlas*. Available at: www.qhatlas.com.au/content/johannes-bjelke-petersen-straddling-barbed-wire-fence.

Weller, P. 2005. 'Investigating power at the centre of government: Surveying research on the Australian executive'. *Australian Journal of Public Administration* 64(1): 35–40. doi.org/10.1111/j.1467-8500.2005.00414.x.

Weller, P. 2014. *Kevin Rudd: Twice Prime Minister*. Carlton: Melbourne University Press.

Wells, D. 1979. *The Deep North*. Collingwood: Outback Press.

Whip, R. and C. A. Hughes (eds). 1991. *Political Crossroads: The 1989 Queensland Election*. St Lucia: University of Queensland Press.

Whitton, E. 1993. *The Hillbilly Dictator: Australia's Police State*. Revised edition. Pymble: ABC Books.

Williams, P. D. 2007. 'Defying the odds: Peter Beattie and the 2006 Queensland election'. *Australasian Parliamentary Review* 22(2): 212–220.

Williams, P. D. 2009. 'Leaders and political culture: The development of the Queensland premiership, 1859–2009'. *Queensland Review* 16(1): 15–34. doi.org/10.1017/S1321816600004943.

Williams, P. D. 2011. 'Editorial'. In 'Labor in Queensland, 1989–2011', special issue. *Queensland Review* 18(2): v–viii. doi.org/10.1375/qr.18.2.v.

Williams, P. D. 2012. 'Political chronicles: Queensland, January to June 2012'. *Australian Journal of Politics and History* 58(4): 638–645.

Williams, P. D. 2018a. 'Back from the brink: Labor's re-election at the 2017 Queensland state election'. *Queensland Review* 25(1): 6–26. doi.org/10.1017/qre.2018.3.

Williams, P. D. 2018b. 'Leadership or policy? Explaining the 2015 Queensland election result'. *Australian Journal of Politics and History* 64(2): 260–276. doi.org/10.1111/ajph.12462.

Williams, P. D. 2018c. 'One, two or many Queenslands? Disaggregating the regional vote at the 2017 Queensland state election'. *Australasian Parliamentary Review* 33(2): 57–79.

Williams, P. D. 2019. 'Queensland'. In P. J. Chen, N. Barry, J. Butcher, D. Clune, I. Cook, A. Garnier, Y. Haigh, S. C. Motta and M. Taflaga (eds) *Australian Politics and Policy: Senior Edition*. Sydney: Sydney University Press.

Williams, P. D. 2020. 'Raising guardrails: The role of the political commentator in a post-expert age'. *Queensland Review* 27(1): 100–115. doi.org/10.1017/qre.2020.7.

Yarrow, S. 2015. 'Split, intervention, renewal: The ALP in Queensland 1957–1989'. MPhil Thesis. Brisbane: School of Historical and Philosophical Inquiry, University of Queensland.

Young, I. 1971. *Theodore: His Life and Times*. Sydney: Alpha Books.

Young, S. 2008. 'Politics and the media in Australia today'. Senate Occasional Lecture, 11 July. Canberra: Australian Parliament.

8

Policymaking, party executives and parliamentary policy actors

Marija Taflaga

Public policy and policymaking discussions often de-emphasise the role of 'capital P' politics, which scholars typically think of as occurring within political parties or on the floor of parliaments. There is a good reason for this — much of the traditional focus on policymaking examines the interaction between the executive and the bureaucracy. Recently, scholars have acknowledged the institutionalised influence of third-party policy communities that orbit executives, such as interest groups, quangos, other tiers of government and non-executive actors within parliament itself. Nevertheless, given the executive's critical place in decision-making and within chains of delegation and accountability, this core relationship remains the point of tension between two sets of actors: ministers as principals and decision-makers, and bureaucrats as their agents, tasked with design, implementation and evaluation. Politics is always there, as wildcard, trump card, perhaps a spanner in the works or worse still a wrecking ball. But the perception appears to be that politics – by which I mean the interplay between the executive and parliament through party conflict – *gets in the way* of business as usual, of good practice, of the real work of policymakers.

Over decades, policymaking has been conceptualised in multiple ways: as a cycle (Lasswell 1956; Jones 1970; Althaus, Bridgman and Davis 2007); or a garbage can (Cohen, March and Olsen 1972); as multiple streams (Kingdon 1984); as multi-levelled (Rhodes 1997; Richards and Smith 2004); or as the result of policy networks (Rhodes 1997, 2006) distributed largely outside the reach of government. Given that much of the interest in public policy relates to the overall success of implementation and evaluation of outcomes, it makes sense that the political dimensions, such as they are, should be viewed through a public policy–focused lens. Yet, discounting the political dimension leaves the question about how public policy and 'capital P' politics interrelate underdeveloped, and the answer not quite complete, for citizens seeking to understand how power is wielded.

In Westminster parliamentary democracies like Australia, executives do not arrive from nowhere. They are party members, elected to parliament under party labels. Governments are really party governments (Lucy 1993; Kopecký et al. 2012; Mair 2007), just as the official opposition is party opposition. It's important not to forget the reality that it is political parties that inhabit both legislative and executive roles, animating these institutions and interpreting their norms and conventions. It remains the case that political parties overwhelmingly exercise, and sometimes even reshape, the powers of the executive and legislature.

Since the 1970s, ministers have demanded increased 'responsiveness' from the public service, as a strategy to reassert the role of elected representatives over the work of governments. Over this same time period, political scientists have discussed the growing professionalisation of the political elite (King 1981; Pakulski and Tranter 2015; Cairney 2007; Miragliotta and Errington 2012; Best and Cotta 2000). Today, there is growing evidence that ministerial selection is linked to a previous career in the 'persuasion industries' – such as in a political office, think tank or advocacy organisation (Allen 2013, 2014; Cowley 2012; Goplerud 2015). Further, political staff have become an institutionalised third pillar (Maley 2015) of executive governance (Craft 2016, 2015; Connaughton 2010, 2015; Wilson 2015). The pathway into executive government appears to be becoming more networked and politicised. The opportunity parliament presents as a platform for elected elites has important policy implications.

One of the calling cards of John Wanna's work is to readily acknowledge not only the importance of party and parliamentary politics, but also to engage with the way in which it complicates relationships. Wanna's work fits into a tradition that straddles public policy and a more traditional political science view of how government works. This is most evident in Rhodes and Wanna's critique of public value, where they argue that politics is portrayed as a problem rather than integral to advisory systems (Rhodes and Wanna 2007). This broader view, conceptualising policymaking and government management systems as part of a wider policy advisory system (Craft and Halligan 2017) that is shaped by tradition, myths and 'capital P' politics (Rhodes, Wanna and Weller 2009) offers an important touchstone for our understanding of how decisions are made – and by whom – over time. In this chapter, I argue in favour of a greater recognition of the place of party and parliamentary politics in broader discussions of public policy and explain why it matters for policy researchers.

Institutional design and policymaking

The rise of disciplined two-party systems within Westminster democracies has seen a long-running discussion about the decline in the importance of parliament as the preeminent site for policy debate (Uhr and Wanna 2000). Parliaments are dominated by the executive, akin to 'elected dictatorships', able to ram through their policy agendas with minimal opposition from the legislature. This trend is amplified by the increasing expectations on government and the assumption that its work is becoming more complex. While this remains a broad generalisation across Westminster, the reflexive referral to parliament – a technical and (often) perfunctory step – in the policy development and legitimation process is overly simplistic. The argument is often used as a way to differentiate between different political systems and/or as a ready justification to ignore the political dimensions of policymaking in order to focus on bureaucratic or third-sector actors (e.g. see Cairney 2012; or from an Australian perspective Althaus, Bridgman and Davis 2007). Indeed, 40 years ago Richardson and Jordan (1979) went as far as to argue that polities such as the UK are 'post-parliamentary' and that policy formulation is the result of negotiation between government and advocacy groups.

Yet, as Uhr and Wanna (2000) have argued, parliament is now a 'theatre of action', where its role has become more diffuse and is, arguably, far broader than originally conceptualised by Bagehot (1963), Dicey (1982) or Jennings (1966). Further, recent work on policy agendas (Dowding and Martin 2017) demonstrates that there remains a close link between what executives say they want to do, and what they attempt to legislate in parliament for policy domains such as economics, defence, immigration and workplace relations. They also found differences between the executives' policy focus compared with the opposition and the media. These differences highlight both the agenda setting and accountability functions of parliament. Ultimately, major policy initiatives must make it to parliament for legitimation and parliament remains an important site to pressure governments for change and to reform existing policy structures.

Handwaving over parliament as executive-dominated and therefore tangential to policymaking ignores important political system differences in institutional design and their impact on policy outcomes. This is perhaps even more important as the scope of parliament's remit has become broader, and the notion of parliament's boundaries more porous. Indeed, deliberation appears to have spilled over beyond parliament into the media (Uhr and Wanna 2000), creating an effective 'third chamber' (Taflaga 2016). Rhodes, Wanna and Weller (2009) have noted that over the twentieth century, internal party deliberations have become more robust as a larger proportion of parliamentary deliberations have become 'rehearsed theatre'. This reflects the long-term trend over the twentieth century where the relative balance of deliberation within parliament is shifting between public and private domains – from the parliamentary chamber to debates within party rooms. However, this picture is becoming somewhat more complex in the twenty-first century, as parliament finds new ways to reassert itself and political parties' internal machinery is increasingly sidelined by party elites (Gauja 2013).

In Australia, the Senate is a powerful upper chamber – one of the most powerful in the world (Kaiser 2008). As Ganghof, Eppner and Pörschke (2018) argue, the reality that both the House and Senate are equally legitimate with near-equal powers, but that confidence in the government need only be secured in the Lower House, has allowed actors within both chambers to pursue different normative goals. That is, actors in the House are focused on asserting and maintaining the chamber's confidence in the government. But in the Senate, where confidence in the government is not required, this chamber is free to pursue tasks aimed at increasing deliberation and accountability. Reflecting these theoretical observations, research by Halligan, Miller and Power (2007) documents the growing role of the parliamentary committee system, particularly in the Senate. Halligan and colleagues note a resurgence of parliamentary institutions' capacity to reach out to the public when discussing policy proposals or evaluating outcomes. They have also documented the way committee processes have opened up policymaking opportunities for backbench MPs to redefine policy problems and solutions, particularly in domains where agendas are new and policy stances are undergoing refinement and clarification.

Indeed, the emergence of a modern committee system from the 1970s onwards, in multiple Westminster jurisdictions, has also reasserted the policymaking role of Westminster parliaments. In the UK, reforms to parliamentary debate in the Commons, reforms to the House of Lords and changes to the committee system have increased the potential for parliamentary actors to influence outcomes, though most argue that reforms have not gone far enough (Bates, Goodwin and McKay 2017; Goodwin and Bates 2016). Recent evidence suggests that committee work is increasingly seen as a policy training ground and as a pathway into ministerial office (Goodwin, Bates and McKay 2018; Maley 2018). Further, committees provide meaningful opportunities for parliamentary actors, particularly oppositions, to influence policy outcomes. For actors locked out of established policy networks, committees are alternative sites to 'venue hop', in the hope of winning a receptive audience.

From a top-down perspective, policymaking is largely seen as the preserve of governments. In Westminster contexts, this tendency is exaggerated by tension between responsible government, which emphasises the role of executives, and parliamentary government, which encompasses more actors, but where responsible government's legitimacy resides (Halligan 2008). Further, Westminster executive–bureaucratic relationships are explicitly hierarchical (Wanna and Weller 2003). In this light, policymaking functions as a means of hypothesis-testing and deliberate choice-making on the part of political actors, most commonly conceptualised in the literature as ministers or executive actors. Policy formulation is facilitated by a set of structured processes undertaken by the public service, political party infrastructure or outside third parties such as think tanks, interest groups or organised policy communities. Importantly, actors' choices are made consciously in the dynamic context of government and the political dimensions of policy decisions (Althaus, Bridgman and Davis 2007, 6–7).

In this sense, for political actors, policy functions as a tool to reconcile philosophical and ideological aims with real world realities. It could be the need for a solution to a public scandal, to satisfy an important interest group or to simply appear to be doing something. These political motivations can coexist with policy choices that may be the product of long-running deliberations to deliver outcomes to citizens. Ultimately, which policies are pursued reflect political actors' priorities – indeed, as Wanna has argued, political parties can even 'prevent wider policy debate by internalising disputes or options' (Wanna 1993, 52). Put another way, policymaking sorts out political problems, and policy is ultimately a means to an end.

However, ministers, prime ministers, executives and governments are not the only 'capital P' political actors with important influence on policy outcomes. For parliamentary actors (Prosser and Denniss 2015), and particularly the official opposition (Haddon 2012; Prasser 2010; Taflaga 2016), parliament is a key venue to influence policy debate either directly via the chamber floor, or more commonly, indirectly through the media. Parliamentary actors are able to use their resources for agenda setting and public education opportunities.

For the official opposition, their role as an alternative government is important in terms of agenda setting, policy development and legislating and evaluating outcomes. As Brendan McCaffrie (2012) has argued, a portion of government leaders' success can be attributed to the actions of their opposition, whether through ineptitude, timely support of a discrete policy or a long-term reform agenda. The last leads to reform consolidation – that is, accepting and building on the reforms of previous governments. This is because oppositions are seeking to replace the government, but are not by default always in permanent opposition to the government's actions. Indeed, oppositions may seek, or be invited, to contribute to the development of government policy (Norton 2008, 246). The opposition's capacity to influence outcomes is not necessarily dependent on their size, but is more to do with their successful exploitation of opportunities that parliamentary political systems offer (Kaiser 2008, 35). Given that successful governments regularly appropriate policy ideas from their opponents and adopt them with modifications, failure to consider the role of policymaking by non-government political actors understates the role of the political dimension in which actors that design, advocate and implement policy operate.

Oppositions have gradually institutionalised their role since the nineteenth century. First as an institution of the parliament and more recently as an institutionalised alternative government via the shadow cabinet system (Punnett 1973; Bateman 2008). Over time, oppositions have received more resources to undertake this work, though their resource envelope remains modest compared with that of governments. Ultimately, opposition is the principal apprenticeship most ministers receive and one that they value (Tiernan and Weller 2010). Oppositions have been the principal beneficiaries of an increase in parliamentary scrutiny infrastructure, such as the modernisation of the Australian Senate committee system in 1970 and the Wright reforms in the UK. This is in addition to other parliamentary infrastructure to support policymaking such as the parliamentary budget office (which was first implemented in Canada). Despite parliament's overall decline in status, parliamentary actors actually have more resources to challenge the claims of executives and to make meaningful contributions to policy debates than at any time in the past. Further, the incentive structure for one unified and single message is increasingly under challenge by the rise of social media and the desire for authenticity in political leaders. It is not surprising then that, slowly, political institutions are adapting to create more space for political actors to have a say and influence policy outcomes.

But there are doubts as to how genuine oppositions are in their policymaking efforts. Uhr (2009, 74) has argued that over time oppositions have chosen to invest principally in election campaign planning rather than alternative policy platforms. Indeed, a Liberal political adviser, Scott Prasser (2010, 154–58), has argued that perhaps we expect too much from oppositions, who are ill-equipped to adequately develop policy and meet interest groups' and voter's expectations. In the mid-1990s, Wanna himself was pessimistic about the policymaking capacity of parties generally, in part driven by a lack of policy development practice in opposition (Wanna 1993, 48–49). Others disagree; for instance, Catherine Haddon argued forcefully that policymaking was a key exercise for political parties in opposition. Through the policymaking process, parties interpret and renew their principles (Haddon 2012, 4). They also develop contacts with the policy sectors that they can draw upon on in government (Riddell and Haddon 2009, 16; Tiernan and Weller 2010), and opposition policymaking represents an alternative option for those advocacy sector actors seeking to influence policy outcomes.

Recent political experience suggests that interest by 'capital P' political actors in policymaking is likely cyclical – reflecting political circumstances and the skill sets of political leaders. As Australia's 'climate wars' made clear, 'blood and guts' politics still shapes many important policy outcomes, even as government's capacity to control outcomes has receded. Indeed, recent Australian experience has underlined the critical role both parliamentary actors and oppositions can play in derailing policy proposals that have undergone careful consultation, design, development and coordination. If policy measures, especially new initiatives, cannot consolidate parliamentary support, no amount of careful design and consultation can compensate.

Actors and policymaking:
The de-separation of political careers

'Capital P' political actors are often decisive actors in the policymaking process. Typically, in Westminster systems, elected political actors are key decision-makers, veto players or actors with a greater capacity to increase the salience of issues than most others in a crowded policymaking field. As political scientists are increasingly uncovering, the career paths of elected elites have changed in profound ways in parallel to major changes in the policy advisory system.

Just as the consolidation of the party system changed the balance of parliamentary institutions, it has also changed the nature of who gets elected. Political parties were, and remain significant – but not the only – gatekeepers between the public and government. As party organisations have evolved over time, their roles as democratic linkages (Dalton, Farrell and McAllister 2011) have become weaker over time and parties have begun to act more like cartels (Katz and Mair 2009), political scientists have observed that elected elites are drawn from a narrower class (Best and Cotta 2000) with a narrower skill base gained from working within 'instrumental' occupations that orbit the world of the political offices (Cairney 2007). The implications of this are not trivial – there are distinct changes in the way decision-making occurs within parties (Gauja 2013). This trend is exacerbated further as parties become more personalised and elections more focused on party leaders than party brands, which are likely to be less complex and focused on policy (Karvonen 2010).

Career structures are also having a material impact on who is successful in becoming a member of the executive, in charge of making or vetoing key decisions (Dowding and Dumont 2015).

Another important aspect of the change in the career structure of elected elites in Westminster systems is the rise of political advisers. In part this relates to advisers' specific role in the policymaking process (Maley 2015; Craft 2015), acting as gatekeepers, brokers, generators of ideas and, most concerningly, as proxies for ministers. While there have undoubtedly been some positive outcomes, there are also well-documented concerns about their impact on the policy advisory system and the traditions of Westminster's professional and nonpartisan civil service (Peters and Pierre 2004). These are exemplified by the poor consequences of policy decisions taken by actors who are increasingly driven by short-term incentives and the decoupling of policy design from policy implementation (King and Crewe 2014).

Another aspect is the fact that political advising is increasingly a pathway to elected political office. As noted, the expansion of political offices and the broadening of the policy advisory system beyond the public service into the world of interest groups, think tanks and lobbyists has led to a proliferation of 'instrumental careers'. While it remains unclear what, if any, specific links exist between interest groups and the world of elected politics, there is growing evidence of the importance of political advising in elected careers. Evidence from the UK highlights how a career in staffing increases the likelihood of being selected as a candidate, elected to parliament and appointed to the executive (Goplerud 2015). Similar trends are being uncovered in Australia (Miragliotta and Errington 2012; Taflaga and Kerby 2020), though there are distinct differences in patterns in recruitment and the structure of career paths between men and women, for example.

As I have argued elsewhere with Keith Dowding (Dowding and Taflaga 2020), Westminster systems appear to have undergone a de-separation of careers at the top of government. That is, there were once two distinct career paths. On the one hand, a political path that had higher risks and, on the other, a professional path that existed to consider long-term consequences and restrain the worst excesses of popularly elected executives. Now these career paths are increasingly blurred, as increasing numbers of people move back and forth between partisan and nonpartisan roles (Maley 2017). The effect over decades has been to shift the balance of decisive decision-making power towards more amateur and partisan-minded actors – or actors we would think of as 'capital P' political actors like elected elites and political advisers, which has a deleterious impact on the quality of policy formulation. While governments might be struggling to retain control as government becomes large, more diffuse and/or more complex, the need to look like they are in control is ever-pressing, as policy debate has increasingly become about 'political management'. This has led to what Patrick Diamond (2019) argues is government by permanent campaign. John Wanna's (1993, 49, 53) own assessment in the mid-1990s was perhaps even more pessimistic, where parties were seen to 'preen' before the media to burnish their alternative government credentials and were made up of 'careerist politicians intent on surviving above doing anything else'.

Taken together, perhaps it is not surprising that the changing nature of political careers has moved in parallel to changes in policy advisory systems, with a greater emphasis on managerialism by bureaucrats (O'Faircheallaigh, Wanna and Weller 1999). Perhaps what is understated is that these processes are likely intertwined, with changes on one side of the political–professional divide impacting and shaping decisions and changes on the other.

Conclusion

Political policy actors outside of the executive, and those within the executive but who are not ministers, can and do assert their right and insert themselves into the policy development, legitimation and, in a more limited way, evaluation. Or as Rod Rhodes and John Wanna (2009, 168) have put it: 'large "P" politics frames the decision structures for small "p" politics', within the world of policymakers. Over recent decades, political institutions have adapted to grant previously marginalised political actors more scope to influence policy debate. Under some conditions, political actors' influence can have disproportionate impact. At the same time that policy advisory systems have expanded, political career structures have also changed. It is likely that changes occurring on the 'capital P' politics side are impacting and interacting with processes underway within public policy institutions and systems. Public policy scholars obviously know that politics and political dimensions remain important. In large part, the lack of emphasis on 'capital P' actors is one of differences in focus:

that is, the different choices researchers make when they investigate policymaking processes, which may favour one set of actors over others or specific policy sites over others, or which may simply look at higher or lower levels of abstraction. However, as argued above, changes in the institutional framework of policy advisory systems often do originate with 'capital P' actors, or it is these actors that force changes as they attempt to assert their role. In following the example of John Wanna's body of work, accounting for the role of 'capital P' politics enriches and deepens our understanding of policymaking processes and the evolution of policy advisory systems.

References

Allen, P. 2013. 'Linking pre-parliamentary political experience and the career trajectories of the 1997 general election cohort'. *Parliamentary Affairs* 66(4): 685–707. doi.org/10.1093/pa/gss030.

Allen, P. 2014. 'Bring in the professionals: How pre-parliamentary political experience affects political careers in the House of Commons'. PhD thesis. Birkbeck: University of London. Available at: vufind.lib.bbk.ac.uk/vufind/Record/482473.

Althaus, C., P. Bridgman, and G. Davis. 2007. *The Australian Policy Handbook*. Crows Nest: Allen & Unwin.

Bagehot, W. 1963. *The English Constitution*. London: Collins.

Bateman, J. 2008. *In the Shadows: The Shadow Cabinet in Australia*. Canberra: The Parliamentary Library.

Bates, S., M. Goodwin and S. McKay. 2017. 'Do UK MPs engage more with Select Committees since the Wright reforms? An interrupted time series analysis, 1979–2016'. *Parliamentary Affairs* 70(4): 780–800. doi.org/10.1093/pa/gsx007.

Best, H. and M. Cotta (eds). 2000. *Parliamentary Representatives in Europe, 1848–2000 : Legislative Recruitment and Careers in Eleven European Countries*. Oxford and New York: Oxford University Press.

Cairney, P. 2007. 'The professionalisation of MPs: Refining the "politics-facilitating" explanation'. *Parliamentary Affairs* 60(2): 212–233. doi.org/10.1093/pa/gsm006.

Cairney, P. 2012. *Understanding Public Policy: Theories and Issues*. Houndmills, Basingstoke, Hampshire and New York: Red Globe Press.

Cohen, M., J. G. March and J. P. Olsen. 1972. 'A garbage can model of organizational choice'. *Administrative Science Quarterly* 17(1): 1–25. doi.org/10.2307/2392088.

Connaughton, B. 2010. '"Glorified gofers, policy experts or good generalists": A classification of the roles of the Irish ministerial adviser'. *Irish Political Studies* 25(3): 347–369. doi.org/10.1080/07907184.2010.497636.

Connaughton, B. 2015. 'Navigating the borderlines of politics and administration: Reflections on the role of ministerial advisers'. *International Journal of Public Administration* 38(1): 37–45. doi.org/10.1080/01900692.2014.952820.

Cowley, P. 2012. 'Arise, novice leader! The continuing rise of the career politician in Britain'. *Politics* 32(1): 31–38. doi.org/10.1111/j.1467-9256.2011.01422.x.

Craft, J. 2015. 'Conceptualizing the policy work of partisan advisers'. *Policy Sciences* 48(2): 135–158. doi.org/10.1007/s11077-015-9212-2.

Craft, J. 2016. *Backrooms and Beyond: Partisan Advisers and the Politics of Policy Work in Canada*. University of Toronto Press. doi.org/10.3138/9781442617636.

Craft, J. and J. Halligan. 2017. 'Assessing 30 years of Westminster policy advisory system experience'. *Policy Sciences* 50(1): 47–62. doi.org/10.1007/s11077-016-9256-y.

Dalton, R. J., D. M. Farrell and I. McAllister. 2011. *Political Parties and Democratic Linkage: How Parties Organize Democracy*. Oxford: Oxford University Press. doi.org/10.1093/acprof:osobl/9780199599356.001.0001.

Diamond, P. 2019. *The End of Whitehall? Government by Permanent Campaign*. Springer. doi.org/10.1007/978-3-319-96101-9.

Dicey, A. V. 1982. *Introduction to the Study of the Law of the Constitution*. Reprint of the original 8th edition. Indianapolis: Liberty Classics.

Dowding, K. and P. Dumont (eds). 2015. *The Selection of Ministers around the World*. London and New York: Routledge. doi.org/10.4324/9781315757865.

Dowding, K. and A. Martin. 2017. *Policy Agendas in Australia*. Switzerland: Palgrave Macmillan. doi.org/10.1007/978-3-319-40805-7.

Dowding, K. and M. Taflaga. 2020. 'Career de-separation in Westminster democracies'. *Political Quarterly* 91(1): 116–124. doi.org/10.1111/1467-923X.12812.

Ganghof, S., S. Eppner and A. Pörschke. 2018. 'Australian bicameralism as semi-parliamentarism: Patterns of majority formation in 29 democracies'. *Australian Journal of Political Science* 53(2): 211–233. doi.org/10.1080/10361146.2018. 1451487.

Gauja, A. 2013. *The Politics of Party Policy: From Members to Legislators*. Houndmills, Basingstoke, Hampshire and New York: Palgrave Macmillan.

Goodwin, M. and S. Bates. 2016. 'The "powerless parliament"? Agenda-setting and the role of the UK Parliament in the Human Fertilisation and Embryology Act 2008'. *British Politics* 11(2): 232–255. doi.org/10.1057/bp.2015.37.

Goodwin, M., S. Bates and S. McKay. 2018. 'Electing to do women's work? Gendered divisions of labour in UK Select Committees, 1979-2016.' In *Politics & Gender*. Cambridge: Cambridge University Press. doi.org/ 10.1017/S1743923X19000874.

Goplerud, M. 2015. 'The first time is (mostly) the charm: Special advisers as parliamentary candidates and Members of Parliament'. *Parliamentary Affairs* 68(2): 332–351. doi.org/10.1093/pa/gst033.

Haddon, C. 2012. *Making Policy in Opposition: Lessons for Effective Government*. The Institute for Government. Available at: www.instituteforgovernment.org. uk/publications/making-policy-opposition.

Halligan, J. 2008. 'Parliamentary committee roles in facilitating public policy at the Commonwealth level'. *Australasian Parliamentary Review* 23(2): 135–156.

Halligan, J., R. Miller and J. M. Power. 2007. *Parliament in the Twenty-First Century: Institutional Reform and Emerging Roles*. Carlton: Melbourne University Press.

Jennings, I. 1966. *The British Constitution*. 5th edition. Cambridge: Cambridge University Press.

Jones, C. 1970. *An Introduction to the Study of Political Life*. Berkeley: Duxberry Press.

Kaiser, A. 2008. 'Parliamentary opposition in Westminster democracies: Britain, Canada, Australia and New Zealand'. *The Journal of Legislative Studies* 14(1): 20–45. doi.org/10.1080/13572330801920887.

Karvonen, L. 2010. *The Personalisation of Politics: A Study of Parliamentary Democracies*. ECPR Press.

Katz, R. and P. Mair. 2009. 'The cartel party thesis: A restatement'. *Perspectives on Politics* 7(4): 753–766. doi.org/10.1017/S1537592709991782.

King, A. 1981. 'The rise of the career politician in the UK'. *British Journal of Political Science* 11(3): 249–85.

King, A. S. and I. Crewe. 2014. *The Blunders of Our Governments*. London : Oneworld. Available at: trove.nla.gov.au/version/216213164.

Kingdon, J. 1984. *Agendas, Alternatives and Public Policies*. New York: Harper Collins.

Kopecký, P., P. Mair, M. Spirova and European Consortium for Political Research. 2012. *Party Patronage and Party Government in European Democracies*. Oxford : Oxford University Press. doi.org/10.1093/acprof:oso/9780199599370.001.0001.

Lasswell, H. 1956. *The Decision Process: Seven Categories of Functional Analysis*. College Park: University of Maryland Press.

Lucy, R. 1993. *The Australian Form of Government: Models in Dispute*. South Melbourne: Macmillan.

Mair, P. 2007. 'The challenge to party government'. Working Paper. EUI SPS 2007/09. European University Institute. Available at: cadmus.eui.eu//handle/1814/7158.

Maley, M. 2015. 'The policy work of Australian political staff'. *International Journal of Public Administration* 38(1): 46–55. doi.org/10.1080/01900692.2014.907311.

Maley, M. 2017. 'Temporary partisans, tagged officers or impartial professionals: Moving between ministerial offices and departments'. *Public Administration* 95(2): 407–420. doi.org/10.1111/padm.12290.

Maley, M. 2018. 'Parliamentary experience in Australian ministerial careers 1996–2007'. *Australian Journal of Politics and History* 64(2): 241–259. doi.org/10.1111/ajph.12464.

McCaffrie, B. 2012. 'Understanding the success of presidents and prime ministers: The role of opposition parties'. *Australian Journal of Political Science* 47(2): 257–271. doi.org/10.1080/10361146.2012.677005.

Miragliotta, N. and W. Errington. 2012. 'Legislative recruitment and models of party organisation: Evidence from Australia'. *The Journal of Legislative Studies* 18(1): 21–40. doi.org/10.1080/13572334.2012.646708.

Norton, P. 2008. 'Making sense of opposition'. *The Journal of Legislative Studies* 14(1–2): 236–250. doi.org/10.1080/13572330801921257.

O'Faircheallaigh, C., J. Wanna and P. M. Weller. 1999. *Public Sector Management in Australia: New Challenges, New Directions*. South Yarra: Macmillan Education Australia.

Pakulski, J. and B. Tranter. 2015. *The Decline of Political Leadership in Australia? Changing Recruitment and Careers of Federal Politicians*. New York: Palgrave Macmillan.

Peters, B. G., and J. Pierre (eds). 2004. *The Politicization of the Civil Service in Comparative Perspective: A Quest for Control*. Taylor & Francis. doi.org/10.4324/9780203799857.

Prasser, S. 2010. 'Opposition one day, government the next: Can oppositions make policy and be ready for office?' *Australasian Parliamentary Review* 25(1): 151–161.

Prosser, B. and R, Denniss. 2015. *Minority Policy: Rethinking Governance When Parliament Matters*. Carlton: Melbourne University Press.

Punnett, R. M. 1973. *Front-Bench Opposition: The Role of the Leader of the Opposition, the Shadow Cabinet and Shadow Government in British Politics*. London: Heinemann Educational Books Ltd.

Rhodes, R. A. W. 1997. *Understanding Governance: Policy Networks, Governance, Reflexivity and Accountability*. Buckingham: Open University Press.

Rhodes, R. A. W. 2006. 'Policy network analysis'. In M. Moran, M. Rein and R. Goodin (eds) *The Oxford Handbook of Public Policy*. Oxford: Oxford University Press.

Rhodes, R. A. W. and J. Wanna. 2007. 'The limits to public value, or rescuing responsible government from the platonic guardians'. *Australian Journal of Public Administration* 66(4): 406–421. doi.org/10.1111/j.1467-8500.2007.00553.x.

Rhodes, R. A. W. and J. Wanna. 2009. 'Bringing the politics back in: Public value in Westminster parliamentary government'. *Public Administration* 87(2): 161–183. doi.org/10.1111/j.1467-9299.2009.01763.x.

Rhodes, R. A. W., J. Wanna and P. Weller. 2009. *Comparing Westminster*. Oxford: Oxford University Press. doi.org/10.1093/acprof:oso/9780199563494.001.0001.

Richards, D. and M Smith. 2004. 'The "hybrid state"'. In S. Ludlam and M. Smith (eds) *Governing as New Labor*. Basingstoke: Palgrave Macmillan.

Richardson, J. J. and G. Jordan. 1979. *Governing Under Pressure*. First edition. Oxford: Blackwell Publishers.

Riddell, P. and C. Haddon. 2009. *Transitions: Preparing for Changes of Government*. London: Institute for Government. Available at: www.instituteforgovernment. org.uk/publications/transitions.

Taflaga, M. 2016. 'Policy, policy development and political communication during opposition: The Federal Liberal Party of Australia 1983–1996 and 2007–2013'. PhD thesis. Canberra: The Australian National University.

Taflaga, M. and M. Kerby. 2020. 'Who does what work in a ministerial office: Politically appointed staff and the descriptive representation of women in Australian political offices, 1979–2010'. *Political Studies* 68(2): 463–485. doi.org/10.1177/0032321719853459.

Tiernan, A. and P. Weller. 2010. *Learning to Be a Minister: Heroic Expectations, Practical Realities*. Carlton: Melbourne University Press.

Uhr, J. 2009. 'Parliamentary oppositional leadership'. In P. 't Hart, J. Kane and H. Patapan (eds) *Dispersed Democratic Leadership: Origins, Dynamics, and Implications*. New York: Oxford University Press. doi.org/10.1093/acprof:oso/9780199562992.003.0004.

Uhr, J. and J. Wanna. 2000. 'The future roles of parliament'. In J. Wanna, P. Weller and M. Keating (eds) *Institutions on the Edge? Capacity for Governance*. St Leonards: Allen & Unwin.

Wanna, J. 1993. 'Political parties and the policy process'. In S. Prasser and A. Hede (eds) *Policy-Making in Volatile Times*. Sydney: Hale & Iremonger.

Wanna, J. and P. Weller. 2003. 'Traditions of Australian governance'. *Public Administration* 81(1): 63–94. doi.org/10.1111/1467-9299.00337.

Wilson, R. P. 2015. 'Research note: A profile of ministerial policy staff in the Government of Canada'. *Canadian Journal of Political Science/Revue Canadienne de Science Politique* 48(2): 455–471. doi.org/10.1017/S0008 423915000293.

9

Models of government– business relations: Industry policy preferences versus pragmatism

Michael de Percy

Introduction

I first came to know John Wanna in 2005 when he acted as an assessor for my doctoral confirmation seminar. I had just started as an associate lecturer at the time, teaching a large first-year class in government– business relations, and my research was focused on government–business relations in the Australian and Canadian telecommunications sectors. I had conducted strategic planning seminars with several small Australian internet service providers and it was clear that regulatory issues were stifling their ability to innovate and to deliver services outside of the traditional provider models, even if the smaller firms had the technological capacity and human capital to deliver to areas that were under-served by the major players. Canada was a world leader in broadband at the time and I had conducted interviews with Canadian telecommunications businesspeople and policymakers: the 'culture' of the relationships between government and businesses was significantly different there and this seemed worth exploring. But I was struggling to find the research supervision I needed. After a discussion with Professor Ian Eddie, then the head of my school at the University of Canberra, Ian asked John if I could transfer across to The Australian National University under John's supervision. And thus, my education in government–business relations began.

Often students would tell me they did not need to know anything about government–business relations because they were going to be accountants. Having worked as an accountant in a suburban practice, and later with the Royal Australian Army Pay Corps and in government financial management, I knew this was incorrect. Time and again I had seen accountants, especially in the public sector, make mistakes because they had commercial training but no experience working in government. So, I set about trying to convince students that, since the market liberalisation agenda had gathered pace from 1983, understanding the relationship between government and business had become more important than ever (Catley 1996, 129). With the establishment of the Business Council of Australia during Bob Hawke's Labor Government, various Prices and Incomes Accords were able to be negotiated, involving tripartite, consensus-based power sharing arrangements between the government, the Business Council of Australia and the Australian Council of Trade Unions (ACTU). By this time, the traditional industries could no longer rely on government protection (which the Whitlam Government had started to dismantle during the early 1970s), and it was recognised that they would need to become internationally competitive if they were to survive. The nature of the government–business relationship in Australia that had been heavily focused on targeted industry policy now had to adjust to a climate of international engagement and competition (competition regulation within Australia had only been seriously pursued since the establishment of the *Trade Practices Act 1974* [Cth]).

John Wanna introduced me to the academic subdiscipline of government–business relations. The notes from our first meeting record the scholars I was to read: Frank Stilwell, Ted Wheelwright, Greg Crough, William Byrt, Ann Capling and Brian Galligan,[1] Bob Catley, Gwynneth Singleton, Stephen Bell, Kenneth Dyson and Stephen Wilks, among others. But it was Frank Stilwell's model of the capitalist economic system that become the basis for my understanding of the nature of government–business

---

1   Sadly, Professor Brian Galligan passed away on 14 December 2019. With co-author Ann Capling, his work *Beyond the Protective State: The Political Economy of Australia's Manufacturing Industry Policy* is one of the most important works in the study of Australian government–business relations (see Capling and Galligan 1992).

relations, especially in cross-national comparative work, and also for my approach to teaching the subject to first-year students (Stilwell 2006, 49–52). Stilwell's model is founded on the private ownership of the means of production, with a distinctive ideology and a distinctive role of the state that shape the labour, financial, land and property, and goods and services markets, all of which have an expansionary tendency. Using Stilwell, I introduced students to a history of political and economic ideas, the major political ideologies, comparisons of national industrial cultures and how these impact ways of organising markets, political parties' preferences in relation to trade agreements and industry policy, how governments regulate for externalities, the impact of globalisation and international institutions, and later the links between the public, private and voluntary sectors and the impact of climate change.

In a podcast for John's festschrift, I interviewed John and asked him to reflect on his career (de Percy 2019). During the discussion, John suggested that the great ideological battles between the two major political parties were a thing of the past, and that there had been significant convergence (outside of perhaps climate change and immigration or socially divisive issues such as same-sex marriage and euthanasia), to the point where the major political parties tend to agree on the role of the state in the economy. In this chapter, I want to consider the nature of this convergence from the perspective of the interactions of government and business since the 2007 election. I draw on Stilwell's model of capitalism to frame the concept of government–business relations and to establish a framework for analysing the convergence of the major parties' preferences in dealing with businesses. The empirical discussion follows with a comparison of the various Labor and Coalition[2] governments since 2007, focusing on four areas of industry policy: the telecommunications industry, the automotive manufacturing industry, trade policy and reducing carbon emissions. I have chosen these industry policies because each represented significant policy challenges for the major parties following John Howard's 11 years in office, two involving particular industries and two having broader or horizontal impact. I conclude by examining the extent of convergence in the major political parties' preferences towards the role of the state in the economy and argue that short-term governments face powerful policy legacies that are difficult to remake in the space of one or two electoral

---

2   Although the Liberal and National parties have separate policy platforms and members of the respective parties can and do come into conflict over policy issues, for the purposes of this chapter, the Coalition will be treated as one entity based on its actions when in government.

terms. The analysis suggests that the convergence in ideas about the role of the state in the economy is the result of pragmatism in response to rapidly changing circumstances rather than inherent ideological preferences.

A model of capitalism

Stilwell's model of capitalism acknowledges a distinctive ideology about the role of the state in shaping the market. While some consider capitalism an ideology (Grey 2013), Stilwell's model makes better sense when capitalism is viewed as an economic system with ideologies incorporated into the model. Ball and Dagger (2004) also suggest moving beyond the explanatory function of political ideologies (such as Cunningham's definition of an ideology as an 'integrated system of beliefs by which we make sense of our lives' [2003, 234]), to include the evaluative, orientative and programmatic functions that ideologies perform. The main political ideologies explored by Ball and Dagger can be understood in relation to the 'proper' role of the state within the economic system. In the West, debates have been between democratic socialism (in its Fabian reformist sense), conservatism (emphasising traditions and incremental reform rather than radical change) and liberalism (stressing individual freedoms combined with equality of opportunity). However, within the confines of the capitalist economic system, political ideologies manifest differently in specific policies. Strict adherence to the programmatic function of political ideologies at the level of political parties, then, ignores the extent of pragmatism at other levels of economic and social policymaking and is not helpful in identifying distinct models of government–business relations.

Nevertheless, when a cross-national perspective is adopted, democratic socialism and liberalism bring to light some of the differences in government–business relations. For example, Hall and Soskice (2001) referred to these differences as 'varieties of capitalism', with countries such as Sweden working to a consensus-based, collective system of 'coordinated capitalism' and the US favouring 'rugged individualism' in a system of 'competitive capitalism'. Countries such as Australia and Canada are regarded as 'mixed economies', somewhere between the two extremes, with Japan's 'statist' model reflecting neither socialism nor liberalism but a unique blend of conservatism and business acumen (Curran and Van Acker 2007; Ryan, Parker and Brown 2003, 61–69). The problem with macro- or national-level generalisations is that, on the one hand, there will be several industries that do not comply with the particular variety of capitalism (such as agriculture in the US), while on the other hand, the 'culture' of government–business relations may not necessarily reflect the type of capitalism practised in a particular country in general (e.g. the extent of industry interest group lobbying in the US). At some meso or industry levels, however, clear patterns of government–business interaction can be discerned over time. For example, what is the role of the state in the Australian telecommunications industry? Historical practice suggests that politicians, policymakers and citizens have a preference for government control of the network, as practised from the time of the telegraph up until the privatisation of Telstra in 2006. Such habits are hard to break and, following the 2007 election, the traditional government control approach to telecommunications policy was reinstated. The same can be said of the health sector in Australia. Despite the introduction of Medicare, now with bipartisan support, private health insurance continues to exist with substantial government regulation and subsidisation. When the automotive industry requested further subsidisation, then prime minister Tony Abbott refused on liberal economic grounds, but later refused to establish a market-based carbon trading scheme, preferring to subsidise the energy industry as a way of reducing carbon emissions. Such contradictions suggest pragmatism rather than preferences based purely on ideological platforms.

At the meso or industry level (see de Percy and Batainah 2019), political ideologies can shed some light on government–business relations as practised, whereas at the macro level, ideology as a defining characteristic does not. Similarly, normative ideas about the role of the state in 'the economy' in general do not exhibit the characteristics of a peculiar model of government–business relations. Stilwell's model does, however, provide a framework for analysis when both the ideological components and normative ideas about the role of the state are considered at the meso level. The final element of Stilwell's model of capitalism, the expansionary tendency of the economic system, reflects the traditional economic problem – endless wants and finite resources – and to some extent explains concerns about the sustainability of the postwar welfare state and the necessity for both sides of politics to address environmental concerns. Government–business interaction about social and environmental policies are better described as horizontal industry policy, as distinct from targeted industry policy – whether anticipatory or passive (de Percy and Batainah 2019).

In constructing a particular model of government–business relations, Jacoby (1975) lists a number of interactions from the perspectives of both business and government. These interactions reflect the underpinning ideologies and the 'proper' (or expected) roles of the state in given contexts and circumstances. This approach is adopted in analysing two targeted (telecommunications and automotive) and two horizontal (trade and carbon emissions) industry policy case studies below. First, however, 'models' of government–business relations are outlined in relation to the policy preferences of the federal Liberal/National Coalition and Labor parties.

Models of government–business relations

At the meso level, industry policy is a major component of the government–business relationship. The policymaking process involves various institutions, interest groups and competing claims for legitimacy amid differing ideologies. Traditionally, governments have had to juggle between their party's policy platform, interest groups (including voters and rent-seekers), economic ideas and international arrangements about how to implement industry policy in a given situation. A fundamental issue in the provision of government assistance to specific industries is the impact on the economy and often the unintended consequences that may result. For example, long-term, institutional protectionism is no longer deemed appropriate for supporting 'ailing' industries such as the textiles, clothing and footwear (TCF) and automotive industries in developed nations, where such government intervention might prove 'politically attractive in the short term, but globally harmful in the long term' (Agah 2015; Productivity Commission 2017, 56). Short-term 'sunset' industry policy measures to facilitate industry transition (such as retraining workers) or 'sunrise' industry policy measures (such as providing tax incentives for investment in information technology or research and development) to assist emerging industries, however, are typically World Trade Organization (WTO) compliant. These internationally accepted arrangements may still involve different government–business relationships in different industries and different countries, and under different governing parties.

A model may help to represent the ways in which governments and businesses interact within a given jurisdiction, incorporating the characteristics of government–business relations within a particular country or industry. The Australian TCF sector provides an interesting example of traditional party preferences in industry policy. The TCF industries had been protected by tariffs that were gradually reduced over time, and, in line with a significant increase in global competition, employment in the sector had decreased significantly (Karanikolas 2014). Nevertheless, the industries remain supported by organised lobby groups, many that were established during the protectionist era, and these groups remain a powerful voice in sector-specific policymaking. Pacific Brands (including Bonds), for example, was a major employer in Australia, but moved its manufacturing operations offshore in 2010 (Sharp and Zappone 2009) and continued to be involved in industry lobbying. Tariffs of around 5 per cent remain on many imported TCF items (for imports from countries outside of extant trade agreements)[3] and grant programs – such as the Howard Coalition Government's 2005 TCF Small Business Program and later the Rudd Labor Government's 2009 Building Innovative Capability – provided significant funding as part of a drawn-out, decades-long process of the TCF sector adjusting to an 'open economy' (Karanikolas 2014). Each political party's policy approach was influenced by its respective preferences.

The Australian Labor Party's (ALP) historical formal commitment to democratic socialisation did not inhibit the 1983 Hawke Government's ability to tackle stagflation (ALP 1979; Singleton 1990, 120). Recently, the party has attempted to 'renew' this commitment – being prepared to intervene in the economy in order to achieve social and economic objectives 'to the extent necessary to eliminate exploitation and other anti-social features in those fields' (and therefore within the bounds of the rules-based trading regime established later by the WTO) (Johnson 2015). Yet democratic socialism tends not to represent the reality of Labor's policies in the last four decades; or, in the words of Labor's George Campbell: 'Does anyone seriously believe that our policy agenda since 1983 was governed by the socialist objective?' (Campbell, Smith and Puig 2002). In 2016, Labor's objectives were formally reconsidered for the first time since 1981, although the term 'democratic socialisation' retains a degree of vagueness that has fallen short of the original desire to 'nationalise' industries (Johnson 2015). Clearly, the absence of any attempt at nationalisation by a Labor government since Chifley's prime ministership suggests there are certain limits to intervention in industry by any potential Labor government.

---

3   See, for example, Australian Border Force website: www.abf.gov.au/importing-exporting-and-manufacturing/tariff-classification/current-tariff/schedule-3/section-xi/chapter-61.

Nevertheless, consistent preferences in industry policy are evident in the political parties' approaches to providing industry assistance. The Howard Government's assistance to the TCF sector was provided as part of a larger package of support for small businesses, a preference that is clearly stated in the Liberal Party's (2002, 11) *Federal Platform*, rather than the TCF sector in particular. For the Coalition, assistance tends to be both 'horizontal' in that it focuses on, for example, small-to-medium enterprises (SMEs) across sectors, and 'passive' in that it does not attempt to 'pick winners' or influence the choices of industry. As revealed under the Rudd Labor Government, however, Labor's assistance tends to be 'targeted' in that it applies to a specific industry, and 'anticipatory' in that it attempts to align firms' behaviours with specified policy objectives. While these contrasting preferences were evident up until the first Rudd Government, the discussion below examines two sets of targeted and two sets of horizontal industry policies to assess the extent that policy legacies can be overcome in the short term to implement the major parties' policy preferences.

Telecommunications policy: The National Broadband Network

Traditionally, Australia's telecommunications sector has been dominated by government, and not necessarily because of market failure (Trubnikov and Trubnikova 2018). This historical policy approach is often justified due to Australia's geographic remoteness and the lack of a local industry capable of manufacturing and maintaining the necessary technologies to support telecommunications networks (Barr 2000, 79). Yet this view ignores the extent of local inventiveness that existed in Australia in the early days of telecommunications (Moyal 1984, 78). An alternative view suggests that Australian governments have habitually adopted telecommunications policy as social or economic policy, rather than industry policy per se (de Percy 2008; see also Quiggin 1998, 427). For example, the Howard Government set about privatising Telstra and using the economic returns to shore up the 'Future Fund', a sovereign wealth fund designed to make 'provision for unfunded superannuation liabilities' (Department of Finance 2020). Telstra's sale, along with numerous other reforms, had been on the political agenda for the major parties for some time, albeit with Labor wanting to retain majority public ownership (Lewis 1997). Nevertheless, in-principle, bipartisan support existed for privatisation (Aulich and O'Flynn 2007).

When the Rudd Government came to power in 2007 amid growing controversy over Australia's expensive and limited broadband services with lagging internet speeds (Crowe 2006), Labor was faced with two challenges. First, Telstra had not been structurally separated to distinguish between the monopoly infrastructure and the competitive retailers (so an effective market structure had not been established); and, second, privatisation had not delivered the connectivity required to support the emerging digital economy. In response to a 2008 Request for Proposal to build a high-speed broadband network, Telstra's noncompliant proposal response encouraged the Rudd Government to increase its initial $4.7-billion government contribution to the network to some $43 billion after opting for a fibre to the home (FTTH) network in 2009. Effectively, the Rudd Government decided to structurally separate Telstra by bypassing the existing copper network and building a wholesale-only fibre network with the aim of increasing competition in retail broadband services (Taylor 2014). While not 'nationalisation' in the traditional sense of the word (as the government intended to privatise the network in the future) the National Broadband Network (NBN) re-established government control of the telecommunications sector (see Aston 2019) and took much of the risk.

After Labor won the 2010 federal election, the Abbott opposition appointed Malcolm Turnbull, an acknowledged telecommunications industry expert, as the communications spokesman with 'orders' to 'demolish' the government's NBN (Rodgers 2010). However, soon after winning the 2013 federal election and following a series of reviews, the Abbott Government announced that Labor's NBN plan to deliver fibre to 93 per cent of the population (with 4 per cent delivered via fixed wireless and the remaining 3 per cent via satellite) would be modified to a 'multi-technology mix' rather than replaced (Knezevic 2016). In a 2014 press briefing, Malcolm Turnbull and Ziggy Switkowski outlined their cost-benefit analysis and the multi-technology mix plan (de Percy 2014). In effect, the NBN would be delivered faster and cheaper, but at slower speeds and with fibre to the node (FTTN) delivered to the 93 per cent, rather than FTTH as proposed by Labor. By this stage, and as pointed out by the cost-benefit analysis, the sunk costs of the NBN were such that it would be more difficult to scrap the plan or continue with the FTTH option, rather than adopt the multi-technology mix proposed by the Coalition. In effect, the Coalition's preference to leave telecommunications infrastructure predominantly to the market could not be achieved because of the lock-in from the former Labor Government's plan. At the time of writing the Coalition is also planning to introduce what some have referred to as a 'broadband tax' to subsidise satellite and fixed wireless services in regional and remote areas, thereby increasing state intervention in the telecommunications sector (Duckett 2020; Hendry 2020; Lane 2020). The cost recovery model used to fund the NBN was inherited from previous Labor governments and has been extended by the Coalition despite its traditional industry policy preferences.

Automotive manufacturing policy: From 'green car' to 'goodbye'[4]

Protectionism in the Australian manufacturing sector has a long history of contestation between political party preferences. In the early days of federation, Australian political economy was contested between the free traders, protectionists and labour. Protectionism developed as a form of 'tariff ratchet', where protection only escalated rather than declined. Behind the protection wall, wages were highly regulated. Despite recommendations to address the growth of protectionism by the Brigden Report in 1927 and later the Vernon Report in 1965, it was not until the 1972 Whitlam Government that the reform direction advocated by G. A. Rattigan, then chairman of the Tariff Board, could be pursued. The Tariff Board became the Industries Assistance Commission (IAC) and, despite Labor's historic predilection for protectionism, Whitlam decided on an across-the-board tariff reduction of 25 per cent. This led to the IAC being dubbed by critics the 'Industries Assassination Commission' as part of a strong political backlash. The subsequent Fraser Government was ineffective in implementing further reforms as it remained mired in the politics of protectionism (Capling and Galligan 1992, 108–111; Catley 1996, 63–64). It was not until the 1983 Hawke Government that trade liberalisation got back on the agenda, this time not through unilateral tariff reductions but more carefully designed industry restructuring.

---

4   Interestingly, John Wanna's 1984 doctoral thesis focused on the car industry, metal unions and vehicle builders and the negotiations for the first accord between the ACTU and a Labor government. John's interest in government–business relations was inspired by Doug McEachern, Professor of Politics at the University of Adelaide. After a lifetime career as an academic, McEachern completed a PhD in creative writing at the University of Adelaide and published his first novel, *Stardust and Golden*, in 2018. The novel explores the culture of resistance during the during the Vietnam War era from the perspective of a group of students living in a commune (McEachern 2018).

The IAC became (symbolically) the Industry Commission in 1990, and subsequently the Productivity Commission in 1998 under the Howard Government and, in the space of three decades, decades of protectionism were unwound. Australia's industry policy environment changed from structural protection to economic liberalisation (Productivity Commission 2003). However, the automotive industry,[5] like the TCF sector, continued to be assisted by governments.

Up until 2007, government assistance to the Australian automotive manufacturing industry consisted predominantly of tariffs that had for many years restricted international competition to some 20 per cent of the market (Industry Commission 1997, xxvi). Indeed, under the Button Plan, the Hawke Government continued to assist the industry to become more competitive and to increase exports by rationalising the industry, although most of the export growth was related to specialised automotive parts manufacture rather than passenger vehicle manufacturing and assembly (Thomas 1993).[6] By the late 1990s, however, an inquiry into the automotive industry noted that: 'History shows that the higher the level of assistance to the industry the poorer the industry's performance' and that as the industry was 'now nearing the end of a 20-year adjustment plan', no further inquiries should be conducted (Industry Commission 1997, xxii). Yet, in the late 1990s, the Howard Government paused further reductions in tariffs for a five-year period, and, while providing some relief to the industry as a whole, the action led to increased lobbying efforts by the industry and by the mid-2000s the industry was receiving special industry assistance as a series of cash payments (Scales 2017). Nonetheless, the payments were then on the public record, and therefore transparent, achieving a long-held objective of industry policy reform that had not been realised despite repeated recommendations since the time of the 1927 Brigden Report. Bill Scales (2017), appointed to implement the Button Plan[7] and later chair of the Industry Commission, suggested that the transparency and greater scrutiny of the cost of industry assistance

---

5 I use the term automotive manufacturing industry loosely here to mean the passenger vehicle industry (PVI) and associated industries. Despite the loss of the PVI industry, other facets of the industry such as design and advisory services continue to operate. Robert Bosch Australia, for example, recently invested in its Clayton factory, albeit as part of an evolution strategy following the demise of passenger vehicle manufacturing in Australia (AuManufacturing 2020).

6 The 'Button Plan' influenced a unique period in Australian automotive history, where government-led rationalisation resulted in, among other brands, the Holden Commodore being rebadged as the Toyota Lexcen, and such creations being referred to as 'Buttonmobiles' (Oastler 2018).

7 Scales was appointed as the head of the Automotive Industry Authority of Australia, the body designed to implement what was referred to as the 'Button Plan'.

(and therefore economic trade-offs elsewhere), signalled the death knell for the automotive manufacturing industry. The industry was offered a transitional compromise with a further decade of support ('at diminishing levels') but no support guaranteed beyond 2015 (Colebatch 2013).

Yet when the Rudd Government came to office, Rudd announced that Labor would implement a 'green car initiative' designed to utilise Australia's highly skilled labour and manufacturing capability to overcome the challenge of competition from low-income manufacturers offshore. The general plan was that Australian automotive manufacturers would take advantage of their 'high-tech' capabilities and develop efficient vehicles that would enable the Australian manufacturing industry to remain competitive despite the obvious higher cost of wages. By mid-2013, however, the first Gillard Government had reduced the amount of the 'green car innovation fund' once, then again in response to the flooding disasters in Queensland, and refused to increase tariffs to protect the industry further (Borrello and Kirk 2013). Later, the second Rudd Government, while still desirous of the benefits of a manufacturing sector, was out of ideas for the automotive industry and automotive manufacturing was effectively off the policy radar (Sales 2013).

Accordingly, the Rudd Government's initiative failed (Preistley 2010); and the subsequent Gillard Government had no interest in continuing the protectionist agenda to the automotive industry, despite what may have been considered Labor's traditional preference for industry policy. While the Rudd Government's anticipatory attempts aligned with Labor's industry policy preferences, the actions taken by the Gillard Government and second Rudd Government had little to do with party preferences, and more to do with a necessary response to contemporary events: subsequent events had turned attention towards pragmatism. And while the demise of passenger vehicle manufacturing in Australia has not signalled an end to government support for the industry as a whole, by the time the Abbott Government came to power in 2013, government assistance to the industry had run its course, and soon after the remaining manufacturers announced their intention to cease operations in Australia by the end of 2017.[8]

---

8   Holden announced its intention to cease operations on 11 December 2013. Followed by Toyota on 10 February 2014. Ford had made their announcement on 23 May 2013 while the Gillard Government was in power, months before the Abbott Coalition Government won the 2013 federal election.

Although the former Labor industry minister Kim Carr (2016) blamed neoliberal 'ideologues' in the Coalition Government for the demise of the passenger vehicle industry, he was quick to accept Ford's decision to leave on the basis of the higher dollar affecting exports during Labor's time in government. Yet the time frame for the end of industry assistance had been foreshadowed a decade earlier and Carr's claims about the efficacy of ongoing industry assistance to support automotive manufacturing were not supported by the evidence (RMIT ABC Fact Check 2013). Further, industry assistance did not cease under the subsequent Turnbull and Morrison Coalition governments. For example, in late 2019, the Morrison Coalition Government implemented the Manufacturing Modernisation Fund (Department of Industry, Innovation and Science 2019), focused on small-to-medium manufacturing firms. While this program reflected the Coalition's preference for passive, 'horizontal' policy, as it applied to the manufacturing sector as part of a broader package focused on SMEs, other packages designed to assist the automotive industry such as the Automotive Diversification Programme (funding to assist supply chain firms to find new markets) and the Automotive Industry Structural Adjustment Programme (funding to assist redundant automotive industry workers transition to new jobs) were targeted and anticipatory and therefore pragmatic in their intent. But none of these pragmatic initiatives were able to halt the industry's decline.

Trade policy: Preferences, lock-in and international pressure

Trade policy has a major influence on firms and industries – and therefore may be considered a form of horizontal industry policy – and is 'passive' in that it focuses on improving the economic conditions in which firms operate. To be sure, anticipatory industry policy may result from trade policy; for example, the Australia–United States Free Trade Agreement resulted in the Sugar Industry Reform Programme 2004 to assist cane growers to exit the industry following the Howard Government's inability to secure concessions on sugar from the US. Nevertheless, the trade policy preferences of the major parties can be considered from the perspectives of multilateralism versus bilateralism, and the overall cultural and national identity priorities communicated by different governments. As with industry policies, Labor and Coalition governments have displayed particular preferences for engagement in the global economy; for example the Hawke Government's focus on multilateralism led to its role in founding the Asia-Pacific Economic Cooperation (APEC) group, and the Howard Government's 1997 foreign and trade policy white paper set out its preferences for bilateralism (Department of Foreign Affairs and Trade 1997). Similarly, Paul Keating had argued that Australia must identify itself as an Asian country, whereas John Howard vigorously opposed Keating's ideas and instead fostered a 'practical' or 'transactional' (rather than 'cultural') regionalism, where history (including shared Anglo-Saxon values) was privileged over geography (Gulmanelli 2014, 590). When the Rudd Government came to power in 2007, the trade minister, Simon Crean, reinstated Australia's preference for multilateralism, stating that the government would only pursue bilateral agreements where these were in line with the aims of multilateralism.

Several key issues influence preferences for multilateralism versus bilateralism. Multilateralism became the norm following the Bretton Woods conferences, supported by the multilateral institutions that emerged after World War II. By creating a rules-based trading system, multilateralism ameliorates the asymmetries of power that exist when a powerful nation negotiates with a less-powerful nation. That is not to say that bilateral free trade agreements are not WTO-compliant, but that multilateralism promotes fairness in the global trading system (Capling 2003, 379). Multilateralism does have its weaknesses, however, and the history of the Bretton Woods institutions is testament to this fact. In particular, multilateralism requires a degree of consensus that is difficult to achieve at a global level in the short term, more so since the number and hence the diversity of its membership has increased. The failed attempt at establishing the International Trade Organization in the late 1940s meant that the General Agreement on Trade and Tariffs (GATT), a temporary measure, remained in place until the establishment of the WTO in 1995 (de Percy 2020). In addition, multilateral arrangements have been subject to populist sentiment since the 1990s, claiming national policies are controlled by 'unelected' international institutions; the Howard Government responded by reinforcing Australia's national interest through statements of 'core values' (de Percy 2020). This is not to say that party preferences are at odds with multilateralism per se; rather that, much like earlier bipartisan support for protectionism, subtle differences in the relevant approaches to trade policy represent different party preferences in the conduct of trade policy agendas (Conley 2007, 165).

The different policy preferences exhibited by Labor and Coalition governments in the trade liberalisation era can be summarised as follows: (1) Labor has a preference for regionalism leading towards multilateralism, perhaps reflecting its traditional trade union consensus-based decision model; whereas (2) the Coalition has a preference for strengthening traditional, cultural ties through bilateral agreements where other policy objectives, such as strategic and security alliances, can be reinforced, and the benefits of these agreements can be realised faster than through multilateral arrangements (Capling 2008). These preferences stem from long-term governments and were not implemented consistently during periods of shorter-term governments. From the first Rudd Government in 2007 to the present Morrison Government in 2020, nine trade agreements have become operational, including two 'plurilateral' (meaning more than two countries, as opposed to multilateral, meaning global) trade agreements. But rather than reflecting party preferences, Australia's trade policy tends to be the result of long-term negotiations that have more to do with the temporal aspect of trade policy development than deliberate design by particular governments.

While history certainly matters in the ability of the major parties to implement trade policy preferences, statements concerning national identity in their national and international context are somewhat easier to expound. For example, the various foreign and trade policy white papers that have been produced over the years reveal Labor's preference for engagement with Asia on a cultural level and the Coalition's preference for engagement on a practical or transactional level.[9] Yet the practicalities of domestic politics combined with the obstacles to multilateralism on the global stage led to the Howard Government establishing the Joint Standing Committee on Treaties within weeks of coming to power in 1996, partly as a reaction to the success of Pauline Hanson's One Nation party and the promise in her first speech to 'find out how many treaties we have signed with the UN, have them exposed and then call for their repudiation'.

---

9   White papers are generally regarded as a government's 'declaration of intent' or a commitment to a policy (Senate Foreign Affairs, Defence and Trade References Committee 2003, 2). The Howard Government produced two, *In the National Interest* (1997) and *Advancing the National Interest* (2003), whereas the Hawke Government had adopted its approach from Garnaut (1989). The Gillard Government more or less adopted Paul Keating's idea of 'the Asian century' in its white paper (Department of Foreign Affairs and Trade 2012). Equally interesting is that Julia Gillard's foreword mentions 'drifting' versus 'planning' – the same language used previously by Paul Keating (1992).

Australian governments tend to reflect their global aspirations through domestic policy statements. The Howard Government, for example, in its 1997 and 2003 foreign and trade policy white papers, established a list of core values as part of a wider project to establish an Australian identity in the region. In contrast, the Gillard Government's white paper mentioned Australian values in a general sense rather than in the context of a preconceived national identity (Department of Foreign Affairs and Trade 2012). Further, party preferences are complicated by the long-term nature of ongoing negotiations between nation-states. In trade policy at least, negotiations over multilateralism, regionalism and bilateralism seem to be temporally specific and do not necessarily indicate a policy preference of a particular political party. Rather, major political parties tend to communicate a sense of national identity through trade deals, as opposed to how they operationalise their trade policy preferences in practice. The long time frame required by negotiations with other nation-states means that the way a nation-state presents its policies externally can be distinctly different from the inward representation as communicated to its constituents. Hence, trade policy, as far as it represents horizontal industry policy, suggests that Australian governments of all persuasions tend to be pragmatic in their pursuit of trade policy goals rather than deliberately pursuing party preferences.

Reducing carbon emissions: Left–right, right–left

One of the more bewildering debates in horizontal industry policy in Australia has been the approach to pricing carbon emissions. Australia is one of the highest per capita greenhouse gas emitting nations and has been a laggard internationally in capturing the cost of carbon emissions. Australia's power sector emits more carbon than any other, yet fossil fuel consumption continues to be supported by the government while not being subjected to emission reduction constraints (OECD 2019). To be sure, the mining industry is a powerful lobby group concerned about reduced demand for fossil fuels, and any attempt at reducing carbon emissions could risk the industry using 'advocacy advertising', a technique it has used in the past to influence public policy to great effect (McKnight and Hobbs 2013). Nevertheless, since 2007, the major parties have each attempted to address carbon emissions using either pricing, to capture the externality, or direct subsidisation, to assist industry to reduce emissions.

Based on the ideological preferences of the major parties, one might reasonably expect the Coalition to pursue a market-based strategy, with Labor more likely to adopt a 'democratic socialisation' strategy through some form of direct action. But whether because of the threat of advocacy advertising by the mining industry or other reasons, the major parties have overturned their traditional preferences since 2007.

Australia ratified the Montreal Protocol (to reduce the use of ozone-depleting substances) in the late 1980s and first announced a greenhouse gas emission reduction strategy in 1990. The Hawke Government 'adopted an Interim Planning Target to stabilise greenhouse gas emission at 1988 levels by 2000 (known as the Toronto target)' and the approach became known as a 'no regrets' strategy: Australia would not, in the absence of similar actions by other countries, put its economy or international competitiveness at risk unless there were benefits beyond greenhouse emissions reductions to be gained (CSIRO 2019). The Howard Government adopted a similar approach, with a focus on businesses adopting 'voluntary reductions' promoted by the Greenhouse Challenge (Kay 1997). Little else happened in terms of policy action on emissions reduction and it was not until just before the 2007 election when the Howard Government, with Malcolm Turnbull as environment minister, announced a 'cap and trade' emissions trading scheme. Such a scheme fits with the Coalition's usual policy preferences, as it provides an economic incentive and a market pricing mechanism to constrain carbon emissions. Put simply, the 'cap' refers to a limit to the amount of emissions allowed, and the 'trade' refers to the market where companies can buy and sell the allowances to emit, and supply and demand set the price. As the cap is reduced over time and the price of allowances increases, companies have strong incentives to reduce emissions (Environmental Defense Fund 2020). Clearly, such a market-based solution suits the traditional preferences of the Coalition.

In an interesting turn of events, soon after the Rudd Labor Government came to power in 2007, it released the 2008 white paper *Carbon Pollution Reduction Scheme: Australia's Low Pollution Future*. Labor would implement the Carbon Pollution Reduction Scheme (CPRS) – effectively a cap and trade emissions trading system (ETS) – in 2010. In 2009, however, the mining industry launched its first major advocacy advertising campaign against the government and the CPRS bill was twice rejected by the Senate (McKnight and Hobbs 2013, 308). Rather than go to a double-dissolution election, Prime Minister Rudd shelved the legislation, but with pressure mounting from the Abbott opposition and the mining industry lobby also campaigning against Rudd's proposed Resource Super Profits Tax, Rudd was deposed as party leader because of fear of election loss, and was replaced by Julia Gillard as prime minister (Manne 2019). Gillard's policy response was to replace the CPRS with the Clean Energy Bill 2011, setting, among other measures, an initial price on greenhouse gas emissions of $23 per tonne to be paid from 1 July 2012 by the nation's largest 500 emitters, transitioning to a cap and trade system by 1 July 2015 (Swoboda, Tomaras and Payne 2011).

Before the 2010 election, the Gillard Government had campaigned on a range of measures to address climate change, but Gillard specifically stated that there would be no 'carbon tax'. The Tony Abbott–led Coalition, on the other hand, had campaigned for a direct action package with some form of payment or subsidy to businesses. Gillard was able to form minority government after the election. Subsequently, Abbott called on the mining industry to mount a two-year campaign against her government's 'carbon tax', which it did successfully (McKnight and Hobbs 2013, 308). To be fair, the Gillard Government's attempt at carbon pricing was confusing, to the extent that even Parliamentary Library researchers had difficulty deciding how and when to use the terms 'carbon price' or 'carbon tax' in the Clean Energy Bill briefing for parliamentarians (Swoboda, Tomaras and Payne 2011). Abbott won the 2013 election convincingly, and his government's emissions reduction fund white paper (Commonwealth of Australia 2014) set out the direct action plan in detail.

While the replacement of Abbott by Turnbull in 2015 was not directly related to climate change policy, the ongoing internal debate within the Coalition was very much concerned with climate policies. While paying lip service to the need to contain greenhouse emissions, some in the Coalition parties were unconvinced of the need for any substantial action that might have short- or medium-term costs. The debate ostensibly centred on the form of the action to be taken, but the underlying differences related to the extent of any action. In any case, Turnbull was replaced by Morrison in 2018, two years after a narrow election win in 2016.

As the policy currently stands under the Morrison Government, firms voluntarily participate in a 'reverse auction' where the Clean Energy Regulator secures 'contracts for the provision of carbon offsets'; firms then report on their offsetting project's outcomes, then claim Australian Carbon Credit Units (ACCUs) for the reductions achieved and either hold or sell these on secondary markets (CSIRO 2019). Major emitters that exceed their baseline emissions are required to surrender ACCUs, thus creating a secondary market. While not a price on carbon per se, the latest Energy Reduction Fund (ERF) auctions resulted in a price of $16.14 per tonne being paid by the ERF (much lower than Labor's $23 per tonne) (Clean Energy Regulator 2020). To date, demand for compliance offsets is low and unlikely to increase under the current policy (Tyers 2019), and, despite falling for a brief period during the term of the Gillard Labor Government's 'carbon tax', Australia's carbon emissions began to rise again (Slezak 2017). But what does this say about the major parties' policy preferences?

Compared to the Coalition, Labor has generally demonstrated more of a commitment to international greenhouse gas reduction obligations. The Coalition, despite Turnbull's 'almost' deal with Rudd for an ETS (Crabb 2019), has continued to pursue a 'no regrets' strategy and an unwillingness to sacrifice the economy for the environment (in the short term at least). While the economic impact of the recent bushfires and, at the time of writing, the global COVID-19 crisis will provide an interesting counterpoint for the next federal election, the lack of action on environmental policy may well be something Australians come to regret. But in terms of policy preferences in this case, the Coalition's anti-Greens stance took precedence over its support for markets, whereas Labor's 'democratic socialisation' agenda was ignored in an attempt to move to an ETS. In the absence of regulations to the contrary, the power of the mining industry to sway public policy outcomes in Australia has been a major driver of pragmatism over policy preferences for the major parties. The clash of preferences in environmental policy, especially for the Coalition, suggests that pragmatism takes precedence in this case, and it will be difficult for any future Labor Government to avoid accusations of, for example, 'Carbon Tax 2.0' (Murphy 2019).

Short-termism: Pragmatism versus preferences

The purpose of analysing the cases above was to test the extent that party preferences in industry policy are converging as a result of pragmatism and to what extent short-term governments and rapid leadership changes prevent the major parties from implementing those preferences. Since the 1980s, following the demise of the Soviet Union and China's expanding involvement in the global economy, there seemed to be some international convergence of ideas about the role of the state in the economy. This has since been upset by, among other events, the 2008 global financial crisis and the COVID-19 pandemic. Once again, governments are expected to play a much larger role. But whether that intervention is market- or state-based, the overall strategy that the major Australian parties have adopted in industry policy has traditionally reflected their ideological differences (Byrt and Bowden 1989, 190–192). With different approaches to government–business relations, one might expect Labor to adopt an 'internationalist' commitment (hence multilateralism), targeted state industry assistance or anticipatory intervention and consensus-based decision-making, and be more likely to consider negotiating with the Greens on environmental issues. For the Coalition, one might expect less state intervention in the market, passive industry policy, a focus on horizontal rather than targeted industry policy, and a commitment to traditional allies in trade policy. Of course, these preferences have never been static (Colebatch 1997, xiv–xvi; Parkin and Hardcastle 2006, 344), but looking to the past and the earlier capacity to implement reforms due to 'continuity of office-holding' during the long-term Hawke–Keating and Howard governments, short-termism has certainly resulted in the major parties adopting more politically pragmatic rather than preference-programmatic responses to industry (Halligan 1995, 6).

In the cases examined, the Rudd Government attempted a state-controlled solution to the broadband problem, which subsequently forced the Coalition to modify but not undo the state's intervention in the industry; the Morrison Government seems to be going even further considering an additional tax to cross-subsidise the NBN. In the automotive industry, we see the preferences more clearly with the Rudd Government focusing on targeted, anticipatory measures to support manufacturing, but this policy tinkering was insufficient to stop the inevitable demise of the automotive industry. The Abbott Coalition Government certainly followed its preferences in leaving the outcome to market forces. The ongoing assistance to the industry by the Morrison Government has been largely passive and horizontal, thus following the traditional party preferences.

In trade policy, Labor's preference for multilateralism was not fully realised, with 'plurilateral' agreements set in train well before the party returned to power in 2007. For the Coalition, the economic realities of Australia's reliance on China meant that both siding with the US and preferring bilateralism could not stop Australia's involvement in the successor to the Trans-Pacific Partnership. It would seem that in targeted industry policy, policy preferences are easier to implement, but are still difficult when changes in government occur in quick succession. The most pragmatic of all responses to reducing carbon emissions was the Coalition's avoidance of a market-based solution and opting for direct action by the state. Even for Malcolm Turnbull as prime minister, who preferred an ETS, pragmatism won the day in response to the party and the power of the mining industry and any talk of an ETS was shelved. Labor, on the other hand, had attempted to implement a market-based solution that was contrary to its traditional preferences and faced an aggressive mining industry protecting its own interests. Governments have taken decisions 'based on immediate electoral advantage, rather than long term "public" or "national" interest' (Davis et al. 1993, 158). In terms of public policymaking in this field, it seems, a 'mix of principle and pragmatism' may well be prudent (Halligan 1995, 12–13).

Conclusion

It is interesting that the decline in the study of government–business relations as a standalone academic subject has coincided with a period of high turnover in prime ministers. Further, the decline of faith in Australia's political system has coincided with a period in which federal governments have lost their appetite for major economic reforms (Grattan 2014; Howard 2017). Contemporary bipartisanship on politically risky issues resembles failed attempts of the past (GST in the 1980s, Workchoices in the 2000s), or those that remain too politically unpalatable to tackle (such as road pricing, see de Percy 2018). Most reforms are too politically risky for short-term governments to pursue, until a tipping point occurs and their time has come. Although some policies have received bipartisan support (e.g. the National Disability Insurance Scheme, national security and border policy, and health and education policy generally), deeper economic reform has taken a back seat while the major parties squabble over the reality of budget surpluses (Wanna 2015). Almost a decade ago, Lindquist and Wanna (2011, 1) observed that flu epidemics represented 'tipping-point challenges [that] seem to be increasing'. Given the nation and most of the world is under lockdown due to the COVID-19 pandemic, a major tipping point may have arrived. Does the current crisis mean that party preferences will further converge? Or is it simply a case of the circumstances demanding government be pragmatic? If the Morrison Government's recent decision to introduce a Labor-style economic stimulus package that is effectively doubling welfare payments is any indication, there is certainly evidence of convergence (Hutchens 2020). But whether party preferences return once the crisis is over and the nation tries to rebuild the economy remains to be seen. In the words of Davis, Wanna, Warhurst, and Weller (1993, 157):

> There is no single best way of making choices, no method guaranteed to deliver the right answer every time. Values, interests and resources, mediated through institutions and determined by politics, are too volatile a mix to allow agreement on process.

Finally, to paraphrase Hal Colebatch (1997, xvi), we have to ask not only what is the model of government–business relations, but what is the process that shapes them? Based on recent experience, and more so now in the present circumstances, the necessity for pragmatic responses to global crises may well drive the convergence of the major parties' industry policy preferences in the foreseeable future.

References

Agah, Y. F. 2015. 'An insurance policy against protectionism'. *G7 Germany: The Schloss Elmau Summit*. World Trade Organization. Available at: www.g7g20.utoronto.ca/books/g7elmau2015.pdf.

Aston, J. 2019. 'Rear window: Kevin Rudd rewrites history – again'. *Australian Financial Review*, 10 February. Available at: www.afr.com/rear-window/kevin-rudd-rewrites-history--again-20190210-h1b2vs.

Aulich, C. and J. O'Flynn. 2007. 'From public to private: The Australian experience of privatisation'. *The Asia Pacific Journal of Public Administration* 29(2): 153–171. doi.org/10.1080/23276665.2007.10779332.

AuManufacturing. 2020. 'Robert Bosch invests $17 million in Clayton factory'. *@AuManfacturing*, 18 February. Available at: www.aumanufacturing.com.au/robert-bosch-invests-17-million-in-clayton-factory.

Australian Labor Party (ALP). 1979. *Platform, Constitution and Rules as Approved by the 33rd National Conference, Adelaide 1979*. Canberra: Australian Labor Party.

Ball, T. and Dagger, R. 2004. *Political Ideologies and the Democratic Ideal*. New York: Pearson.

Barr, T. L. 2000. *Newmedia.com.au: The Changing Face of Australia's Media and Communications*. St Leonards: Allen & Unwin.

Borrello, E. and A. Kirk. 2013. 'PM Julia Gillard rejects calls to raise import tariffs as car industry struggles for survival after Ford closure'. *ABC News*, 24 May. Available at: www.abc.net.au/news/2013-05-24/actu-calls-for-emergency-talks-on-car-industry/4710100.

Byrt, W. and P. Bowden. 1989. *Australian Public Management: Principles and Cases*. South Melbourne: Macmillan.

Campbell, G., P. Smith and G. V. Puig. 2002. 'The socialist objective: Should it go? A challenge for 21st century Labor'. *Evatt Foundation*, 22 April. Available at: web.archive.org/web/20200403041550/evatt.org.au/news/socialist-objective-should-it-go.html.

Capling, A. 2003. 'Democratic deficit, the global trade system and 11 September'. *Australian Journal of Politics and History* 49(3): 372–379. doi.org/10.1111/1467-8497.00292.

Capling, A. 2008. 'Australia's trade policy dilemmas'. *Australian Journal of International Affairs* 62(2): 229–244. doi.org/10.1080/10357710802060576.

Capling, A. and B. Galligan. 1992. *Beyond the Protective State: The Political Economy of Australia's Manufacturing Industry Policy*. Cambridge: Cambridge University Press.

Carr, K. 2016. 'Setting the record straight on the Ford closure'. *Sydney Morning Herald*, 6 October. Available at: www.smh.com.au/opinion/setting-the-record-straight-on-the-ford-closure-20161006-grw8vn.html.

Catley, B. 1996. *Globalising Australian Capitalism*. Cambridge: Cambridge University Press. doi.org/10.1017/CBO9780511597145.

Clean Energy Regulator. 2020. 'Successful tenth ERF auction secures more carbon abatement for Australia'. *Clean Energy Regulator*, 3 April. Available at: www.cleanenergyregulator.gov.au/ERF/Pages/News%20and%20updates/NewsItem.aspx?ListId=19b4efbb-6f5d-4637-94c4-121c1f96fcfe&ItemId=771.

Colebatch, H. K. 1997. 'Introduction'. In H. K. Colebatch, S. Prasser and J. R. Nethercote (eds) *Business–Government Relations: Concepts and Issues*. South Melbourne: Nelson.

Colebatch, T. 2013. 'How we lost our place in the global car industry'. *Sydney Morning Herald*, 28 May. Available at: www.smh.com.au/politics/federal/how-we-lost-our-place-in-the-global-car-industry-20130527-2n7a1.html.

Commonwealth of Australia. 2014. *Emissions Reduction Fund White Paper*. Canberra: Commonwealth of Australia.

Commonwealth Scientific and Industrial Research Organisation (CSIRO). 2019. 'Evolving Australian carbon markets'. 6 May. Available at: research.csiro.au/ digiscape/evolving-australian-carbon-markets/.

Conley, T. 2007. 'Australian trade policy: From multilateralism to bilateralism'. In G. Curran and E. Van Acker (eds) *Globalising Government Business Relations*. Sydney: Pearson.

Crabb, A. 2019. The day that plunged Australia's climate policy into 10 years of inertia. *ABC News,* 24 November. Available at: www.abc.net.au/news/2019-11-24/10-years-of-climate-change-inertiaand-the-role-of-andrew-robb/11726072.

Crowe, D. 2006. 'Fraudband, it's slow and it's expensive: Stuck in the Internet slow lane [Australians pay more and get less from their Broadband Internet service than any other developed country]'. *Australian Financial Review,* 8–9 April: 1, 17–19.

Cunningham, A. 2003. 'Autonomous consumption: Buying into the ideology of capitalism'. *Journal of Business Ethics* 48(3): 229–236. doi.org/10.1023/B:BUSI.0000005784.48184.d6.

Curran, G. and E. Van Acker (eds). 2007. *Globalising Government Business Relations*. Sydney: Pearson.

Davis, G., J. Wanna, J. Warhurst and P. Weller. 1993. *Public Policy in Australia*. Second edition. St Leonards: Allen & Unwin.

de Percy, M. A. 2008. 'Broadbanding the nation: Lessons from Canada or shortcomings in Australian federalism?' In J. Butcher (ed.) *Australia Under Construction: Nation-Building Past, Present and Future*. Canberra: ANU E Press. doi.org/10.22459/AUC.04.2008.10.

de Percy, M. A. 2014. 'NBN cost-benefit analysis signals the end of an era'. *The Conversation,* 26 August. Available at: theconversation.com/nbn-cost-benefit-analysis-signals-the-end-of-an-era-30909.

de Percy, M. A. 2018. 'Introduction: Shaping the road pricing and provision debate'. In M. A. de Percy and J. Wanna (eds) *Road Pricing and Provision: Changed Traffic Conditions Ahead*. Canberra: ANU Press. doi.org/10.22459/RPP.07.2018.

de Percy, M. A. (producer). 2019. 'Special edition: Interview with Professor John Wanna: Career reflections'. *Le Flâneur Politique*. Podcast. Available at: soundcloud.com/madepercy/special-edition-professor-john-wanna-career-reflections.

de Percy, M. A. 2020. 'Populism and a New World Order'. In V. Jakupec, M. Kelly and J. Makuwira (eds) *Rethinking Multilateralism in Foreign Aid: Beyond the Neoliberal Hegemony*. New York: Routledge. doi.org/10.4324/9780367853808-3.

de Percy, M. A. and H. S. Batainah. 2019. 'Government–business relations'. In P. J. Chen, N. Barry, J. R. Butcher, D. Clune, I. Cook, A. Garnier, Y. Haigh, S. C. Motta and M. Taflaga (eds) *Australian Politics and Policy: Senior Edition*. Sydney: Sydney University Press.

Department of Finance. 2020. 'Future Fund'. *Department of Finance*, 1 May. Available at: www.finance.gov.au/government/australian-government-investment-funds/future-fund.

Department of Foreign Affairs and Trade. 1997. *In the National Interest: Australia's Foreign and Trade Policy White Paper*. Canberra: Commonwealth of Australia.

Department of Foreign Affairs and Trade. 2012. *Australia in the Asian Century*. Canberra: Commonwealth of Australia.

Department of Industry, Innovation and Science. 2019. 'Manufacturing Modernisation Fund'. *Business.gov.au*. Canberra. Available at: www.business.gov.au/Grants-and-Programs/Manufacturing-Modernisation-Fund.

Duckett, C. 2020. 'Committee leaves door open for expanding broadband tax to mobiles in future'. *ZDNet*, 18 February. Available at: www.zdnet.com/article/committee-leaves-door-open-for-expanding-broadband-tax-to-mobiles-in-future/.

Environmental Defense Fund. 2020. 'How cap and trade works'. *EDG.org*. Available at: www.edf.org/climate/how-cap-and-trade-works.

Garnaut, R. 1989. *Australia and the North-East Asian Ascendancy*. Canberra: Australian Government Publishing Service.

Grattan, M. 2014. 'John Howard and Bob Hawke find a lot to agree on'. *The Conversation*, 4 June. Available at: theconversation.com/john-howard-and-bob-hawke-find-a-lot-to-agree-on-27594.

Grey, J. 2013. 'The ideology of capitalism'. *AmeriQuests* 10(1). doi.org/10.15695/amqst.v10i1.186.

Gulmanelli, S. 2014. 'John Howard and the "Anglospherist" reshaping of Australia'. *Australian Journal of Political Science* 49(4): 581–595. doi.org/10.1080/10361146.2014.965658.

Hall, P. A., and D. Soskice. 2001. *Varieties of Capitalism: The Institutional Foundations of Comparative Advantage*. Oxford: Oxford University Press.

Halligan, J. 1995. 'The process of reform: Balancing principle and pragmatism'. In J. Stewart (ed.) *From Hawke to Keating: Australian Commonwealth Administration 1990–1993*. Canberra: Centre for Research in Public Sector Management, University of Canberra and Royal Institute of Public Administration, Australia.

Hendry, J. 2020. 'Broadband tax bill gets senate committee green light'. *IT News*, 17 February. Available at: www.itnews.com.au/news/broadband-tax-bill-gets-senate-committee-green-light-538103.

Howard, J. 2017. 'Hawke and Howard: In conversation with Annabel Crabb'. *ABC News*, 16 August.

Hutchens, G. 2020. 'Australia's net debt likely to jump to more than $500 billion as massive coronavirus stimulus unleashed'. *ABC News*, 31 March. Available at: www.abc.net.au/news/2020-03-31/how-will-130-billion-dollar-coronavirus-stimulus-be-paid-for/12105774.

Industry Commission. 1997. *The Automotive Industry, Volume 1: The Report, Report No. 58*. Melbourne: Industry Commission.

Jacoby, N. H. (ed.). 1975. *The Business–Government Relationship: A Reassessment*. Los Angeles: Goodyear Publishing.

Johnson, C. 2015. 'Reviewing an anachronism? Labor to debate future of socialist objective'. *The Conversation*, 31 July. Available at: theconversation.com/reviewing-an-anachronism-labor-to-debate-future-of-socialist-objective-45233.

Karanikolas, E. 2014. 'Textile, Clothing and Footwear Investment and Innovation Programs Amendment Bill 2014'. *Bills Digest* 87(2013–14). Available at: www.aph.gov.au/Parliamentary_Business/Bills_Legislation/bd/bd1314a/14bd087.

Kay, P. 1997. *Australia and Greenhouse Policy – A Chronology*. Background Paper 4 1997–98. Canberra: Parliamentary Library.

Keating, P. 1992. *Australia and Asia: Knowing Who We Are*. Paper presented at the Asia-Australia Institute, Sydney, 7 April.

Knezevic, E. 2016. 'National Broadband Network'. In D. Heriot (ed.) *Parliamentary Library Briefing Book – 45th Parliament*. Canberra: Parliament of Australia.

Lane, I. 2020. 'Broadband tax: NBN Co accused of "sneakily" slashing regional spending'. *The New Daily*, 26 February. Available at: thenewdaily.com.au/life/tech/2020/02/26/regional-broadband-tax-nbn/.

Lewis, S. 1997. 'Labor prepares to backflip on Telstra'. *Australian Financial Review*, 24 October. Available at: www.afr.com/politics/labor-prepares-to-backflip-on-telstra-19971024-k7oxk.

Liberal Party of Australia. 2002. *The Federal Platform of the Liberal Party of Australia*. Canberra: Liberal Party of Australia.

Lindquist, E. A. and J. Wanna. 2011. 'Delivering policy reform: Making it happen, making it stick'. In E. A. Lindquist, S. Vincent and J. Wanna (eds) *Delivering Policy Reform: Anchoring Significant Reforms in Turbulent Times*. Canberra: ANU Press. doi.org/10.22459/DPR.04.2011.01.

Manne, R. 2019. 'Rats, heroes and Kevin Rudd's "The PM Years"'. *The Monthly*. Available at: www.themonthly.com.au/issue/2019/march/1551445200/robert-manne/rats-heroes-and-kevin-rudd-s-pm-years#mtr.

McEachern, D. 2018. *Stardust and Golden*. Perth: UWA Publishing.

McKnight, D. and M. Hobbs. 2013. 'Public contest through the popular media: The mining industry's advertising war against the Australian Labor Government'. *Australian Journal of Political Science* 48(3): 307–319. doi.org/10.1080/10361146.2013.821101.

Moyal, A. 1984. *Clear Across Australia: A History of Telecommunications*. Melbourne: Nelson.

Murphy, K. 2019. 'Labor's climate change policy explained: Here's what we know'. *The Guardian*, 1 April. Available at: www.theguardian.com/australia-news/2019/apr/01/labors-climate-change-policy-explained-heres-what-we-know.

Oastler, M. 2018. 'The "Buttonmobiles" – where are they now?' *Shannons.com.au*, 23 July. Available at: www.shannons.com.au/club/forum/general/the-button mobiles-where-are-they-now/.

Organisation for Economic Cooperation and Development (OECD). 2019. *OECD Environmental Performance Reviews: Australia 2019*. Paris: OECD Publishing.

Parkin, A. and L. Hardcastle. 2006. 'Government–business relations'. In A. Parkin, J. Summers and D. Woodward (eds) *Government, Politics, Power and Policy in Australia*. Frenchs Forest: Pearson.

Preistley, M. 2010. *How Green is the Green Car Innovation Fund?* Canberra: Parliamentary Library.

Productivity Commission. 2003. *From Industry Assistance to Productivity: Thirty Years of 'The Commission'*. Canberra: Productivity Commission.

Productivity Commission. 2017. *Rising Protectionism: Challenges, Threats and Opportunities for Australia, Canberra*. Canberra: Productivity Commission.

Quiggin, J. 1998. 'The premature burial of natural monopoly: Telecommunications reform in Australia'. *Agenda* 5(4): 427–440. doi.org/10.22459/AG.05.04. 1998.04.

RMIT ABC Fact Check. 2013. 'Would losing the car industry cost more than maintaining it, as Kim Carr claims?' *RMIT ABC Fact Check*, 22 November. Available at: www.abc.net.au/news/2013-11-15/kim-carr-car-industry-cost/ 5075988.

Rodgers, E. 2010. 'Abbott orders Turnbull to demolish NBN'. *ABC News*, 14 September. Available at: www.abc.net.au/news/2010-09-14/abbott-orders-turnbull-to-demolish-nbn/2260320.

Ryan, N., R. Parker and K. Brown. 2003. *Government, Business and Society*. Frenchs Forest: Pearson.

Sales, L. 2013. 'Kevin Rudd takes leadership "with humility and energy"'. Available at: www.abc.net.au/7.30/kevin-rudd-takes-leadership-with-humility-and/4783952.

Scales, B. 2017. 'Bill Scales: The rise and fall of the Australian car manufacturing industry'. *Australian Financial Review*, 19 October. Available at: www.afr. com/opinion/bill-scales-the-rise-and-fall-of-the-australian-car-manufacturing-industry-20171018-gz3ky4.

Senate Foreign Affairs, Defence and Trade References Committee. 2003. *The (Not Quite) White Paper: Australia's Foreign Affairs and Trade Policy, Advancing the National Interest*. Canberra: Commonwealth of Australia.

Sharp, A. and C. Zappone. 2009. 'Pac Brands exits Australian manufacturing'. *Sydney Morning Herald*, 25 February. Available at: www.smh.com.au/business/ pac-brands-exits-australian-manufacturing-20090225-8hei.html.

Singleton, G. 1990. *The Accord and the Australian Labour Movement*. Melbourne: Melbourne University Press.

Slezak, M. 2017. 'Australia's greenhouse gas emissions soar in latest figures'. *The Guardian*, 4 August. Available at: www.theguardian.com/australia-news/2017/aug/04/australias-greenhouse-gas-emissions-soar-in-latest-figures.

Stilwell, F. 2006. *Political Economy: The Contest of Economic Ideas*. South Melbourne: Oxford University Press.

Swoboda, K., J. Tomaras and A. Payne. 2011. *Bills Digest no. 68 2011–12: Clean Energy Bill 2011*. Canberra: Parliamentary Library.

Taylor, J. 2014. '"Absolutely right": Gillard stands by Labor's NBN vision'. *ZDNet*, 23 September. Available at: www.zdnet.com/article/absolutely-right-gillard-stands-by-labors-nbn-vision/.

Thomas, C. 1993. 'Car-part makers staging rapid boost in export performance'. *The Age*, 29 March: 1, 24.

Trubnikov, D. and E. Trubnikova. 2018. 'Is universal service justified by the public interest? From the early days to the digital age'. *Economic Affairs* 38: 185–196. doi.org/10.1111/ecaf.12290.

Tyers, P. 2019. 'Evolving Australian carbon markets'. *Digiscape Future Science Platform*, 6 May. Available at: research.csiro.au/digiscape/evolving-australian-carbon-markets/.

Wanna, J. 2015. 'An impecunious election: The significance of fiscal and economic issues'. In C. Johnson, J. Wanna and H.-A. Lee (eds) *Abbott's Gambit: The 2013 Australian Federal Election*. Canberra: ANU Press. doi.org/10.22459/AG.01.2015.18.

SECTION 3: PUBLIC POLICY AND ADMINISTRATION

Introduction to Section 3: Public policy and public administration

John Wanna's contribution to public policy has been primarily related to the process of policymaking, primarily in Australia, rather than on any particular policy subject. He has followed developments and debates about the roles of the public service and ministerial advisers, the increasing level of consultation and collaboration with customers/clients/citizens and other stakeholders, and the consideration of implementation in the policy development process. These have been the subject of the Australia and New Zealand School of Government (ANZSOG) conferences and workshops John has organised, many of which have led to ANU Press books he has edited.

Policymaking is just one area of public administration (PA) that has gained his attention. As mentioned in the first section, Wanna specialised in budgeting and financial management, emphasising the important link between budgeting and managing more generally. He has closely followed in Australia and elsewhere similarities and differences in approaches to what might be seen as the broad trends over the last 50 years, from traditional Weberian PA through new public management (NPM) and on to new public governance (NPG).

Rod Rhodes, a long-time collaborator who also shares many personal and professional interests including as long-term editors of PA journals, has himself made a major contribution in identifying and analysing these broad trends, particularly the increasing extent of 'networking' across jurisdictions and with external organisations and interests. His chapter in this section explores further the different waves of NPG and his expectation that 'decentring' will become increasingly important.

This involves much more localised decision-making based on local 'stories', presenting central elites with considerable challenges. He does not present this as a panacea, but as a relevant and effective analytical tool for examining the practices of elected and accountable decision-makers as they respond to bottom-up pressures.

Andrew Podger and Hon Chan are two of the principals (with Wanna, Tsai-tsu Su, Ma Jun and Meili Niu) of the Greater China Australia Dialogue on Public Administration, which has organised annual workshops since 2011 and led to a large number of publications. Podger has known Wanna since the 1990s, when Wanna edited the *Australian Journal of Public Administration* and Podger was president of the ACT division of the Institute of Public Administration Australia; Chan has known Wanna since the early 2000s as Wanna began to include China in the countries whose financial management practices he was keen to explore.

In their chapter, Podger and Chan review and update developments in PA in the People's Republic of China. Since the opening up reforms commencing in 1978, China has not only embraced markets but accepted the associated need to reframe the role of government (the 'state' as Jim Jose would call it). China has consciously drawn from Western PA reform movements but, as Podger and Chan emphasise, it would be wrong to assume some long-term shift away from authoritarianism to a Western-style democracy. Instead, China has been selectively adopting and then adapting Western approaches to its own institutional and cultural practices as the impact of marketisation has taken hold. So far, the result has been extraordinarily successful in terms of poverty alleviation and many aspects of personal wellbeing of its citizens, but there are signs of a slowing down of reforms and some back-sliding associated with the current pursuit of a more centralised and nationalistic approach.

Jim Jose was a fellow postgraduate student of Wanna in 1981, and they have remained friends ever since. In his chapter, Jose stands back from the more practical aspects of PA and management that he believes Wanna has been pursuing since his time at the University of Adelaide, and explores whether such a practical perspective reflects a broader shift in PA scholarly work away from the role of the state itself. In concluding that it does, Jose is clearly uncomfortable, particularly as he sees NPM and the more recent focus on 'governance' as raising serious questions about the legitimacy of the state and its role vis-à-vis that of the market. Indeed, he echoes

Peter Aucoin's concerns about 'new political governance' and related problems with the governance paradigm, namely politicisation of the public sector and the concomitant decline of trust in government generally (Aucoin 2012). The very measures aimed at improving the state's flexibility, responsiveness and efficiency, he says, present the potential to weaken the state's legitimacy.

In his writings, Wanna has not, of course, endorsed all the developments and practices under NPM or NPG but has drawn attention to various shortcomings, most famously in the criticisms he and Rhodes made of 'public value' as applied in a Westminster system like Australia's (Rhodes and Wanna 2007). But Jose raises a more fundamental issue that is worth further consideration by both scholars and practitioners: whether aspects of recent and current PA reforms are going too far.

The three chapters provide an interesting 'umbrella' to the PA issues that Wanna has contributed so much to: the broad international trends that Australia has both contributed to and followed, the possible implications for the state itself and the widening scope of international PA studies. Much of Wanna's work, however, has been at a more detailed level below this umbrella, encompassing not only developments in policymaking processes but also changes in service delivery, human resource management, intergovernmental relations, the use of the 'third sector' of non-government organisations and the civil service as an institution. This work, like much of his scholarship, draws heavily on practitioners' experience and talks to practitioners in ways that are most likely to influence future practice. But these chapters remind us also of Wanna's appreciation of broader and higher-level aspects of PA, and the importance of linking practice to theory and vice versa.

References

Aucoin, P. 2012. 'New political governance in Westminster systems: Impartial public administration and management performance at risk'. *Governance* 25(2): 177–199. doi.org/10.1111/j.1468-0491.2012.01569.x.

Rhodes, R. A. W. and J. Wanna. 2007. 'The limits to public value, or rescuing responsible government from the platonic guardians'. *Australian Journal of Public Administration* 66(4): 406–421. doi.org/10.1111/j.1467-8500.2007. 00553.x.

10

Beyond new public governance[1]

R. A. W. Rhodes

Introduction

I met John Wanna through his colleague Pat Weller of Griffith University. I met Pat at the Public Administration Committee annual conference held at the University of York on 3–5 September 1990. That meeting led to an invitation for me and my family to go to Australia. We went for July and August 1991 and I met John at the (then) Centre for Australian Public Sector Management – now the Centre for Governance and Public Policy. I reciprocated by inviting John Wanna and his partner, Jenni Craik, from Griffith to the University of York for a sabbatical term. We continued to meet regularly after that, mainly because I was a regular visitor to the centre.

In 2003, I emigrated to Australia and became Head of the Department of Politics at The Australian National University (ANU) (2003–07), then Director of the Research School of Social Sciences (2007–08). Between times, I was the temporary Research Coordinator of the Australia and New Zealand School of Government (ANZSOG). In this capacity, I had the task of recruiting a permanent director. The job required a demanding

---

1   The origins of this chapter lie in a keynote address to the conference on 'Democracy and Public Administration', Institute for Futures Studies, Holländargatan 13, Stockholm, 14–15 March. Also, I have drawn also on material in Rhodes (2016, 2017a, 2017b).

set of skills. ANU insisted on high intellectual quality. ANZSOG wanted someone who could work with the public service. We appointed John Wanna from Griffith University. I thought he was a 'catch'. I could not think of anybody better suited to bridge the gap.

John and I actively collaborated on several projects. We have published one book, *Comparing Westminster* (Rhodes, Wanna and Weller 2009) and five articles or chapters. The articles included 'The limits to public value, or rescuing responsible government from the platonic guardians' (Rhodes and Wanna 2007). It was the 2008 winner of the Sam Richardson Prize for the best article published in the *Australian Journal of Public Administration* (see also: Rhodes and Wanna 2008, 2009a, 2009b; Rhodes, Wanna and Weller 2008). From 2004 to 2009, we edited a series for UNSW Press, entitled the *ANZSOG Book Program in Government, Politics and Public Administration*. We published 12 books before the publisher withdrew. It was a happy and productive partnership that ended only because I left ANU. He – although I detect Jenni Craik's good taste – bought me a striking glass sculpture as a farewell present. It is in my study to this day. This blizzard of acronyms and academic publications may be relevant but it is a tad dry. It does not tell you anything about John's personality or what he was like to work with.

On my 2000 trip, I stayed in John's lovely Queenslander house in Bardon. Of course, I paid a modest rent, but my real job was to look after the cat, Billy, who was an independent old stray tom. He just wandered into the house one night when John was away, leapt on Jenni's bed, and gave her the shock of her life. Billy forgave her this discourtesy and allowed Wanna and Craik to look after him. With John, I took him to the vet to have an electronic chip inserted. He forgave us too. We bonded. He was there every night when I came home. A good ol' cobber.

The house came not only with a stray cat but also with a shonky old car. I was allowed to drive it, provided I could prise the keys from his daughter's reluctant fingers. The car became a saga. I took my girlfriend to Noosa for the weekend and, driving back, a speed camera clocked me. John got the speeding ticket. He explained to the police that, at the time, the car was on loan to me. The Queensland police, trusting wee souls that they are, thought it was a scam. Because I was back in the UK by now, the police thought John was blaming me to avoid the points on his license. I had to go to a notary public and sign a 'stat dec' (statutory declaration) that John was not a born liar and that I was driving the car. What was galling was the fact that the car could only have exceeded the speed limit on the Bruce Highway because there was a strong tailwind. Six months later, I was 'allowed' to pay the fine, I was not docked any points, and I am sure the Queensland police still did not believe us. Not a word of a lie. I was driving, and John's reputation was unfairly besmirched.

On occasion, the cultural divide between England and Australia separated us. John has a penchant for loud beach shirts reminiscent of Hawaii. The shirt I disliked the most displayed drunken koalas, holding 'tinnies', lounging around under palm trees in the most garish green, yellow and blue colours. John assures me the shirt is by Mambo, and famous. I think it is ghastly, but what does an Englishman who dresses in a black suit with a black shirt know about fashion?

Festschrifts, like weddings, are an excuse for friendly, hopefully amusing, stories, but enough frivolity. In this chapter, my task is to talk about the John's work on public sector management. He held the Sir John Bunting chair at ANU and his brief was to engage with the public sector. He did so successfully by organising large ANZSOG conferences for public servants, not academics, and initiating the ANU E Press series of monographs. Beyond the necessary scene setting, I do not intend to summarise this work. Both were a great success and the number of downloads reached staggering proportions. I acknowledge his skill and success in working with the public sector but my brief is to talk about his academic work on public management.

I provide a brief history of the shift from traditional public administration to new public management to new public governance. I identify three waves of new public governance – network governance, metagovernance and decentred governance. I discuss John's work against the backcloth of these trends. This chapter describes the first two waves briefly before focusing on decentred governance. I argue for a bottom-up approach to the study of governance that focuses on local knowledge and uses storytelling as its main method for collecting data. As every approach to the study of governance has its limits, the chapter concludes by discussing the usefulness of local knowledge to central policymakers.

Table 10.1. Public administration, new public management and new public governance compared

Paradigm/Key elements	Theoretical roots	State tradition	Unit of analysis	Key focus	Resource allocation mechanism	Core beliefs
Public administration	Political science and public policy	Unitary/federal	The political–administrative system	Policy advice and implementation	Hierarchy	Public sector ethos
New public management (NPM)	Rational choice theory and management studies	Regulatory	The organisation	Management of organisational resources and performance	Markets	Efficiency, competition and the market
New public governance (NPG)	New institutionalism and network theory	Differentiated	The network	Negotiation of values, meanings and relationships	Networks	Trust and reciprocity

Source: Compiled from Osborne (2010) and Rhodes (1998).

From traditional public administration to new public governance

Table 10.1 summarises the shift from traditional public administration to new public management (NPM) to the latest wave of reform, new public governance (NPG).

Traditional public administration

We turned our backs on traditional public administration; it was seen as the problem, not the solution. Of course, the bureaucracies of yesteryear had their faults and the reformers had a case (see e.g. Osborne and Gaebler 1992; Pollitt 1993; Pusey 1991). Yet, the defining characteristics of traditional public administration are not red tape, cost and inefficiency. Rather, the phrase refers to classic bureaucrats working in a hierarchy of authority and conserving the state tradition. In Table 10.1, their task is to provide policy advice for their political masters and to implement the politician's decision. Politicians, political staffers and even some public servants continue to hold important misconceptions about the past of our public services. They forget that bureaucracy persists because it provides 'consistent, stable administration', 'equity in processes', 'expertise' and 'accountability' (Meier and Hill 2005, 67; see also Goodsell 2004).

New public management (NPM)

The last 40 years have seen three waves of NPM reforms (and for a more detailed account see: Pollitt and Bouckaert 2011, Chapter 1). In Table 10.1, the first wave of NPM was managerialism or hands-on, professional management; explicit standards and measures of performance; managing by results; and value for money. That was only the beginning. In the second wave, governments embraced marketisation or neoliberal beliefs about competition and markets. It introduced ideas about restructuring the incentive structures of public service provision through contracting out, and quasi-markets. The third wave of NPM focuses on service delivery and citizen choice. Nothing has gone away. We have geological strata of reforms. Thus, Hood and Lodge (2007, 59) suggest we have created the 'civil service reform syndrome' in which 'initiatives come and go, overlap and ignore each other, leaving behind residues of varying size and style'. As one senior civil servant said 'the inoculation theory of reform does not work – you are not immune after one bout'. Although the extent of the reforms varies from country to country, the Westminster countries were among the most enthusiastic. Pollitt and Bouckaert (2011, 9) conclude NPM 'has become a key element in many ... countries. It has internationalised ... In short, it has arrived.'

NPM arrived in Australia too and John Wanna was at the forefront in documenting the changes.[2] The book he co-authored with Ciaran O'Faircheallaigh and Pat Weller on public sector management in Australia (1992) was the first in the field in Australia. He also contributed books on implementation and project management (Wanna 2007; Butcher, Freyens and Wanna 2010). Both were topics central to NPM. However, his most significant contribution, and the most cited, is his critique of Mark Moore's (1995) notion of 'public value' (see Rhodes and Wanna 2007, 2008 and 2009a; cf. Alford 2008). The idea was that public managers should initiate and reshape public sector enterprises to increase their value to the public (Moore 1995, 52–55). I do not propose to summarise the debate. For my purposes, I need to make two points. First, it was a prominent debate. Second, the scope for initiative and reshaping by non-elected public servants was severely constrained by not only the party political context of management in Westminster systems, but also by the key relationship between ministers and their departmental heads. The corpse of public value lies in the elephants' graveyard of so many reforms of the public service. The big game hunter that put it there is the elected party politician for whom management is an incidental sideshow. The article was prescient.

New public governance (NPG)

In Table 10.1, managing networks is at the heart of NPG. For example, both the Dutch school (Kickert, Klijn and Koppenjan 1997) and the Anglo governance school (Rhodes 1997a) posit a shift from hands-on to hands-off steering by the state. Hands-off steering refers to working with and through networks or webs of organisations to achieve shared policy objectives. It involves continuously negotiating beliefs and exchanging resources within agreed rules of the game (see also: Torfing et al. 2012, 14; Koliba, Meek and Zia 2011, 60).

---

2   For a full list of John Wanna's publications see Appendix 1. Many of these publications can be downloaded free at: press.anu.edu.au/publications/series/anzsog.

The first point to note is that, whereas NPM inspired a vast array of management reforms, NPG inspired relatively few reforms in Westminster governments. Pollitt and Bouckaert (2011, 212) see joining-up in its various forms as one of the main themes of reform that has 'grown in prominence internationally since the turn of the century' (see e.g. Management Advisory Committee [MAC] 2004). So, the neutral, competent servants of the political executive must now master the skills for managing the complex, non-routine issues, policies and relationships in networks: that is, metagoverning, boundary-spanning and collaborative leadership. The task is to manage the mix of bureaucracy, markets and networks (Rhodes 1997b). The public service needs these new skills, although it is a step too far to talk of these new skills requiring 'a full-blown cultural transformation' (Goldsmith and Eggers 2004, 178).

I identify three waves of waves of NPG. The first wave of *network governance* originated in the 1990s. The second wave of *metagovernance* came to prominence in the 2000s. As the wave metaphor implies, it did not supplant network governance. Both waves kept on rolling and were joined by the third wave of *decentred governance*. I discuss each in turn.

Network governance

There are several accounts of this trend for Britain, continental Europe and the US, too many to warrant yet another extended summary (see Börzel 1998 and 2011; Klijn 2008; Klijn and Koppenjan 2015, Chapter 2; Rhodes 2017a, Chapter 3). In Britain, there has been a shift from government by a unitary state to governance by and through networks. The boundary between state and civil society changed. Commonly, it is understood as a shift from hierarchies, or the bureaucracies of the welfare state, through the marketisation reforms of the Conservative governments of Thatcher, to the networks and joined-up government of New Labour.[3]

There is also a large European literature on 'guidance', 'steering' and 'indirect coordination', which predates both the British interest in network governance and the American interest in reinventing government. For example, Kaufmann, Majone and Ostrom's (1986) edited volume on guidance, steering and control is Germanic in size,

---

3   See for example: Rhodes (1997a, 2017a); Stoker (2004); and for a review of the literature and citations see Marinetto (2003).

scope and language. It focuses on how a multiplicity of interdependent actors can be coordinated in the long chains of actions typical of complex societies (see also Kooiman 1993; Scharpf 1997). Also, the distinctive and productive 'Rotterdam School' focused on network management (Kickert, Klijn and Koppenjan 1997; Klijn and Koppenjan 2015).

For the US, Osborne and Gaebler (1992, 20 and 34) distinguish between policy decisions (steering) and service delivery (rowing), arguing bureaucracy is a bankrupt tool for rowing. In its place, they proposed entrepreneurial government, with its stress on working with the private sector and responsiveness to customers. This transformation of the public sector involves 'less government' or less rowing but 'more governance' or more steering. In his review of the American literature, Frederickson (1997, 84–85) concludes the word 'governance is probably the best and most accepted metaphor for describing the patterns of interaction of multiple-organisational systems or networks' (see also Kettl 1993, 206–207; Salamon 2002). There is also a methods divide between European and American scholars. The latter brought their characteristic quantitative skills to bear on networks and governance. They combined 'large N' studies of networks (Meier and O'Toole 2005) with an instrumental or tool view that sought to make the study of networks relevant to public managers (Agranoff 2007). Their European counterparts preferred comparative case studies, although there was a shared focus on network management and the allied subject of collaboration. The interested reader will have no difficulty finding practical advice. Running a network may have its challenges but it is not rocket science (see e.g. Ansell and Gash 2007; Goldsmith and Eggers 2004; Rhodes 2017a, and citations).

This necessarily brief skim through an extensive literature shows that network governance abounds. The topic prospers because it can provide advice to governments on how to manage networks. There is an odd Australian challenge to the network governance narrative that questions whether it is an accurate description (Colebatch 2009; Hughes 2010). Whether the number of networks has grown or whether such networks are new are, frankly, deeply uninteresting questions that miss the point. The central concern is the spread of new ideas about markets and networks and the consequent changes in the role of the state. Torfing et al. (2012, 31–32) deal brusquely and briskly with such sceptics. They argue there have been three 'irreversible changes': in the expectations of stakeholders about their involvement in collaborative policymaking, in the shift of public bureaucracies to 'open organisations ... engaged in joint problem solving and collaborative service delivery', and in the belief that network governance is 'a legitimate alternative to hierarchy and markets'. The new ideas had consequences.[4]

Metagovernance

Metagovernance refers to the role of the state in securing coordination in governance and its use of negotiation, diplomacy and informal modes of steering. As with network governance, metagovernance comes in several varieties (Sørensen and Torfing 2007, 170–180). These approaches address what they see as a weakness in network governance; its emphasis on the hollowing-out of the state. Metagovernance seeks to bring the state back in (see Torfing et al. 2012, Chapters 1 and 7). The meta-role of the state is to regulate the mix of markets, hierarchy, networks and other governing structures: it is not just to manage networks.

However, both network governance and metagovernance share a concern with how the state steers organisations, whether markets or networks, when it no longer directly provides services through state bureaucracies, or rowing. These other organisations undertake much of the work of governing; they implement policies, they provide public services and at times they even regulate themselves. The state governs the organisations that govern civil society; 'the governance of government and governance' (Jessop 2000, 23). Moreover, the other organisations characteristically have a degree of autonomy from the state. They are often voluntary or private sector groups or they are governmental agencies or tiers of government separate from the core executive. So, the state cannot govern them solely by the instruments that work in bureaucracies.

Torfing et al. (2012, 156–159 and Chapter 7) suggest the traditional role of the public service is supplemented (not replaced) with that of the 'meta-governor managing and facilitating interactive governance'. Their task is to 'balance autonomy of networks with hands-on intervention'. They have various specific ways of carrying out this balancing act. They become 'meta-governors', managing the mix of bureaucracy, markets and networks (see also: Koliba, Meek and Zia 2011, xxxii and Chapter 8; and Rhodes 1997b; Rhodes 2017a, Chapter 11).

---

4   For critiques of network governance, see, for example: Bell and Hindmoor (2009); Jessop (2000); Kjær (2004); Pierre and Peters (2000); Peters and Pierre (2009); and Torfing et al. (2012). For a reply, see: Rhodes (2017a).

Tools of the metagovernor

The problem with the neologisms of the social sciences is that they can seem a world away from the experience of practitioners. While there is a wealth of literature on how to manage a network, there is little work on how to be a metagovernor. There are several ways in which the state can steer the other actors involved in governance (see e.g. Jessop 2000, 23–24, and 2003; Koliba, Meek and Zia 2011, xxxii and Chapter 8; Torfing et al. 2012, Chapter 7). The state is not limited to any one of these tools. It can use different tools, and combinations of tools, in different settings at different times.

First, the state can set the rules of the game for other actors and then leave them to do what they will within those rules; they work 'in the shadow of hierarchy'. So, it can redesign markets, reregulate policy sectors or introduce constitutional change.

It can supplement such hands-on measures with, second, hands-off steering through storytelling. It can organise dialogues, foster meanings, beliefs and identities among the relevant actors, and influence what actors think and do.

Third, the state can steer by the ways in which it distributes resources such as money and authority. It can play a boundary-spanning role, alter the balance between actors in a network, act as a court of appeal when conflict arises, rebalance the mix of governing structures and step in when network governance fails.

Finally, public servants can play a political role. Of course, they cannot play a *party political* role but they can campaign for a policy and form alliances with (say) local politicians. Of course, the state need not adopt a single uniform approach to metagovernance; it can pick and mix.

John Wanna documented equivalent changes in the Australian public sector in his discussions of collaborative governance and putting citizens first. He disseminated these ideas widely in the public service. Both are responses to the problems of NPM. So, collaboration is necessary because policies are delivered by different agencies, across jurisdictions, with third-party providers and with citizens. Policymakers 'recognise new dependencies', and collaboration became 'a widely used policy instrument across the fields of public policy' that 'took on the mantle of managing mutual dependencies using diplomacy, dialogue and deliberation' (Wanna 2008, 6–7). The drive to put citizens first has its root in the problems that 'emerged with attempting to treat clients of public programs as "customers"'. Putting citizens first means 'extending citizens' participation and engagement directly into policymaking and program administration, and improving responsiveness through greater use of third parties to deliver services' such as NGOs (non-government organisations) (Podger et al. 2012, 103; see also Lindquist, Vincent and Wanna 2013; Wanna, Butcher and Freyens 2010). With this shift came changing roles for public servants, from bureaucrat to the '"in-between" operator, the entrepreneur or diplomat, or the NGO motivator' (Podger et al. 2012, 110). In short, we are in the heartland of networks and network governance, with the focus on the problems for the practitioner and helping them to manage their dependencies.

Decentred governance

For all their different emphases, the first and second waves of governance have two shared weaknesses relevant to this chapter – essential properties, and instrumental knowledge (and for a more detailed account see Bevir and Rhodes 2010 and Rhodes 2017a).

First, proponents of metagovernance take for granted the characteristics or essential properties of network governance. They agree networks are characterised by trust and diplomacy. They accept that states are becoming increasingly fragmented into networks based on several different stakeholders. They accept the dividing line between the state and civil society is becoming more blurred because the relevant stakeholders are private or voluntary sector organisations. So, Jessop (2000, 24) concedes, 'the state is no longer the sovereign authority … [it is] less hierarchical, less centralised, less *dirigiste*'. There is a shared description of the characteristics of network governance (see also Sørensen and Torfing 2007; Torfing et al. 2012).

Second, in the analysis of metagovernance, the state governs the other actors involved in governance. It concedes them the power to self-regulate but keeps the capacity to exert macro control over that self-regulation. In other words, metagovernance heralds the return of the state by reinventing its governing role; it is 'bringing the state back in (yet again)' (Jessop 2007, 54). This return to the state opens opportunities for instrumental knowledge or policy advice on the practice of metagovernance. The two waves share a common concern with instrumental knowledge on network governance; both assume the role of the state is to manage, directly and indirectly, the networks of service delivery. The literature on network management assumes that government departments, state governments, local authorities, markets and networks are fixed structures with essential properties that governments can manipulate by using the right tools. It seeks to improve the ability of the state to manage the mix of hierarchies, markets and networks and of state managers to steer these structures.

A decentred account of governance overcomes these problems by providing a different description of governance. It does not have essentialist features like trust or reciprocity, only 'family resemblances' that are constructed, contested and contingent (Wittgenstein 2009, 17–20). It does not describe recurring patterns of action or systematise with typologies; it focuses on the everyday practices of agents whose beliefs and actions are informed by traditions. In a phrase, it shifts away from a top-down focus on the intentions of central elites to a bottom-up analysis of the beliefs and practices of citizens and street-level bureaucrats. It explains shifting patterns of governance by focusing on the actors' own interpretations of events, not external causes such as a global financial crisis. It explores the diverse ways in which such situated agents change the boundaries of state and civil society by constantly remaking practices as their beliefs change in response to dilemmas. It highlights a more diverse view of state authority and its exercise by recovering the contingent and contestable narratives or stories that people tell. The decentred account of governance is summarised in Table 10.2.

Table 10.2 Decentred analysis

1.	It represents a shift of *topos* from institutions to *meanings* in action.
2.	Institutions whether a policy network or a prime ministerial office or a policy do not have essentialist features, only *family resemblances* that are *constructed, contested and contingent*.
3.	Decentred analysis explains shifting patterns of policy and policymaking by focusing on the actors' own interpretations of their *beliefs and practices*, not external causes such as a global financial crisis.
4.	The everyday practices arise from agents whose beliefs and actions are informed by *traditions*.
5.	It explores the diverse ways in which *situated agents* are changing policies by constantly remaking practices as their beliefs change in response to *dilemmas*.
6.	It reveals the *contingency* and *contestability* of policy narratives. It highlights both the importance of local knowledge and the diversity of policymaking and its exercise.
7.	It provides instrumental knowledge expressed in *stories*.

Source: Rhodes (2017b).

All patterns of rule arise as the contingent products of diverse actions and political struggles informed by the varied beliefs of situated agents. So, the notion of a monolithic state in control of itself and civil society was always a myth. The myth obscured the reality of diverse state practices that escaped the control of the centre because they arose from the contingent beliefs and actions of diverse actors at the boundary of state and civil society. The state is never monolithic and it always negotiates with others. Policy always arises from interactions within networks of organisations and individuals. Patterns of rule always traverse the public, private and voluntary sectors. The boundaries between state and civil society are always blurred. Transnational and international links and flows always disrupt national borders. In short, state authority is constantly being remade, negotiated and contested in widely different ways in widely varying everyday practices (and for a more detailed account see Bevir and Rhodes 2010, Chapter 5). Awareness of such limits to state action are recognised by its practitioners. A former head of the UK civil service acknowledged:

> I have a very strong suspicion that governments are nothing like as important as they think they are, and that the ordinary work of making things and moving things about, of transport, manufacture, farming, mining, is so much more important than what the Government does. (cited in Theakston 2017, Chapter 5)

This conception of decentred governance avoids the shared weaknesses of network governance and metagovernance. There are no essential properties. The state is not reified. Both the first and second waves have an instrumental approach to networks; they are top-down approaches supporting central steering. A decentred view challenges this approach with its bottom-up approach. Local networks are no longer local when run from the centre. The relationship is better described as an exercise in official consultation; at least this phrase does not imply any local discretion or local ownership. The effect is that central management of local networks threatens their autonomy, distinctiveness and effectiveness. This threat arises because any pattern of governance is a product of diverse practices that are themselves composed of multiple individuals acting on all sorts of conflicting beliefs. The bottom-up approach of decentred governance suggests that central intervention will undermine the bottom-up construction of governance, provoking resistance and generating unintended consequences (and see Rhodes 2018 for several examples of decentred analysis in action).

So far, so abstract – on which parallel Planet Earth is this conception of the state useful? First, this decentred view of the state is its own justification because it directs our attention to new topics; to local knowledge and bottom-up accounts of the state. Edification is more than enough.

But, and second, we live in an era where 'impact' and 'relevance' rule. Decentred analysis is 'relevant' because it supplements the views of the elite and the expert with giving voice to the silent. A decentred approach undercuts the idea of network steering as a set of tools by which we can manage governance. If governance is constructed differently, contingently and continuously, we cannot have a toolkit for managing it. However, decentred narratives offer a different approach to policy advice. Instead of revealing policy consequences through insights into a social logic or law-like regularities, they enable policymakers to see things differently. They display new connections in governance and new aspects of governance. In other words, a decentred approach treats policy advice as stories that enable listeners to see governance afresh (Bevir 2011).

Storytelling

To counter the criticism of 'irrelevance', the next section harnesses the analysis of storytelling to the decentred analysis of governance and its practices. It offers a different version of instrumental or useful knowledge.

A storytelling approach encourages us to give up management techniques and strategies for learning by telling stories and listening to them. While statistics, models and claims to expertise all have a place in such stories, we should not become too preoccupied with them. On the contrary, we should recognise that they too are narratives about how people have acted or will react given their beliefs and desires. No matter what rigour or expertise we bring to bear, all we can do is tell a story and offer plausible conjecture on what the future might bring.

The starting point is the idea that any organisation 'always hinges on the creation of shared meaning and shared understandings'. Metaphors exercise a 'formative impact' when constructing meanings (Morgan 1993, 11 and 276–280). Stories spell out the shared meaning and shared understandings. Of course, stories come in many versions and often have no clear beginning and no ending. They are provisional and unfolding. In telling the stories, we freeze them so they can appear set in stone, but they unfold constantly.

In a British government department, there is at least one departmental philosophy and it is the storehouse of many stories. It is a form of folk psychology. It provides the everyday theory and shared languages for storytelling. It is the collective memory of the department. Institutional memory lives in the stories people tell one another; 'stories are to the storytelling system what precedent cases are to the judicial system'. Such narratives were like 'precedent cases … to the judicial system'. They were used to 'formulate recognizable, cogent, defensible and seemingly rational collective accounts that will serve as precedents for individual assumption, decision and action' (Boje 1991, 106).

Civil servants and ministers learn and filter current events through the stories they hear and tell one another. It is an integral part of the everyday practice of civil servants. Stories explain past practice and events and justify recommendations for the future. It is an organised, selective retelling of the past to make sense of the present. Public servants know they tell the minister stories. Stories come in many forms. Some stories are short. They take a single sentence. When you belong to the same organisation, the listener can unpack these stories. They do not need to be recounted in full. The shortest example is 'you know', as in 'you know the story already'. For example, one short story told recruits there 'is a bit of mystique around ministers and they make you feel inferior'. It invokes the idea of hierarchy, the subordinate role of civil servants, and the ceremonial side of being the Queen's minister. Its meaning is clear: 'you are a subordinate'. Gossip is another form of storytelling; personalised with a variable regard for accuracy. Submissions and briefs are stories by another name and recognised to be so by the civil servants who tell them. When the minister resigned, the civil servants asked: 'What is our story?' They wanted to find out what had happened. They talked of 'getting the story straight', 'getting it together', 'we've got the story', 'when you have the narrative' and 'we've reached agreement on some of the main story-lines'. Officials were invited to tell a story. Managers recognise that storytelling provides guides for managerial action (Rhodes 2011, 130–131).

Storytelling is linked to performance. In Rhodes (2011, 289) storytelling had three characteristics: a language game, a performing game and a management game. The language game identified and constructed the storyline, answering the questions of what had happened and why. The performing game told the story to a wider audience, inside and outside the department. Officials tested the facts and rehearsed the storyline in official meetings to see how their colleagues responded. They had to adapt the story to suit the minister, and both ministers and officials had to judge how the story would play publicly. They then performed that agreed story on a public stage to the media, parliament and the public. Finally, there was the management game, which both implemented any policy changes and, perhaps even more important, let them get on with 'business as usual' as quickly as possible. The resulting story had to be reliable, defensible, accurate and consistent with the department's traditions. Moreover, the analysis of storytelling requires us to understand not only their construction and performance of stories but also their reception; 'why do some stories capture the imagination when others fail?' If storytelling is an important metagoverning tool, we need to examine the successes and failures of different types of stories and ways of telling them. We need also systematic ways of collecting and analysing stories.

Collecting stories

Recovering stories can be treated as a technique like a survey; a means for getting data for policymakers. For central elites, the question is how can we collect such data? In a phrase, the answer is 'policy narratives'. Storytelling is a tool for collecting data about local knowledge to be used by central elites; an addition to the modernist social science toolbox. It is about providing information for policymakers so they can make rational decisions (Van Willigen 2002, 150 and Chapter 10).[5]

There are several ways to collect stories to provide advice to policymakers, including observation, questionnaires and focus groups. Observational field work is the best way of collecting stories but involves deep hanging out (see Rhodes 2017b, Chapter 3). The problem is that such field work is time-consuming. So, deep hanging out is supplemented, even replaced, with hit-and-run ethnography – short repeat visits. An alternative way of collecting stories is to use a questionnaire (see Gabriel 2000, Chapter 6). The questions are reassuringly obvious; for example: 'if a new member of staff asks you "how do things work around here?", what do you tell them?' Focus groups are another effective method for collecting stories. Focus groups involve getting a group of people together to discuss their beliefs and practices. The groups are interactive and group members are encouraged by a facilitator to talk to one another. The researcher does

---

5   Storytelling, or narratives, as a tool of management is an established part of the business toolkit and there is a burgeoning literature. See, for example: Czarniawska (2004); Gabriel (2000); and Denning (2007). There is even a *Dummies* book (Dietz and Silverman 2013).

not interview the group members but facilitates their discussion. It is important the focus group should be coherent, comprised of people from the same organisation and with shared experiences in that organisation. There has to be a shared history from which they can draw stories. The focus group is shaking the bag of organisational stories to identify its dramas (see Rhodes 2017b, Chapter 5 for an extended discussion).

Such applied ethnography is now the stuff of management consultants (Dietz and Silverman 2014). There are also specialised government units. The aim may not be to collect stories, although they do, but it is always to provide advice for policymakers. However, many parties are involved in, or affected by, public policymaking. They can resist and subvert the aims of central elites. A second reason for collecting stories about governance is to specify the voices of the silent others.

Inscribing: Recover, recount and review

Recovering local stories about governance is not only about providing data for policymakers: it is also about giving voice to those who are seldom heard. The toolkit is the same whether one is collecting stories to advise policymakers or to give voice. The differences lie in whom we ask, for whom we collect the data and how we use those data. The role is not limited to advising policymakers. The researcher has many roles. The research does not privilege any one voice but represents the several voices in public policymaking. Instead of advice to policymakers, the aim can be to recover, recount and review. We recover the stories told to us by politicians, public servants and citizens. We systematise these accounts, telling our version of their stories and recounting them. Storywriter and storyteller review this version jointly to identify errors, divergences and lessons. The aim is a fusion of horizons that covers both agreement and where we agree to disagree.

We derive practical lessons from such lived and shared experiences. In late 2009, Pat Weller and Anne Tiernan brought together 11 former Chiefs of Staff (CoS) of the Australian prime minister. They came together to take part in two closed, roundtable focus group discussions facilitated by Tiernan and Weller. Each session aimed to elicit participants' views on such topics as how different individuals approached the task of working with the prime minister, the key duties and responsibilities that they performed, and the challenges confronting the CoS. Rhodes and Tiernan conducted interviews with serving CoS. They then analysed both the 230 pages of transcripts and the interviews to identify the lessons for future CoS – see Table 10.3.

Table 10.3. Lessons for Chiefs of Staff

1. **Know the boss; supporting and protecting the prime minister** Support the position Support the person
2. **Coping and surviving** Run the office Day-to-day management Crisis management
3. **Policy coordination** Set and stick to priorities Control the agenda Get the right people in the room Policy coordination
4. **Political management: managing dependencies** The cabinet and the ministry The party-room The media The public service

Source: Rhodes and Tiernan (2014, 13).

We circulated, discussed and modified drafts with the CoS before agreeing the contents of Table 10.3. We used the analysis as the basis of several workshops for political appointees in Australian state and federal government.

The term 'local knowledge' does not refer to only geographical localities. Yanow (2004, s10–s11) sees local knowledge as 'typically developed within a community of practitioners' that 'makes it "local" knowledge – that is, specific to a context and to a group of people acting together in that context at that time'. CoS are specific to a context and share tacit local knowledge about working with the prime minister. It is tacit because they do not have a public voice – they would have to get permission from their prime minister to speak in public. Their work is officially 'secret'. It is local because it is confined to the networks around the prime minister. The focus groups were the mechanism that gave them voice because they could remain anonymous as individuals yet share their experience in public. In fact, after the research was completed, they waived anonymity.

Truth and lies

Pat Weller reminded me that, as kids, when our parents said we were telling stories they meant we were lying. My account of storytelling is benign; it assumes reasonable people tell the truth. In politics that assumption is naïve. We know that politicians tell whopping great lies. Also, they tell stories for malign purposes: to justify the unjustifiable. So, how do we know when a story is reliable? How do we distinguish between the different stories people tell about the same events? How do we discredit fake news stories?

The search for, and the criteria of, objective knowledge lie at the core of these questions and I do not have the space to develop the argument (see Bevir 1999, Chapter 3; and Rhodes 2017b, 30–33, 50–51 and 100–102). The simple point is that stories must be forensically challenged. As Collini (2012, 62) argues, all inquiry including storytelling 'is governed by broadly similar canons of accuracy and precision, of rigour in argument and clarity in presentation, of respect for the evidence and openness to criticism'. Facts must be checked. The story must be documented. The argument should be interrogated. We compare stories by putting them on trial and interrogating the quality of the evidence. 'Truth' may 'multifaceted, theoretically loaded, and embedded in historically situated language games and ordinary practice' (Wagenaar 2016, 134), but we can still strive for 'plausible conjectures' (Boudon 1993). In other words, stories are plausible when they rest on good reasons and the reasons are good when they are inferred from relevant evidence.

Conclusions

This chapter discusses three waves of governance: network governance, metagovernance and decentred governance. For each wave, it discusses the implications for practitioners: the tools they can use to steer governance. All three waves coexist today. Frankly, network governance continues to dominate because of its demonstrable relevance to practitioners on managing networks. Metagovernance suggests some important additions to the network governance toolkit. However, there are significant weaknesses with both network governance and metagovernance. This chapter seeks to move beyond NPG by highlighting decentred governance – an edifying third wave. Decentred governance focuses on the diverse ways in which such situated agents change the boundaries of state and

POLITICS, POLICY AND PUBLIC ADMINISTRATION IN THEORY AND PRACTICE

civil society by constantly remaking practices as their beliefs change in response to dilemmas. It highlights a more diverse view of state authority and its exercise. It suggests that tools based on collecting and analysing stories are the best way to steer contingent and contested narratives of governance. It describes how to collect and analyse stories.

Instrumental knowledge is a much-valued goal of social science research today and it lies at the heart of John Wanna's contribution. He plays the role of commentator, identifying and commenting on trends for public servants. He points to possible limits to reforms. He identifies promising lines of inquiry. He engages with theoretical debates that help him carry out his role of bridging the gap between academic and public servant. He is a dancer on the edges of theory, but a player in the game of reform.

Instrumental knowledge is not the heart and soul of decentred analysis. Rather, the approach is valuable in its own right, for its own sake, because it unpacks what is taken for granted by inscribing complex specificity in its context. However, like any approach in the social sciences, it has its limits. I can decentre my decentred account of governance by asking two questions. Is local knowledge useful to central policymakers? What are the barriers to giving voice to the silent?

Local knowledge is seen as 'good' and an essential complement to other forms of knowledge – hence the interest in putting citizens first. It is seen as another way for elite decision-makers to 'improve' policymaking by adapting national decisions to local conditions. Such advice *confronts* politicians and bureaucrats who are scarcely sympathetic to other previously silent voices. They see the stories as 'coming forward with awkward observations' and 'as wishing to preserve "traditional" ways' (Sillitoe 2006, 10). Politicians and bureaucrats criticise stories because the stories fail to conform to their expectations about the causes of problems and their solutions. Stories are dismissed as 'irrelevant or disruptive' (Sillitoe 2006, 14).

Any aphorism such as 'recover, recount and review' courts the danger of oversimplification. My aphorism is no exception because it sets local stories in stone when such knowledge is often elusive and ambiguous. Thus, Vohnsen (2015, 158) argues that 'local knowledge and practice is a tricky phenomenon' because it is 'dispersed and, not possessed equally by all'. It is also shifty: 'what one person holds to be of importance in one specific situation is not necessarily what the same person might attribute importance to in a different situation' (Vohnsen 2015, 158). Moreover, the street-level bureaucrats do not have clear, fixed identities. They 'swap identities all the time'. Thus, 'one minute they are advocating the project like true politicians, while the next moment they are criticising it like detached academic scholars'. They are not local experts confronting a central plan. They know the plan cannot be implemented so 'implementation happens hand-in-hand with street-level planning'. There is 'a second, highly unstable planning phase' locally, which continuously plans and redrafts the policy (Vohnsen 2015, 157–158; see also Vohnsen 2017). Local knowledge is 'shifty' or, more formally, it is contested, contingent and generative (Rhodes 2017b, 173–177). It is not amenable to central collection or direction. Collecting stories to advise policymakers raises the question of whose local knowledge in what context. To recover local knowledge through stories is to inscribe these complex specificities in their ever-varying contexts, but at the cost of being dismissed as irrelevant by central elites.

Proponents of decentred governance can provide advice to policymakers by collecting stories and through the systematic analysis of those stories. However, buyers beware. Today's conventional wisdom may assert that local knowledge should be relevant to policymakers but policymakers define relevance, not citizens. Moreover, local knowledge is not a given. It may be seen as disruptive by governments, but it is legitimate to focus on other people's definition of relevance and on people who hold views contrary to the government of the day. We can choose to be servants of power and help the state win consent, but it is not required. We can choose to contribute to debates that will enhance the capacity of citizens to consider and voice differing perspectives in policy debates. Social scientists, like cobblers, should stick to their lasts and focus on diagnosing ills and criticising policies and policymaking. They should leave problem-solving and policymaking to those elected, *and accountable*, for those tasks. Decentred governance and its stories encapsulating local knowledge offer no easy panacea for decision-makers, but it is an effective analytical tool for unpacking state practices from the bottom up.

Acknowledgements

I would like to thank Anne Tiernan, John Wanna and Pat Weller for their corrections and constructive comments.

References

Agranoff, R. 2007. *Managing within Networks: Adding Value to Public Organizations.* Washington, DC: Georgetown University Press.

Alford, J. 2008. 'The limits to traditional public administration, or rescuing public value from misrepresentation'. *The Australian Journal of Public Administration* 67: 357–366. doi.org/10.1111/j.1467-8500.2008.00593.x.

Ansell, C. and A. Gash. 2007. 'Collaborative governance in theory and practice'. *Journal of Public Administration Theory and Practice* 18: 543–571. doi.org/10.1093/jopart/mum032.

Bell, S. and A. Hindmoor. 2009. *Rethinking Governance: The Centrality of the State in Modern Society.* Cambridge: Cambridge University Press. doi.org/10.1017/CBO9780511814617.

Bevir, M. 1999. *The Logic of the History of Ideas.* Cambridge: Cambridge University Press.

Bevir, M. 2011. 'Public administration as storytelling'. *Public Administration,* 89: 183–195. doi.org/10.1111/j.1467-9299.2011.01908.x.

Bevir, M. and R. A. W. Rhodes. 2010. *The State as Cultural Practice.* Oxford: Oxford University Press. doi.org/10.1093/acprof:oso/9780199580750.001.0001.

Boje, D. 1991. 'The storytelling organization: A study of story performance in an office-supply firm'. *Administrative Science Quarterly* 36: 106–126. doi.org/10.2307/2393432.

Börzel, T. A. 1998. 'Organizing Babylon: On the different conceptions of policy networks'. *Public Administration* 76: 253–73. doi.org/10.1111/1467-9299.00100.

Börzel, T. A. 2011. 'Networks: Reified metaphor or governance panacea?' *Public Administration* 89: 49–63. doi.org/10.1111/j.1467-9299.2011.01916.x.

Boudon, R. 1993. 'Towards a synthetic theory of rationality'. *International Studies in the Philosophy of Science* 7: 5–19. doi.org/10.1080/02698599308573439.

Butcher, J., B. Freyens and J. Wanna. 2010. *Policy in Action: The Challenge of Service Delivery.* Sydney: UNSW Press.

Colebatch, H. K. 2009. 'Governance as a conceptual development in the analysis of policy'. *Critical Policy Studies* 3: 58–67. doi.org/10.1080/19460170903158107.

Collini, S. 2012. *What Are Universities For?* London: Penguin Books.

Czarniawska, B. 2004. *Narratives in Social Science Research.* London: Sage. doi.org/10.4135/9781849209502.

Denning, S. 2007. *The Secret Language of Leadership: How Leaders Inspire Action Through Narrative.* San Francisco: Jossey-Bass. doi.org/10.1108/sd.2009.05625aae.001.

Dietz, K. and L. L. Silverman. 2013. *Business Storytelling for Dummies.* New York: Wiley.

Frederickson, H. G. .1997. *The Spirit of Public Administration.* San Francisco: Jossey-Bass.

Gabriel, Y. 2000. *Storytelling in Organizations: Facts, Fictions and Fantasies.* Oxford: Oxford University Press.

Goldsmith, S. and W. D. Eggers. 2004. *Governing by Networks.* Washington, DC: Brookings Institution Press.

Goodsell, C. T. 2004. *The Case for Bureaucracy.* Fourth edition. Washington, DC: CQ Press.

Hood, C. and M. Lodge. 2007. 'Civil service reform syndrome – Are we heading for a cure?' *Transformation* (Spring): 58–59.

Hughes, O. 2010. 'Does governance exist?' In S. Osborne (ed.) *The New Public Governance: Emerging Perspectives on the Theory and Practice of Public Governance.* London and New York: Routledge/Taylor and Francis.

Jessop, B. 2000. 'Governance failure'. In G. Stoker (ed.) *The New Politics of British Local Governance.* Houndmills, Basingstoke: Macmillan.

Jessop, B. 2003. 'Governance and metagovernance: On reflexivity, requisite variety, and requisite irony'. In H. P. Bang (ed.) *Governance as Social and Political Communication.* Manchester: Manchester University Press.

Jessop, B. 2007. *State Power.* Cambridge: Polity.

Kaufman, F. X., G. Majone and V. Ostrom (eds). 1986. *Guidance, Control, and Evaluation in the Public Sector.* Berlin, de Gruyter.

Kettl, D. F. 1993. *Sharing Power: Public Governance and Private Markets.* Washington, DC: The Brookings Institution.

Kickert, W. J. M., E.-H. Klijn and J. F. M. Koppenjan (eds). 1997. *Managing Complex Networks: Strategies for the Public Sector.* London: Sage.

Kjær, A. M. 2004. *Governance*. Cambridge: Polity.

Klijn, E-H. 2008. 'Governance and governance networks in Europe: An assessment of 10 years of research on the theme'. *Public Management Review* 10: 505–525. doi.org/10.1080/14719030802263954.

Klijn, E.-H. and J. Koppenjan. 2015. *Governance Networks in the Public Sector. A Network Approach to Public Problem Solving, Policy making and Service Delivery.* Abingdon, Oxon: Routledge.

Koliba, C., J. W. Meek and A. Zia. 2011. *Governance Networks in Public Administration and Public Policy*. Boca Raton: CRC Press.

Kooiman, J. 1993. *Modern Governance*. London: Sage.

Lindquist, E. A., S. Vincent and J. Wanna (eds). 2013. *Putting Citizens First: Engagement in Policy and Service Delivery for the 21st Century*. Canberra: ANU E Press. doi.org/10.22459/PCF.08.2013.

Management Advisory Committee (MAC). 2004. *Connecting Government: Whole of Government Response to Australia's Priority Challenges*. Canberra: Australian Public Service Commission.

Marinetto, M. 2003. 'Governing beyond the centre: A critique of the Anglo-Governance school'. *Political Studies* 51: 592–608. doi.org/10.1111/1467-9248.00443.

Meier, K. J. and G. C. Hill. 2005. 'Bureaucracy in the twenty-first century'. In E. Ferlie, L. Lynn and C. Pollitt (eds) *The Oxford Handbook of Public Management*. Oxford: Oxford University Press. doi.org/10.1093/oxfordhb/9780199226443.003.0004.

Meier, K. J. and L. J. O'Toole. 2005. 'Managerial networking: Issues of measurement and research design'. *Administration & Society* 37: 523–541. doi.org/10.1177/0095399705277142.

Moore, M. 1995. *Creating Public Value: Strategic Management in Government*. Boston: Harvard University Press.

Morgan, G. 1993. *Images of Organisation*. London: Sage.

O'Faircheallaigh, C., J. Wanna and P. Weller. (1992) 1999. *Public Sector Management in Australia: New Challenges, New Directions*. Second edition. Melbourne: Macmillan.

Osborne, D. and T. Gaebler. 1992. *Reinventing Government: How the Entrepreneurial Spirit Is Transforming the Public Sector*. Reading: Addison-Wesley.

Osborne, S. P. 2010. 'Introduction. The (new) public governance: A suitable case for treatment'. In S. Osborne (ed.) *The New Public Governance: Emerging Perspectives on the Theory and Practice of Public Governance*. London and New York: Routledge and Taylor and Francis. doi.org/10.4324/9780203861684.

Peters, B. G. and J. Pierre. 2009. 'Governance approaches'. In A. Wiener and T. Diez (eds) *European Integration Theory*. Second edition. Oxford: Oxford University Press.

Pierre, J. and B. G. Peters. 2000. *Governance, Politics and the State*. Houndmills, Basingstoke: Macmillan.

Podger, A., J. Wanna, H. Chan, J. Ma and T.-T. Su . 2012. 'Putting the citizens at the centre: Making government more responsive'. *Australian Journal of Public Administration* 71(2): 101–110. doi.org/10.1111/j.1467-8500.2012.00773.x.

Pollitt, C. 1993. *Managerialism and the Public Services*. Second edition. Oxford: Blackwell.

Pollitt, C. and G. Bouckaert 2011. *Public Management Reform. A Comparative Analysis: New Public Management, Governance and The Neo-Weberian State*. Third edition. Oxford: Oxford University Press.

Pusey, M. 1991. *Economic Rationalism in Canberra: A Nation-Building State Changes Its Mind*. Sydney: Cambridge University Press.

Rhodes, R. A. W. 1997a. *Understanding Governance: Policy Networks, Governance, Reflexivity and Accountability*. Buckingham: Open University Press.

Rhodes, R. A. W. 1997b. 'From marketization to diplomacy: It's the mix that matters'. *Australian Journal of Public Administration* 56: 40–53. doi.org/10.1111/j.1467-8500.1997.tb01545.x.

Rhodes, R. A. W. 1998. 'Different roads to unfamiliar places: UK experience in comparative perspective'. *Australian Journal of Public Administration* 57(4): 19–31. doi.org/10.1111/j.1467-8500.1998.tb01558.x.

Rhodes, R. A. W. 2011. *Everyday Life in British Government*. Oxford: Oxford University Press.

Rhodes, R. A. W. 2016. 'Recovering the craft of public administration'. *Public Administration Review* 76(4): 638–647. doi.org/10.1111/puar.12504.

Rhodes, R. A. W. 2017a. *Network Governance and the Differentiated Polity: Selected Essays. Volume I.* Oxford: Oxford University Press. doi.org/10.1093/oso/9780198786108.001.0001.

Rhodes, R. A. W. 2017b. *Interpretive Political Science: Selected Essays. Volume II.* Oxford: Oxford University Press. doi.org/10.1093/oso/9780198786115. 001.0001.

Rhodes, R. A. W. (ed.). 2018. *Narrative Policy Analysis: Cases in Decentring Policy.* London: Palgrave Macmillan. doi.org/10.1007/978-3-319-76635-5.

Rhodes, R. A. W. and A. Tiernan. 2014. *The Gatekeepers.* Carlton: Melbourne University Press.

Rhodes, R. A. W. and J. Wanna. 2007. 'The limits to public value, or rescuing responsible government from the platonic guardians'. *Australian Journal of Public Administration* 66(4): 406–421. doi.org/10.1111/j.1467-8500.2007. 00553.x.

Rhodes, R. A. W. and J. Wanna. 2008. 'Stairways to Heaven: A reply to Alford'. *Australian Journal of Public Administration* 67: 367–370. doi.org/10.1111/ j.1467-8500.2008.00594.x.

Rhodes, R. A. W. and J. Wanna. 2009a. 'Bringing the politics back in'. *Public Administration* 87(2): 161–183. doi.org/10.1111/j.1467-9299.2009.01763.x.

Rhodes, R. A. W. and J. Wanna. 2009b. 'The executives'. In R. A. W. Rhodes (ed.) *The Australian Study of Politics.* Houndmills, Basingstoke: Palgrave Macmillan. doi.org/10.1057/9780230296848_9.

Rhodes, R. A. W., J. Wanna and P. Weller. 2008. 'Reinventing Westminster: How public executives reframe their world'. *Policy & Politics* 36(4): 461–479. doi.org/10.1332/030557308X313705.

Rhodes, R. A. W., J. Wanna and P. Weller. 2009. *Comparing Westminster.* Oxford: Oxford University Press. doi.org/10.1093/acprof:oso/9780199563494.001. 0001.

Salamon, L. M. (ed.). 2002. *The Tools of Government: A Guide to the New Governance.* Oxford: Oxford University Press.

Scharpf, F. W. 1997. *Games Real Actors Play. Actor-Centred Institutionalism in Policy Research.* Boulder: Westview Press.

Sillitoe, P. 2006. 'The search for relevance: A brief history of applied anthropology'. *History and Anthropology* 17: 1–19. doi.org/10.1080/02757200500501066.

Sørensen, E. and J. Torfing (eds). 2007. *Theories of Democratic Network Governance.* Houndmills, Basingstoke: Palgrave Macmillan. doi.org/10.1057/ 9780230625006.

Stoker, G. 2004. *Transforming Local Governance.* Houndmills, Basingstoke: Palgrave. doi.org/10.1007/978-0-230-21368-5.

Theakston, K. 2017. *William Armstrong and British Policy Making.* London: Palgrave. doi.org/10.1057/978-1-137-57159-5.

Torfing, J., B. G. Peters, J. Pierre and E. Sørensen. 2012. *Interactive Governance: Advancing the Paradigm.* Oxford: Oxford University Press. doi.org/10.1093/acprof:oso/9780199596751.001.0001.

Van Willigen, J. 2002. *Applied Anthropology: An Introduction.* Third edition. Westport: Bergin & Garvey.

Vohnsen, N. H. 2015. 'Street-level planning; The shifty nature of "local knowledge and practice"'. *Journal of Organizational Ethnography* 4: 147–161. doi.org/10.1108/JOE-09-2014-0032.

Vohnsen, N. H. 2017. *The Absurdity of Bureaucracy: How Implementation Works.* Manchester: Manchester University Press. doi.org/10.7228/manchester/9781526101341.001.0001.

Wagenaar, H. 2016. 'Extending interpretivism: Articulating the practice dimension in Bevir and Rhodes's differentiated polity model'. In N. Turnbull (ed.) *Interpreting Governance, High Politics, and Public Policy.* New York: Routledge.

Wanna, J. (ed.). 2007. *Improving Implementation: Organisational Change and Project Management.* Canberra: ANU E Press. doi.org/10.22459/II.02.2007.

Wanna, J. 2008. 'Collaborative government: Meanings, dimensions, drivers and outcomes'. In J. O'Flynn and J. Wanna (eds) *Collaborative Governance: A New Era of Public Policy in Australia?* Canberra: ANU E Press. doi.org/10.22459/CG.12.2008.01.

Wanna, J., J. Butcher and B. Freyens. 2010. *Policy in Action: The challenge of service delivery.* Sydney: UNSW Press.

Wittgenstein, L. (1953) 2009. *Philosophical Investigations.* Fourth edition. Edited by P. M. S. Hacker and J. Schulte. Oxford: Wiley-Blackwell.

Yanow, D. 2004. 'Translating local knowledge at organizational peripheries'. *British Journal of Management* 15: s9–s25. doi.org/10.1111/j.1467-8551.2004.t01-1-00403.x.

11

Chinese public administration developments and prospects: An Australian (and Hong Kong) perspective

Andrew Podger and Hon Chan[1]

Introduction

John Wanna has undertaken a number of comparative studies in his career, particularly on budget management (Wanna, Jensen and de Vries 2003, 2010; Wanna, Lindquist and de Vries 2015) and on 'Westminster' systems of government (Patapan, Wanna and Weller 2005; Rhodes, Wanna and Weller 2009). The budget management studies focus mainly on selected Organisation for Economic Cooperation and Development (OECD) countries though at least one includes China, and the 'Westminster' studies focus on former British dominions (and the UK).

Over the last decade and a half, Wanna has also become increasingly interested in China: the mainland People's Republic of China, the PRC's special zones of Hong Kong and Macau, and Taiwan. The main (but not sole) forum for this interest has been the annual workshops since 2011 of the Greater China Australia Dialogue on Public Administration, of which

1   This work was supported by the Ministry of Education of the Republic of Korea and the National Research Foundation of Korea (NRF-2017S1A3A2067636).

he and the authors of this paper are principals (along with professors Jun Ma, Tsai-tsu Su and Meili Niu). A body of work arising from these workshops and the network of scholars Wanna helped to develop was published in the *Australian Journal of Public Administration* (*AJPA*) while he was the editor, and in ANU Press's Australia and New Zealand School of Government (ANZSOG) series of books, which Wanna has been responsible for as ANZSOG's research director. Wanna has also supervised PhD candidates from across Asia, and been involved in teaching and training Asian government officials, particularly in Taiwan.

There is an art in addressing the challenges of comparative research and teaching public administration and financial management for people working in very different institutional arrangements and with very different cultures and histories. Even in his 'Westminster' work, where there might seem considerable commonality of concepts derived from shared history, Wanna's work highlights just how far countries' systems have diverged, the UK itself evolving its system so significantly as to raise questions as to whether it still models some of the attributes most often associated with the term 'Westminster' (e.g. the role of cabinet). The British settlement dominions (Australia, Canada and New Zealand) have also diverged considerably, while the other former British colonies have more radically adapted 'Westminster' traditions in light of their own indigenous cultures and histories.

The art in comparative research is to identify theoretical concepts and/or challenges that are sufficiently relevant across the countries being compared, while also sufficiently specific, to allow meaningful comparisons to be made of each country's systems and practices. It also requires great care in describing each country's arrangements: as Rudolph Klein emphasised about cross-border learning, it is essential to 'learn about' before 'learning from' (Klein 2009).

Examining public administration in the PRC (referred to as 'China' below) from an Australian perspective is particularly problematic given the scale of the differences, not only in our respective political institutional arrangements but in our cultures, histories, geography, population size and wealth.

China and Australia

As Podger and Yan highlight, the contexts in which public administration operates in China and Australia are fundamentally different (Podger and Yan 2013). Perhaps the only contextual similarity is their geographic size, both being among the six largest countries in the world, but even in terms of geography it is important to note that China is full of mountains and rivers and has multiple borders while Australia is flat and mostly dry and is an island continent with no land borders. While Australia's Indigenous history is ancient, the dominant European settlement is relatively recent and many people still debate Australia's identity; China has an ancient history of which it is proud and there is virtually no debate about its identity. Australia's culture today is mostly of European origin while China's is mostly of Han origin; Australia's population is remarkably homogeneous across its states and territories despite being increasingly multicultural, while China is quite heterogeneous with multiple languages and dialects and widely differing incomes and wealth across and within its provinces; Australia is mainly Christian-secular while China is officially non-religious but with strong influences from Confucianism, Buddhism and Taoism; most importantly, Australia's population has just surpassed 25 million, while China's is approaching 1,400 million. Australia is among the more wealthy countries in the world while China, despite its rapid economic growth, has average income per capita around one-quarter of Australia's (on a purchasing power parity basis).

These and other contextual features impact public administration in the two countries in many ways. One of the significant impacts is the different emphases on individual and collective rights, Australia giving priority to individual rights and the rule of law, derived from its Christian and Anglo-Saxon heritage, while China (like many Asian countries) gives priority to harmony, filial piety and personal relationships and obligations (and the rule of morality), derived from Confucian, Buddhist and Taoist philosophies.

China of course is also a country in transition, from a command economy with an inward focus to a more market-based, globalised economy, its public administration also undergoing transformation as it adjusts to the requirements of a more open market economy. Its public administration arrangements are therefore not as easy to describe as Australia's, being more of a 'moving target'; Australia has a more mature framework, with clearer understanding of the respective roles of the market, government and civil society, and firmly embedded institutional structures. It is easier to describe what China has been moving away from than to describe how it operates today or where it might be heading in the future.

It is also difficult to identify concepts that have sufficiently common meanings to allow valid comparisons to be made of practice in the two countries. One of the authors, Podger, recalls discussions at various seminars as he and Yan presented drafts of their 2013 paper, a key concern expressed by some Chinese scholars being the danger of trying 'to fit (Chinese) round poles into (Western) square holes'. The criticism led to an important shift in the paper's approach and title, from suggesting some convergence in public administration to focusing on 'different worlds but similar challenges' (a shift suggested by Wanna and this paper's co-author, Chan). This paper also uses 'common challenges' as a useful means for comparing public administration practice.

Yet it is important also to recognise two contrasting truths about China's transition. Firstly, that its shift to a more market-based economy *has* led to a series of political reforms that resonate to some degree with Western experience and have delivered considerable personal freedoms as well as enhanced standards of living. There is more transparency in government, if not the formal approaches to accountability that apply in Western democracies; the social responsibilities of government are clearer; and a better informed and mobile population is able to place more pressure on government. Secondly, however, despite much conventional wisdom, there is *no basis* to assume that economic growth through a more market-oriented approach will necessarily cause a shift from China's one-party state authoritarianism to a Western-style, multi-party democracy.

This paper explores key aspects of China's shifting approach to public administration, drawing in part on the Dialogue workshops held since 2011 and research by the Dialogue's network of scholars. Recognising the dangers outlined above, it includes some comparisons with Australia's systems and practices, focusing on the following key issues:

- China's party system and approach towards accountability
- China's bureaucratic machinery and approach towards merit and performance management
- China's intergovernmental arrangements and approach towards subsidiarity and responsiveness.

We conclude with some discussion about the challenges and prospects for China under President Xi Jinping.

China's party system and accountability

Article 36 of the 2018 amended *Constitution of the People's Republic of China* for the first time has written the phrases 'Communist Party of China (CCP)' – and its 'leadership' – into the main body of the Constitution. In the previous version of the Constitution, the party is only mentioned in the Preamble. While people in China would not say that the Preamble has no legal force, the reference to the party now in the body of the Constitution confirms the indisputable reality of the party's leadership in China. Article 36 now reads: 'The socialist system is the basic system of the People's Republic of China. The defining feature of socialism with Chinese characteristics is the leadership of the Communist Party of China'. Like the 2006 Civil Service Law, the Constitution gives the principle of party control of cadres (cadres and civil servants are the same body under the 2006 Civil Service Law) the requisite state and legal mandate, which has turned the CCP into a political institution that has become the source of both civil service empowerment and control. Some will subscribe to the view that China is expanding its political control to ensure greater leverage over the bureaucracy. In that regard, China has seemingly displayed a tendency partly in line with the global trend, including in Australia.

As a one-party state, China's institutions reflect that the party, together with the people's congresses, the people's political consultative conferences and the procuratorial organisations, constitute the principal and indispensable parts of an integrated political system. The widespread references to the party's leadership and the status and usefulness of its organisation in many laws, including the 2006 Civil Service Law and now the amended 2018 Constitution, may simply reflect a natural outcome to better fit the legal description with facts. They acknowledge and underscore the leading role of the party and its organisational divisions at various levels in cadre personnel management (Chan 2007, 391).

Through amending the Constitution, the guiding thought behind the Chinese leadership is to assert that integration between politics and administration is a unique feature (expressed by the term 'Chinese characteristics'), which contradicts some long-held assumptions with regard to the civil service and its relationship with politics in Western democracies (going back to the Northcote-Trevelyan Report in the UK in the 1850s and Woodrow Wilson's lecture in the US in the 1880s [Podger 2017]). Chinese leaders do not see the fusion of politics and administration as a threat to or being incompatible with a modern, permanent and competent bureaucracy. Instead, this landmark combination of politics and administration is considered a positive step towards developing a stable, adaptable, highly competent, rule-based, and legitimacy-enhancing administration (Chan 2016).

The party and the civil service

The CCP has adjusted itself to meet with the needs of its changing society in the last two decades or so. In order to establish regular adjustments in response to societal change and to guard against corruption and irregularity in its cadre personnel management system, Chinese leaders have carried out two sets of activities since 1997. The first was internal competition for posting cadres, and the second was open recruitment. Three parallel sets of regulations and laws have been introduced comprising the cadre examination syllabus and questions (2000), public announcement of employment decisions (2000), and appointment and probation arrangements (2001). All these measures were intended to build administrative capacity and to inculcate 'vitality' and 'liveliness' into the cadre personnel management system. Because politics is still taking centre stage, China has undertaken more limited administrative rationalisation. This needs to be understood within China's peculiar political configurations. Administrative capacity-building can be understood as efforts geared towards improving the operational efficiency of the administrative offices of party, state and other units in other sectors in society and, at the same time, retaining political authority over all sectors (Chan 2003).

Another major policy measure introduced by the CCP was to establish a party-led, merit-based talent management system in an effort to address China's talent deficit in the reform era. Since the opening up of China to the West in 1978, Chinese leaders have striven to develop a talent market that places more emphasis on merit, rather than relying solely on political loyalty. The market reform that began in the late 1970s has substantially reshaped state–market relations in China. Because the traditional nomenklatura no longer extends to the workforce in the private sector, the rising expansion of the private sector workforce has prompted the party to adjust its own governance mechanism. More fundamentally, the need for talents – expertise – in the rapidly developing economy of China is increasingly pressing. In response to these developments and pressures, the CCP began to look for ways to attract new talents into the cadre personnel management system. In September 1995, CCP leaders started to consider defining talents more broadly under the stance of two fundamental shifts in Chinese society: a shift from a planned economy into a socialist market economy, and a shift from extensive economic growth to intensive economic growth. The crux of the issue was a mismatch between its market-oriented economic system and its HRM (human resources management) system.

As of today, talent is categorised into two groups: cadre talent (in Chinese terminology, talent within the system, or those who are managed according to the traditional nomenklatura) and non-cadre talent (talent outside the system). With the introduction of these categories, in line with the system of 'party controlling cadres', a new system began to take shape in the early 2000s: the system of 'party management of experts'. The two systems differ in terms of the role of the party's organisation departments and the ways in which they manage talent (Chen et al. 2015).

'Social accountability'

In any comparative study, one intriguing issue is how accountability operates and how it might be enhanced. This issue is particularly interesting in relation to China. Ma (2009 and 2012) has addressed it directly, arguing that, despite the absence of competitive elections, society itself is a powerful force for enhancing accountability in China. He referred to the impact of China's 1999 budgetary reforms, which facilitated a greater role for peoples' congresses in oversight of government financial management and introduced a degree of 'horizontal accountability' as well as internal 'bureaucratic accountability', preconditions for more 'citizen participatory budgeting' or 'social accountability' (Ma 2009). Tsai (2007) made a similar argument by drawing attention to the interactions between formal and informal institutions, social structures and state structures, and social boundaries and political boundaries in ways that improve our understanding of governmental performance and public goods provision. Both scholars make a case that, when state–society is in a crisis (e.g. rampant corruption or serious invasion of citizen rights), society may rise up to protect itself. In a way, the CCP understands this and the seriousness of potential social problems. It is in the interest of the CCP to support some forms of social action to ameliorate state–society relationships. Ma's papers showed that two forms of activities, either society-led action or state-led, take place simultaneously. In that regard, 'social accountabilities' seem to have provided a channel for citizens and/or civil society (however defined in China) organisations, formerly excluded from political participation, to engage in the process of governing. Particularly noteworthy is the growing importance of non-government organisations (NGOs). The case of Nu River in Yunnan Province was described by Ma as a turning point in China's policymaking, in that China has begun to witness an increase in the policy influence of environmental NGOs. Citizens and NGOs have begun to impose a form of societal control over the government, and the latter has become more accountable and more responsive to citizens' needs (Ma 2012, 119–120).

This development is still emerging. The growth in the number of NGOs in China has continued exponentially since Ma's papers, and the former 'dual registration' system that required NGOs to be tied to an associated ministry has been substantially relaxed. Some NGOs are now engaged by government to deliver public services and to fill capability gaps within government (Shen and Yu 2016). There remain sensitivities about NGOs' advocacy activities, however, and, most recently, pressure has been placed on NGOs to establish CCP branches within their organisations (Shen, Yu and Zhou 2020).

Party, government and the market

Since the opening of China to the West, China-watchers often raise the question of how an authoritarian regime can sustain itself in the global market. A common assumption is that, without liberating Chinese companies from bureaucratic control, China's overall economy is likely to be constrained and less effective (Koppell 2007). On the other hand, Stent (2017) argues that this line of thought is ungrounded and that continued economic growth is only partly reliant on removing CCP involvement in commercial activities, and is mainly contingent on the performance of other aspects of China's growing economy.

Since the founding of the PRC, there has been a strong tie between politics and business. The five central nomenklatura processes (disseminated in 1955, 1980, 1984, 1990 and 1998, respectively) consistently featured such a tie. In 1993, Chinese leaders had differentiated its public sector into three types – state organs, social institutions and enterprises. Because the leadership groups of all state-owned enterprises (SOEs) are party members, they continue to be managed by the party body. The policy measure of retaining control of the large (enterprises) while releasing the small (enterprises), adopted since the 15th Party Congress, in fact unveiled the attempt by Chinese leaders to strike a balance between political primacy and economic flexibility (Chan 2004; Song 2018).

Chan and Rosenbloom (2010) argue that Chinese public enterprises of fundamental and strategic importance to national security and economic livelihoods have always been part of the party-controlled compounds. CCP has shown no intention to privatise them in domestic and international markets or to reduce leverage over them. In making a comparison between Chinese and American public enterprises, they note that countries all over the world have adopted different public enterprise reforms with different plans and objectives. These are pursued in each country's specific political and ideological contexts and reflect the embedded relationships between public enterprises and the wider political institutions in each country. Notwithstanding the wide variations in countries' approaches to SOEs, however, including across Western market economies, a common reform theme is to improve efficiency whether the SOEs stay in public ownership or not. This is particularly important for those SOEs involved in international trade and subject to international laws and conventions. That so far is not imminent in China.

Chinese public enterprise reform is primarily a reflection of local economic nationalism, rather than efficiency alone. What Chinese leaders are trying to do is to maximise China's position in the international economic order and become strong (but not necessarily competitive, at least in the short term), especially in terms of meeting the urgent need for resources to fuel and sustain China's economic growth, through its main strategies to date of exports and investment. In the absence of a pluralist democracy in China, the pursuit of economic growth and prosperity is seen as an effective way to maintain its legitimacy. The strong tie between politics and business is also important to the entire governance mechanism at this point in China's transition, which has historically relied upon SOE revenues and assets to fund policy objectives such as social security, free education and affordable health care and the government's economic and administrative bureaucracies, and to avoid the costs of policy-induced redundant workforces. While more efficient SOEs combined with further tax reform might, in time, lead to greater increases in productivity along with a new, more sustainable revenue base, the transaction costs and transitional risks would be significant. China's rapid economic growth does not necessarily at this stage require making China's SOEs fully competitive in global markets and, unlike in the US, there is no political opposition to extensive government involvement in the economy. In China, many 'backbone' and 'key' public enterprises, which are considered important to the lifeline of the Chinese economy, are likely to remain under strict nomenklatura control.

On the flip side of the policy of CCP control of large enterprises, there is a need to clarify the policy of releasing small enterprises. It is difficult to spell out this policy, as the general idea is not to leave all small SOEs unattended. The CCP does not want to define strictly what constitutes a large or a small SOE. A backbone or key SOE that is not important to the central government could be a backbone or key enterprise essential to a local government. The CCP wants to strategise its resources to enable backbone or key enterprises to corporatise and be publicly listed both in domestic and global markets. The orientation of the policy of releasing the small enterprises hence could be understood as measures to enable enterprises to meet their challenges on their terms under the auspices of the respective party body. The current policy of grasping the large while releasing the small enterprises is not based on an intention to liberate Chinese enterprises from party-state bureaucratic control.

China's bureaucratic machinery

China's continued blurring of politics and administration through the overriding role of the CCP discussed above is also reflected in its approaches to personnel management in the public sector, its concept of 'merit' and its performance management system. This is notwithstanding efforts made over the last four decades to examine the challenges and problems of the cadre personnel management system in China. The promulgation of the 1993 Provisional Regulations of Civil Servants and the 2016 Civil Service Law clearly manifests different approaches taken by Chinese leaders in striking a balance between politics and administration. Core to this endeavour is the question of how far measures might be taken to reduce the direct power and authority of the CCP, such that a state civil service can function fully and effectively.

A central issue here is the future of the rank-in-person approach in the cadre personnel management system, adopted since the founding of the nation. The rank-in-person approach, also known as the rank classification system, is a system in which every cadre is assigned a rank (instead of a particular job) and attached to a pertinent party committee. This contrasts with the rank-in-job approach, also known as the post-classification system, in which HRM is conceived as a set of jobs while a prospective employee is treated as a set of skills, knowledge and abilities that may or may not fit a particular job. Instead, a rank-in-person approach conceives HRM as a collection of people. Under the system, rank directly determines a cadre's status, fringe benefits and other monetary and political entitlements. This approach appears to support a management method that associates one's political orientation, attachment, affiliation and other related attributes to a job. A rank-in-person approach is designed chiefly to manage people but not to manage a job. When a cadre has achieved a certain rank, s/he will be locked into and controlled by respective nomenklatura. This approach clearly integrates politics and administration in enshrining the importance of political and other related attributes in personnel management.

It cannot be denied that this rank-in-person approach has become the target of criticisms. But one needs to put the background in perspective. Chinese leaders do not contemplate a Weberian type of bureaucracy. Politics, instead of administrative rationality, always takes command in China. It seems that this approach is presently able to build strong cohesion of leadership groups at each level of administration. In that light, the approach remains instrumental to any attempt to theorise how accountability is being shaped in China (Chan and Su 2009).

In today's Chinese bureaucracy, cadres are divided into two types – ordinary and leading cadres. Respective civil service divisions manage respective ordinary cadres and the respective organisation departments manage respective leading cadres. In this way, the cadre personnel management system for leading cadres is theoretically tasked with the accomplishment of political accountability. Cadre personnel management for ordinary cadres is targeted more at the fulfillment of organisational and program objectives, or 'social accountability'. One caveat that must be made here is that in every level of administration and in every agency, 'leading cadre' is a relative term. An ordinary cadre in a central ministry (such as bureau-level official) may be a leading cadre in a lower-level administration. At a grassroots organisation level of administration (such as village or street unit), an office-level official is a leading cadre, though an office-level official is by default, and status, a non-leading cadre.

Performance management and the concept of 'merit'

An intriguing issue may be raised: is it possible to embrace a merit principle in personnel management in China given the blurring of politics and administration? This was a key focus of the Dialogue's 2013 workshop (Podger and Chan 2015) where it was noted that the use of examinations to enter the civil service goes back far longer in China than in the West. In recent decades, China has drawn upon and adapted new public management's emphasis on performance management to refine its cadre personnel management system. The system now sets a range of performance items, targets and indicators for officials and organisations at different levels of administration and uses all these for selection, appointment and promotion purposes. Many are 'mission-based' including economic targets (e.g. the total amount of industrial output, per capita annual net income of peasants) and public service targets (e.g. the percentage of rural residents vaccinated against infectious diseases). The system also sets a range of 'non-mission-based' targets, some of which would be regarded as 'political' in Australia or elsewhere. Three types of such targets are in place: (1) anti-corruption targets (e.g. ensuring that expenditures on items like meals and entertainment are less than the amount spent in the previous year), (2) social solidarity targets (e.g. implementing family planning policies, limiting the number of mass petitions to the central government), and (3) explicit political targets (e.g. conducting ideological indoctrination through regular study sessions). While sometimes it is very difficult to differentiate mission- and non-mission-based targets, the proliferation of different types of performance items, targets and indicators in China provides evidence of continuing to embrace a merit principle in personnel management in China. It is nonetheless a very different concept of merit to that used, for example, for the Australian Public Service. There, 'political' factors have no direct bearing (though skills in communications and relationship management may well be relevant) and a range of administrative skills and capabilities as well as proven performance is used to identify the best candidate for a position.

The focus on rank-in-person rather than rank-in-job, and the emphasis on individual-based performance within the personnel management system, has affected China's adoption of performance management across government. While an increasing proportion of the targets, whether mission-based or non-mission-based, relate to economic or social or environmental outcomes, they have tended to date to be government-wide rather than organisation- or program-specific. Progress on organisational and program performance has been slow, though examples exist (e.g. Niu 2018; Ye and Ni 2016). Nonetheless, the National Development and Reform Commission has been promoting more systematic performance monitoring and evaluation and, as discussed below, China has been at the forefront of experimentation and evaluation to inform national policy development.

As in many OECD countries (including Australia) and some East Asian countries, China is developing sets of quantified targets with open reporting on achievements across a range of economic, social and environmental fields that offer increased capacity for social accountability, and an increased oversight role for people's congresses. With respect to work safety, for example, Chinese officials have promulgated annual performance indicators level by level down the bureaucracy in work safety. The establishment of fatality indicators to local governments is characterised by three features: (1) control by precise numbers, (2) control by zones and (3) control by hierarchical accountability. In a way, this system requires compliance from all levels of government but at the same time gives flexibility for the goalposts to be accomplished (Chan and Gao 2012). As discussed below, such arrangements involve a mix of vertical performance contracts between levels of government and horizontal reporting and related social accountability.

Intergovernmental relations

China's population and geographic size demands a multi-level system of government, notwithstanding its authoritarian party-state approach. It has forever been such, as explained in an ancient Cantonese saying: 'Mountains are high and the Emperor is far away'.

As discussed at the Dialogue workshop held in Canberra in 2012, China adopts a unitary system with decentralised administration through five layers of government, but with only the central level having 'sovereignty', as implied in federal systems of government (see the symposium of papers in *AJPA* Volume 72, Issue 3, 2013). Each national ministry is replicated down each level of government with strong vertical controls, while, at each level, there are also horizontal structures to ensure coordination and responsiveness to local circumstances. Nonetheless, managing this decentralised system involves similar challenges to those faced by federations such as Australia's: the degree of autonomy allowed to (or exercised by) different levels of government, the distribution of financial powers, both vertically and horizontally, the respective roles and responsibilities at different levels, and accountability both between levels of government and to the public. Australia's experience demonstrates that success requires more than institutional stability; it also requires adaptability, responsiveness, accountability, trust and the wellbeing of the citizens being served.

The Dialogue workshop held in Hangzhou in 2014, which focused on decentralisation, explored some of the principles that may guide judgement on when devolved or decentralised administration is likely to be most efficient and effective. The principles may be grouped under three headings: subsidiarity, differentiation and experimentation, along with local capabilities (Woods and Wanna 2014). These are interdependent, the success of subsidiarity (with local authority and local provision) being dependent upon sufficient local capabilities, and with differentiation and experimentation being reliant on a degree of autonomy and local capabilities.

China faces added challenges relating to its transition from a command economy to a market economy (with some socialist characteristics). This has required redefinition of the role of government, and consequential changes to the relationships among the different levels of government.

Intergovernmental finances

The first major fiscal reform came with the 1994 tax reforms. While replacing the complex old Soviet system, separating SOE arrangements from government revenues and repairing China's fiscal decline since the reform era began (Wong 2018a and 2018b), these reforms had an enormous impact on intergovernmental financial relations. The introduction of the new system of taxes, including a national value-added tax, greatly increased the revenues of the national government, beyond that needed for its own expenditures, giving the centre a lot more power and allowing the national government to transfer some revenues to sub-national governments; in so doing, the national government was also able to take steps towards horizontal fiscal equity, addressing some of the variations in revenue-raising capacity among the provinces and in their development needs, and also to place conditions on some of the transfers. At the same time, market-based reforms were increasing public expenditure pressures most on local governments, as the old collectives disappeared along with the social protections they provided, and as SOEs were being commercialised.

Table 11.1 illustrates the shifts in revenue and expenditure levels and shares between the central government and local (or sub-national) governments over the reform era.

Table 11.1. Government revenues and expenditures for selected years in the reform era

Year	Revenues			Expenditures		
	Total billion RMB (%)	Central government billion RMB (%)	Local government billion RMB (%)	Total billion RMB (%)	Central government billion RMB (%)	Local government billion RMB (%)
1978	113.2 (100%)	17.6 (16%)	95.6 (84%)	112.2 (100%)	53.2 (48%)	59.0 (52%)
1993	434.9 (100%)	95.8 (22%)	339.1 (78%)	464.2 (100%)	131.2 (28%)	333.0 (72%)
1995	624.2 (100%)	325.7 (52%)	298.6 (48%)	682.4 (100%)	199.5 (29%)	482.8 (71%)
2016	15,960.5 (100%)	7,236.6 (45%)	8,723.9 (55%)	18,775.5 (100%)	2,740.4 (15%)	16,035.1 (85%)
2018	18,336.0 (100%)	8,617.9 (47%)	9,718.1 (53%)	22,090.4 (100%)	3,313.6 (15%)	18,776.8 (85%)

Source: National Bureau of Statistics of China 2019.

Central government's share of expenditure has continued to trend downwards, while its share of the revenues sharply increased with the 1994 reforms (this share falling a little in more recent years).

Not readily apparent from Table 11.1 is that the transfers to sub-national governments have not been nearly sufficient to allow them to meet their expenditure requirements without resort to (hidden) debts and unsustainable 'extra-budgetary revenues' particularly from land sales. The debts and implicit liabilities have remained a serious concern for future sustainable economic growth, even though the debts are mostly owed to domestic lenders (Ma 2012; Wong 2018a, 2018b).

A series of public financial management (PFM) reforms were pursued from the late 1990s, including changes to budget preparation and classification and Treasury management, strengthening of procurement processes and the implementation of new fiscal information systems (Wong 2009). These reforms involved the consolidation of all government revenues and expenditures and (at least in theory) the outlawing of unauthorised debt. They also strengthened the role of the National People's Congress (the legislature).

While strong economic growth fuelled overall revenues, financial pressures on sub-national governments (some more than others) continued to increase as the party leadership from 2004 looked to spread the gains of economic growth to support a 'harmonious society', addressing mounting social issues such as social security, health insurance and access to education, and growing environmental concerns. Financial responsibility for these measures has fallen mainly on local governments.

More recent PFM reforms, particularly under the 2014 Budget Law, try to address concerns about hidden debts and unsustainable extra-budgetary revenues, and to regain oversight of fiscal resources, ensure greater transparency and improve accountability. The Law also addressed intergovernmental transfers, specifying principles and objectives and emphasising the need for regular appraisals (Wong 2018a). Rather than outlaw local government debt, the new Budget Law is a 'call to "open the front door, lock the back door and build walls around it"' (Wong 2018a, 73), by stipulating that local governments must report on the purpose, size and mode of debt and specify the mechanisms of supervision and legal liabilities. As Wong highlights, implementation of the new round of reforms presents major challenges because local governments have become reliant on their off-budget revenue sources and may need to radically reduce investments to meet the new requirements; they also face capability deficits for implementing the new comprehensive financial reporting system.

Roles and responsibilities

Associated with these moves to clarify and make transparent governmental financial arrangements at all levels, and intergovernmental financial relationships, is the need for clarification of respective roles and responsibilities, and the degree of local government autonomy China will allow in its unitary system. There have been no moves to distinguish responsibilities in terms of different policy functions, but provinces and lower levels of government have varying degrees of freedom in implementing the policies set by the national government.

Those policies also allow considerable differentiation reflecting differences in provincial economic development and financial capacity. From the beginning of the reform era, the national government has also actively promoted experimentation and piloting of reforms, allowing some provinces to move ahead of others and drawing on their experience in setting and refining subsequent national policies. Decentralisation, and localised policy innovation, as well as the market reforms themselves, would seem to have been behind China's remarkable economic success including the lifting of so many people out of poverty.

Health insurance example

Proactive experimentation has continued as a strategy for developing and reviewing national policies, including the 'harmonious society' policies of the last decade to improve social and environmental wellbeing and spread the benefits of economic success. Developments in health insurance provide an interesting example not only of experimentation but also of the continuing constraints arising from China's past command economy and its social control arrangements. This 'path dependency' continues to shape China's approach not only to healthcare and health insurance but also to its system of decentralised government in a unitary state.

Health systems are large and complex, and their design is inevitably contextually shaped. In China's case, the design has to date been greatly influenced by its longstanding household registration system (*hukou*) that determines the local government to which each person is related and that in turn is responsible for providing relevant services and benefits. Under *hukou*, each person is tied to his or her household, which is registered with a village government (the lowest level of government). As a result of urbanisation, huge numbers of people now living in one place remain registered in another. The sending jurisdiction continues to have formal responsibility for their public services, but may be unable to provide them, while the receiving jurisdiction may lack the authority and financial resources to provide the services. This situation is made more complex because some families choose to have split arrangements, some members working in the cities and others staying in their rural villages dependent on remittances sent home, and some also are only resident in the cities while work is available.

In many respects, health care deteriorated in the first decades of economic reform as villages could no longer rely on collectives to provide services, and SOEs also cut back support for current and former employees' health and social security. Local health services began to rely on profits from pharmaceutical sales and other out-of-pocket payments by patients, reducing access to affordable care and undermining the quality of care.

The first steps towards a national health insurance system were taken in the 1990s with the establishment of the Urban Employees Basic Medical Insurance (UEBMI) scheme, part of a new approach to social security. It was managed by provincial and city governments through the Ministry of Labour and Social Security (MLSS), later the Ministry of Human Resources and Social Security (MoHRSS), reimbursing urban employees for a substantial part of the costs of health care through approved hospitals. In practice, however, only around 25 per cent of migrant workers were ever covered by this scheme (Müller 2016).

In 2002, a New Rural Cooperative Medical System (NCRMS) was introduced, managed at the county level through the Ministry of Health, providing reimbursements for costs at county hospitals and village health centres, with funding support via intergovernmental transfers. By 2013, 99 per cent of the rural population was covered (Müller 2016) but it became apparent much earlier that there remained major gaps in real access to healthcare services by migrant workers and their families. Sending jurisdictions received higher-level government transfers for those registered with them, but no incentive to ensure access to services in their new location, while receiving jurisdictions did not receive the relevant transfers and had no financial incentive to offer support.

In 2007, a new Urban Residents Basic Medical Insurance (URBMI) scheme was introduced aimed at city residents not covered by UEBMI, who could choose to be covered by the NCRMS or the new scheme, which provided assistance for those visiting hospitals in the cities. Like UEBMI, URBMI was managed through the MLSS (now the MoHRSS). While few have taken up membership of this third scheme, a series of experiments has been undertaken to find a way to ensure more complete coverage and access to health services (Müller 2016). These include experiments involving:

- extending 'approved services' that attract NCRMS benefits, including particular hospitals in cities with numbers of migrant workers from the relevant counties
- delegating NCRMS administration to urban social insurance managers, or transferring URBMI management to the Ministry of Health, which was responsible for NCRMS
- pooling of city-level funding across NCRMS and the new URBMI
- merging of schemes across counties and even provinces.

From 2013, all three schemes have come under the responsibility of MoHRSS, facilitating greater interoperability or mergers and more complete coverage, but problems still remain particularly for migrants who have crossed provincial boundaries. The most recent reforms are aimed to provide urban registration by 2020 for around 100 million migrant workers now registered with rural villages.

Different context, similar challenges

This example illustrates aspects of China's unique approach to intergovernmental relations when addressing challenges common to other countries with tiers of government. As in Australia, the intergovernmental financing arrangements require substantial revenue transfers to ensure capacity to fund access to affordable health care, with higher transfers to poorer provinces (and counties in China's case) to achieve a degree of horizontal equity. China's unitary system involves greater shared responsibility across tiers of government for health insurance and health services delivery, with the centre providing the policy framework and local governments the insurance management (increasingly at the provincial level) and service delivery (increasingly at the city and county levels).

The example also illustrates China's considered, almost systematic, approach to developing, testing and adapting high-level policies through differentiation and experimentation, allowing a considerable degree of local autonomy in applying and adapting central policies. There remain significant legacy issues from China's former command economy and population control arrangements that present additional challenges and will take many more years of reform to settle. And there are significant capability issues to address to ensure effective management of both financing and delivery (as Wong [2018a] has emphasised, this is true more generally about implementation of China's PFM reforms).

Other examples discussed at various Dialogue workshops, such as environmental management (Meng, Chen and Yeophantong 2020), illustrate the ongoing tensions between vertical and horizontal management in China's decentralised arrangements, and the ongoing cycles of local autonomy, experimentation and firm top-down policy direction under China's authoritarian government structure. They also highlight the challenges of local capability and the increasing importance of forms of accountability to local people including through local peoples' congresses. Informal processes (such as 'small leading groups' [Yan and

Wu 2020]) as well as formal institutional arrangements provide means for horizontal management at local levels. And to enhance local capability, there is increasing use of external support from civil society and academia (Zhao 2018; Shen and Yu 2016) though there are also moves to increase party involvement in NGOs (Shen, Yu and Zhou 2020).

Given China's size, and its huge transition agenda constrained by legacies such as its historic rural/urban divide, its intergovernmental arrangements are understandably complex and fluid. It has some way to go to achieve institutional stability with reasonably clear financial arrangements and roles and responsibilities, but it has demonstrated that decentralisation and systematic experimentation can achieve considerable economic and social success. There remain considerable challenges regarding local capabilities, and the basic authoritarian structure of government continues to give emphasis to upwards accountability over downwards accountability to the people.

Challenges and prospects in the Xi era

China's 'socialist market economy' has always embraced a dilemma – some would even suggest an oxymoron. How far towards a free market economy is China's leadership prepared to go?

The shift from a command economy has been profound and has delivered extraordinary success including the relief from poverty of hundreds of millions of people and personal freedoms unheard of in the Mao era. It has also required fundamental reform to China's political system, as the role of government has changed to take over social responsibilities previously met by collectives, party and state agencies and SOEs; to facilitate the emerging market; and to address its inevitable failures and limitations through regulation, the provision of public goods and appropriate macroeconomic settings to ensure a degree of stability. The scale of the task is difficult for outsiders to grasp, and China's leadership has been highly conscious of the risks involved. Inevitably there have been swings in the pace of reform, rapid change followed by consolidation (sometimes a reversal) followed by new waves of reform.

China is still in transition, with many agreed reforms still in the long process of implementation and with further reforms probably inevitable. Challenges of accountability, public sector capability and performance and intergovernmental relations remain, some of these not dissimilar to the challenges Australia continues to face. Some of the measures being taken to address them may superficially appear also to be similar to those on the agenda in Australia but, as explained here, there is no reason to expect China's reforms will lead to a political system remotely similar to Australia's or that of any other Western democracy.

Questions certainly remain about President Xi Jinping's leadership and reform intentions. He would seem to be going further than just ensuring the Constitution and legal system reflect existing reality about CCP's overall control, to be strengthening that control over the civil service, public enterprises, academia and the expanding civil society (Podger 2019; J. Garnault 2018). In addition, he has taken a stronger nationalist perspective both within China and in international relations, as signified, for example, through the Belt and Road Initiative (Cheng 2018). At the same time, he is continuing to pursue reforms aimed at enhancing capability and professionalism within the public sector, and to talk about further economic reform including increased support for free trade and the international order regulated by the World Trade Organization (Cheng 2018). He has also surrounded himself with experts with strong free market credentials (Zhang 2017).

These developments under Xi highlight the dilemma China continues to face. The strengthening of CCP control and the nationalistic approach that seems apparent are likely to constrain the further economic reforms needed for China to move on to the next stage of economic prosperity. They may also constrain both domestic pressures for improved social protection and personal freedoms and also international goodwill about China's global leadership intentions (J. Garnault 2018; R. Garnault 2018; Paulson 2018).

But it is equally important not to misunderstand the scope for further productivity improvement and increased living standards in China within its particular framework, nor the scope for improving accountability, capability and performance notwithstanding firm CCP control. The dilemma many outside observers see need not come to a head for a long time, and even then we should not expect that the balance of government and market and civil society that is chosen will look like any of the models we see across the West.

References

Chan, H. S. 2003. 'The civil service under one country, two systems: The cases of Hong Kong and the People's Republic of China'. *Public Administration Review* 63(July/August): 405–417. doi.org/10.1111/1540-6210.00304.

Chan, H. S. 2004. 'Cadre personnel management in China: The *nomenklatura* system, 1990–1998'. *The China Quarterly* 179(September): 703–734. doi.org/10.1017/S0305741004000554.

Chan, H. S. 2007. 'Civil service law in the People's Republic of China: A return to cadre personnel management'. *Public Administration Review* (May/June): 383–398. doi.org/10.1111/j.1540-6210.2007.00722.x.

Chan, H. S. 2016. 'The making of Chinese civil service law: Ideals, technicalities, and realities'. *American Review of Public Administration* 46(4): 379–398. doi.org/10.1177/0275074016634877.

Chan, H. S. and J. Gao. 2012. 'Death versus GDP! Decoding the fatality indicators on work safety regulation in post-Deng China'. *The China Quarterly* 210(June): 355–377.

Chan, H. S. and D. H. Rosenbloom. 2010. 'Public enterprise reforms in the US and the People's Republic of China: A drift towards constitutionalization and departmentalization of enterprise management'. *The Journal of Institution of Public Enterprises* 33(1–2): 133.

Chan, H. S. and T.-T. Su. 2009. 'Accountability and public governance in Greater China'. *Australian Journal of Public Administration* 68(S1): S1–S4. doi.org/10.1111/j.1467-8500.2009.00618.x.

Chen, L., H. Chan, J. Gao and J. Yu. 2015. 'Party management of talent: Building a party-led, merit-based talent market in China'. *Australian Journal of Public Administration* 74(3): 298–311. doi.org/10.1111/1467-8500.12141.

Cheng, D, 2018. *Trade Governance of the Belt and Road Initiative: Economic Logic, Value Choices, and Institutional Arrangement*. Abingdon UK: Routledge. doi.org/10.4324/9780203701911.

Garnault, J. 2018. 'Australia's China Reset', *The Monthly*, August.

Garnault, R. 2018. '40 years of Chinese economic reform and development and the challenge of 50'. In R. Garnault, L. Song and C. Fang (eds) *China's 40 Years of Reform and Development 1978–2018*. Canberra: ANU Press. doi.org/10.22459/CYRD.07.2018.02.

Klein, R. 2009. 'Learning from others and learning from mistakes: Reflections on health policy making'. In R. M. Theodore, R. Freeman and K. Okma (eds) *Comparative Studies and the Politics of Modern Medical Care*. Yale University. doi.org/10.12987/yale/9780300149838.003.0012.

Koppell, J. G. S. 2007. 'Political control for China's state-owned enterprises: Lessons from America's experience with hybrid organizations'. *Governance* 20(2): 255–278. doi.org/10.1111/j.1468-0491.2007.00356.x.

Ma, J. 2009. 'The dilemma of developing financial accountability without election – A Study of China's Recent Budget Reforms'. *Australian Journal of Public Administration* 68(1): 62–72. doi.org/10.1111/j.1467-8500.2009.00622.x.

Ma, J. 2012. 'The rise of social accountability in China'. *Australian Journal of Public Administration* 71(2): 111–121. doi.org/10.1111/j.1467-8500.2012.00770.x.

Meng, F., Z. Chen and P. Yeophantong. 2020. 'Assessing the vertical management reform of China's environmental system: Progress, conditions and prospects'. In A. Podger, T.-T. Su, J. Wanna, H. S. Chan and M. Niu (eds) *Designing Government Structures for Performance and Accountability: Developments in Greater China and Australia*. Canberra: ANU Press. doi.org/10.22459/DGSPA.2020.09.

Müller, A. 2016. 'Hukou and health insurance coverage for migrant workers'. *Journal of Current Chinese Affairs* 45(2): 53–82. doi.org/10.1177/18681026 1604500203.

National Bureau of Statistics in China. 2019. *China Statistical Yearbook 2018*. Beijing: People's Republic of China.

Niu, M. 2018. 'Adoption or implementation? Performance measurement in the City of Guangzhou's Department of Education'. In A. Podger, T.-T. Su, J. Wanna, H. S. Chan and M. Niu (eds) *Value for Money: Budget and Financial Management Reform in the People's Republic of China, Taiwan and Australia*. Canberra: ANU Press. doi.org/10.22459/vm.01.2018.07.

Patapan, H., J. Wanna and P. Weller (eds). 2005. *Westminster Legacies: Democracy and Responsible Government in Asia and the Pacific*. Sydney: UNSW Press.

Paulson, H. M. 2018. 'United States and China at the crossroads'. Address to the Bloomberg New Economy Forum in Singapore, 7 November. Paulson Institute. Available at: www.paulsoninstitute.org/news/2018/11/06/statement-by-henry-m-paulson-jr-on-the-united-states-and-china-at-a-crossroads/.

Podger, A. 2017. 'Revisiting the relationship between politics and administration'. *Wuhan University Journal of Social Science* 3(May). (Chinese translation of paper presented to CPAS/ASPA Conference on Modern National Governance at Wuhan University in October 2016).

Podger, A. 2019. 'Engaging with China and the US: An increasingly complex challenge, including for public administration scholars and practitioners'. *Public Administration Review* 79(2): 277–280. doi.org/10.1111/puar.13013.

Podger, A. and H. S. Chan. 2015. 'The concept of "merit" in Australia, China and Taiwan'. *Australian Journal of Public Administration* 74(3): 257–269. doi.org/10.1111/1467-8500.12148.

Podger, A. and B. Yan. 2013. 'Public administration in China and Australia: Different worlds but similar challenges'. *Australian Journal of Public Administration* 72(3): 201–219. doi.org/10.1111/1467-8500.12023.

Rhodes, R. A. W., J. Wanna and P. Weller. 2009. *Comparing Westminster.* Oxford: Oxford University Press. doi.org/10.1093/acprof:oso/9780199563494.001.0001.

Shen, Y. and J. Yu. 2016. 'Local government and NGOs in China: Performance-based collaboration'. *China: An International Journal* 15(2): 177–191.

Shen, Y., J. Yu and J. Zhou. 2020. 'The Administration's retreat and the Party's advance in the new era of Xi Jinping: The Politics of the ruling party, the government, and associations in China'. *Journal of Chinese Political Science* 25: 71–88. doi.org/10.1007/s11366-019-09648-5.

Song, L. 2018. 'State-owned enterprise reform in China: Past, present and prospects'. In R. Garnault, L. Song and C. Fang (eds) *China's 40 Years of Reform and Development 1978–2019.* Canberra: ANU Press. doi.org/10.22459/CYRD.07.2018.19.

Stent, J. 2017. *China's Banking Transformation: The Untold Story.* Oxford: Oxford University Press. doi.org/10.1093/acprof:oso/9780190497033.001.0001.

Tsai, L. L. 2007. *Accountability without Democracy.* Cambridge, New York, Melbourne: Cambridge University Press.

Wanna, J., L. Jensen and J. de Vries. 2003. *Controlling Public Expenditure: The Changing Roles of Central Budget Agencies – Better Guardians?* Cheltenham, UK: Edward Elgar.

Wanna, J., L. Jensen and J. de Vries. 2010. *The Reality of Budgetary Reform in OECD Nations: Trajectories and Consequences.* Cheltenham, UK: Edward Elgar. doi.org/10.4337/9781849805636.

Wanna, J., E. A. Lindquist and J. de Vries. 2015. *The Global Financial Crisis and its Budget Impacts in OECD Nations: Fiscal Responses and Future Challenges.* Cheltenham, UK: Edward Elgar. doi.org/10.4337/9781784718961.

Wong, C. 2009. 'Rebuilding government for the 21st century: Can China incrementally reform the public sector?' *China Economic Quarterly* 14(2): 22–27. doi.org/10.1017/S0305741009990567.

Wong, C. 2018a. 'Budget reform in China: Progress and prospects in the Xi Jinping era'. In A. Podger, T.-T. Su, J. Wanna, H. S. Chan and M. Niu (eds) *Value for Money: Budget and Financial Management Reform in the People's Republic of China, Taiwan and Australia.* Canberra: ANU Press. doi.org/10.22459/VM.01.2018.04.

Wong, C. 2018b. 'An update on fiscal reform'. In R. Garnault, L. Song and C. Fang (eds) *China's 40 Years of Reform and Development 1978–2018.* Canberra: ANU Press. doi.org/10.22459/CYRD.07.2018.15.

Woods, M. and J. Wanna. 2013. 'Decentralisation of Public Administration: An Introductory Overview'. Paper presented to Greater China Australia Dialogue on Public Administration, 2013 Workshop, Hangzhou. Available via www.anzsog.edu.au/preview-documents/research-output/5350-decentralisation-of-public-administration-an-introductory-overview/file and the 2014 workshop on Decentralisation.

Yan, B. and J. Wu. 2020. 'Meetings matter: An exploratory case study on informal accountability and policy implementation in mainland China'. In A. Podger, T.-T. Su, J. Wanna, H. S. Chan and M. Niu (eds) *Designing Government Structures for Performance and Accountability: Developments in Australia and Greater China.* Canberra: ANU Press. doi.org/10.22459/DGSPA.2020.10.

Ye, L. and X. Ni. 2016. 'Assessing agency-level performance evaluation reform in China: Can it truly serve as a management innovation?' *Chinese Public Administration Review* 7(1): 7–34. doi.org/10.22140/cpar.v7i1.117.

Zhang, D. D. 2017. *Understanding China's Politics, Economic Policy Makers, and Policy Making under Xi Jinping.* Treasury Paper. Canberra: Australian Treasury, Commonwealth of Australia.

Zhao, Z. 2018. 'Case study of the role of third party evaluators in performance-based budgeting reform at the local government level in China'. In A. Podger, T.-T. Su, J. Wanna, H. S. Chan and M. Niu (eds) *Value for Money: Budget and Financial Management Reform in the People's Republic of China, Taiwan and Australia.* Canberra: ANU Press. doi.org/10.22459/VM.01.2018.14.

12

Coming to terms
with the state

Jim Jose

Introduction

It is an honour to be asked to contribute to this festschrift for Professor John Wanna. His distinguished career spans almost 40 years and I am pleased to be able to say that I was there more or less at the beginning, circa 1981, when John and I met as postgraduate students at the University of Adelaide and became firm friends. Since that time, John has produced an enormous body of work that has contributed greatly to our understanding of Australian politics and public policy. He has nurtured and mentored many young scholars launching them into careers of their own. By any measure his contributions to the study of public policy and the profession of political science have been substantial. The diversity of his work, and its depth, is such that I find myself somewhat daunted by the prospect of saying something beyond the obvious about its significance.

Reflecting on the trajectory of John's research publications I noticed something that seemed a little unexpected. Discussion of the state more or less disappears. In 1981, in *Defence not Defiance*, an important early monograph, the state occupies a central conceptual, explanatory and instrumental place. By 2016, in a collection of essays entitled *Sharpening the Sword of State* (Podger and Wanna 2016), there is no state to speak of. It has neither conceptual nor instrumental presence, despite what the title might be thought to imply. In that collection of essays, including John's co-authored piece (Allen and Wanna 2016), the state has a presence, certainly, but as a taken-for-granted term that can be deployed in an unproblematic way, as a background condition for the analysis of other phenomena. This is not to suggest that he was (or is) unaware or neglectful of its importance. Over the course of his career there were a few works (e.g. in 1986, 1988/1993, 1994 and 2006) where he explicitly discussed the state and considered it as a phenomenon in its own right rather than as something to be taken for granted in a merely instrumental way. Granted, *Public Policy in Australia* (1988/1993) is multi-authored and hence its discussion of the state might not be attributable solely to him, but it does not affect the argument I am advancing. These few papers notwithstanding, the state no longer held a key strategic place in his research. Instead, his research centred on a range of mechanisms and instruments of the various apparatuses of the state such as those concerned with budgeting and budget processes, the delivery of services, the executive and its role, and the like – a very different proposition.

This gave me pause for thought. Is this something that is simply peculiar to his research trajectory, a reflection of his particular choices along the way as to subject matter and research problematic? Or might it indicate something deeper going on, something about the nature of how we might research and understand politics and public policy in the twenty-first century? Since answering yes to the first question would make for a short and very uninteresting paper, I opted for the second question, especially as it offered an opportunity to reflect on the trajectory of efforts to theorise the state from the late 1970s into the first decades of the twenty-first century. Prompting that reflection is an underlying suspicion that the place of the state within John's scholarship mirrors a parallel decline in its prominence within public policy and public administration. Exploring that suspicion is the focus for this chapter.

Of course, one might object with the standard 'so what?' question. The suspicion might be misplaced because for much of the twentieth century the state, as an object of empirical and conceptual analysis, remained a non-issue within political science, internationally until the early 1970s (Almond 1988) and in Australia until the early 1980s (Galligan 1984, 82) – though possible exceptions might be Hancock (1930), Barraclough (1940), Mayer (1952) and Encel (1960). One might also object that the problem is really one of the appropriate level and field of analysis. At a macro level, especially for fields like comparative politics, international relations or political economy, the concept of the state remains central, a core unit of analysis with considerable analytic value. But at a micro level, where research and analysis explores the particulars of how the institutions and apparatuses of the state actually operate, the term loses its centrality as a unit of analysis. However, such objections mix up key questions about the nature of modern states with the minutiae of governing. They also obscure the possibility that there is something significant about its minimisation within public policy discourses. This is not to say that research on the state as such has been non-existent, since many scholars both within and on the boundaries of public policy and public administration have attempted to take the measure of the contemporary state (see e.g. Jessop 2015, 2004; Bevir and Rhodes 2010; Bell and Hindmoor 2009; Lister and Marsh 2006; Weiss 2005; Crouch 2004; Pierre and Peters 2000; McEachern 1990).

Common to these and other discussions of the state is the central (though often unstated) problematic of explaining how the power of the state is organised and exercised in the service of policy development and implementation, and on whose behalf and in whose interests that power might be exercised. Attempts to answer those questions, whether directly or indirectly, constituted the brief efflorescence of arguments in the 1970s and early 1980s about the state, which in turn saw other concepts emerge that appear to have displaced a concern with the state as such. In what follows I will consider four such concepts: 'political regime', 'governmentality', 'new public management' and 'governance'. I will begin with a brief overview of the state of the state within political science research (broadly construed) to contextualise John's views on the state, which will be outlined in the second section. I will then discuss briefly each of these four terms before drawing these threads together in the concluding section.

Political science/public administration and the state

For much of the twentieth century most political scientists seemed agreed that conceptual questions about the nature of the state were largely settled. Within mainstream political science the state could be accounted for in terms of pluralist theory (i.e. as a neutral umpire mediating between contending interests) or elite theory (i.e. where elite groups competed for control of state institutions). Central to both these approaches was a view that there were two spheres of activity – a private sphere of civil society where individuals pursued their private (i.e. economic) interests, and a public sphere of state activity, the domain of institutional politics. The revival of Marxist theory in the late 1960s amid the revolutionary decolonisation processes and growing economic turmoil accompanying the end of the post–World War II long boom generated significant rethinking about how to theorise the state, or more specifically the capitalist state (e.g. Miliband 1969; Poulantzas and Miliband 1972; O'Connor 1973; Yaffe 1973; Offe and Ronge 1975; Poulantzas 1978; Holloway and Picciotto 1978; Frankel 1979; Nordlinger 1981; and Jessop 1982). The key issues centred mostly on how one should understand the nature and role of the state in managing a capitalist society, and in particular managing conflicting class relations and interests to ensure optimised conditions for profitability. Paralleling these debates were at least two other threads also worth noting.

One of these threads was similarly a response to the economic crises of the 1970s. A number of political scientists began arguing that modern society was becoming ungovernable because government was overloaded with contradictory demands, especially from citizens demanding a greater say in how their governments exercised their authority (e.g. Crozier, Huntington and Watanuki 1975; King 1975, 1978; Rose 1975). These ideas provided the political framing for a suite of emerging economic ideas that eventually 'moved from the margins of influence to become conventional political wisdom with world-transforming effects' (Block and Somers 2016, 3–4; see also Blyth 2002; Bevir 2010; Jones 2014). This constellation of ideas is today more commonly referred to as 'neoliberalism' (Harvey 2007). This worldview became not just 'conventional political wisdom', but the common sense of our time (Jose 2003).

The other thread to note is more to do with the impact of the Marxist debates about the state on the then prevailing pluralist and elite theories of the state. Given the Marxist critiques noted above and the steadily growing empirical evidence pointing to the untenability of key assumptions of the pluralist paradigm, a number of mainstream political scientists rethought the weaknesses of pluralist and elitist approaches to theorising the state (e.g. Lindblom 1977; Dahl 1982, 1985). Interestingly, the impact and influence of Marxist scholarship on the state on emerging neopluralist scholarship on power and the state appears not to have registered in mainstream US accounts of neopluralism (McFarland 2007). That observation notwithstanding, as if in response to this thread of scholarly debates, the US Social Science Research Council, through its Committee on States and Social Structures, underwrote a new research program under the theme of 'bringing the state back in' that produced a number of key works (e.g. Skocpol 1979; Evans, Rueschemeyer and Skocpol 1985). In the somewhat melodramatic view of one US political scientist, 'the concept of the state ... had risen from the grave to haunt us once again' (Easton 1981, 303).

But the state was not all that began to 'haunt' political science. The women's liberation movement of the late 1960s and early 1970s challenged all of the above approaches by asking 'was the state patriarchal?', or at least was the state a manifestation of masculinist interests and biases? Their answers to these questions entailed critical scrutiny of the institutions of law, the family, domestic labour, paid work, politics and political power (see e.g. Firestone 1971; Gornick and Moran 1971; Millett 1971; Morgan 1970; Summers 1975). The so-called public/private dichotomy and its privileging of the idea of civil society was revealed as gendered: the idea of 'the private' involved not just the already acknowledged civil society activities of the market but the reality of the domestic spaces of interpersonal relations between women and men and children (Pateman 1983). With the exception of what became known as radical feminism (see e.g. MacKinnon 1982, 1983, 1989), most of these early critiques drew on one or another of the contesting political ideologies of the times (such as liberalism, socialism, Marxism, anarchism and so on).

The reverberations from all of these debates began to be reflected within Australian political science by the early 1980s (see e.g. Frankel 1983; Sawer 1983; Head 1984; Galligan 1984), notwithstanding the earlier consideration of Marxist debates by Barbalet (1974) and Frankel (1979). Various works of political economy (e.g. Connell 1977; Catley and McFarlane 1981; Crough and Wheelwright 1982; and Wheelwright and Buckley's five-volume edited collections of essays 1975–83) as well as those by Australian feminists (Sawer 1983, 1990; Game and Pringle 1983; O'Donnell 1984; Franzway, Court and Connell 1989; Watson 1990) all presupposed these international debates and contributed to a broader understanding of the Australian state. Finally, and in addition to the unfolding debates within Australian political science, two other interrelated dimensions contributed (and continue to contribute) to shaping these debates and ongoing ideas about the state. On the one hand there is the ever-changing dynamics of global market forces (conveniently but misleadingly described as 'globalisation'). On the other hand, and itself a response to these global dynamics, is the ongoing reorganisation of particular state functions, their institutional design and institutionalised practices. This is the background against which the decline in the use of the state as a key conceptual term within John's scholarship parallels its decline within public policy and public administration.

Wanna and the state

In his first monograph, *Defence not Defiance* (1981), Wanna understood the state as an entity encompassing:

> the instruments of government: both policy-making bodies (cabinet, parliament and government departments), and the bureaucracy (public service and local councils). In addition, the state also includes the judiciary (the court system in each of its various branches; criminal, civil and industrial), and the legal structure, the agencies of social control (police, military and intelligence organisations), the public financial institutions and to a lesser extent the public statutory authorities. (Wanna 1981, 42)

Variations on this summary were also sketched in both editions of *Public Policy in Australia*, though these also expanded the scope of 'the institutions of the state' to include entities one might ordinarily have thought should be excluded such as the church, political parties, pressure groups and trades unions (Davis et al. 1993, 24). These were the means to create, implement and enforce whatever policies might be needed to maintain and reproduce the state's particular social order, and in particular to resolve whatever conflicts might arise between various competing social, economic and political interests. The state remains obligated to upholding the social order in which it is embedded, while managing whatever degrees of social change might be needed.

Unsurprisingly, as Wanna subsequently pointed out, no matter what action the state takes it 'continually exerts significant influence over the economy and patterns of economic activity' (Wanna 1994, 227). However, for Wanna, this did not really amount to the state having control over the economy, since on his analysis in 1994, 'the management of the macroeconomy seems generally beyond state capacities' (Wanna 1994, 243). He suggested a number of reasons for this but chief among them were, on the one hand, the international global dynamics that shape and impact the domestic economy, and on the other, that the private sector 'serves as the reciprocal dimension of state capacities' (Wanna 1994, 243) insofar as it exercises considerable control of key economic resources. This is further reinforced by the fact that there is more or less agreement on the fundamental values of the political-economic order such as the sanctity of private property, a significant degree of corporate autonomy, a minimalist approach to the redistribution of wealth and the subordination of the demands of labour to those consistent with business profitability (Lindblom 1977, 233, 205).

Nonetheless, Wanna was not suggesting that the state remains powerless, or that the ongoing processes of globalisation have necessarily weakened the state's ability to act, though it has 'transformed the means through which the state seeks to influence outcomes' (Mintrom and Wanna 2006, 162; see also Keating 2004). To the extent that the state is responsible for maintaining and reproducing the social order it also has to take policy positions that at any given time will favour some interests at the expense of others. Far from being a means to resolve conflict this is often a source of conflict on a number of levels: between the state and various interest groups, within the state and its various instruments of government concerning the strategies and policies to be developed and pursued, and between the political parties vying to represent the interests of their supporters. As Wanna (1981, 1994) has variously pointed out, the state is not neutral in the adjudication of such conflicts. The dominant influence of the fundamental values noted above ensures that the state cannot be neutral, especially as the state is the only entity with the authority and legitimacy to impose and enforce society-wide 'solutions'.

And so, it is fair to say that in Wanna's view the state is still a central actor, but how should one characterise that centrality? Should the state now be considered merely as a rule-setter, a guarantor of order, a facilitator, a coordinator, some sort of relay station, something else again or a combination of some or all of the above? How should we understand the diverse ways in which the state operates in terms of its administrative capacity and practices, its policymaking and delivery? Explanations attempting to take these issues into account have led away from a state-based language of analysis to other ways of conceptualising the state's activities and the various processes by and through which it has undergone various transformations. This is partly because the concept of the state, though important for the reasons already noted, operated at a fairly high level of abstraction. Its use seemed limited for explaining how its power might be manifested (and in particular how policies were developed and implemented), or how government and its agencies actually behaved. Yet even then its explanatory value might be considered questionable. The rest of the chapter will now consider some of these other ways of coming to terms with the state, of how we might understand the multiple, diverse activities of the state. What follows is not so much a history of these approaches as a series of snapshots summarising key aspects of their conceptualising and understanding of the machinations of the state and, by extension, the exercise of political rule.

Political regime

The first approach I would like to consider is the concept 'political regime'. Political scientists use this concept in a number of ways. The most common is to identify a particular coalition of political groups or individuals that exercises the prevailing sovereign power and accepts the rules legitimising and constraining that power. In this sense 'political regime' captures those empowered to rule. But this is a bit too limited, given that conceptually speaking, the idea of 'political regime' would seem to encompass more than just a means to describe who rules. Another quite common use of the idea of 'political regime' is as a means to classify different types of rule such as a democracy, or oligarchy, or monarchy, and so on. This second sense then aims to tell us something about the nature of political rule. It gives some idea of the organisational terrain, 'the locus of decision-making' to borrow Przeworski and Limongi's (1993, 58) phrase, in which a given government is required to operate.

Yet despite this second approach covering more than those who rule, whether singly or as coalitions, it 'is more than the government of the day' (Pempel 1997, 338). It also involves the determinations about who gets what share of the difference between the total wealth generated and the cost of running the government, the 'fiscal residuum' as Przeworski and Limongi's (1993, 58) term it. Thus on this reckoning, the idea of 'political regime' fuses together an understanding of political institutions, aspects of the prevailing socio-economic order, and a specific mixture of public policies. Accordingly, this interpretation of 'political regime' allows the identification of 'a regularized pattern of political and economic interactions that are synergistic in character' such that all three aspects of the fusion noted above inform and reinforce one another (Pempel 1997, 338). Implicitly at least, this understanding of the idea of 'political regime' carries with it an alignment to a particular social order (Pempel 1997, 338).

Yet even this conceptualisation omits dimensions that need to be included. Apart from diluting the class relations that might be of some significance for an understanding of how these three aspects actually interact, there is no reason to assume any definitive correlation between a given regime and any particular social order. To make that correlation, some sort of normative or value dimension must already be present within the concept of 'political regime'.

A different conception of 'political regime', developed from a neo-Marxist perspective, emerged in the late 1980s in the work of McEachern (1990, 13–41). His aim was to develop a conceptual approach that would make it possible to explain how and in what ways capitalist social relations and, by extension, the relations between classes, changed over time (1990, 41). This would then enable him to develop a way of understanding the nature and articulation of state power, class power and class interests so that it could be adequately theorised in terms of explaining specific policy outcomes developed by the state. Given that the state has the organisational power and social legitimacy, in theory at least, to act on and advance its own interests, McEachern (1990, 30) asked why the state has not made real its potential for 'full autonomy and social dominance'? The short answer is that while the potential for such an authoritarian outcome is always ever-present, in a healthy liberal democracy there are constitutional limits to guard against such unfettered autonomy on the part of the state. In most normal circumstances, and even in so-called states of emergency, a state is hard-pressed simply to impose its will come what may, provided that it maintains a reasonable level of 'performance legitimacy' by sustaining its citizens' faith in its institutions of government, including its bureaucracy and its capacity 'to initiate and implement the requested policies' (Andersen et al. 2014, 1308).

Even though it might be the case that a given state action or policy 'may bear the marks of the influence or initiative of one section of a class, its organisations or political party' it does not follow from this that we can read off 'the consequences of the policy, understood in terms of its impact on classes and class interests' (McEachern 1990, 32). There are no guarantees as to how the mix of powers, interests, ideas and political locations will play themselves out. Situating his account explicitly within the problematic of capitalist social relations, McEachern's notion of 'political regime' goes beyond the above two conceptions because it does not shy away from the class dynamics that shape and are shaped by the prevailing social order.

Implicit in McEachern's notion of 'political regime' is a sense in which continuously contested guiding principles and norms are built into it. Both in principle and practice, McEachern's idea of 'political regime' has distinctly prescriptive dimensions. When talking about a political regime one is also talking about a particular alignment of class forces. Each conditions the other such that the shift from one political regime to another maps at the same time a reconfiguration of class forces and their political manifestations. Thus, McEachern's notion of a 'political regime' ensures that the analysis does not lose sight of the complex interplay of the social relations that give rise to the formation and shifts in political regimes (cf. Dean and Villadsen 2016, 20–21).

Yet despite the explanatory potential of McEachern's concept of 'political regime', its emphasis on class relations perhaps positioned it on the wrong side of history. For all its sophistication it seemed to leave hanging the key question of how the state's bureaucracy might be constituted in order to contribute to and implement any given policy. In some respects, the explicit class focus left considerations of the bureaucracy in much the same place as Miliband (1969) some 20 years earlier, and, in a slightly different way, Pusey (1991) a couple of years later. While I would argue that one cannot understand the nature of contemporary politics without some understanding of the prevailing class dynamics and hence McEachern's concept of 'political regime' retains some contemporary relevance, concern about the state qua state did not have much resonance at a time when the end of history had arrived and liberal democracy was being repositioned as the only game in town (cf. Fukuyama 1989). In that context, other ways of coming to terms with the state began to find favour.

Governmentality

A totally different approach to thinking about the state emerged from the work of French philosopher Michel Foucault and his concept of 'governmentality' (Foucault 1979, 1982). At a first approximation, it could be said that Foucault aimed to capture the specific understandings and practices of political rule adopted or developed by those empowered to govern. This oversimplifies the conceptual complexities involved in Foucault's research agenda, but it nevertheless provides an initial orientation for the concept.

In Foucault's view, the then prevailing approaches to theorising the state drew on particular understandings of sovereignty shaped by strategic and/ or juridical conceptualisations of power, irrespective of the particular form of sovereignty, be it monarchical, republican or some other popular form (Foucault 2004). On these understandings power was a property to be possessed, to be struggled over, and so on, and conceived 'in terms of law, prohibition, liberty, and sovereignty', emanating from a singular centre (Foucault 1984, 90). What was needed was a different theory of power, one that was neither beholden to nor derived from whatever was theorised as the sovereign authority, one that could conceive of 'power without the king' (Foucault 1984, 91; see also Foucault 2004, 34–40). Rejecting this juridical and strategic approach, Foucault conceptualised power as being 'exercised from innumerable points, in the interplay of nonegalitarian and mobile relations' (Foucault 1984, 94). The locus of sovereignty came to be de-centred and de-individualised as the art of government came to embrace more and more domains previously subsumed under the pre-modern governmental model of the family (Foucault 1982, 1981).

Power relations could be creative, productive, repressive or destructive, or a contradictory admixture of all four. But significantly for Foucault (1979, 27), there could be 'no power relation without the correlative constitution of a field of knowledge, nor any knowledge that does not presuppose and constitute at the same time power relations'. Power–knowledge relationships were products of language and discourse, since these were the means by which power and knowledge relations became known, or at least theorised and understood. For Foucault, language is organised into specific discourses, which then created what he called disciplinary practices, understood in a double sense: (1) as a body of knowledge and (2) as a mode of practice situating and constituting humans as beings in the world. The disciplinary practices created through a particular discourse (or intersecting sets of discourses) also refracted back on to the discourse to help regulate it. Space precludes expanding these important aspects of Foucault's philosophy, but suffice it to say that he was concerned with the multiple ways in which language and discourse produced 'the different modes by which in our culture, human beings are made subjects', a process he termed 'subjectification' (Foucault 1982, 777). Through this process people are disciplined both as individual consciousnesses or agents and as members of a given social and political community (Foucault 1982, 777). The dynamic between discourse and discipline was at one and the same time the dynamic between knowledge and power and as such challenged the idea that our knowledge was either certain or grounded on incontestable foundations.

In developing his concept of governmentality, Foucault brought together four crucial dimensions: (1) the link between the idea of government and modes of political rationality; (2) the relationship between forms of power and processes of subjectification; (3) the complex ways in which technologies of self (ideas and practices through which individuals crafted their subjectivities) and technologies of domination (the ideas and practices through which governing powers enforced particular outcomes) were enmeshed in the workings of the modern state; and, finally, (4) the necessity of freedom for effective political rule. This provided Foucault with a way of conceptualising the art of governing in terms of 'guiding the possibility of conduct and putting in order the possible outcome' (Foucault 1982, 789), an art he termed the 'conduct of conduct' (Foucault 2008, 186). He regarded governmentality as a 'method of decipherment', meaning the means to uncover and analyse the specific and dominant rationalities of governing and the technologies or practices that enabled such rationalities to be made real, regardless of the scale involved (Foucault 2008, 186). In short, governments govern by influencing 'the actions of others', though for Foucault it was governing in a very much broader sense than had come to be accepted by scholars in their analyses of government in the modern era (Foucault 1982, 790; 1997, 156). Such an approach enabled him to move beyond the abstract level of the state to call into question the commonly accepted understandings of the constitution and exercise of power (Foucault 2008, 2007, 2000, 1982), and to engage in the 'analysis of micro-powers' (Foucault 2008, 186).

Under the auspices of the concept of governmentality Foucault showed how the state was not the exclusive locus of sovereign power. Rather it was merely one, albeit a significant one, of any number of key actors in the multiple circuits of power that 'connect[ed] a diversity of authorities and forces, within a whole variety of complex assemblages' (Rose 1999, 5). Thus, not only did Foucault's governmentality approach decentre the reign of the autonomous individual, it also decentred the state as the locus of sovereign authority with respect to decision-making around policy matters. By decentring is meant the displacement of previously privileged concepts, ideas and practices as organising principles for how we interpret phenomena within our conceptual schemas. Governmentality proved to be very attractive to scholars aiming to understand the workings of public policy and public administration, because it shifted the focus away from 'linear and hierarchical perspective[s] which underl[y] much discussion about policy-making' (Colebatch 2002, 35–36; Dean and Hindess 1998).

Yet there is a tension in Foucault's approach, as is evident from his opening comment in his first lecture in *The Birth of Biopolitics* where he noted that 'the state is at once that which exists and that which does not yet exist enough' (Foucault 2008, 4). That is, governing presupposed 'a state which is already there', but the art of governing, governmentality, meant that the state was constantly being remade. It was but a short step from the idea of remaking the state to decentring the state. For many Foucauldians, and perhaps even for Foucault himself, the idea of decentring the state seemed to sit very easily within various anti-statist (i.e. anarchist or libertarian) perspectives, or what Dean and Villadsen (2016) aptly termed 'state phobia'. While governmentality provided a powerful means to explore the operations of the state, and to identify and analyse the arts of governing, it privileged an anti-statism that diminished attempts, including Foucault's own initial concerns, to understand how the state reproduced itself and its capacities.

Foucault's development of the idea of governmentality presupposed an understanding of governing that went beyond the normally accepted spheres of the political institutions of the state. But as noted above, this understanding of government also underscored forms of anti-statism that worked against positive conceptions of the state. It also saw many Foucauldians uncritically moving towards another conceptual shift that was on the rise at around the same time, and one that seemed to resonate favourably with Foucauldian perspectives. This was the idea of governance. Some have equated Foucault's 'conduct of conduct' with 'governance' (e.g. Sokhi-Bulley 2011, 252, fn 5; Singer and Weir 2006, 449) which in turn led some to treat 'governance' and 'governmentality' as interchangeable terms. But this move is a misreading of Foucault and the radical challenge his concept of governmentality posed (Jose 2010). Foucault's 'governmentality' aimed to displace past views of sovereignty and the state as central organising features of our understanding of political rule. To the extent that his idea of the 'conduct of conduct' could be described as 'governance' it bore little or no relation, either conceptually or politically, to the idea of governance that was gaining prominence as a key concept in the political science and public administration literature in the 1990s. Rather, the non-Foucauldian governance owed much to an already ascendant set of discourses characterised under the name new public management (NPM), and it is to those discourses we will turn to first, before considering 'governance'.

New public management (NPM)

New public management (NPM) was less a worked-out theory or cluster of theories about the state and more 'a conceptual device invented for purposes of structuring scholarly discussion of contemporary changes in the organization and management of executive government' (Barzelay 2005, 16). Over time it became a series of measures developed and applied by governments to reorganise or modernise their public sectors (see e.g. Wilenski 1988; Aucoin 1990; Pollitt 1990; Hood 1991; Dunleavy and Hood 1994; Rhodes 1997 and this volume; Clarke and Clegg 1999; Dent, Chandler and Barry 2004; Torres 2004; Kirkpatrick, Ackroyd and Walker 2005; McLaughlin, Osborne and Ferlie 2005; Lynn Jr 2006; Pollitt, van Thiel and Homburg 2007). The roots of these measures reach back into the economic turmoil and political crises of the 1970s and the concomitant preoccupation with 'government overload' and the feared prospects of 'ungovernability', which in turn saw the post–World War II Keynesian consensus give way to a different constellation of ideas about the role of government and economic management, a consensus now commonly understood as neoliberalism (Skidelsky 2019; Block and Somers 2016; Jones 2014; Bevir 2010; Blyth 2002). Even if it is the case, as is argued by Shergold and Podger in Chapter 14 of this volume, that senior public servants in Australia did not speak about neoliberalism or use the term 'neoliberal' in their deliberations and discussions of policy (or research underpinning such discussions), it is still appropriate for scholars to describe as neoliberalism the dominant ideological and intellectual ideas that comprise the milieu within which such activities take place. Christensen and Laegreid (2002, 268) make a similar point with respect to practitioners' non-use of the term 'new public management' in the two decades prior to it being coined by Hood in 1991.

NPM signifies a paradigm-like shift in thinking shaped by what Roberts (2010) has termed a 'logic of discipline' in which governments are seen as a significant part of the problem. This logic has two key prongs. The first is a recognition that conventional methods of democratic government and public administration have failed to deliver what is expected of them (cf. Rhodes this volume). The problem is sheeted home in governments' and politicians' inability to think outside their need for re-election and a propensity to make irresponsible decisions. Hence the rhetoric of reform emerges as a major discursive force to shape the thinking of practitioners and politicians alike. The second prong involves devising means or tactics to give effect to these reforms in ways that constrain the democratic impulse of politicians and voters on the one hand, and on the other, enable key decisions to be removed from the hurly-burly of everyday politics, a process of 'depoliticization' as Roberts terms it. In addition, he notes:

> there are strong substantive commonalities in the way that reform is justified … that sometimes go unrecognized by the stakeholders themselves, and certainly none would refer to a 'logic of discipline' itself. (Roberts 2010, 13–14)

The commonalities that Roberts had in mind were everyday tropes, like most politicians are ignorant of the realities of doing business, most politicians lack an understanding of basic economic dynamics, politicians are prone to pork-barrelling at the expense of the long-term health of the economy, politicians are poll-driven, and so on (I am sure readers can add more to the list). There were four interrelated propositions that provided the intellectual rationalisations for the application of the 'logic of discipline', which underwrote a reshaping of what Roberts termed 'the architecture of government'.

These four propositions were central to the international thinking around the development of NPM, at least within those circles in which the Keynesian consensus had given way to the dominance of monetarist-informed neoclassical economics (Buchanan and Wagner 1977; Skidelsky 2019) and a predominantly neoliberal form of politics. First, all alternatives to the market were deeply flawed. Market-based decisions were nearly always more reliable and effective than government planning. Second, government failure was more prevalent than market failure. Third, government-imposed regulatory frameworks were mostly counterproductive, that is, government intervention did not work. And fourth, government intervention was unjust as it usually resulted in the transfer of resources to the undeserving. In one way or another these propositions reflected the dominant input of public choice theory and private sector management theory that together with the above propositions might be 'best described as [a] "paradigm"', because they 'combine both intellectual and ideological dimensions' (Aucoin 1990, 116). This does not deny that governments, in varying degrees, abandoned the need to address market failures or provide public goods and social protection. Governments were mindful, most of the time, of the social dimension and potential political fallout from their pursuit of particular policies. Social justice sentiments were not ruled out of considerations within the NPM paradigm, they just carried a different weighting in the political calculus.

Another defining characteristic of NPM was its focus on 'modernising' (i.e. reforming) the public sector. This was understood to mean remaking it in the image of the private sector by drawing on 'private sector-derived accounting and management technologies in the pursuit of public sector efficiency' (Lapsley 2009, 2). Across most of the Organisation for Economic Cooperation and Development (OECD) nations and beyond, government bureaucracies were transformed in varying degrees into market-oriented organisations that were to be competitive, performance-focused, cost-effective and audit-oriented (Bale and Dale 1988; Aucoin 1990; Hood 1991; Lynn Jr 2006), though in the UK context McLaughlin and Osborne (2005, 2) suggest that it was less about marketisation and more about the diversification of the 'unitary government provision and management of public services'. Nonetheless, the modernising dynamic of NPM and its accompanying rhetoric was both a rationale for and a consequence of governments' efforts to commercialise, corporatise or privatise a wide range of its activities. This also saw formal commitments to develop and implement competition policies such as occurred in Australia in 1994, which, among other provisions, introduced the principle of competitive neutrality to ensure that private sector companies and government-owned businesses and departments operated within the same commercial framework.

A third defining characteristic of NPM was the devolution of everyday levels of decision-making to lower echelons while effecting a greater level of centralisation (and political control) of the decision-making capacity of the senior executives of the bureaucracy (Aucoin 1990, 120–125). Despite their seemingly contradictory nature these dynamics very much reflected the influence of private sector management practices. It also reflected the view articulated forcefully by Osborne and Gaebler (1992) in their influential, though fanciful, book *Reinventing Government* that policymaking and its implementation are separate activities. Setting the policy agenda is what governments should do and implementing it should be left to market-sensitive entities, whether private or public. According to Osborne and Gaebler, echoing the views of Drucker (1968) from three decades earlier, governments are not good at rowing, hence they should steer and leave the rowing (i.e. the delivery of their services) to those with the requisite expertise and capacities. That their evidence for a lack of ability to row was more anecdotal assertion than demonstrable fact was neither here nor there.

Much more could be said about the minutiae of NPM, but it is clear from the above that NPM informed much of the thinking enabling the shift away from traditional public administration practices to allow public sector agencies and departments to become more like those operating in the private sector. Yet the outcomes have not turned out as intended insofar as the promised benefits have proved difficult to achieve (Lapsley 2009), despite there being some evidence of a positive impact in terms of assisting many state entities to improve their efficiency levels, to become more cost conscious and to become more creative or entrepreneurial in discharging their responsibilities (Diefenbach 2009, 896). On the other hand, the increased turn to auditing requirements, for example, has arguably resulted in increased costs, a preoccupation with compliance and a decline in attending to core activities (Lapsley 2009, 12–13).

Perhaps more worrying is the potential for governments (and the politicians who comprise them) to undermine 'their own legitimacy and that of the democratic state' (Lynn Jr 2006, 130) through a lack, or at least minimalist forms, of democratic accountability. And while it is the case that NPM emerged from deliberate choices undertaken by politicians and others within their respective nations, the long march of the NPM reforms and the changes they have put in place were not a result of the state and its agencies *removing* themselves from economic activity and the market. Rather it was a result of the state *reconstructing* the market regime and redefining its role within that regime. This is a point made in a slightly different context by Wanna when he and his co-author argued, perhaps echoing Keating (2004), that the '"nation-building" state has not disappeared but remains active in shaping and redirecting market mechanisms' (Mintrom and Wanna 2006).

Even so, for NPM it seems that its time has passed in terms of being 'the torch of leading-edge change', its embeddedness and institutionalisation notwithstanding (Dunleavy et al. 2006, 468). As a conceptual frame for interpreting the operations of the state then, NPM has lost its lustre. Its possibilities as a paradigm (Aucoin 1990) seem to have been exhausted as events have forced a rethink of its intellectual capacities and its particular practices – though this is not to deny its significant influence and part in helping redesign the architecture of government. Just what is lining up to take its place remains to be seen, though Dunleavy et al. were opting for what they called 'digital era governance', stressing that it was 'about governance, it is not solely or even primarily about digital changes' (Dunleavy et al. 2006, 469). This is because they see an increased role for the state, one that within an enhanced digital environment needs to be holistic and integrative. Similarly, Rhodes (this volume) sees variations on the networked governance theme as having moved beyond NPM, in particular what he terms 'decentred governance'. What can be noted here is that the concept of 'governance' emerged within the discursive formation of NPM and rapidly developed a key terminological place within it. It is to the concept of 'governance' to which I now turn.

Governance

The appeal of 'governance' as a term was that it seemed to provide a convenient means of settling conflicting debates over theorising the dynamics of the state and its institutions. In part, this was because it appeared to offer a way of examining and explaining the interrelated processes of government and governing without putting the state at the centre of the analyses. In that sense, it offered the capacity to decentre the state in much the same way as Foucault's governmental approach. But 'governance' offered other advantages. It was (and still is) a conceptually slippery term. It could circulate within and between disparate disciplines and fields of study with apparent ease, which allowed scholars to ascribe diverse and conflicting content and meanings to it. This was part of its appeal. Its conceptual slipperiness, even disciplinary promiscuity, meant that it could 'be applied to almost everything', though whether it 'describes and explains nothing' (Jessop 2003, 4) is a matter of considerable debate (cf. Offe 2009). Nonetheless, the extent to which 'governance' remains a prominent term can be seen from the discussion offered by Rod Rhodes in Chapter 10 of this volume.

Stoker (2019, 13–14) suggests that governance, both as concept and practice, arose as a response to 'globalisation, [a] weakening of national sovereignty and the emergence of more challenging citizens'. But this ignores a number of things. First, responses to the 'emergence of more challenging citizens' had been unfolding since the mid-1970s (cf. Crozier, Huntingdon and Watanuki 1975; King 1975), and found concerted expression within various NPM strategies. Second, the challenges of globalisation and the concerns over national sovereignty were also unfolding long before the idea of 'governance' emerged. And this is the third point. 'Governance' as a term only came to prominence within political science discourse in the early 1990s (Jose 2007), partly as a result of its promotion by World Bank publications (1989, 1992), and partly by scholars reworking the discourses within and around NPM and public administration. This does not mean that the term had no currency prior to that time. It did, but it was mostly within a corporate management setting where the concern was about management structures and corporate accountability. And so it is not surprising that it enters contemporary political discourse via various World Bank publications (1989, 1992).

For it was the World Bank that provided a 'go to'(and seemingly innocent) definition of 'governance' as 'the manner in which power is exercised in the management of a country's economic and social resources for development' (World Bank 1992, 1). The political nature of that definition was revealed in a footnote in which the bank noted that its focus was with 'the processes by which authority is exercised in the management of a country's economic and social resources' and 'the capacity of governments to design, formulate, and implement policies, and, in general, to discharge government functions' (World Bank 1992, 58 n 1). The nature or type of government was supposedly not its concern as it was 'outside the Bank's mandate' (World Bank 1992, 58, n 1). Notwithstanding its supposed apolitical positioning, the bank's core focus was with how governing was both organised and exercised, political in all but name. The World Bank's focus was similarly reflected in the works of many scholars who came to exercise significant influence in shaping contemporary understandings of governance (see e.g. Bevir and Rhodes 2003; Richards and Smith 2002; Hill and Hupe 2002; Lynn Jr, Heinrich and Hill 2000; Pierre and Peters 2000; Rhodes 1997; Stoker 1998; Kooiman 1993; McGregor Jr 1993; Wamsley 1990).

Over time, 'governance', like NPM, became more than just a concept. It generated a language of political discourse, at least within the fields of public policy and public administration, that formed its own paradigm for framing scholarly (and practitioner) understanding of contemporary modes of governing (Peters 2003; Stoker 1998). But 'governance' represented more than a shift in scholarly terminology; it also signified a technology of governing, a 'specific modality of government' (Prozorov 2004, 268). Governance both described and helped effect 'the restructuring of the relationship between the political and economic spheres' in which both the nature of the 'political' and its relationship to the 'economic' was redefined in ways that enhanced the latter at the expense of the former (Jessop 1997, 572). Though regarded by many scholars as a 'descriptive label' (e.g. Richards and Smith 2002, 2), 'governance' inscribed prescriptive imperatives onto the cluster of meanings attributed to it that helped shape understandings of both the theory and practice of governing. While this was similar to the impact of NPM, 'governance' more explicitly enabled political problems to be redefined as technical issues relating to administration and management. That is to say that political rule by governments and their relevant state apparatuses, when understood in terms of a governance lens, were merely a matter of economic management. In itself this gave governance great conceptual appeal.

This appeal was further enhanced by the fact that NPM could be recalibrated in terms of the emerging language of governance. Some of NPM's key features such as marketisation and an emphasis on the state steering rather than rowing were easily accommodated within the newly emerging governance discourses. But whereas NPM emphasised that state entities should reinvent or re-engineer themselves by adopting private sector practices, within the emerging governance literature the emphasis was on 'partnerships between governmental, para-governmental and non-governmental organizations in which the state apparatus is often only first among equals' (Jessop 1997, 574–575). The state was to be less a central sponsor of government activities and more a facilitating partner. There is some resonance here with the governmentality approach in terms of decentring of the state. However, the key difference is that governmentality displaces the state rather than subordinates it, whereas governance (and to a lesser extent NPM) makes a virtue of the reconfigurations of public–private partnerships while simultaneously asserting the overall political authority of the state.

The nature of these public–private partnerships is not simply a matter of mutual convenience, because it also involves significant organisational change within the administrative apparatuses of the modern state. The NPM impetus to redesign organisational structures of state institutions, in particular enhancing the management authority of senior public sector executives, found a ready resonance within the rising governance discourses. These too created new and consolidated existing opportunities for non-state actors to join with state officials to become integral parts of state decision-making and policymaking processes. Private interests were then enabled to participate as legitimate insiders within the state's policymaking apparatuses. In that context, 'governance', both as concept and practice, is more than just 'the manner in which power is exercised in the management of a country's economic and social resources for development' (World Bank 1992, 1). It designates a form of political authority that is exercised through various administrative apparatuses and decision-making processes that are shared with private sector actors, in effect transforming political processes. This has implications for the forms of political authority that might be possible within those reconfigurations as these arrangements have the potential to transform political institutions in unanticipated and perhaps unwanted ways, in particular where the sovereign political authority of the elected government might be concerned (Jose 2011). Politicians may well see themselves as setting policy agendas, objectives and performance measures, but the basis for their decisions and pronouncements still depend on advice from others (e.g. party apparatchiks, personal assistants, media advisers, so-called independent consultants and so on), all of whom think, write and advise within various contexts in which neoliberal ideas are the norm.

Furthermore, the decision-making processes within public sector organisations become subject to two competing but not necessarily incompatible tensions. On the one hand, decision-making processes become subordinated to the logic of the market rather than to a logic authorised by democratic political processes in which policy decisions are entrusted to elected politicians. On the other hand, the decision-making processes become subject to a different political logic driven by elected politicians' attempts to seek 'partisan advantage over their competitors', an outcome described by Aucoin (2012, 178) as 'new political governance'. Space precludes exploring this aspect further. Suffice it to say that it underscores one of the problem areas of the governance paradigm (Peters 2003; Stoker 1998, 2019), namely the politicisation of the public sector and the possible concomitant decline of trust in government generally. The very measures aimed at improving the state's flexibility, responsiveness, and efficiency present the potential to weaken the state's legitimacy as they form part of a mindset as to how those charged with acting in the public interest, in particular politicians and perhaps to a lesser extent senior bureaucrats, understand and discharge their roles and responsibilities.

Conclusion

My discussion began from a suspicion that the place of the state within Wanna's scholarship mirrored a parallel decline in its prominence within public policy and public administration scholarship. Scholars turned to other conceptual means of analysis such as 'political regime', 'governmentality', 'NPM', and 'governance'. Considered individually, each of these had particular appeal. But considered in the context of a trajectory of public policy and public administration scholarship over the past six or seven decades, a less appealing picture emerges. Two concepts, 'political regime' and 'governmentality', could be described as heuristic in their deployment in theorising the operations of the state (though it could also be argued that the latter has its own paradigm of sorts). The other two concepts, 'NPM' and 'governance', were more than simply heuristic terms. Not only did they provide a means to explain what was happening within the state's organisational and political architecture, they assisted in shaping and providing justifications for those reconfigurations to become practices of governing.

As products of the post-Keynesian zeitgeist, both NPM and governance enjoyed what might be considered a form of conceptual hegemony, to the extent that they formed paradigms in the Kuhnian sense (Kuhn 1970, 35–42). That is, each concept provided 'an organizing ... framework for understanding changes in governing', as Stoker (1998, 18) asserted in the case of governance, that involved a fusion of 'intellectual and ideological dimensions', as Aucoin (1990, 116) noted in relation to NPM. Thus, both concepts set the boundaries defining the puzzles and activities that could be explored, the legitimacy of the questions that might be asked and the answers that might be permitted. In such a context concerns about theorising the state as a focus for research receded as the seemingly more practical concerns about policy and administration appeared more accessible.

This did not mean that all such consideration of the state disappeared, as I have already noted above. But it did mean that the state became more of a taken-for-granted term, deployed by scholars in an unproblematic way, as a background condition for the analysis of other phenomena within frameworks shaped by terms like 'NPM' or 'governance'. Hence the diminishing importance of the state qua state within Wanna's research trajectory was not something peculiar to his individual choices about the particular objects of his research. It was part of a wider (inter-)disciplinary phenomenon in which ideas about the nature and practices of governing came to be rethought and reconfigured.

References

Allen, P. and J. Wanna. 2016. 'Developing leadership and building executive capacity in the Australian public services for better governance'. In A. Podger and J. Wanna (eds) *Sharpening the Sword of State: Building Executive Capacities in the Public Services of the Asia-Pacific*. Canberra: ANU Press. doi.org/10.22459/SSS.11.2016.02.

Almond, G. 1988. 'The return to the state (and critiques)'. *American Political Science Review* 82(3): 853–874. doi.org/10.2307/1962495.

Andersen, D., J. Møller, L. L. Rørbæk and S.-E. Skaaning. 2014. 'State capacity and political regime stability'. *Democratization* 21(7): 1305–1325. doi.org/10.1080/13510347.2014.960204.

Aucoin, P. 1990. 'Administrative reform in public management: Paradigms, principles, paradoxes and pendulums'. *Governance: An International Journal of Policy, Administration, and Institutions* 3(2): 115–137. doi.org/10.1111/j.1468-0491.1990.tb00111.x.

Aucoin, P. 2012. 'New political governance in Westminster systems: Impartial public administration and management performance at risk'. *Governance: An International Journal of Policy, Administration, and Institutions* 25(2): 177–199. doi.org/10.1111/j.1468-0491.2012.01569.x.

Bale, M. and T. Dale. 1998. 'Public sector reform in New Zealand and its relevance to developing countries'. *The World Bank Research Observer* 13(1): 103–121. doi.org/10.1093/wbro/13.1.103.

Barbalet, J.M. 1974. 'Political science, the state and Marx'. *Politics* (now *Australian Journal of Political Science*) 9(1): 69–73. doi.org/10.1080/00323267408401441.

Barraclough, H. 1940. 'Engineering the state'. *Australian Journal of Public Administration* 2(3): 173–195. doi.org/10.1111/j.1467-8500.1940.tb01932.x.

Barzelay, M. 2005. 'Origins of the new public management: An international view from public administration/political science'. In K. McLaughlin, S. P. Osborne and E. Ferlie (eds) *New Public Management: Current Trends and Prospects*. London: Routledge.

Bell, S. and A. Hindmoor. 2009. *Rethinking Governance: The Centrality of the State in Modern Society*. Cambridge: Cambridge University Press. doi.org/10.1017/CBO9780511814617.

Bevir, M. 2010. *Democratic Governance*. Princeton: Princeton University Press. doi.org/10.1515/9781400836857.

Bevir, M. and R. A. W. Rhodes. 2003. *Interpreting British Governance*. London: Routledge.

Bevir, M. and R. A. W. Rhodes. 2010. *The State as Cultural Practice*. Oxford: Oxford University Press. doi.org/10.1093/acprof:oso/9780199580750.001.0001.

Block, F. and M. Somers. 2016. *The Power of Fundamentalism: Karl Polanyi's Critique*. Cambridge, MA: Harvard University Press.

Blyth, M. 2002. *Great Transformations: Economic Ideas and Institutional Change in the Twentieth Century*. Cambridge: Cambridge University Press. doi.org/10.1017/CBO9781139087230.

Buchanan, J. M. and R. E. Wagner. 1977. *Democracy in Deficit: The Political Legacy of Lord Keynes*. New York: Academic Press.

Catley, R. and B. McFarlane. 1981. *Australian Capitalism in Boom and Depression*. Chippendale: Alternative Publishing Cooperative.

Christensen, T. and P. Laegreid. 2002. 'New public management: Puzzles of democracy and the influence of citizens'. *Journal of Political Philosophy* 10(3): 267–295. doi.org/10.1111/1467-9760.00153.

Clarke, T. and S. R. Clegg. 1999. 'Changing paradigms in public service management'. *Administrative Theory & Praxis* 21(4): 485–459. doi.org/10.1080/10841806.1999.11643406.

Colebatch, H. K. 2002. *Policy*. Revised edition. Buckingham: Open University Press.

Connell, R. W. 1977. *Ruling Class, Ruling Culture: Studies of Conflict, Power and Hegemony in Australian Life*. Cambridge: Cambridge University Press. doi.org/10.1017/CBO9781139085076.

Crouch, C. 2004. *Post-Democracy*. Cambridge: Polity Press.

Crough, G. and E. L. Wheelwright. 1982. *Australia: A Client State*. Ringwood: Penguin Books.

Crozier, M., S. Huntington and J. Watanuki. 1975. *The Crisis of Democracy: Report on the Governability of Democracies to the Trilateral Commission*. Triangle Paper No. 8. New York: New York University Press.

Dahl, R. 1982. *Dilemmas of Pluralist Democracy*. New Haven: Yale University Press.

Dahl, R. 1985. *A Preface to Economic Democracy*. Cambridge: Polity Press. doi.org/ 10.1525/9780520341166.

Davis, G., J. Wanna, J. Warhurst and P. Weller. (1988) 1993. *Public Policy in Australia*. Second edition. Sydney: Allen & Unwin.

Dean, M. and B. Hindess (eds). 1998. *Governing Australia: Studies in Contemporary Rationalities of Government*. Cambridge: Cambridge University Press.

Dean, M. and K. Villadsen. 2016. *State Phobia and Civil Society: The Political Legacy of Michel Foucault*. Stanford: Stanford University Press.

Dent, M., J. Chandler and J. Barry (eds). 2004. *Questioning the New Public Management*. Aldershot: Ashgate.

Diefenbach, T. 2009. 'New public management in public sector organizations: The dark sides of managerialistic "enlightenment"'. *Public Administration* 87(4): 892–909. doi.org/10.1111/j.1467-9299.2009.01766.x.

Drucker, P. 1968. *The Age of Discontinuity: Guidelines to Our Changing Society*. New York: Harper and Row.

Dunleavy, P. and C. Hood. 1994. 'From old public administration to new public management'. *Public Money and Management* 14(3): 9–16. doi.org/10.1080/ 09540969409387823.

Dunleavy, P., H. Margetts, S. Bastow and J. Tinkler. 2006. 'New public management is dead—Long live digital-era governance'. *Journal of Public Administration Research and Theory* 16(3): 467–494. doi.org/10.1093/jopart/ mui057.

Easton, D. 1981. 'The political system besieged by the state'. *Political Theory* 9: 303–325. doi.org/10.1177/009059178100900303.

Encel, S. 1960. 'The concept of the state in Australian politics'. *Australian Journal of Politics and History* 6(1): 62–76. doi.org/10.1111/j.1467-8497.1960. tb00782.x.

Evans, P., D. Rueschemeyer and T. Skocpol (eds). 1985. *Bringing the State Back In*. Cambridge: Cambridge University Press. doi.org/10.1017/CBO978051162 8283.

Firestone, S. 1971. *Dialectic of Sex: The Case for Feminist Revolution*. London: Jonathan Cape.

Foucault, M. 1979. 'Governmentality'. *Ideology & Consciousness* 6: 5–21.

Foucault, M. 1981. 'Omnes et singulatum: Towards a criticism of "political reason"'. In S. M. McMurrin (ed.) *The Tanner Lectures on Human Values, II*. Salt Lake City: University of Utah Press.

Foucault, M. 1982. 'The subject and power'. *Critical Inquiry* 8(4): 777–795. www.jstor.org/stable/1343197.

Foucault, M. 1984. *The History of Sexuality Volume 1: An Introduction*. Translated by R. Hurley. Harmondsworth: Penguin Books.

Foucault, M. 1997. 'What our present is'. In S. Lotringer and L. Hocbroth (eds) *The Politics of Truth*. New York: Semiotext(e).

Foucault, M. 2000. 'The ethics of the concern for the self as a practice of freedom'. In M. Foucault, *Ethics: Essential Works of Foucault 1954–1984*. Volume 1 of 3 volumes. Edited by P. Rabinow. London: Penguin Books.

Foucault, M. 2004. *Society Must Be Defended? Lectures at the College de France, 1975–1976*. Translated by D. Macey. Harmondsworth: Penguin Books.

Foucault, M. 2007. *Security, Territory, Population: Lectures at the Collège de France 1977–1978*. Translated by G. Burchell. Basingstoke: Palgrave Macmillan.

Foucault, M. 2008. *The Birth of Biopolitics: Lectures at the Collège de France 1978–1979*. Translated by G. Burchell. Basingstoke: Palgrave Macmillan.

Frankel, B. 1979. 'On the state of the state: Marxist theories of the state after Leninism'. *Theory and Society* 7(1/2): 199–242. doi.org/10.1007/BF00158682.

Frankel, B. 1983. *Beyond the State? Dominant Theories and Socialist Strategies*. London: Macmillan Press.

Franzway, S., D. Court and R. W. Connell. 1989. *Staking a Claim: Feminism, Bureaucracy and the State*. Sydney: Allen & Unwin.

Fukuyama, F. 1989. 'The end of history?' *The National Interest* 16(Summer): 3–18.

Galligan, B. 1984. 'The state in Australian political thought'. *Politics* (now *Australian Journal of Political Science*) 19(2): 82–92. doi.org/10.1080/00323268408401923.

Game, A. and R. Pringle. 1983. *Gender at Work*. Sydney: Allen & Unwin.

Gornick, V. and B. K. Moran (eds). 1971. *Woman in Sexist Society: Studies in Power and Powerlessness*. New York: Basic Books.

Hancock, K. 1930. *Australia*. London: Benn.

Harvey, D. 2007. *A Brief History of Neoliberalism*. Oxford: Oxford University Press.

Head, B. 1984. 'Recent theories of the state'. *Politics* (now *Australian Journal of Political Science*) 19(1): 36–45. doi.org/10.1080/00323268408401906.

Hill, M. and P. Hupe. 2002. *Implementing Public Policy: Governance in Theory and Practice*. London: Sage Publications.

Holloway, J. and S. Picciotto (eds). 1978. *State and Capital: A Marxist Debate*. London: Edward Arnold.

Hood, C. 1991. 'A public management for all seasons?' *Public Administration* 69(1): 3–19. doi.org/10.1111/j.1467-9299.1991.tb00779.x.

Jessop, B. 1982. *The Capitalist State: Marxist Theories and Methods*. Oxford: Martin Robertson & Co.

Jessop, B. 1997. 'Capitalism and its future: Remarks on regulation, government and governance'. *Review of International Political Economy* 4(3): 561–581. doi.org/10.1080/096922997347751.

Jessop, B. 2003. 'Governance, governance failure and metagovernance'. Paper presented to the Politics, Governance and Innovation for Rural Area International Seminar, Università della Calabria, Arcavacata di Rende, 21–23 November. Available at: www.researchgate.net/publication/228960146_Governance_Governance_Failure_and_Meta-Governance.

Jessop, B. 2004. 'Multi-level governance and multi-level meta-governance'. In I. Bache and M. Flinders (eds) *Multi-level Governance*. Oxford: Oxford University Press.

Jessop, B. 2015. *The State: Past, Present and Future*. Cambridge: Polity Press.

Jones, D. S. 2014. *Masters of the Universe: Hayek, Friedman, and the Birth of Neoliberal Politics*. Princeton: Princeton University Press.

Jose, J. 2003. 'Revisioning the logic of industrialisation: Contesting the common sense of our time'. In E. Carlson (ed.) *The Full Employment Imperative*. Callaghan, NSW: University of Newcastle, Centre of Full Employment and Equity.

Jose, J. 2007. 'Reframing the "governance" story'. *Australian Journal of Political Science* 42(3): 455–470. doi.org/10.1080/10361140701513588.

Jose, J. 2010. 'A (con)fusion of discourses? Against the governancing of Foucault'. *Social Identities* 16(5): 689–703. doi.org/10.1080/13504630.2010.509574.

Jose, J. 2011. 'Responding to terrorism in the era of the governance state'. In B. B. Hawks and L. Baruh (eds) *If It Was Not for Terrorism: Crisis, Compromise, and Elite Discourse in the Age of War on Terror*. Newcastle, UK: Cambridge Scholars Press.

Keating, M. 2004. *Who Rules? How Government Retains Control of a Privatised Economy*. Sydney: Federation Press.

King, A. 1975. 'Overload: Problems of governing in the 1970s'. *Political Studies* 23: 284–296. doi.org/10.1111/j.1467-9248.1975.tb00068.x.

King, A. (ed.). 1978. *The New American Political System*. Washington, DC: American Enterprise Institute.

Kirkpatrick, I., S. Ackroyd and R. Walker (eds). 2005. *The New Managerialism and Public Service Professions*. New York: Palgrave Macmillan. doi.org/10.1057/9780230503595.

Kooiman, J. (ed.). 1993. *Modern Governance: New Government-Society Relations*. London: Sage.

Kuhn, T. S. 1970. *The Structure of Scientific Revolutions*. Second edition, enlarged. Chicago: University of Chicago Press.

Lapsley, I. 2009. 'New public management: The cruellest invention of the human spirit?' *Abacus: A Journal of Accounting, Finance and Business Studies*. 45(1): 1–21. doi.org/10.1111/j.1467-6281.2009.00275.x.

Lindblom, C. 1977. *Politics and Markets*. New York: Basic Books.

Lister, M. and D. Marsh. 2006. 'Conclusion'. In C. Hay, M. Lister and D. Marsh (eds) *The State: Theories and Issues*. Basingstoke: Palgrave Macmillan.

Lynn Jr, L. E. 2006. *Public Management: Old and New*. New York: Routledge. doi.org/10.4324/9780203964774.

Lynn Jr, L. E., C. J. Heinrich and C. J. Hill. 2000. 'Studying governance and public management: Challenges and prospects'. *Journal of Public Administration Research and Theory* 10(2): 233–261. doi.org/10.1093/oxfordjournals.jpart.a024269.

MacKinnon, C. 1982. 'Feminism, Marxism, method, and the state: An agenda for theory'. *Signs: Journal of Women in Culture and Society* 7(3): 515–524. doi.org/10.1086/493898.

MacKinnon, C. 1983. 'Feminism, Marxism, method, and the state: Toward feminist jurisprudence'. *Signs: Journal of Women in Culture and Society* 8(4): 635–658. doi.org/10.1086/494000.

MacKinnon, C. 1989. *Towards a Feminist Theory of the State*. Cambridge, MA: Harvard University Press.

Mayer, H. 1952. 'Notes on Marxism and the state'. *Australian Journal of Public Administration* 11(3): 129–142. doi.org/10.1111/j.1467-8500.1952.tb01592.x.

McEachern, D. 1990. *The Expanding State: Class and Economy Since 1945*. London: Harvester Wheatsheaf Press.

McFarland, A. 2007. Neopluralism. *Annual Review of Political Science* 10: 45–66. doi.org/10.1146/annurev.polisci.10.072005.152119.

McGregor Jr, E. B. 1993. 'Toward a theory of public management success'. In B. Bozeman (ed.) *Public Management: The State of the Art*. San Francisco: Jossey-Bass.

McLaughlin, K. and S. P. Osborne. 2005. 'Current trends and future prospects of public management: A guide'. In K. McLaughlin, S. P. Osborne and E. Ferlie (eds) *New Public Management: Current Trends and Future Prospects*. London: Routledge. doi.org/10.4324/9780203996362.

McLaughlin, K., S. P. Osborne and E. Ferlie (eds) 2005. *New Public Management: Current Trends and Future Prospects*. London: Routledge. doi.org/10.4324/9780203996362.

Miliband, R. 1969. *The State in Capitalist Society*. New York: Basic Books.

Millett, K. 1971. *Sexual Politics*. London: Granada Publishing.

Mintrom, M. and J. Wanna. 2006. 'Innovative state strategies in the Antipodes: Enhancing the ability of governments to govern in the global context'. *Australian Journal of Political Science* 41(2): 161–176. doi.org/10.1080/10361140600672410.

Morgan, R. (ed.). 1970. *Sisterhood is Powerful: An. Anthology of Writings from the Women's Liberation Movement*. New York: Vintage Books.

Nordlinger, E. 1981. *On the Autonomy of the Democratic State*. Cambridge, MA: Harvard University Press.

O'Connor, J. 1973. *The Fiscal Crisis of the State*. New York: St Martin's Press.

O'Donnell, C. 1984. *The Basis of the Bargain: Gender, Schooling and Jobs*. Sydney: Allen & Unwin.

Offe, C. 2009. 'Governance an "empty signifier"?' *Constellations* 16(4): 550–562. doi.org/10.1111/j.1467-8675.2009.00570.x.

Offe, C. and V. Ronge. 1975. 'Theses on the theory of the state'. *New German Critique* 6: 137–147. doi.org/10.2307/487658.

Osborne, D. and T. Gaebler. 1992. *Re-Inventing Government: How the Entrepreneurial Spirit is Transforming the Public Sector*. New York: Harper.

Pateman, C. 1983. 'Feminist critiques of the public/private dichotomy'. In S. I. Benn and G. F. Gaus (eds) *Public and Private in Social Life*. New York: St Martin's Press.

Pempel, T. J. 1997. 'Regime shift: Japanese politics in a changing world economy'. *Journal of Japanese Studies* 23(2): 333–361. doi.org/10.2307/133160.

Peters, B. G. 2003. 'The changing nature of public administration: From easy answers to hard questions'. *Viešoji Politika ir Administravimas* 5: 7–20.

Pierre, J. and B. G. Peters. 2000. *Governance, Politics and the State*. London: Macmillan.

Podger, A. and J. Wanna (eds). 2016. *Sharpening the Sword of State: Building Executive Capacities in the Public Services of the Asia-Pacific*. Canberra: ANU Press. doi.org/10.22459/SSS.11.2016.

Pollitt, C. 1990. *Managerialism and the Public Services: The Anglo-Saxon Experience*. Oxford: Basil Blackwell.

Pollitt, C., S. van Thiel and V. Homburg (eds). 2007. *New Public Management in Europe: Adaptation and Alternatives*. London: Palgrave Macmillan. doi.org/10.1057/9780230625365.

Poulantzas, N. 1978. *State, Power, and Classes*. Translated by P. Camiller. London: NLB.

Poulantzas, N. and R. Miliband. 1972. 'The problem of the capitalist state'. In R. Blackburn (ed.) *Ideology in Social Science: Readings in Critical Social Theory*. London: Fontana/Collins.

Prozorov, S. 2004. 'Three theses on "governance" and the political'. *Journal of International Relations and Development* 7(3): 267–293. doi.org/10.1057/palgrave.jird.1800023.

Przeworski, A. and F. Limongi. 1993. 'Political regimes and economic growth'. *Journal of Economic Perspectives* 7(3): 51–69. doi.org/10.1257/jep.7.3.51.

Pusey, M. 1991. *Economic Rationalism in Canberra: A Nation-Building State Changes its Mind.* Melbourne: Cambridge University Press.

Rhodes, R. A. W. 1997. *Understanding Governance: Policy Networks, Governance, Reflexivity and Accountability.* Buckingham: Open University Press.

Richards, D. and M. J. Smith. 2002. *Governance and Public Policy in the United Kingdom.* Oxford: Oxford University Press.

Roberts, A. 2010. *The Logic of Discipline: Global Capitalism and the Architecture of Government.* Oxford: Oxford University Press.

Rose, R. 1975. 'Overloaded government: The problem outlined'. *European Studies Newsletter* 5: 13–18.

Rose, R. 1999. *Powers of Freedom: Reframing Political Thought.* Cambridge: Cambridge University Press. doi.org/10.1017/CBO9780511488856.

Sawer, M. 1983. 'From the ethical state to the minimal state: State ideology in Australia'. *Politics* (now *Australian Journal of Political Science*) 18(1): 26–35. doi.org/10.1080/00323268308401870.

Sawer, M. 1990. *Sisters in Suits: Women and Public Policy in Australia.* Sydney: Allen & Unwin.

Singer, B. C. J. and L. Weir. 2006. 'Politics and sovereign power: Considerations on Foucault'. *European Journal of Social Theory* 9(4): 443–465. doi.org/10.1177/1368431006073013.

Skidelsky, R. 2019. *Money and Government: The Challenge to Mainstream Economics.* Harmondsworth: Penguin Books.

Skocpol, T. 1979. *States and Social Revolutions: A Comparative Analysis of France, Russia, and China.* Cambridge: Cambridge University Press. doi.org/10.1017/CBO9780511815805.

Sokhi-Bulley, B. 2011. 'Government(ality) by experts: Human rights as governance'. *Law Critique* 22: 251–271. doi.org/10.1007/s10978-011-9091-4.

Stoker, G. 1998. 'Governance as theory: Five propositions'. *International Social Science Journal* 50(155): 19–28. doi.org/10.1111/1468-2451.00106.

Stoker, G. 2019. 'Can the governance paradigm survive the rise of populism?' *Policy & Politics* 47(1): 3–18. doi.org/10.1332/030557318X15333033030897.

Summers, A. 1975. *Damned Whores and God's Police: The Colonization of Women in Australia*. Ringwood: Penguin Books.

Torres, L. 2004. 'Trajectories in public administration reforms in European continental countries'. *Australian Journal of Public Administration* 63(3): 99–112. doi.org/10.1111/j.1467-8500.2004.00394.x.

Wamsley, G. L. 1990. 'The agency perspective: Public administrators as agential leaders'. In G. L. Wamsley, R. N. Bacher, C. T. Goodsell and P. S. Kronenberg (eds) *Refounding Public Administration*. Newbury Park: Sage.

Wanna, J. 1981. *Defence Not Defiance: The Development of Organised Labour in South Australia*. Adelaide: CAE Government Printer.

Wanna, J. 1986. 'The state and industrial relations in South Australia'. In K. Sheridan (ed.) *The State as Developer: Public Enterprise in South Australia*. Adelaide: Royal Australian Institute of Public Administration in association with Wakefield Press.

Wanna, J. 1994. 'Can the state "manage" the macroeconomy?' In S. Bell and B. Head (eds) *State, Economy and Public Policy*. Melbourne: Oxford University Press.

Watson, S. (ed.). 1990. *Playing the State: Australian Feminist Interventions*. Sydney: Allen & Unwin.

Weiss, L. 2005. 'The state-augmenting effects of globalisation'. *New Political Economy* 10(3): 345–353. doi.org/10.1080/13563460500204233.

Wheelwright, E. L. and K. Buckley (eds). 1975–1983. *Essays in the Political Economy of Australian Capitalism*. 5 volumes. Sydney: ANZ Book Publishing.

Wilenski, P. 1988. 'Social change as a source of competing values in public administration'. *Australian Journal of Public Administration* 47(3): 213–222. doi.org/10.1111/j.1467-8500.1988.tb01062.x.

World Bank. 1989. *Sub-Saharan Africa: from Crisis to Sustainable Growth*. Washington DC: World Bank Publications.

World Bank. 1992. *Governance and Development*. Washington DC: World Bank Publications.

Yaffe, D.S. 1973. 'The Marxian theory of crisis, capital and the state'. *Economy and Society* 2(2): 186–232. doi.org/10.1080/03085147300000009.

SECTION 4:
WORKING WITH PRACTITIONERS

Introduction to Section 4: Working with practitioners

A recurring theme throughout this book is John Wanna's determination to observe close at hand the world of the practitioner – whether the politicians or the mandarins or the public servants down the line – to listen to them and watch as they respond to events, to see the processes and systems they use. He does this without in any way compromising his role as an academic, independently relating what he observes to theories of power, management and finance, questioning the assumptions and claims of the practitioners while recognising the messiness of the world in which they operate.

Perhaps John's key legacy will be his demonstration of the value, indeed the essentiality, of bridging the worlds of the academics and the practitioners. In a sense this legacy, and its appreciation of the pragmatism that so often guides contemporary practitioners, reflects a broader shift in politics and public administration over the last 30 or 40 years: a meta-narrative.

The ideological divide that characterised the twentieth century collapsed almost as quickly as the Berlin Wall and the Soviet Union. Within the space of a decade, pragmatism was on the rise in the crafting and administering of public policy. Markets were given a greater role in economic activities as governments around the world focused more on policy and financing and less on the actual delivery of services, especially where the private sector already provided similar services. Early, somewhat naïve references to 'customers' have over time evolved as the ideas of 'co-design' and 'co-production' of policy and social services delivery have been embraced by governments of all persuasions, where the state plays a greater role as facilitator. Long gone are institutions like the Postmaster-General's Department and the Commonwealth Employment Service, representing monolithic political-administrative forces. And, because hindsight is often blind when comparing today's public administration to the 'good old days' or some 'golden era', it is easy to forget that Australian levels of consumption have increased substantially over the last 30 years, along with the wellbeing of the vast majority of Australians, and that this has coincided with the advent of what is too often referred to, pejoratively, as 'neoliberalism'.

The academic debate about neoliberalism (and, previously, 'managerialism' and 'economic rationalism') focused in particular on whether the pursuit of neoliberal goals involved abandonment of public service ethics. This portrayal of the reforms as an ideological debate contrasts with the practitioners' perspective of an ongoing pragmatic struggle to find what works, or what works better. In this meta-narrative of ideology versus pragmatism, Wanna has generally sided with the pragmatists. He still looks to identify the theories that might explain how pragmatism is applied, and he is also conscious of the context of differing political philosophies, but he eschews the emphasis of some fellow academics on an ideological divide that assumes a disposition of practitioners, including unelected officials. Framed in ideological terms, the debate too often degenerates into echo chambers where participants speak to their own audience.

In the midst of the COVID-19 pandemic, even the politicians have largely abandoned ideology in favour of pragmatism. John Howard reportedly informed the Treasurer, Josh Frydenberg, that 'there are no ideological constraints at this time'. While times of crisis may be particularly conducive to pragmatism, the electorate's interest in ideological debate seems more generally to be secondary to government performance and the credibility of the opposition to perform better. Arguably, this is more the case since the 1980s than previously.

John Wanna's work went against the grain of the aloof critic of public administration by actively engaging with the public service. At first, this approach was not popular among political scientists (notwithstanding the pioneering work of earlier postwar academics such as Robert Parker, Dick Spann, Gordon Reid and Fin Crisp, as well as Martin Painter, David Corbett, John Halligan and Jonathan Boston in New Zealand). But Wanna became a leader and has developed a following of research students who have adopted the same ethos (some transitioning or on leave from the public service and some of whom are authors in this volume). In parallel, there has been considerable effort from government to strengthen links with academia, including through the establishment of the Australia and New Zealand School of Government (ANZSOG) with John as its inaugural head of research (as the Sir John Bunting Professor of Public Administration at The Australian National University [ANU]); governments have also introduced incentives for academics to undertake research relevant to 'national priorities' and likely to have impact, working with government practitioners and wider networks.

The chapters in this section address the complex relationship between academics and practitioners, and the contribution John has made. Paul 't Hart opens with a personal account of his involvement with John, and the antagonism he found, to his dismay, among political scientists in Australia, including at ANU, towards close interaction with practitioners. Public administration in the Netherlands is accepted as a standalone discipline. His own interest is in 'useable knowledge', combining traditional academic pursuits with contributing to the professional development of public servants. In this regard, he refers to John Wanna as a 'trailblazer'.

Peter Shergold and Andrew Podger in a shared chapter respond directly and firmly to academic critics who claim a neoliberal basis for public sector reform over the last 30 years. Shergold's essay highlights the exclusively pejorative use of the 'neoliberal' tag, its lack of clear definition and the failure of the critics to engage with the practitioners. Podger complements the Shergold essay providing a detailed history of the reforms as described by public service practitioners themselves, demonstrating the iterative processes involved and the emphasis on pragmatism.

While firmly rejecting any conscious ideological agenda among the public service leaders, Shergold and Podger acknowledge the influence of economics and the use of its language of prices and efficiency. In a sense, this does reflect an underlying appreciation of liberalism, but not the implied ideology the critics claim of a 'neoliberal' desire to roll back the state. A more careful academic assessment of the direction of public sector reform over recent decades may well present it differently to how those involved in it directly portray it, as Jose suggests in his chapter in the previous section; but that would be very different from the loaded and almost indiscriminate use of the term 'neoliberal'.

Isi Unikowski examines the interaction between research and practice, and the lessons to be drawn from John's approach. These include the importance of consciously and explicitly grounding collaboration in the norms, values and principles of public sector work. A major contribution of the researcher is in ensuring practitioners understand their own public service history, which is increasingly important as modern public sector practices make it more difficult for the public service to be the custodian of its history. The researcher also provides essential support by helping to frame the questions, problems and issues facing practitioners, taking a step back to contextualise current concerns.

Linking research to practice is not easy. The chapters in this section do not explore in any detail the challenges involved; rather they focus on how John Wanna has succeeded where so many others have failed. The problems, however, are not purely the fault of academics: often practitioners too quickly dismiss the relevance of research to the matters at hand. This has been the subject of much research itself, drawn upon by Meredith Edwards and others (including John Wanna) in a review for ANZSOG some years ago (Research Reference Group 2007). A particular challenge is to bridge different cultures based in part on different time horizons. The academic studies the past, the practitioner is focused on the present and near future; the academic needs time to undertake new research and is generally unable to provide responses in the time frames practitioners work to so that, by the time a practitioner's research question is answered, the practitioner has moved on to a new issue and problem. This is a perennial challenge for ANZSOG and it requires ongoing, iterative, two-way engagement where practitioners should be asking what is already known about a current issue, and researchers can be motivated to redirect future research as they discern from practitioners emerging research questions.

It is this messy, iterative, mutually respectful approach to engagement and collaboration that John Wanna has excelled at over his career, including nearly 20 years as editor of the *Australian Journal of Public Administration* and nearly 15 years as the inaugural Sir John Bunting Professor of Public Policy and ANZSOG's director of research, where he has guided ANZSOG conferences and orchestrated the publication of more than 50 ANU Press books (gaining well over 2 million downloads) that combine the work of academics and practitioners.

Notwithstanding this contribution, and John's efforts to develop new public administration scholars, there remains a significant capability deficit in public administration scholarship in Australia compared with earlier eras, a deficit likely to worsen as current leaders like John Wanna retire.

Public administration scholarship requires 'fox skills' (as Pat Weller describes Wanna's approach in Chapter 6), encompassing history, politics, law, economics, sociology and management, a mix not easily achieved in academia today. But the public service also has a capability deficit: submissions by Australian Public Service (APS) agencies to the recent Independent Review of the APS (Thodey Review) had nowhere near the depth or breadth of those made to the Coombs Royal Commission in the 1970s. There was little evidence of knowledge of the history of the public service, its evolving role as an institution of Australian government or the impact of economic and social change on its structures, personnel and relationships.

ANZSOG clearly has some way to go in building public administration capacity in both government and academia, as well as in connecting the two.

Reference

Research Reference Group. 2007. *Enhancing ANZSOG's Contribution to Better Government: Future Research Directions*. Report to ANZSOG Board by M. Edwards (Chair), G. Hawke, O. Hughes, A. Podger and J. Wanna, 14 October.

13

Engaging with government:
A confessional tale

Paul 't Hart

In the aloof and lofty heights of the political science program at the Research School of Social Sciences (RSSS) at The Australian National University (ANU) – we were a global 'top 10' department, I was told upon my arrival there in late 2005 – John Wanna was really the only one among my new colleagues who had a serious commitment to working with and for government. His research agenda and his editorial efforts at the *Australian Journal of Public Administration*, in running the ANZSOG book series at UNSW Press and later ANU E Press, were in no small measure shaped by what he knew was topical in political and administrative practice. He published self-consciously for the local market and maintained an active presence in the broadsheet and electronic media. The more academically snobbish colleagues at RSSS, of which there were plenty, were very disparaging *for that very reason*. I thought they were mad.

After a year's worth of the allegedly blissful, monk-like 'research-only' existence (meaning: no need for teaching or external engagements) while working on the kind of 'A-list' journal articles and weighty academic monographs that my colleagues appeared to regard as the be-all and end-all of life as a political scientist, I found myself bored stiff. I mean, I enjoy doing research as much as the next academic, but to be mimicking my RSSS colleagues and do it ad infinitum – there was no retirement age that I could see – from the stuffy confines of the claustrophobic Coombs building with my door closed to the world outside, did feel like stretching it. I had had my professional socialisation in the Netherlands, where public administration is a standalone social science discipline rather than, as was the case in Australia, a condescendingly tolerated little pocket within the majestic realm of political science.

Working in that discipline, I had seen my mentors define its role as one of producing and communicating 'usable knowledge' (Cohen and Lindblom 1979). At the tender age of 20, as a research assistant, I got to follow my boss, Professor Uriel Rosenthal, around to ministry boardrooms, invitation-only seminars and hands-on field work of observing decision-making during crises in real time. We studied how governments prepare for and respond to disasters, riots, acts of terrorism and other major disturbances in an otherwise stable and prosperous polity. At 26, I found myself lecturing to police, fire and military commanders in Holland and, inconceivably yet fortuitously, Australia. It seems a daunting thing to do now but of course back then I didn't think twice about it. When the European Cup final of 1985 in Brussels turned into a horrific crowd disaster, I went out with a colleague to reconstruct what had happened *and* used it to write a book in which we adapted and applied academic theories of disaster causation and crisis management to explain the course of events, which then informed years of executive teaching on such matters. When a 747 crashed into a multicultural suburb in Amsterdam, we observed and evaluated the city's response *and* published widely about what we had learned in academic settings.

And so, through many other ventures and experiences – some hard and humbling ones included – I had learned to take pride in combining the traditional academic pursuits with making an active contribution to the professional development of public servants, to public debate about government and politics and to the design and evaluation of public policies and programs. It's what you did, and it was appreciated by one's academic peers as well as by practitioner constituencies (even though the latter may not have always felt comfortable about what we had to say). And it was all based on a firm academic ethos of robust research and mental independence from the powers that be.

Mysteriously, to me at least, none this of appeared to be valued in my new surroundings. It was perhaps not actively despised, it was simply not contemplated as a viable way of being a 'political scientist'. Did I not realise that I had landed in a researcher's version of heaven with my 'research-only' appointment? Why would I bother with engagement with practice when the opportunity was there to do nothing other than churn out Oxford University Press books and articles for revered periodicals such as the *American Political Science Review*? Engaging with practitioners was left to the likes of the Crawford School, which was always spoken about as if it was a bit of a lower life form at the university. I have never been able to quite make up my mind whether it was intellectual conviction that was driving this stance, ideological dislike of government or simply a convenient cover for utter introversion. I should add that the guy who had appointed me, Rod Rhodes, was the only one with what I regarded was an acceptable excuse for what I considered to be the deplorable aloofness of my colleagues: he had 'been there and done it' over a long career in the UK that had involved extensive engagement with government. He had come to Australia to now single-mindedly focus on harvesting all he had learned in the process. He had earned his stance, and he became a close collaborator (and friend) from whom I have learned an awful lot.

Of all the others, Wanna was the exception who confirmed the rule, and perennially risked their derision for it. Unsurprisingly, considering the fact that he occupied the Sir John Bunting Chair in Public Administration funded by the Australia and New Zealand School of Government (ANZSOG), a joint venture of governments and universities entirely devoted to active engagement on the academia–practice interface, it was Wanna who gave me the golden tip that would rid me of my predicament. He told me to get in touch with Allan Fels, the then ANZSOG dean, to explore the possibilities of doing some executive education teaching for them. As one who had been present at the creation of the Netherlands School of Administration (in 1989), which had a similar mission and comparable structure to ANZSOG, it was music to my ears.

I met Fels at the ANZSOG annual conference. I was lucky in two ways. I had presented myself to him as an expert in public leadership, and it turned out ANZSOG had a vacancy for the leadership course in its Executive Master of Public Administration. And Fels was courageous enough to consider a 'nobody from Holland' for the spot – though I remember him asking me in his seemingly casual, almost offhand way to 'remind me again why it is that I should land you this role'. I must have thought of something, because he gave me the opportunity. It made me feel relevant again. It was at that same conference that I saw Peter Shergold, as secretary of the Department of Prime Minister and Cabinet, the then head of the Australian Public Service, making an impassioned speech – which included forceful and repeated banging of the rostrum –

exhorting his colleagues in the audience to get on with the job to 'deliver, deliver, deliver'. It felt like coming home. These were the settings, the people, the discourses and the stakes that I had lived and breathed in Holland. It emboldened me to bring the world of 'Canberra' back to that of RSSS in other ways. I started organising 'policy breakfasts' where key ANU academics strutted their stuff for large and captivated public service audiences, and – importantly – vice versa.

Teaching at ANZSOG was – and still is – a privilege. I returned to live in Holland in 2011, but I still make the big trek twice a year (at least) to deliver several courses, lectures and events for ANZSOG. I have written and commissioned case studies – with Wanna – for its John L Alford case library, a brilliant, open access asset for giving a hands-on empirical grounding to teaching the art and craft of public policy, public management, leadership, collaboration, evaluation and the like. And it has inspired me to finally write that textbook on public sector leadership I had been procrastinating on for years on end.

May 2018. I co-chair a workshop on Successful Public Policy in Melbourne. Esteemed academics and 'pracademics' from around Australia and New Zealand present case studies of government policies, programs and reforms that have done well and have 'created public value', as the Harvard guru of engaged public administration scholarship Mark Moore would have it. The vibe is great. The scholars present talk about how it was almost a relief to be invited to write about the 'upside' of government, as so much of their energy – and incentive structure – appears to gravitate towards naming and explaining its challenges, dilemmas, paradoxes and failures. There should be a place for both, we all agree. At the margins of the sessions I chat with one of the smartest people in the room. He asks me about my whereabouts. I feed him my enthusiasm for the ANZSOG work, and the remarkable keenness to learn, share and reflect that I meet among the Australian and New Zealand practitioners that I teach there. I tell him it's not quite so in some other countries where I do similar work. He stares at me in amazement. Why would a guy like you spend so much time doing that, he wonders. 'I am lucky', he says, 'I don't have to do all that. I have a research-only appointment …'

The moral of the story? There's two. First: let it be a matter of record that John Wanna has been a trailblazer for engaged, grounded, policy-relevant scholarship in Australia, carving out against the odds a path in a landscape that – at least at ANU at the time – was disturbingly barren. And he has accomplished this in his own way (a, well, idiosyncratic, endearing and occasionally enraging fashion, as all who have had experience with his unique correspondence habits will be able to testify) and on his own terms. Second: in the highly competitive institutional environment of modern academia, where publishing in highly specialised and mostly American and British journals that maintain 95 per cent rejection rates and charge authors for the privilege of sharing their own published output forms the backbone of its economy of esteem (and its economy of 'dough', I should add), it clearly takes continued determination and vigilance to persuade academics to allocate their time and energy to ill-understood and ill-appreciated activities such as applied research, executive education, and the somehow denigrating act of engaging with 'government'.

References

Lindblom, C. E. and D. K. Cohen. 1979. *Usable Knowledge: Social Science and Social Problem Solving*. New Haven: Yale University Press.

14

Neoliberalism? That's not how practitioners view public sector reform

Peter Shergold and Andrew Podger

The Government is establishing an independent review to ensure the APS is fit-for-purpose for the coming decades. The APS needs to be apolitical and professional, agile, innovative and efficient – driving both policy and implementation through coherent, collaborative, whole-of-government approaches. (Independent Review of the APS 2018)

'A clear-eyed and objective look at the Australia Public Service is clearly needed, but we have real concerns that this review will be subservient to neoliberal orthodoxy and the bizarre and damaging policies … imposed in pursuit of that extreme ideology,' said CPSU National Secretary, Nadine Flood. (Donaldson 2018)

Introduction

This chapter is in two complementary parts, bookended by this co-authored introduction and a short co-authored conclusion.

In the first part, Peter Shergold challenges the too-common view of academics and other outside observers that governments, and the public service in particular, have consciously pursued a 'neoliberal' ideological agenda over the last 30 years. The 'neoliberal' tag is not consistently defined – indeed, it is rarely defined at all and few who use it appreciate its peculiar history. People do not ever call themselves neoliberal; instead, they only use the term to tag their enemies.

Public servants may recognise the key features of political change that are identified by the academics but would be surprised at their framing as part of a neoliberal agenda. Public servants live in a world of continuous political debate and compromise. Their world is one of iteration. They are not driven by ideological purity, but are schooled in pragmatism; they focus on achievement of results, key performance indicators, value for money. Their role is not to advocate for particular policies – that is the province of elected ministers – but to explain the measures being taken and to implement them. Moreover, behind the scenes there is healthy debate among officials about the reform measures being pursued.

Andrew Podger expands on Shergold's description of the world of public servants by setting out in some detail what the practitioners who have led much of the public sector reform agenda have actually said. Each reform step has been taken pragmatically, to increase efficiency or improve the quality and effectiveness of government programs. At times, the steps have involved unwinding previous actions that had proved unsuccessful but more often they have built on previous steps, as ways to make new incremental improvements were discovered.

The focus of the practitioners is best described as 'management for results'. It is true that the means for achieving results have shifted with more willingness to use market-type mechanisms, and that this was consistent with broader economic policy changes pursued by successive governments in the face of global competition. But changing the means did not mean limiting the role of government or its capacity to achieve the policy objectives governments set, notwithstanding suggestions to the contrary by outsiders claiming a neoliberal agenda.

John Wanna is the exception to the rule: he is the academic outsider who listens to the insiders, is willing to embed himself in public service organisations to observe exactly how they behave, what they say to each other, why they pursue their management reforms. His is still an independent voice, willing to criticise when actions do not meet claimed improvements; and to relate what is happening to scholarly theories of public administration and historical experience, and to international experience. It is why he is trusted by practitioners – he understands their business and eschews vague and unsubstantiated typecasting such as the charge of 'neoliberalism'.

The thunder of outside voices shouting: Has the Australian Public Service really become a 'neoliberal' public service?

Peter Shergold

Talking to public servants

The oeuvre of John Wanna's published research on Australian public administration reflects his lifetime interest in how 'bureaucracy has been substantively reformed … to make it more efficient and effective and to improve its responsiveness to both members and the public' (Wanna, Weller and Keating 2000, 236). He has not always been an admirer of aspects of that process. Indeed, on occasion he has been strongly critical both of the reasons for change and of the manner in which it has been implemented. Always, however, his arguments have been well-informed.

There is a reason for that. Wanna's great academic strength has been his conscious efforts to understand the reform undertaking from the inside. His underlying concern, which his writing has sought to ameliorate, is that 'today's public entrepreneurs are taking part in revolutionary changes but often without recording their experiences' (Wanna, Forster and Graham 1996, x). His unremitting goal has been fully to understand the 'evolving genus of public employees' just as much as the 'inspired few' at the top. Together they have driven 'a conscious and deliberate movement within the Australian public sector' (Wanna, Forster and Graham 1996, 14).

It has not been an easy path for Wanna to tread. As he emphasised back in the mid-1990s, 'such momentous changes are highly controversial and have attracted avid supporters and detractors' (Wanna, Forster and Graham 1996, x). They still do. Wanna's approach, increasingly rare, has been to get himself 'embedded' with public servants as an insider without sacrificing his outsider perspective. He exhibits empathy for the reformers although not necessarily for their goals.

He worked for a time in the Commonwealth Department of Finance, observing the manner in which the agency performed its functions. He has observed the work of the Australian Public Service Commission from within. In all his research he has talked to public servants about how they go about their business. And, in general, public servants have reciprocated his interest, welcoming the opportunity to converse, be interviewed and even co-author articles. Sometimes he agrees with their arguments. Sometimes he does not. But their views, written or oral, are always taken seriously. They are accorded respect. Public servants are given a voice.

Wanna's strength – and the reason public servants actually read his scholarly work – is that he recognises that a public service is not an anonymous and amorphous institution but a multitude of officials doing their work. In Wanna's sympathetic portrayal, they are people: employees who gather information, establish priorities, test assumptions, share dialogue, seek to persuade others, develop narratives, learn how to anticipate shifting political circumstance and respond to the agenda of the government of the day. To understand the Australian Public Service (APS) requires 'a fair and accurate assessment of the Canberra-based SES ... the non-Canberra-based managers and those often in crucial discretionary positions below the SES' (Wanna 1992, 44).

Even the mandarinate of secretaries, he notes, has always been a far more diverse group than their counterparts in France or the UK. They are:

> human beings coping with the pressure of managing careers and personal lives ... in their careers they were sometimes fortunate, lucky, exasperated, disappointed, proud of their achievements, worried that things are getting away from them or becoming harder to manage. (Wanna, Vincent and Podger 2012, xi)

He understands how they seek to influence the decisions by which public policy is created and executed. He is sensitive to the complex interplay of overt and covert power in which they ply their vocation.

His fascination with how these forces are reflected in organisational structures breathes life into complex issues of policy design, program implementation and regulatory intervention. Without bringing together practitioners and scholars, he asks, how can one truly 'explain the beliefs and ideas local political actors maintained about their own system'? From an anthropological or 'ethno-methodological' perspective, one needs to comprehend the 'operational "myths" or belief-systems … through which actors shape their world and ideas' (Patapan, Wanna and Weller 2005, 245, 247).

I emphasise these qualities not simply to accord respect to the person honoured in this festschrift. I do so because it is a virtue that is relatively uncommon within academia and becoming less so.

Elsewhere, on a number of occasions, I have explored (and bemoaned) the manner in which so much potentially valuable scholarly research gets 'lost in translation' (Shergold 2011). Too rarely does it inform evidence-based policy. In this essay my concern runs deeper. I seek to understand why the fashion in which public servants articulate the need for change, and the manner in which academics critique it, rarely engage. Too often both sides talk past each other. Indeed, it is sometimes hard to countenance that they are talking about the same phenomena. Frequently, the philosophical worldview that frames how university researchers and opinion writers portray the changing nature and purpose of public service employs language and intellectual constructs with which most practitioners do not identify.

The words used by external observers to describe the managerial culture within which public servants operate would almost never be employed by those who are observed. In the late 1980s the evolution of public service in Western democracies was generally portrayed as symptomatic of the emergence of 'new public management', although sometimes the terms 'postmodern' or 'post-bureaucratic' public administration were used as alternatives. These trends – and particularly the outsourcing of service delivery – were seen to give rise to the 'Enterprising State', the 'Contract State' or the 'Hollow State'. The changes were presented as the products (particularly in Australian jargon) of 'economic rationalism' or (in American parlance) of 'new paternalism'. They claimed 'the ground once occupied by the old state-bureaucratic paradigm' (Considine 2001, 5).

Rarely did I hear public servants employ those idioms themselves. Perhaps that is not surprising given that each of the terms tended to convey a pejorative rather than a neutral character. But language moves on. Increasingly, the preferred framework of academic discourse on Australian democracy centres on 'neoliberalism'. Australia's modern political parties, we are told, 'have changed around the dominant paradigm of neo-liberalism' (Kefford 2015, 200). And so, too, the world. 'Forget every conspiracy theory that you've read' warns one Australian commentator, for 'nothing will prepare you for the nightmare ideology of neoliberalism' (Stinson 2014).

The ideological construct of neoliberalism is used to name and shame. Indeed, it is almost never used by those politicians and public servants who are the objects of the criticism. It has become a swearword dressed up as polemic (Hartwich 2009). It tends to convey a sense of judgemental superiority. It is a term redolent of political decline, societal inequality, decaying administrative standards and rotting ethical foundations. It is 'a lazy term (used only pejoratively)' (Lawson 2018). But what precisely does the term seek to convey? And to what extent have Australian public services really transformed themselves into institutions fit for neoliberal purpose?

The peculiar history of neoliberalism

The history of economic thought is a fascinating but arcane world. The intellectual roots of ideas shoot, develop and intertwine: the woodland paths get lost in the trees. Concepts rarely have a certain beginning. As they grow and develop, their scholarly proponents reassess and rearticulate different ways of imagining the economic order of the world, as it is or how it might be. A 'school of thought' nearly always turns out to be more complex and internally riven at any given moment than the unifying nomenclature suggests. Over time places, events and personal circumstances create a chronology marked by predictable twists and unexpected turns.

Historical analysis reveals agreements and arguments, amiable consensus and fierce disputation, intellectual consensus and bitter fissures. No sooner is a philosophical position clarified than it morphs into something else, subtly familiar or entirely different. Personal acrimony plays a role. Individuals identify with a position, argue with those who seek to subscribe to or modify it and, not infrequently, end up rejecting the description (and sometime the intellectual substance) of the view attributed to them. The history of ideas is messy.

So it is with neoliberal economics. Its intellectual paradigm has a disputed history complicated by geopolitical diversity. In the late nineteenth century it emerged as a term used by the French economist, Charles Gide, to describe the economic beliefs of an Italian colleague, Maffeo Pantaleoni.

It indicated a break with the classical liberalism of Adam Smith. It was best espoused perhaps by the Austrian economist Ludwig van Mises and German social market economists such as Eucken, Röpke, Rüstow and Müller-Armack. As the twentieth century progressed, neoliberalism sought to position itself between the polar opposites of laissez-fairism and state control.

A key event, the Walter Lippman Colloquium of 1938, brought together a group of intellectuals who shared a deep-seated resistance to prevailing economic mores and who organised themselves – briefly – around the 'neoliberal project'. They were united, briefly, around the priority of the price mechanism, free enterprise and the benefits of competition (Aalbers 2016, 569).

Unity did not prevail for long. Clashes on political economy and social philosophy soon surfaced. Within the agreed framework of polemical discourse there emerged profound points of intellectual difference. Some proponents believed that there was a need for a strong, impartial and constructivist state to create and supervise the necessary conditions for a competitive market free of monopolistic cartel behaviour ('ordo-interventionism') (Hartwich 2009, vii). Others argued that it was better to leave the competitive market largely unregulated, relying on its intrinsic structural mechanisms to generate the societal information necessary to empower individuals and corporations to make rational economic decisions.

The exemplar of that position, certainly to those critical of the ethos, was Friedrich Hayek and the views he espoused, most particularly in *Road to Serfdom* (Hayek 1944), and echoed later by Milton Friedman (1962) in *Capitalism and Freedom*. Hayek's influential but hotly contested proposition was that any centralised control of economic activities by the state was likely to be misused and tended to be associated with political repression. Democracy was best protected by an unfettered market.

Meanwhile, in the US, a group of prominent Americans began to build a body of economic thought that challenged the postwar Keynesian consensus. It is often associated with University of Chicago economists such as George Stigler, Gary Becker and Ronald Coase. The university's doyen, Milton Friedman, initially subscribed to the term neoliberal as a characterisation of his own views. By the late 1960s, however, he had rejected it as a useful descriptor of his intellectual position on monetarism and supply-side economics. Nevertheless, opponents continued to draw a strong link between the Chicago School's espousal of limited government intervention and the premises of neoliberal economics.

Then, in the 1970s, an odd transmutation occurred. It essentially transformed a school of economic thought into a marker for ideological confrontation. A group of Spanish-speaking scholars, opposed to the influence of the 'Chicago Boys' on the economic policies associated with General Pinochet's autocratic rule in Chile, identified the enemy they faced as neoliberalism. It was from that circumlocutious genesis that left-leaning English scholars found themselves attracted to the term, predominantly as a means of rejecting its avowed political menace.

And so it has come to pass that in the last 40 years neoliberalism has become a term generally associated with those economic policies that are seen as creating increased inequalities in income, wealth and power. Kean Birch, who has identified at least seven variants of neoliberalism, is indubitably correct in arguing that it is 'tricky to identify neoliberalism with any one particular school of thought without missing out a whole lot of the story' (Birch 2017). But it is too late: the word has become the intellectual weapon of choice. The more amorphous the concept the greater its power to condemn.

It is a term often identified with the economic policies of 'the apostles of neoliberalism – state withdrawal, and surrender of control of economic factors to the private sector – Margaret Thatcher and Ronald Reagan' (Strangio, 't Hart and Walter 2017). But its pernicious influence stretches beyond 'Thatcherism' and 'Reaganomics', and is applied also to many of the policies pursued by Jimmy Carter and Bill Clinton in the US. It is seen as central to Tony Blair's 'Third Way' and 'Modernising Government' initiatives in the UK. It is the preferred term used to characterise the policies pursued by the 1980s Labour Government of David Lange and the strong deregulatory impulse of 'Rogernomics' in New Zealand. Lange, it is argued, was 'the affable and charming salesman' for a neoliberalism which out-Thatchered Thatcher (Marcetic 2017).

For similar reasons, it has become the common epithet applied by critics to the successive Labor and Liberal governments of Australia led by Bob Hawke, Paul Keating and John Howard and beyond. To opponents, what Paul Kelly (2011) has characterised as the 'March of Patriots' took place to the drumbeat of neoliberalism. Critics are appalled that Kelly, who never uses the term, 'commends the neo-liberal political economy that prompts governments to deregulate markets … to privatise public assets, to impose new obligations on welfare recipients, and to open Australia to global flows of people, goods and finance' (Rowse 2003).

Neoliberalism as political shorthand for horror

Today, neoliberalism has become largely an expression of political opposition. The provenance of its complex intellectual origins have been lost and its arguments simplified. The term is most often deployed as the object of a rather crude form of sloganeering. In the last 30 years it 'has rapidly become an academic catchphrase' (Boas and Gans-Morse 2009, 138). In its simplest form it represents: 'markets good, government bad' (Jones, Parker and ten Bos 2005). Often it is employed as a pejorative term for 'hyper-capitalism', 'capitalism with the gloves off' or 'liberalism … with a vengeance'. It is 'a catch-all shorthand for the horrors associated with globalization and recurring financial crises' (Jones 2014, 2).

'Much maligned, often misunderstood, neoliberalism is frequently in the eye of the beholder. And that beholder is often a hostile one.' Thus argues Bernard Keane (2018), seeking to explain how Australian politics has gone to hell and dragged us with it. 'Neoliberal', he recognises, 'has become a term of abuse for the left, denoting virtually any economic or fiscal policy disliked by progressives'.

Neoliberalism has emerged, within the treatises of angry academic discourse, as an international phenomenon. It represents 'the contemporary form of capitalism which now dominates the world economy' (Dunlop 2016). It is 'a political project carried out by the corporate capitalist class' since the late 1970s (Harvey 2016). Almost every public policy crisis can be attributed to neoliberal economic principles. From this jaundiced perspective, global financial recession is interpreted as symptomatic of the 'crisis of neoliberal capitalism'.

What was the cause of the disastrous bushfires in Australia 2019–20? The answer: 'It's neoliberalism that lit the fires' (Gibson 2019). And coronavirus? The COVID-19 pandemic is 'exposing the plague of neoliberalism' (Giroux 2020). And climate change? That, too, reveals the destructive assaults waged by neoliberal globalisation on the ecosystem. By contributing to untrammelled environmental degradation, 'the era of neoliberalization also happens to be the era of the fastest mass extinction of species in the Earth's recent history' (Harvey 2016, 172). Even the recent moral crisis of Australian cricket reveals neoliberalism's nefarious hand (Williams 2018).

Neoliberalism is the spectre that haunts governments around the globe. From urban water privatisation in Bolivia (Spronk 2007) to the collection of television tax in Bosnia and Herzegovina (Delic 2016), from land conversion in Guyana's gold fields (Canterbury 1977) to timber production in south-eastern Mexico (Klepeis and Vance 2009), from workforce policy in New Zealand (Marcetic 2017; Perry 2007) to welfare consumerism in Denmark (Anderson 2019), from the contamination of water in Ontario (Prudham 2004) to the undermining of municipal unionism in San Francisco and Toronto (Travis 2017; Fanelli 2014) – the roots of pernicious public policy can most often be sourced to the worldwide proliferation of neoliberalism.

International institutions and their policy objectives have also been captured. The undermining of public health by the International Monetary Fund (IMF) can be attributed to 'the deadly ideas of neoliberalism' (Rowden 2009). Similarly, the World Trade Organization and the World Bank 'have attracted excoriating criticism for supposedly representing the vanguard of a particularly vicious brand of neo-liberalism' (Anonymous 2000). All the institutions, it is suggested, have become exponents of the neoliberal agenda (Mentan 2015, 298).

In Australia, Job Network (now jobactive) is also tarred with the same brush. So, too, are welfare reform, health services and aged and community care. Education policy is 'increasingly infused and driven by the logic of profit' (Davidge 2016) inspired by a neoliberal set of financial practices and exchanges (Ball 2012). Australia, from 1975 until today, has been in the grip of 'neo-liberal policy hegemony' (Haworth and Hughes 2015, 122; Lloyd 2008, 40): Richard Denniss (2018b) argues that 'for thirty years, the *language* of neoliberalism has been applied to everything from environmental protection to care of the disabled'. 'The only issue that matters' in Australia today is 'the galloping inequality, the public squalor and private splendour of a neoliberal deregulated capitalism' (Roberts 2017).

In short, the perceived application of neoliberalism to public policy is now couched almost exclusively in a negative form. The extensive literature suggest that its pernicious influence comes in 'waves', that its manifestation involves 'excesses', and that its effects are 'repressive'. It is portrayed as a source of brutal government inaction. Its 'neoliberal penalty' is exhibited in economic inequality and social instability, the increasing insecurity of wage labour and the widening incarceration of the poor. It represents, according to *The Handbook of Neoliberalism*, 'a seemingly ubiquitous set of market-orientated policies ... being largely responsible for a wide range of social, political, ecological and economic problems' (Springer, Birch and MacLeavy 2016, 2). It is 'the ideology at the root of all our problems' (Monbiot 2016).

The case for the prosecution

So what, more precisely, do critics of neoliberalism wish to convey? In essence, it is argued, its ethos is predicated upon the superiority of the market and its pursuit has been driven ruthlessly by the exigencies of public government austerity. Government proponents seek to reduce deficits and lower spending. They eschew redistributive polices. They see the social protections of a welfare safety net as a hindrance to economic growth. They imagine that state regulation, especially of the labour and capital markets, produces rigidities. They argue that all sectors of the economy should be opened up to competition. Neoliberalism is symbolised by 'its uncritical worship of free markets and its determinedly wasteful consumerist culture' (Mackay 2014).

Neoliberals as characterised show little interest in constraining the free movement of goods and services across sovereign borders. Nor do they believe that the state should intervene in foreign trade to protect domestic economic enterprises (or their workforces) from global competition. Neoliberals do not wish the state to control international financial markets or, domestically, to establish price controls. They believe that taxation should be reduced to provide an incentive to work and invest. Monetary policy should focus on inflation.

For critics, this ideological bent has had disastrous consequences for citizens. While economic growth has resulted, its benefits have gone overwhelmingly to the privileged. Under the ideological pretence of individual freedom and self-reliance, neoliberals espouse policies that engender increasing inequality of income, wealth and opportunity, and result in ever-greater concentration of economic power. The pursuit of labour market flexibility is a smokescreen for the casualisation and exploitation of paid work.

Neoliberalism, from this perspective, is defined as blind faith in unrestrained market competition. Its deleterious ambition is to drive 'the extension of the competitive markets into all areas of life, including the economy, politics and society' (Springer, Birch and MacLeavy 2016, 2). It is not just that 'spheres of life are colonized by the market': the state actually creates new markets for commoditised public goods (Meagher, Connell and Fawcett 2009, 333). It is an ethos that is 'privileging market competition over moral considerations' (Hil 2014). The world is imagined as 'a vast supermarket' in which citizens are treated merely as consumers. Indeed, Tom Christensen (2005), assessing critically Norway's move to new public management and privatisation adopts the term 'supermarket state' to characterise the future he fears (Olsen 1988, cited in Christensen 2005, 725).

The Australian version of the neoliberal impulse, it is argued, intends to 're-task' the state into a minimalist form (Weiss 2012). Successive governments under its ideological sway have sought to privatise and commercialise the public sphere by breaking up and selling state assets. They have transferred responsibility for the construction of public infrastructure and delivery of public programs to a contestable environment of outsourced providers.

And neoliberalism is not just reflected in public policy. In pursuit of its goals, neoliberal politicians have undermined the institutional structures of democratic governance and conducted an 'assault against public services and workers' (Fanelli 2014). Everywhere, one can discern a 'pattern of linkage between public service reform and neoliberalism' (Clark 2002, 771). Professional expertise has been undermined. In North America, Europe and Australasia, public administration has been in retreat. Officialdom has been captured. Neoliberalism now stalks the corridors of bureaucratic power. Its agenda has been imposed on society through the 'state project' of new public management.

Indeed, public services are characterised as the institutional means by which governments deliver their supposedly neoliberal agendas. Public servants provide advice to frame the policy discussions of governments, design the programs that give effect to their decisions and deliver (directly or through third parties) the services, payments or regulatory interventions that implement their goals.

In Australia, it has been proposed, public servants have done much more than be responsive to their political masters (Pusey 1991). They have led the charge. It was the economic rationalists in senior levels of the APS in the 1980s and 1990s who persuaded their ministers to pursue deregulatory neoliberalism. It was departmental secretaries, the 'shadowy but influential figures in determining how Australia is governed', who struck out in a neoliberal direction (Weller 2001). 'Top public servants are the "switchmen" of history', it is posited: 'when they change their minds the destiny of nations takes a different course' (Pusey 1991, 2). Bureaucrats changed their minds and persuaded their political masters to change theirs.

Whether or not Australian public servants were leaders or led, it has been argued that the institutions in which they work have been transformed by ideology. They have become the most significant method by which to 'introduce neoliberalism policies by a kind of organisational coup' (Meagher, Connell and Fawcett 2009, 333). Critics suggest that public service agencies, like the policies they are required to execute, have been made over by a market-oriented ethos.

The private sector has been looked to as a means by which to drive greater efficiency and effectiveness in public administration. Today 'the profit-seeking corporation is promoted as the admired model for the public sector' (Connell 2010, 25). A public service agency now functions like a profit-making firm. The structures, operational systems and workplace culture of public services have been given neoliberal guise.

Performance measures have been introduced, by which managers are held accountable for value-for-money results that reflect the economic constraints of budgets rather than the quality of social provision. An audit culture prevails (Sparkes 2013). Neoliberals, by constantly emphasising the need for austerity, have lowered expectations of public administration: for 'the past 30 years, Australians have been told we can't afford high quality public services' (Denniss 2018a). They have sought 'to stigmatize and marginalise … public bureaucracy in particular, as being outmoded and as functionally and morally bankrupt' (Fournier and Grey 1999, 108).

Meanwhile, it is argued, the avowed commitment of governments to improve service standards has become a neoliberal mechanism by which citizens are transformed into customers. The public as a collective has been replaced by individual consumers accessing specific public services. By framing governance and the democratic process in market terms, a political culture has emerged that 'casts citizens as autonomous economic agents, relating to each other and to the state as individual entrepreneurs' (Sparrow 2012a).

Many areas of activity previously undertaken by public servants have been outsourced to the private sector. Most profoundly, the delivery of services to the public has increasingly been 'marketised'. Governments have been repositioned as purchasers rather than providers of public services. There is now a preference to privatise services whenever possible (Hil 2014). A quasi-market is created in which third-party organisations are contracted to deliver government programs. Public administrators, placed in charge of the tender process, are forced to become 'program champions'. The consequence 'is to politicize the senior public service' (Langford and Edwards 2001).

In fact, in Australia it is non-profit civil society organisations that have won most of the tendered contracts for the delivery of human services. This might seem at odds with a neoliberal agenda. Yet, through suspicious eyes, this outcome is portrayed simply as a devious way to take advantage of weaker industrial protections and lower salaries in the community sector (Healy 2009). More importantly, it is presented as a means of coopting non-profits to a subservient role. Australian governments 'have utilized the third sector as a means of quelling political opposition by rendering these community organisations dependent on funding tied to performance and outcome measures set by government' (Van Gramberg and Bassett 2005, 2). The National Disability Insurance Scheme might be hailed as socially progressive but 'what on earth is the NDIS, with its opaque bureaucracies and internal market, if not a neoliberal concoction?' (Harris et al. 2014).

From this perspective, advocacy organisations in the pursuit of government contracts, have been silenced. Keen to hang on to their contracts, they are fearful of criticising government. It is a clever tactic that has 'the effect of institutionalising the neoliberal agenda while quashing political opposition' (Van Gramberg and Bassett 2005, 2). In accepting grants and contracts from governments, community organisations have unwittingly 'supped with the Devil'.

Commissioning service provision from external providers has also been presented as driven by 'an agenda of de-professionalization' in which public sector knowledge is outsourced to less-trained staff (Malin 2017). This move has a 'gendered' impact, because work is moved from a predominately female public sector to a predominately male private sector. Even initiatives framed around enhanced community support for volunteerism or greater citizen participation have actually 'further entrenched neoliberalism' (Fawcett and Hanlon 2009). One must not be beguiled, we are warned. This is a world in which the public evocation of social purpose can nearly always be revealed as driven by nefarious motivation.

The case that falls on deaf ears

The power of neoliberal motivation to explain this perceived restructuring of public service goes almost unchallenged in peer-reviewed scholarly journals. It has pervaded much of the social science literature in Australia. Many academics see successive Australian governments as pursing a neoliberal agenda since at least the 1980s, although some believe that their own location within a 'neoliberal university' mutes their voice for public policy change (Cox 2018).

They identify 'new public management' as a structural manifestation of that ideological predisposition to diminish the role of public administration. There has been a conscious effort 'to stigmatise and marginalise … public bureaucracy … as being outmoded and as functionally and morally bankrupt' (Fournier and Grey 1999, 108). 'Applying the lessons learned from neo-liberalism', Australian public services underwent 'a huge and self-conscious project of reinvention' by moving away from procedural governance and enterprising the state' (Considine 2001, 2). Neoliberalism was 'the ideological driver behind the practices and policy of New Public Management' (Fawcett and Hanlon 2009; Roberts 2015).

The contrast in perspective from those active in public life could not be starker. Politicians (rarely) and public servants (almost never) see themselves as subscribers to neoliberalism. Most public policy management textbooks do not employ the term. Pick up the major tomes on Australian public administration – the most recent edition of *The Australian Policy Handbook* (Althaus, Bridgman and Davis 2017), perhaps, or *Policy Analysis in Australia* (Head and Crowley 2015) – and there is not a single reference to neoliberal goals. Nor, indeed, is there in *Public Sector Management in Australia*, to which Wanna was a contributing editor (O'Faircheallaigh, Wanna and Weller 1999).

Politicians, too, either avoid the term or, equally likely, have never come across it. In some 1,400 pages of text relating to his own political life and that of the Liberal's greatest leader, Robert Menzies, John Howard never uses the term neoliberal (although he does acknowledge *en passant* the influence of 'so-called neo-conservatives' close to George Bush). Nor did Bob Hawke reference the term in his biography. Indeed Hawke, questioned about his supposed 'ideological predilection' for neoliberal policies emphatically rejected the proposition: in his view he laid down a new direction for the social democrats (Swan 2017). Nor do the standard biographies of Paul Keating employ the word. Keating himself emphasised that 'we are not "-ists" and we do not believe in "-isms"' (Ramsay and Battin 2005). Nor does Julia Gillard's biography mention neoliberalism. Indeed, it is not a term used by any of the national campaign directors of either of Australia's two major political parties. Nor does it appear in either of David Lange's two New Zealand memoirs.

It is a similar story at the state level. To critics, neoliberalism was 'characterised by the sweeping privatisations that premier Bob Carr championed in NSW' (Sparrow 2012b). By recasting the entire social world on market lines, Carr's government strenuously led the 'neoliberal project' in Australia. The premier, in a scathing indictment, was 'Carr(ion)' (Sparrow 2012b). This is not the world as seen by Carr. 'The prevailing ideologies?' scoffed the ex-premier: 'sorry, too grand a word. Let's call it the prevailing ethos, way of thinking' (Carr 2018).

By contrast, Kevin Rudd as prime minister did use the term. But he did so only to attack his political opponents as foot-soldiers of the neoliberal enemy. In a wide-ranging paper on the global financial crisis, Rudd sought to present his election as a seismic turning point in political history. He offered himself up as the prime minister who would bring to an end the 30-year 'triumph of neoliberalism – that particular brand of free-market fundamentalism, extreme capitalism and excessive greed which became the economic orthodoxy of our time' (Rudd 2009). On reflection, he believed he delivered. Rudd remembers his response to the global financial crisis as a direct attack on the 'prevailing neoliberal orthodoxy' (Rudd 2018).

None of this bone-pointing at others has offered protection to Rudd from the righteous indignation of critics. Labour politicians are adjudged to have been 'supporters of the neoliberal agenda since the Hayden leadership period' (Marsh 2006). In spite of attempts to shake off the legacy, Rudd's government is seen to represent 'continuity in neoliberal thought and policy'. Indeed, it is 'a kind of wild irony' that 'Rudd denounced neoliberalism, shortly before his government introduced a raft of neoliberal measures' that were implemented by Treasurer Swan (Meagher, Connell and Fawcett 2009, 333). In short, those who are keen to direct attention to the neoliberal garb of their political opponents, find that academic writers often drape them in the same attire. The emperors wear clothes but not of their own choosing.

Australian public servants, who have served at senior levels in successive neoliberal government regimes, do not employ the term at all. They do not utter the word in their speeches or writing. Indeed, to the best of my memory, I have not heard neoliberalism mentioned at any ANZSOG (Australia and New Zealand School of Government) seminar or Institute of Public Administration Australia conference that I have attended over the last 25 years. Enter it as a keyword in the search engine of the Australian Public Service Commission website and, yielding no results, it asks you to check the spelling. Similarly, the NSW Public Service Commission site reports '0 results for neoliberalism' (before quickly asking visitors for feedback on the quality of the site).

The failure of senior public servants to identify with the ideological concept for which critics often hold them responsible seems passing strange. Yet it is a particular manifestation of a far deeper phenomenon. Neoliberalism may be 'the idea that swallowed the world' (Metcalf 2017) but it has done so in the most curious of ways. The idiom is generally used now only by those who stridently oppose its avowed consequences: 'People do not call themselves neoliberal; instead they tag their enemies with the term' (Hall and Lamont 2013, xvii). Those who used to identify with the term have vanished. It has become the economic philosophy that dare not speak its name. Silently, its opponents warn us, it is everywhere capturing governments and altering the structure and ethos of the public services that provide advice to them.

There are two obvious reasons why Australian public servants (and the governments they serve) rarely, if ever, identify themselves as neoliberal in orientation. Although I have sought to put flesh on the bones of contention, the meaning of the term has considerable ideological fluidity. Neoliberal is most often used to identify enemies, while implicitly signalling the virtue of its critics' own philosophical and ethical credentials.

Moreover, academic strictures on the application of neoliberal theory tend to be couched in the language of contemporary social science. The scholarly narrative of neoliberal criticism is replete with discursive politics, gendered assumptions, sociocultural logic, market commodification of public value, desocialisation of identity, reappropriation of community, privileging of power and exploitation of a 'precariat' class. Sometimes, in a footnote, there is genuflection before the structuralism and hermeneutics of Michel Foucault. That language increasingly permeates the *Australian Journal of Public Administration*: a recent insightful article on the public policies of bushfire safety was couched in terms of 'the valorisation of hegemonic masculinity' (Reynolds and Tyler 2018, 529). These terms, properly defined, have purpose and meaning but they are not manners of speech that create resonance with most practising public administrators. They widen the gap between the insider and the outsider, between the observation and the observer.

Nor does academic discourse capture public servants' perceived reality. Most would at once recognise the key features of political change that are identified but would be surprised at their framing as part of a 'neoliberal agenda'. Public servants live in a world of continuous political debate but – in part as a consequence – necessary compromise. Their world is one of iteration. Shiny new policies are inevitably tarnished by the need for political negotiation. Second-best solutions to wickedly complex policy conundrums are seen as better than no solutions at all. They are not driven by ideological purity. Nor, they sense, are the ministers they serve.

In fact, a few critics of Australian neoliberalism somewhat grudgingly recognise that political purpose is in practice inconsistent and extraordinarily varied. They acknowledge that in some cases the emphasis on enhanced market-orientation has been counterbalanced by continued commitment to fair and equitable service. Some accept that there is 'no single model of public service reform associated with neoliberal ideological realignment' (Clark 2002). As a special issue of the Australian *Journal of Sociology* admitted, neoliberal concepts:

> have not quite swept all before them in Australian human services … the achievements of reform efforts are partial … [and they] have not been entirely successful in replacing other norms and rationalities. (Meagher, Connell and Fawcett 2009, 335)

In fact, Australia's structural reform policies are a hybrid (Fabian and Breunig 2018).

Academic defenders of the 'Hawke legacy' suggest that 'Hawke never went as far in flirting with neo-liberalism as the Liberal Party did' (Johnson 2009, 7). To some on the centre-left of politics, the views of Hawke (and Keating, Rudd and Gillard) can be distinguished from those of the 'extreme' neoliberal, John Howard. But to others this is simply a false demarcation: party differences 'are not, in fact sides in any meaningful sense but separate cheeks on the same derriere' (Denniss 2018b).

Critics often portray this 'failure' to achieve doctrinal purity as attributable to political opposition and public resistance. They also suggested that political conviction is undermined by self-interested cynicism. While neoliberal language is used to extol the virtues of small government, many of its conservative proponents are actually happy to expend public funds on their own political preferences: they are not ideologues for the simple reason that they 'lack the consistency and strength of principle to warrant the title' (Denniss 2018b). They find themselves brought undone by the rent-seekers of crony capitalism, spruiking government intervention (Keane 2016). Indeed, some argue that it is now conservative politicians, not progressives, that are moving away from market-dominated policies (Bornstein 2017). On such grounds, Richard Denniss postulates that 'neoliberalism is dead'. He argues that Australian politicians of the right have lost confidence in the market and are increasingly attracted to state intervention (Denniss 2018a). But that remains a minority position. Most critics counter that such perspectives do not 'fully appreciate just how deep the market ethos runs in Australian politics' (King 2018). In the eyes of most Australian critics, neoliberalism is alive and well both among politicians and the public servants who work for them.

So, what did the practitioners say?
Andrew Podger

It is time, in John Wanna's words, that we 'tried to allow the actors at the time to present the issues in their own words' (Wanna, Ryan and Ng 2001, xi). He suggested that we should be willing to listen to how 'public servants, government employees, politicians, advisers ... provided their own assessments of the changes taking place in the public sector' (O'Faircheallaigh, Wanna and Weller 1999, v).

Peter Shergold explores above why 'the fashion in which public servants articulate the need for change, and the manner in which academics critique it, rarely engage'. He focuses particularly on the current popular framework of academic discourse that centres on 'neoliberalism'. Let me complement Peter's thesis by referring to the articles and speeches by public servants over the last four decades, a wealth of material in the 1980s and 1990s though sadly more Spartan over the last decade or so.

I should add that practitioner frustration with academics has not been limited to the academics' criticisms of public sector reform. There has been from time to time a denigration of the APS itself with little regard, if any, to facts about the people involved or the work they do. Ian Castles, known within the APS at the time as the most rigorous of academic practitioners, wrote a major rejoinder to criticisms by Donald Horne and Hugh Stretton when Castles was secretary of the Department of Finance defending the record of Australia's civil service and demonstrating by the examples of Treasury secretaries that, unlike many overseas civil services, ours is not dominated by a privileged social class (Castles 1987).

Practitioners' words about reform, not surprisingly, reflect their pragmatic focus. They also demonstrate the particular attributes of public sector reform in Australia from the 1980s: steady, incremental change with occasional punctuations of major measures, but no one big-bang development and few major reversals. These attributes, and the emphasis on pragmatism rather than ideology, have always been highlighted by John Wanna (e.g. Wanna, Kelly and Forster 2000, 311).

This, however, has not stopped other academics from claiming through each stage of Australia's reform process that officials as well as governments have pushed a particular right-wing agenda; many did not concede that the reforms would (and did) lead to improvements in management and public sector efficiency and effectiveness without undermining its fundamental roles.

1980s reforms

The emphasis in the 1980s was on improving efficiency and effectiveness. The genesis of the reforms lay in both the Coombs Royal Commission (RCAGA 1976) and the Reid Report (Review of Commonwealth Administration 1983) that helped to shape the Hawke Government's approach to public expenditure and public sector management

(ALP 1983). David Shand, before he joined the Department of Finance, welcomed the Hawke Government's statements on *Reforming the Public Service* and *Budget Reform*, noting the cautious approach in the latter document and the emphasis on pilot studies including through the Financial Management Improvement Program (FMIP) (Shand 1984).

Shand, together with Malcolm Holmes and under Pat Barrett's leadership within Ian Castles's Finance department, helped shape the FMIP and related management reforms. Following the 1987 machinery of government changes, which both improved cabinet processes and facilitated greater devolution of management authority, Barrett publicly encouraged wide action within line departments to take advantage of the reforms to improve administrative performance (Barrett 1988).

Mike Keating, who replaced Castles as head of Finance in 1987, clarified the objectives of the reforms (Keating 1988):

- to assist the elected government to choose how it wishes to allocate resources best to satisfy its policy objectives
- to improve the effectiveness, equity and efficiency of programs delivered by the public sector directed at meeting these objectives
- to focus the necessary tight restraint in budget outlays on areas where effectiveness, equity and efficiency criteria justify reductions, and embodied in the first three
- to improve the public service as a place to work.

Keating later coined the term 'managing for results' as the underlying basis for the 1980s reforms (Keating 1990).

Academic criticism in the 1980s employed 'managerialism' as the pejorative term for the reforms (Yeatman 1987; Painter 1988; Considine 1988). John Paterson, a senior Victorian public servant, challenged the criticism head-on (Paterson 1988), addressing each of the charges made by one leading critic and declaring firmly that:

- the administrative reforms were not ideologically driven
- no evidence had been presented to support charges of:
  - an internal climate being more masculine than in the past
  - the quality of work downgraded
  - probity declined

- accountability to the parliament, the general public or those aggrieved by bureaucratic decisions being less
- fairness given less weight, or access of minorities or the disadvantaged to public service positions downgraded.

Paterson's assessment, albeit not scientific, was that none of these charges hold.

During this stage of public sector reform, the language of the practitioners could never be described as 'neoliberal'. Practitioners did not emphasise the use of markets: indeed, Paterson made no mention of competition or markets. Even the government's 1986 statement about reforms to government business enterprises and statutory authorities made no mention of privatisation. Only general references were made to the impact of global competition and that the public sector was not immune from competitive pressures by some public servants (e.g. Keating 1989). These implied that the managerialist agenda complemented the government's wider economic agenda, which embraced global competition by reducing protection, floating the Australian dollar and beginning to deregulate the labour market. This, of course, is entirely consistent with Keating's earlier emphasis that the reforms were explicitly intended to ensure the public service was responding to the elected government's priorities.

It is true, nonetheless, that the reforms during the 1980s consciously shifted the emphasis in public administration from processes and legal language to performance in terms of results and the economic language of prices, efficiency and effectiveness.

Early 1990s

After a mostly positive report on the FMIP by a parliamentary committee (Australian Parliament 1990), public service practitioners began to take stock of the wider reform agenda. A major evaluation was undertaken for the Management Advisory Committee (Task Force on Management Improvement 1992), led by Vic Rogers from the Department of Social Security (see also Rogers 1992, 1993). While concluding that further effort was needed to take advantage of the reforms, particularly in the area of human resources management, the evaluation found significant improvements in efficiency and effectiveness, that productivity growth in the APS as a whole had been high, and that the reforms had improved the focus on clients and the quality of services (Sedgwick 1994).

The reform agenda was evolving at that time, with increasing emphasis being paid to the role of markets and competition to improve efficiency as much of the responsibility for financial management was devolved to agencies. Graham Evans, secretary of the Department of Transport and Communications (created in 1987), described his portfolio's reform agenda highlighting the importance of government business enterprises' competitiveness and explaining the department's use of business-type measures such as corporate planning (Evans 1992). John Mellors, a deputy secretary, then secretary of the Department of Administrative Services, described the achievements and challenges from reforms to the common services provided by his department, starting with user pays then user choice of provider and then more commercial approaches to service provision (Mellors 1993, 1996). Mike McNamara and I, then in Defence, described how the department was using competition to drive efficiencies in a wide range of logistical services through the Commercial Support Program (Podger 1994; McNamara 1996). More broadly, the running costs reforms from the 1980s were allowing agencies to determine when contracting out might be more efficient than internal provision of corporate services, and the Department of Finance's procurement rules set out processes for fair competition based on value for money. The reform measures were far more than rhetorical; they involved a cultural change in the management of public moneys, improving value for money by reducing overheads so resources could be focused more on public programs, and paying more attention to program effectiveness.

The shift to greater emphasis on markets and competition was also occurring at the state government level. Sue Vardon in South Australia described the challenges and directions of reform in that state following the collapse of the State Bank (Vardon 1994). Victoria, which had also experienced a financial crisis, restructured its public hospital system introducing a purchaser/provider arrangement to drive efficiencies, led by John Paterson (who had become director-general of the Health Department) and Stephen Duckett. Meredith Edwards, a deputy secretary in the Department of the Prime Minister and Cabinet (PM&C), also examined international trends in using the competition paradigm to reinvent the work of government (Edwards 1996).

As with the 1980s reforms, these further administrative reforms complemented the wider economic reforms being pursued not only by the Commonwealth Government but also by the states, as illustrated by the Council of Australian Governments' Competition Policy (COAG 1995).

The underlying purpose of these reforms was to increase productivity in both the private and public sectors, so as to improve Australian living standards.

Academic criticism of the reforms in this period again assumed that the public service practitioners had their own ideological agenda. Michael Pusey led the attack, claiming that 'economic rationalists' in the public service had had an undue influence over the government and, as a result, 'a nation-building state' had 'change(d) its mind' (Pusey 1991). Wanna was among the few academics to dispute the Pusey thesis, his review of Pusey's book opening with the comment that 'Kicking the Canberra can is obviously alive and well' (Wanna 1992). Fred Argy, by then retired from the APS (he had previously been head of the Economic Planning Advisory Committee and a senior Treasury official), wrote a more gentle review nonetheless firmly rejecting Pusey's central thesis of the government and its advisers being against government intervention and insensitive to social welfare and distribution considerations, highlighting Pusey's failure to refer to the actual writings of senior practitioners (Argy 1992).

Mike Keating, then secretary of PM&C, later felt it necessary to publicly reject the by then widespread characterisation of policy formulation in the last decade as captured by 'neo-classical economic rationalists', noting the critics failed to define an economic rationalist and, 'more importantly, offer little understanding of exactly what has occurred, nor the forces at work' (Keating 1994). It is hard to see how the policies of the previous decade (at least at Commonwealth level), including in the areas of social security, health financing and higher education, or the public management changes that accompanied them, could be viewed then (or now) as in any way rolling back the state or reducing its emphasis on equity.

Later 1990s and early 2000s

Following the election of the Howard Government in 1996, more emphasis was placed on competition and the use of market-type mechanisms in public administration. As through the earlier phases of reform, this reflected in part the government's wider economic reform agenda, in this case a major influence was its controversial agenda to extend labour market reform.

Also, there was growing interest in the quality of services provided to the public. Earlier reforms included service charters to ensure that performance was not measured simply in terms of financial efficiency but also in terms of responsiveness to clients. But the next stage of reform began also to emphasise choice by service 'customers', a 'growing issue' according to Mike Keating and one requiring the development of purchaser/provider administrative arrangements (Keating 1996). By this time, I had become secretary of the Department of Health and Family Services; I referred to this issue and how it might be used to shift the health system's orientation away from providers to patients, and promote better service quality, improving health outcomes (e.g. for people with chronic conditions) as well as efficiency (Podger 1997, 1998). While there was a shared desire to see the public service adopt a more outwards focus, there was also an internal debate about the appropriate term for those receiving services ('clients' or 'customers' or 'citizens').

Perhaps the most significant development in this context was the creation of the Job Network replacing the former Commonwealth Employment Service. This involved the employment department paying providers of employment services (for profit and non-profit organisations and, for a time, a public sector provider) to deliver services to unemployed people based on their performance in getting their clients into jobs, and allowing the clients some choice about their provider of services. The establishment of Centrelink also signalled a strengthened emphasis on those receiving welfare payments and services, improving coordination and responsiveness.

Academic critics claiming a neoliberal agenda might find some limited evidence as some practitioners began to express developments in language that seemed to assume the public sector should embrace private sector practices much more broadly than had been done under earlier reforms. Stephen Bartos (a deputy secretary in Finance) advocated that 'every service of government is potentially open to competition' (Bartos 1998), and there was some suggestion of a 'Yellow Pages' philosophy in Finance at the time (that any activity that could be found in the Yellow Pages should be shifted from the public sector and subject to competition). Peter Boxall (secretary of Finance) and Len Early (another Finance deputy) also advocated more business-like approaches right across the public sector (Boxall 1998; Early 1998), a view continued to be expressed by Boxall after his retirement (Boxall 2012).

All three attracted some criticism from within the APS, perhaps best illustrated by S R Kelleher (a pseudonym for an anonymous public servant), who warned that the allocative powers of markets do not invariably work in the interests of the overall good of the community, and noted the views of past APS leaders that the role of the public service has changed over time 'in degree, not kind' (Kelleher 1998). My strong suspicion is that most public service leaders at the time continued to take a strongly pragmatic approach to reform, eschewing the pockets of ideology that occurred. Indeed, many were continually emphasising the importance of public service values in this period. Peter Shergold (then public service commissioner) noted that traditional values were being retained under the public service reforms being introduced, albeit with more emphasis on performance (Shergold 1997). The values were articulated and placed in the new legislation (*Public Service Act 1999* [Cth]).

Mike Keating, after his retirement, perhaps expressed the most widely held view among the practitioner reformers of the 1990s in his book, *Who Rules? How Government Retains Control of a Privatised Economy* (Keating 2004). In it he argues that 'the shift to marketization largely represents an attempt by government to enhance or restore their power to achieve economic and social objectives, while minimising any loss of efficiency' (Keating 2001, 5); and that 'while marketization may have changed the instruments and policies of governments, governments can still govern: they still command power to determine a course of action and achieve their objectives' (Keating 2004, 12).

Practitioner views since 2000

The importance of the APS Values was constantly highlighted by the APS Commission (Podger 2002; APSC 2003a, 2003b), emphasising that the ends do not always justify the means, and that traditional values of nonpartisanship, impartiality and professionalism remain paramount. The APS Commission also published a report documenting the Australian reforms at both Commonwealth and state/territory levels (APSC 2003c), describing the focus on results and the use of competition. Written for an international audience (at the request of the Commonwealth Association of Public Administration and Management), it presented practical examples of improvements in efficiency and effectiveness that other Commonwealth countries might consider, whatever their political orientation; there was no material that could be considered ideological.

Sue Vardon, then CEO of Centrelink, also published an article on possible international implications of Australian public sector reforms (Vardon 2001); Centrelink was later widely acknowledged as a successful reform (Halligan and Wills 2008).

Some modifications were introduced to the earlier reforms (now seen as moves from new public management to new public governance) to give more emphasis to implementation issues and to whole-of-government management (MAC 2004), but most of the framework of the earlier reforms continued, including the emphasis on managing for results and focusing on clients.

Fewer public speeches and published articles by senior practitioners have appeared since the early 2000s (more's the pity), but valedictory speeches by departing secretaries provide a valuable source of senior practitioners' views. They reveal that senior public servants continue to come from a diverse range of backgrounds, both social and academic (Wanna, Vincent and Podger 2012) and are not characterised either by privilege or a neoliberal, economic education. There is a common emphasis on serving the public interest (e.g. Briggs 2012), distinguishing between the role of the public sector from that of the private sector, and focusing on the long term (e.g. Borthwick 2012).

While some continue to emphasise global competitive pressures (e.g. Henry 2012), none could be characterised as implying any particular ideological position. Some provide constructive criticisms about aspects of the reform agenda. I myself questioned attitudes towards freedom of information (Podger 2012), while Patricia Scott expressed unease about the changing role of ministerial advisers (Scott 2012) and Peter Varghese expressed concern about the quality of policy advising (Varghese 2017). Other more recent speeches by secretaries build on the reforms of earlier eras. Mike Mrdak emphasises the importance of value for money in public infrastructure investment (e.g. Mrdak 2018), Steven Kennedy identifies the trend to more tailored services to meet individual needs and preferences (Kennedy 2018), Martin Parkinson highlights the importance of innovation in the public sector (Parkinson 2018, 2019), and Heather Smith emphasises the importance of taking advantage of new technology and recognising its likely impact on the way government does its business (Smith 2019).

Internal debates

Notwithstanding the occasional flourish in Peter Shergold's speeches and writings, the tone of most practitioners' public statements has been overwhelmingly pragmatic with an emphasis, dully, on efficiency and effectiveness. This may have disguised the extent of internal debate about the reforms of the last 30 years. On occasion the internal debates have been revealed publicly.

In 1999, I admitted before a Senate Estimates Committee the problems the Health Department was struggling with in implementing accrual accounting. Subsequently, I warned that 'expectations about the benefits have been raised excessively' (Podger 2001, 18), a view shared by many colleagues. Allan Hawke was steadfast in his opposition to the introduction of performance-based pay, which, he argued forcefully, was inimical to public service culture and bad for employee morale (Hawke 2012).

Pat Barrett was highly critical of the appropriation of the term 'customer' to the delivery of public services. Barrett thought the term 'client' 'conveys more about the notion of mutual obligations and relationships, and less about the act of purchasing, which act, of course, includes a decision not to purchase' (Barrett 1999, 4). Shergold publicly argued that the term 'citizen' conveys a better sense of the reciprocated balance of rights and responsibilities that exist between the public beneficiary and the state benefactor (Shergold 2006). I held a similar view; also, I was particularly critical of the practice of some colleagues to refer to their ministers as their 'primary customers' (a view I later published [Podger 2009]).

Another translation of private sector language to public sector management was also debated internally. I said in 2000:

> I must admit to continued unease about departmental secretaries being seen as CEOs. Our relationship to ministers, the government and the Parliament is fundamentally different from the relationship between a private sector CEO and the Board ... our role in the Australian democratic system sets the public service apart. (Podger 2000)

The term 'chief executive' appeared in the *Financial Management and Accountability Act 1997* (Cth), which applied to departments, but a number of colleagues felt, as I did, that the term was inappropriate. This was not to deny the lessons that could be learned from private sector experience in such areas as project, risk, finance and human resource management.

There was also vigorous debate about the degree to which the public service should be responsive to the government of the day (and, correspondingly, about its degree of independence). The internal debate became public after I retired from the APS when I publicly argued that the incentives established by secretary appointment and termination processes, and secretary performance pay, was affecting the way advice was (and was not) being provided (Podger 2007). Shergold, still secretary of PM&C at the time, counter-argued that courage was a matter of character not tenure (Shergold 2007). A subsequent secretary of PM&C, Terry Moran, encouraged a greater degree of independence (Advisory Group on Australian Government Administration 2010) and the term 'responsive to the Government' was omitted from the APS Values when they were revised in 2013 (though this still appears in the Commissioner's Directions under the Public Service Act), and significant changes were made to secretary arrangements. This important and healthy debate clearly continues both within the APS and publicly.

Conclusion

The practitioners' perspectives of reforms since the 1980s emphasise the reforms' pragmatism: they do not reveal any ideological agenda but focus on enhancing the capacity of democratically elected governments to set strategic directions and clarify their policy objectives, while also improving the efficiency and effectiveness of administration in delivering the results the government desires.

Perhaps some of the academic critiques we challenge are in part affected by a spillover of political decisions and administration of policy by bureaucrats. Perhaps also, as Pat Weller (1991) suggests, practitioners' pragmatism is not entirely value-free. But from our direct experience, it is not ideological or pursued in order to supplant the elected government's own philosophy and priorities. And there have been, and continue to be, healthy internal debates.

The language of the practitioners in explaining the reforms has been economics-oriented, reflecting in large part the priority successive governments have given to economic policies. This also reflects some of the principles of the economics discipline that professional public administrators (and governments) must not ignore. Importantly, the use of such language and principles should not be seen to reflect a particular view of the role (or size) of government or of the distribution of income and wealth in the community. Rather it reflects concern to make the most from limited resources, to recognise rent-seekers and ensure support is focused on those genuinely in need, and to enhance the public good and limit the distortions of market failures.

If there is a legitimate charge of APS practitioners having a particular and common outlook it would most likely align with some of the original liberal economists (and moral philosophers) from the eighteenth and nineteenth centuries rather than the so-called neoliberals of the late twentieth century. As Ian Castles wrote in 1986 as the first wave of new public management reforms began in Australia, those economists were the radicals of their day, not the conservatives: they were opposed to slavery, keen to improve the wellbeing of workers and the poor, concerned about those suffering from the potato famine in Ireland, supported universal, publicly funded education and the rights of women to contraceptive advice (republished in Castles 2015). Castles's essay, while not explicitly saying so, demonstrated that liberal economics can be employed to maximise the efficiency and effectiveness of government in achieving whatever the policy preferences of the elected government may be, including a progressive agenda.

APS practitioners would never accept the charge of being 'neoliberal' if that necessarily implies support for a lesser role for government or a more unequal distribution of income and wealth. Personal views on these issues among practitioners undoubtedly vary. All those we know or have known believe in a substantial role for government, while leaving to the elected government the right to determine exactly what that role should be and the consequences for income and wealth distribution.

Equally, APS practitioners seem constantly to have had to defend themselves against mostly ill-defined academic criticisms of 'managerialism', 'economic rationalism' and more recently 'neoliberalism'. This is not to deny considerable room for legitimate debate about whether reform measures have been taken too far or involved unintended consequences (or indeed have not gone far enough or have gone backwards). But that debate needs to be based on evidence and to take into account the first-hand experience of the practitioners: the approach John Wanna has always epitomised.

References

Aalbers, M. B. 2016. 'Regulated deregulation'. In S. Springer, K. Birch and J MacLeavy (eds) *Handbook of Neoliberalism*. New York: Routledge.

Advisory Group on Australian Government Administration. 2010. *Ahead of the Game: Blueprint for the Reform of Australian Government Administration*. Canberra: Department of Prime Minister and Cabinet.

Althaus, C., P. Bridgman and G. Davis. 2017. *The Australian Policy Handbook*. Crows Nest: Allen & Unwin.

Anderson, J. G. 2019. 'Denmark: The welfare state as a victim of neoliberal economic failure?' In S. Olafsson, M. Daly, O. Kangas and J. Palme (eds) *Welfare and the Great Recession: A Comparative Study*. Oxford: Oxford University Press. doi.org/10.1093/oso/9780198830962.003.0011.

Anonymous. 2000. 'The IMF and the World Bank: Puppets of the neoliberal onslaught'. *The Thistle* 13(2).

Argy, F. 1992. 'Book review: Michael Pusey, *Economic Rationalism in Canberra: A Nation-building State Changes its Mind*'. *Economic Papers* 11(1): 83–90. doi.org/10.1111/j.1759-3441.1992.tb00033.x.

Australian Labor Party (ALP). 1983. *Labor and Quality of Government*. 1983 election policy statement. R. Hawke and G. Evans. Canberra: Australian Labor Party.

Australian Parliament. 1990. *Not Dollars Alone: Review of the FMIP*. Report of the House of Representatives Standing Committee on Finance and Public Administration. Canberra: Australian Government.

Australian Public Service Commission (APSC). 2003a. *APS Values and Code of Conduct in Practice: A Guide to Official Conduct for APS Employees and Agency Heads*. Canberra: Australian Government.

Australian Public Service Commission (APSC). 2003b. *Embedding the Values*. Canberra: Australian Government.

Australian Public Service Commission (APSC). 2003c. *Australian Experience of Public Sector Reform*. Canberra: Australian Government.

Ball, S. J. 2012. 'Show me the money! Neoliberalism at work in education'. *Forum* 54(1): 27. doi.org/10.2304/forum.2012.54.1.23.

Barrett, P. 1988. 'Emerging management and budgetary issues: The view from the centre'. *Canberra Bulletin of Public Administration* 54(May): 52–57.

Barrett, P. 1999. 'A more systematic approach to effective decision-making for better outcomes or results'. Address to the Institute of Public Administration Australia Conference, Canberra, 10 March. Available at: www.anao.gov.au/sites/default/files/Barrett_a_more_systematic_approach_to_effective_decision%20making_for_better_outcomes_or_results_1999.pdf?acsf_files_redirect.

Bartos, S. 1998. 'Competitive tendering and contracting'. *Canberra Bulletin of Public Administration* 88(May): 63–64.

Birch, K. 2017. 'What exactly is neoliberalism?' *The Conversation*, 3 November. Available at: theconversation.com/what-exactly-is-neoliberalism-84755.

Boas, T. C., and J. Gans-Morse. 2009. 'Neoliberalism: From new liberal philosophy to anti-liberal slogan'. *Studies in Comparative International Development* 44: 137–161. doi.org/10.1007/s12116-009-9040-5.

Bornstein, J. 2017. 'Just as neoliberalism is finally on its knees, so too is the left'. *The Guardian*, 25 February.

Borthwick, D. 2012. 'As if for a thousand years – the challenges ahead for the APS'. In J. Wanna, S. Vincent and A. Podger (eds) *With the Benefit of Hindsight: Valedictory Reflections from Departmental Secretaries, 2004–2011*. Canberra: ANU Press. doi.org/10.22459/WBH.04.2012.10.

Boxall, P. 1998. 'Outcomes and outputs: The new resource management framework'. *Canberra Bulletin of Public Administration* 88(May): 39–43.

Boxall, P. 2012. 'Reflections of an "unabashed rationalist"'. In J. Wanna, S. Vincent and A. Podger (eds) *With the Benefit of Hindsight: Valedictory Reflections from Departmental Secretaries, 2004–2011*. Canberra: ANU Press. doi.org/10.22459/WBH.04.2012.11.

Briggs, L. 2012. 'The boss in the yellow suit – leading service delivery reform'. In J. Wanna, S. Vincent and A. Podger (eds) *With the Benefit of Hindsight: Valedictory Reflections from Departmental Secretaries, 2004–2011*. Canberra: ANU Press. doi.org/10.22459/WBH.04.2012.16.

Canterbury, D. C. 1977. 'The impact of neoliberalism on labour in Guyana: A case from the Caribbean'. *Labour, Capital and Society* 30(2): 260–289.

Carr, B. 2018. *Run for Your Life*. Melbourne: Melbourne University Publishing.

Castles, I. 1987. 'Facts and fantasies of bureaucracy'. *Canberra Bulletin of Public Administration* 53(December): 35–45.

Castles, I. 2015. 'Economics and anti-economics'. In A. Podger and D. Trewin (eds) *Measuring and Promoting Wellbeing*. Canberra: ANU Press. doi.org/10.22459/MPW.04.2014.04.

Christensen, T. 2005. 'The Norwegian state transformed?' *West European Politics* 28(4): 721–739. doi.org/10.1080/01402380500216641.

Clark, D. 2002. 'Neoliberalism and public service reform: Canada in comparative perspective'. *Canadian Journal of Political Science* 35(4): 771–793. doi.org/10.1017/S0008423902778438.

Connell, R. 2010. 'Understanding neoliberalism'. In S. Braedley and M. Luxton (eds) *Neoliberalism and Everyday Life*. Montreal: McGill-Queen's Press.

Considine, M. 1988. 'The corporate management framework as administrative science: A critique'. *Australian Journal of Public Administration* 47(1): 4–18. doi.org/10.1111/j.1467-8500.1988.tb01042.x.

Considine, M. 2001. *Enterprising States: The Public Management of Welfare-to-Work*. Cambridge: Cambridge University Press.

Council of Australian Governments (COAG). 1995. *Competition Principles Agreement*. Canberra: Council of Australian Governments.

Cox, E. 2018. 'The changing politics of feminist academics'. *Australian Journal of Public Administration* 77(4): 525–528. doi.org/10.1111/1467-8500.12321.

Davidge, G. 2016. *Rethinking Education through Critical Psychology: Cooperative Schools, Social Justice and Voice*. Milton Park: Taylor and Francis. doi.org/10.4324/9781315676159.

Delic, V. 2016. 'Dangers of neoliberalism for public services'. *Mediacentar_Online*, 12 August. Available at: www.media.ba/en/magazin-novinarstvo/dangers-neoliberalism-public-services.

Denniss, R. 2018a. 'The big con: How neoliberals convinced us there wasn't enough to go around'. *The Guardian*, 4 June. Available at: www.theguardian.com/australia-news/2018/jun/04/the-big-con-how-neoliberals-convinced-us-there-wasnt-enough-to-go-around.

Denniss, R. 2018b. 'Dead right: How neoliberalism ate itself and what comes next'. *Quarterly Essay* 70: 1–80.

Donaldson, D. 2018. 'APS review a neoliberal stitch-up, says CPSU'. *The Mandarin*, 7 May. Available at: www.themandarin.com.au/92303-aps-review-a-neoliberal-stitch-up-says-cpsu/.

Dunlop, T. 2016. 'The "small government" sucker punch'. *ABC News*, 10 March. Available at: www.abc.net.au/news/2016-03-10/dunlop-the-small-government-sucker-punch/7234168.

Early, L. 1998. 'The changing role of the public service'. *Canberra Bulletin of Public Administration* 88(May): 60–62.

Edwards, M. 1996. 'Competition and the public sector'. *Canberra Bulletin of Public Administration* 81(October): 31–38.

Evans, G. 1992. 'Managing policy and organisational change in the transport and communications portfolio'. *Canberra Bulletin of Public Administration* 70(October): 1–21.

Fabian, M. and R. Breunig. 2018. 'Market v government? In fact, hybrid policy is the best fit for the 21st century'. *The Conversation*, 4 July. Available at: theconversation.com/market-v-government-in-fact-hybrid-policy-is-the-best-fit-for-the-21st-century-98560.

Fanelli, C. 2014. 'Neoliberal urbanism and the assault against public services and workers in Toronto, 2006–2011'. Briefing, 7 March. *Articulo – Journal of Urban Research*. Available at: journals.openedition.org/articulo/2380.

Fawcett, B. and M. Hanlon. 2009. '"The return to community": Challenges to human service professions'. *Journal of Sociology* 45(4): 435. doi.org/10.1177/1440783309346474.

Fournier, V. and C. Grey. 1999. 'Too much, too little and too often: A critique of du Gay's analysis of enterprise'. *Organization* 6(1): 107–128. doi.org/10.1177/135050849961005.

Friedman, M. 1962. *Capitalism and Freedom*. Chicago: University of Chicago Press.

Gibson, S. 2019. 'It's neoliberalism that lit the fires'. *Overland* 237, 21 November. Available at: overland.org.au/2019/11/its-neoliberalism-that-lit-the-fires/.

Giroux, H. A. 2020. 'The COVID-19 pandemic is exposing the plague of neoliberalism'. *Truthout*, 7 April. Available at: truthout.org/articles/the-covid-19-pandemic-is-exposing-the-plague-of-neoliberalism/.

Hall, P. A., and M. Lamont (eds). 2013. *Social Resilience in the Neoliberal Era*. Cambridge: Cambridge University Press.

Halligan, J. and J. Wills. 2008. *The Centrelink Experiment*. Canberra: ANU Press. doi.org/10.22459/CE.12.2008.

Harris, S. P., O. Randall, K. R. Fisher and R. Gould. 2014. 'Human rights and neoliberalism in Australian welfare to work policy'. *Disability Studies Quarterly* 34(4): 1–27.

Hartwich, O. M. 2009. *Neoliberalism: The Genesis of a Political Swearword.* Occasional Paper 114. St Leonards: The Centre for Independent Studies.

Harvey, D. 2016. 'Neoliberalism is a political project'. Interview in *Jacobin*, 23 July. Available at: www.jacobinmag.com/2016/07/david-harvey-neoliberalism-capitalism-labor-crisis-resistance.

Hawke, A. 2012. 'The paradox of performance pay'. *Sydney Morning Herald*, 1 May. Available at: www.smh.com.au/public-service/the-paradox-of-performance-pay-20120430-1xtys.html.

Haworth, N. and S. Hughes. 2015. 'The ILO, Greece, and social dialogue in the aftermath of the GFC'. In S. McBride, R. Mahon and G. W. Boychuk (eds) *After '08: Social Policy and the Global Financial Crisis.* Vancouver: University of British Columbia Press.

Hayek, F. A. 1944. *The Road to Serfdom.* Chicago: University of Chicago Press.

Head, B. and K. Crowley. 2015. *Policy Analysis in Australia.* Bristol: Policy Press. doi.org/10.1332/policypress/9781447310273.001.0001.

Healy, K. 2009. 'A case of mistaken identity: The social welfare professions and new public management'. *Journal of Sociology* 45(4): 403. doi.org/10.1177/1440783309346476.

Henry, K. 2012. 'The opportunities, challenges and policy responses for the Australian economy'. In J. Wanna, S. Vincent and A. Podger (eds) *With the Benefit of Hindsight: Valedictory Reflections from Departmental Secretaries, 2004–2011.* Canberra: ANU Press. doi.org/10.22459/WBH.04.2012.15.

Hil, R. 2014. 'In defence of social service that puts the needs of people first'. *The Conversation*, 23 April. Available at: theconversation.com/in-defence-of-social-service-that-puts-the-needs-of-people-first-24568.

Independent Review of the APS. 2018. 'Terms of reference'. *Independent Review of the APS.* Available at: www.apsreview.gov.au/about.

Johnson, C. 2009. 'The Hawke government and consensus'. In G. Bloustien, B. Comber and A. Mackinnon (eds) *The Hawke Legacy.* Adelaide: Wakefield Press.

Jones, C., M. Parker and R. ten Bos. 2005. *For Business Ethics.* New York: Routledge. doi.org/10.4324/9780203458457.

Jones, D. S. 2014. *Masters of the Universe: Hayek, Friedman, and the Birth of Neoliberal Politics*. Princeton: Princeton University Press.

Keane, B. 2016. 'Neoliberalism is fine, but what we have is crony capitalism'. *Crikey*, 27 April. Available at: www.crikey.com.au/2016/04/27/keane-neoliberalism-fine-crony-capitalism.

Keane, B. 2018. *The Mess We're In: How Our Politics Went to Hell and Dragged Us with It*. Crows Nest: Allen & Unwin.

Keating, M. 1988. 'Managing change in the public sector'. *Canberra Bulletin of Public Administration* 55(June): 59–63.

Keating, M. 1989. 'Quo vadis? Challenges of public administration'. *Australian Journal of Public Administration* 48(2): 123–131. doi.org/10.1111/j.1467-8500.1989.tb02206.x.

Keating, M. 1990. 'Managing for results in the public interest'. *Australian Journal of Public Administration* 49(4): 387–398. doi.org/10.1111/j.1467-8500.1990.tb01984.x.

Keating, M. 1994. 'The role of government economists'. *Canberra Bulletin of Public Administration* 77(December): 1–7.

Keating, M. 1996. 'Past and future directions of the APS: Some personal reflections'. *Australian Journal of Public Administration* 55(4): 3–9. doi.org/10.1111/j.1467-8500.1996.tb02552.x.

Keating, M. 2001. 'National development and the APS'. *Canberra Bulletin of Public Administration* 101(September): 26–29.

Keating, M. 2004. *Who Rules? How Government Retains Control of a Privatised Economy*. Sydney: Federation Press.

Kefford, G. 2015. *All Hail the Leaders : The ALP and Political Leadership*. North Melbourne: Australian Scholarly Press.

Kelleher, S. R. 1998. 'A look at the view from the Department of Finance and Administration'. *Canberra Bulletin of Public Administration* 89(August): 4–7.

Kelly, P. 2011. *The March of Patriots: The Struggle for Modern Australia*. Melbourne: Melbourne University Press.

Kennedy, S. 2018. 'National conference: What's next?' In Institute of Public Administration Australia (ed.) *IPAA Speeches 2017*. Canberra: Institute of Public Administration Australia.

King, R. 2018. 'Paths to a brighter tomorrow'. *Weekend Australian Review*, 8–9 September.

Klepeis, P. and C. Vance. 2009. 'Neoliberal policy and deforestation in southeastern Mexico: An assessment of the PROCAMPO program'. *Economic Geography* 79(3): 221–240. doi.org/10.1111/j.1944-8287.2003.tb00210.x.

Langford, J. and M. Edwards. 2001. *New Players, Partners and Processes: A Public Sector Without Boundaries.* Canberra: National Institute for Governance.

Lawson, D. 2018. 'Review: *Adam Smith: what he thought, and why it matters* by Jesse Norman — defending him from his critics'. *The Sunday Times*, 8 July. Available at: www.thetimes.co.uk/article/review-adam-smith-what-he-thought-and-why-it-matters-by-jesse-norman-a-model-of-enlightenment-8zx909p5g.

Lloyd, C. 2008. 'Australian capitalism since 1992: A new regime of accumulation?' *Journal of Australian Political Economy* 61: 31–56.

Mackay, H. 2014. *The Good Life: What Makes a Life Worth Living.* Melbourne: Macmillan.

Malin, N. 2017. 'Developing an analytical framework for understanding the emergence of de-professionalisation in health, social care and education sectors'. *Social Work & Social Sciences Review* 19(1): 66–162. doi.org/10.1921/swssr.v19i1.1082.

Management Advisory Committee (MAC). 2004. *Connecting Government: Whole of Government Response to Australia's Priority Challenges.* Canberra: Australian Public Service Commission.

Marcetic, B. 2017. 'New Zealand's neoliberal drift'. *Jacobin*, 15 March. Available at: www.jacobinmag.com/2017/03/new-zealand-neoliberalism-inequality-welfare-state-tax-haven.

Marsh, I. 2006. *Political Parties in Transition.* Alexandria: Federation Press.

McNamara, M. 1996. 'Contestability and incentives'. *Canberra Bulletin of Public Administration* 81(October): 7–9.

Meagher, G., R. Connell and B. Fawcett. 2009. 'Neoliberalism, new public management and the human service professions: Introduction to the special issue'. *Journal of Sociology* 45(4): 331–338. doi.org/10.1177/1440783309346472.

Mellors, J. 1993. 'The commercialisation of common services provided by the Department of Administrative Services: Outcomes and emerging issues'. *Australian Journal of Public Administration* 52(3): 329–338. doi.org/10.1111/j.1467-8500.1993.tb00285.x.

Mellors, J. 1996. 'Competitive tendering and contracting'. *Canberra Bulletin of Public Administration* 81(October): 3–6.

Mentan, T. 2015. *Unmasking Social Science Imperialism: Globalization Theory As A Phase Of Academic Colonialism*. Bamenda, Cameroon: Langaa RPCIG. doi.org/10.2307/j.ctvh9vxhh.

Metcalf, S. 2017. 'Neoliberalism: The idea that swallowed the world.' *The Guardian*, 18 August. Available at: www.theguardian.com/news/2017/aug/18/neoliberalism-the-idea-that-changed-the-world.

Monbiot, G. 2016. 'Neoliberalism – The ideology at the root of all our problems'. *The Guardian*, 15 April. Available at: www.theguardian.com/books/2016/apr/15/neoliberalism-ideology-problem-george-monbiot.

Mrdak, M. 2018. 'Secretary series address'. In Institute of Public Administration (ed.) *IPAA Speeches 2017*. Canberra: Institute of Public Administration.

O'Faircheallaigh, C. S., J. Wanna and P. Weller. 1999. *Public Sector Management in Australia: New Challenges, New Directions*. Second edition. South Yarra: Macmillan Education.

Painter, M. 1988. 'Editorial: Public management: Fad or fallacy?' *Australian Journal of Public Administration* 47(1): 1–3. doi.org/10.1111/j.1467-8500.1988.tb01041.x.

Parkinson, M. 2018. '2017 address to the Australian Public Service'. In Institute of Public Administration (ed.) *IPAA Speeches 2017*. Canberra: Institute of Public Administration.

Parkinson, M. 2019. '2018 address to the Australian Public Service'. In Institute of Public Administration (ed.) *IPAA Speeches 2018*. Canberra: Institute of Public Administration.

Patapan, H., J. Wanna and P. Weller (eds). 2005. *Westminster Legacies: Democracy and Responsible Government in Asia and the Pacific*. Sydney: UNSW Press.

Paterson, J. 1988. 'A managerialist strikes back'. *Australian Journal of Public Administration* 47(4): 287–295. doi.org/10.1111/j.1467-8500.1988.tb01072.x.

Perry, L. J. 2007. 'Neoliberal workplace reforms in the Antipodes: What impact on union power and influence?' *Australian Review of Public Affairs* 8(1): 19–46.

Podger, A. S. 1994. 'Partnering: The Defence view'. *Australian Journal of Public Administration* 53: 43. doi.org/10.1111/j.1467-8500.1994.tb01856.x.

Podger, A. S. 1997. 'The charter of government performance and government service charters'. *Canberra Bulletin of Public Administration* 84(May): 32–37.

Podger, A. S. 1998. 'Managing performance: Experience and directions in the Department of Health and Family Services'. *Canberra Bulletin of Public Administration* 89(August): 88–92.

Podger, A. S. 2000. 'The new Public Service Act and the commitment to values'. *Canberra Bulletin of Public Administration* 97: 22–25.

Podger, A. S. 2001. 'Keynote address: Reforms and their significance'. *Canberra Bulletin of Public Administration* 99(March): 14–20.

Podger, A. S. 2002. 'Whole of government innovations and challenges'. *Canberra Bulletin of Public Administration* 61(2).

Podger, A. S. 2007. 'What really happens: Departmental secretary appointments, contracts and performance pay in the Australian Public Service'. *Australian Journal of Public Administration* 66(2): 131–147. doi.org/10.1111/j.1467-8500.2007.00524.x.

Podger, A. S. 2009. *The Role of Departmental Secretaries: Personal Reflections on the Breadth of Responsibilities Today.* Canberra: ANU Press. doi.org/10.22459/RDS.06.2009.

Podger, A. S. 2012. 'My fortunate career and some parting remarks'. In J. Wanna, S. Vincent and A. Podger (eds) *With the Benefit of Hindsight: Valedictory Reflections from Departmental Secretaries, 2004–2011.* Canberra: ANU Press. doi.org/10.22459/WBH.04.2012.02.

Prudham, S. 2004. 'Poisoning the well: Neoliberalism and the contamination of municipal water in Walkerton, Ontario'. *Geoforum* 35(3): 343–359. doi.org/10.1016/j.geoforum.2003.08.010.

Pusey, M. 1991. *Economic Rationalism in Canberra: A Nation-Building State Changes its Mind.* Cambridge: Cambridge University Press.

Ramsay, T. and T. Battin. 2005. 'Labor Party ideology in the early 1990s: Working Nation and paths not taken'. *Journal of Economic and Social Policy* 9(2): 1–13.

Review of Commonwealth Administration. 1983. *Review of Commonwealth Administration* (the Reid Report). Canberra: Australian Government.

Reynolds, B. and M. Tyler. 2018. 'Applying a gendered lens to the stay and defend or leave early approach to bushfire safety'. *Australian Journal of Public Administration* 77(4): 529–541. doi.org/10.1111/1467-8500.12268.

Roberts, J. M. 2015. *New Media and Public Activism: Neoliberalism, the State and Radical Protest in the Public Sphere*. Policy Press Scholarship Online. doi.org/10.1332/policypress/9781447308225.001.0001.

Roberts, J. M. 2017. 'Neoliberalism, neoclassical economics, twinkle-toes Turnbull and a New Year's resolution'. *Pearls and Irritations*, 29 December. Available at: johnmenadue.com/jerry-roberts-neoliberalism-neoclassical-economics-twinkle-toes-turnbull-and-a-new-years-resolution.

Rogers, V. 1992. 'Performance improvement in the Australian Public Service – retrospect and prospects'. *Australian Journal of Public Administration* 51(4): 416–420. doi.org/10.1111/j.1467-8500.1992.tb01088.x.

Rogers, V. 1993. 'Australian Public Service reform: Managing a 1990s-style inquiry'. *Australian Journal of Public Administration* 52(4): 371–375. doi.org/10.1111/j.1467-8500.1993.tb00290.x.

Rowden, R. 2009. *The Deadly Ideas of Neoliberalism: How the IMF Has Undermined Public Health and the Fight Against AIDS*. New York: Zed Books.

Rowse, T. 2003. 'The social democratic critique of the Australian settlement'. In J. Hocking and C. Lewis (eds) *It's Time Again: Whitlam and Modern Labor*. Melbourne: Circa Publishing.

Royal Commission into Australian Government Administrations (RCAGA). 1976. *Final Report* (the Coombs Report). Canberra: Australian Government.

Rudd, K. 2009. 'The global financial crisis'. *The Monthly*, February. Available at: www.themonthly.com.au/issue/2009/february/1319602475/kevin-rudd/global-financial-crisis.

Rudd, K. 2018. *The PM Years*. Sydney: Macmillan.

Scott, P. 2012. 'Our custodial role for the quality of advisory relations at the centre of government'. In J. Wanna, S. Vincent and A. Podger (eds) *With the Benefit of Hindsight: Valedictory Reflections from Departmental Secretaries, 2004–2011*. Canberra: ANU Press. doi.org/10.22459/WBH.04.2012.12.

Sedgwick, S. T. 1994. 'Evaluation of management reforms in the Australian Public Service'. *Australian Journal of Public Administration* 53(3): 341–347. doi.org/10.1111/j.1467-8500.1994.tb01474.x.

Shand, D. A. 1984. *Canberra Bulletin of Public Administration* 11(2): 77–78.

Shergold, P. 1997. 'Ethics and the changing nature of public service'. *Australian Journal of Public Administration* 56(1): 119–124. doi.org/10.1111/j.1467-8500.1997.tb01247.x.

Shergold, P. 2006. *From 'Frank and Fearless' to 'Fumbling and Forgetful'? The Perceived Decline of the Australian Public Service*. London: Menzies Centre for Australian Studies.

Shergold, P. 2007. 'What really happens in the Australian Public Service: alternative view'. *Australian Journal of Public Administration* 66(3): 367–370. doi.org/10.1111/j.1467-8500.2007.00546.x.

Shergold, P. 2011. 'Seen but not heard'. *Australian Literary Review*, 4 May.

Smith, H. 2019. 'Doing policy differently: Challenges and insights'. In Institute of Public Administration (ed.) *IPAA Speeches 2018*. Canberra: Institute of Public Administration.

Sparkes, A. C. 2013. 'Qualitative research in sport, exercise and health in the era of neoliberalism, audit and new public management'. *Qualitative Research in Sport, Exercise and Health* 5(3). doi.org/10.1080/2159676X.2013.796493.

Sparrow, J. 2012a. 'Protests and the hollowing of democracy'. *Overland*, 19 September. Available at: overland.org.au/2012/09/protests-and-the-hollowing-of-democracy/.

Sparrow, J. 2012b. 'So it's Carr(ion)'. *Overland*, 5 March. Available at: overland.org.au/2012/03/so-its-carrion/.

Springer, S., K. Birch and J. MacLeavy (eds). 2016. *Handbook of Neoliberalism*. New York: Routledge.

Spronk, S. 2007. 'Roots of resistance to urban water privatization in Bolivia: The "new working class", the crisis of neoliberalism, and public services'. *International Labour and Working-Class History* 71(Spring): 8–28. doi.org/10.1017/S0147547907000312.

Stinson, S. 2014. 'A country under siege: A brief history of neoliberalism in Australia'. *Australian Independent Media Network*, 28 June. Available at: theaimn.com/country-siege-brief-history-neoliberalism-australia/.

Strangio, P., P. 't Hart and J. Walter. 2017. *The Pivot of Power: Australian Prime Ministers and Political Leadership, 1949–2016*. Melbourne: Melbourne University Publishing.

Swan, W. 2017. 'The Hawke–Keating agenda was Laborism, not neoliberalism, and is still a guiding light'. *The Guardian,* 17 May. Available at: www.theguardian. com/commentisfree/2017/may/14/the-hawke-keating-agenda-was-laborism-not-neoliberalism-and-is-still-a-guiding-light.

Task Force on Management Improvement. 1992. *The Australian Public Service Reformed: An Evaluation of a Decade of Management Reform.* Canberra: Australian Government.

Travis, S. 2017. 'What is neoliberalism?' *San Francisco Examiner,* 25 May.

Van Gramberg, B. and P. Bassett. 2005. *Neoliberalism and the Third Sector in Australia.* Working paper 5/2005. Melbourne: Victoria University.

Vardon, S. 1994. 'The next steps in public management: A South Australian view'. *Australian Journal of Public Administration* 53(3): 355–363. doi.org/ 10.1111/j.1467-8500.1994.tb01477.x.

Vardon, S. 2001. '"Exporting the APS": The international impact of APS innovations'. *Canberra Bulletin of Public Administration* 101(September): 30–34.

Varghese, P. 2017. 'Parting reflections'. In Institute of Public Administration Australia (ed.) *Twelve Speeches 2016.* Canberra: Institute of Public Administration Australia.

Wanna, J. 1992. 'No minister: "Economic rationalism in Canberra: A nation-building state changes its mind" by Michael Pusey'. Book review in *Australian Law Review* February: 43–44.

Wanna, J., J. Forster and P. Graham (eds). 1996. *Entrepreneurial Management in the Public Sector.* South Yarra: Macmillan Education.

Wanna, J., J. Kelly and J. Forster. 2000. *Managing Public Expenditure in Australia.* St Leonards: Allen & Unwin.

Wanna, J., C. Ryan and C. Ng. 2001. *From Accounting to Accountability: A Centenary History of the Australian National Audit Office.* Crows Nest: Allen & Unwin.

Wanna, J., S. Vincent and A. Podger (eds). 2012. *With the Benefit of Hindsight: Valedictory Reflections from Departmental Secretaries, 2004–2011.* Canberra: ANU Press. doi.org/10.22459/WBH.04.2012.

Wanna, J., P. Weller and M. Keating (eds). 2000. *Institutions on the Edge? Capacity for Governance.* Crows Nest: Allen & Unwin.

Weiss, L. 2012. 'The myth of the neoliberal state'. In C. Kyung-Sup, B. Fine and L. Weiss (eds) *In Developmental Politics in Transition: The Neoliberal Era and Beyond*. London: Palgrave Macmillan.

Weller, P. 1991. 'Financial management reforms in government: A comparative perspective'. *Australian Journal of Public Administration* 67 (November): 9–17.

Weller, P. 2001. *Australia's Mandarins: The Frank and the Fearless?* Crows Nest: Allen & Unwin.

Williams, R. 2018. 'Flannelled fools who bend rules'. *Weekend Australian Review*, 29–30 December.

Yeatman, A. 1987. 'The concept of public management and the Australian state in the 1980s'. *Australian Journal of Public Administration* 46(4): 339–356. doi.org/10.1111/j.1467-8500.1987.tb02578.x.

15

Of 'trifles' and 'manhole covers': The practitioner–academic interface[1]

Isi Unikowski

The occasion of John Wanna's festschrift is an opportunity to review the breadth of his interests and research, and his activism at the interface between policy, politics and public administration. On that basis, we may also consider some of the key issues in the interaction between academics and public servants that John's career highlights, while looking forward, of course, to his continuing involvement in driving and contributing to such developments.

It is perhaps worth noting that John's career has broadly coincided with tectonic movements in the relationships between the theoretical and applied fields of political science, policy studies and public administration. The fraught relationship between political science and the field of public administration from which it emerged is a key aspect of that history. The need for a better relationship between scholarship and practice was raised in the very first issue of *Administrative Science Quarterly* in 1956. The editor stressed the need for administrative scholars 'to explore empirical findings in the social sciences which may be pertinent and, when necessary, to translate these into administrative situations' (quoted in Bartunek and

---

1   The author would like to thank Professor Paul 't Hart (Utrecht) and Professor Andrew Podger (ANU) for their helpful comments on an earlier draft of this chapter.

Rynes 2014). But as the field of public administration narrowed down to a focus on 'public management' over the 70s and 80s, the distance between political science and public administration widened, with the debate between them rarely giving much attention to practitioner perspectives (Bartunek and Rynes 2014; Scott 2003; Kettl 2000).

In short, it may seem that not much has changed since a paper prepared for the Committee on Public Administration of the American Political Science Association in 1952 argued:

> there is a feeling among political scientists … that academics who profess public administration spend their time fooling with trifles. It was a sad day when the first professor of political science learned what a manhole cover is! (Martin 1952)[2]

Wanna's career is striking in its divergence from this history. He has demonstrated that professors of public administration do far more than fool with trifles; and not only has he forged a career in lifting manhole covers, in many cases he has jumped right in!

Wanna has insisted that 'the distinctive feature of public administration as a field [is] its dual reliance on practitioners … and academics as contributors' (Scott and Wanna 2005). Moreover, he has been one of those rare scholars whose interest, enthusiasm and output have enriched all three fields: from providing the broadest overviews of the field of public administration (Scott and Wanna 2005; Wanna and Weller 2003), to his history of the practices of the first audit office (Wanna and Ryan 2003), or the implementation of accrual budgeting (Kelly and Wanna 2004);[3] from normative debate, in his polemic over the appropriate role of public managers in the emerging era of public value management (Rhodes and Wanna 2007), to his close empirical studies of the appointments of secretaries (Weller and Wanna 1997), public expenditure (Wanna, Forster and Kelly 2000; Wanna, Jensen and de Vries 2003), implementation (Wanna, Lindquist and Marshall 2015) and so on.

In that work, he has not only been a leading researcher and communicator, but also has actively engaged and communicated with the public service. In this latter context, I had the pleasure of working with John on the first

---

2   See Paul 't Hart's contribution to this volume for his experience of this attitude.

3   *Pace* Rubin's view that 'it is difficult to study budgeting as an academic without either a practitioner background or mindset' (quoted in Posner 2009).

annual research conference organised by the Australia and New Zealand School of Government (ANZSOG), held in Canberra in February 2006 in conjunction with the Department of the Prime Minister and Cabinet (PM&C). The topic of that conference was 'Project Management and Organisational Change' (Wanna 2006) and the series continues to provide an opportunity for the application of research to significant issues in public administration.

As editor of the *Australian Journal of Public Administration* from March 1996 until the end of 2014, he played a leading role in making the synthesis between policy and administration 'the new paradigm', as Ahamed and Davis call it in their overview of the history of Australian scholarship in the field (Ahamed and Davis 2009), even though such a synthesis was considered implausible by earlier commentators.[4] In so doing, he has followed his own precepts for good public policy scholarship: first, that it should engage with real problems without becoming 'sycophantic or clientelist' (Wanna 2003); and second, that the facts should always take priority over the commentary. Even as *The Age* portrayed him as 'a self-described moderate left-winger', sympathetic to Pusey's widely read critique of economic rationalism back in 1993, the paper noted his accusation that 'one of Professor Pusey's central notions is based on bad counting' (Walker 1993).

In sum, although not, strictly speaking, a 'pracademic' in the sense in which Posner popularised the term – that is, someone who has occupied significant positions as both an academic and a public servant – Professor Wanna has nevertheless played a significant role in 'translating, coordinating and aligning perspectives across multiple constituencies' (Posner 2009).

Given such a breadth of interests and his activism at the interface between policy, politics and public administration, the occasion of this festschrift is an opportunity to consider some of the key issues raised by the interaction between academics and public servants.

This interaction takes place in, and responds to, two temporal settings. The first involves the windows of opportunity regularly opened by short-to-medium-term reviews, such as the *Ahead of the Game* review in 2010 (Moran and Department of the Prime Minister and Cabinet 2010),

---

4   This synthesis was also exemplified in textbooks such as *Public Sector Management in Australia* (Wanna, Weller and O'Faircheallaigh 1992).

the Thodey review of the 'capability, culture and operating model of the APS' (Australian Government 2018), and by similar reviews underway or recently completed by state governments. This category also includes responses to catastrophic failures such as the Palmer and Comrie reports on detainees in 2005, the Hammer report on the home insulation program in 2015 and Peter Shergold's wider review of implementation, *Learning from Failure* (Shergold 2015).

The medium-to-longer-term context involves the shift from new public management (NPM) models of public service to emergent new forms, such as new public governance (Rhodes 2016), digital or information-age governance (Wanna and Vincent 2018; Dunleavy et al. 2006), collaborative governance (Shergold 2016) and neo-Weberianism (Pollitt and Bouckaert 2011). The variety and complexity of these post-NPM models is compounded by the emergence of public sector models from outside the Anglosphere and the Organisation for Economic Cooperation and Development (OECD) (Legrand 2016; Pollitt 2015).

These two temporal perspectives are, of course, closely related. The public sector's capacity for 'continual intellectual renewal, through thought and design and implementation' remains as relevant today as when this was a key theme of the Coombs Royal Commission on Australian Government Administration in the mid-70s (Rowse 2002), and will inform the longer-term trajectories I have mentioned. Future demands on and expectations of the public service from governments and citizens will naturally test its capabilities and require further reform measures. In both the short- and longer-term contexts, Posner's prediction that 'the nexus between academics and practitioners will become, if anything, even more important in addressing both research and education needs for the public sector' continues to ring true (Posner 2009).

With those settings in mind, I derive the following learnings from my brief look at Wanna's career.

1. Perhaps most importantly, academics and practitioners need to consciously and explicitly ground their collaboration in the norms, values and principles of public sector work.

That is not to suggest that these normative settings are unchangeable, universal or even necessarily enunciated and articulated. On the contrary, rather than assuming complexity away in *a priori* models of causation that have little interest in the very factors that make public sector work distinctive, academics need to be prepared to recognise the complex, contested wellsprings of public administration. They need to understand and explain how its distinctive formal and informal rules, conventions and values, patterns of interaction, agency and legitimacy are routinely exploited and interpreted in the face of policy challenges, and how practitioners' behaviours and roles reflect the real dilemmas and issues they face.

In a recent interview, the eminent political scientist and economist Francis Fukuyama expressed astonishment that his university, Stanford, and American universities generally, have 'lost a sense of their role in training American elites about their own institutions' (Goldstein 2018).

Wanna's own work has embodied a counter-tradition, such as his examination of the way senior civil servants place themselves in a variety of Westminster traditions that shape their working life, how they re-engaged with and reinvented those traditions (Rhodes, Wanna and Weller 2008); and the need to embody those traditions in public sector responsiveness (Wanna 2008; Lindquist, Vincent and Wanna 2013).

In an editorial Wanna co-wrote with Glyn Davis in 1997 on teaching public administration, he advised 'a chance through study to read and discuss questions of purpose and direction is an important balance to daily demands' (Davis and Wanna 1997). Academics need to help public servants identify and become familiar with the arguments and counter-arguments around concepts like the meaning and measurement of public value;[5] the nature and variety of the ways public servants relate to the political executive, such as through public sector bargains (Hood and Lodge 2006); the challenges and opportunities of alternative paradigms and models of public administration (e.g. Wanna, Butcher and Freyen's analysis (2010) of how the Australian welfare state has developed); how the institutions of our democracy affect, and are affected by, the public sector's work and role (Ventriss et al. 2019); and the role public servants play in maintaining a balance between institutional resilience and stability, on the one hand, and innovation and change in incremental and more fundamental forms, on the other.[6]

---

5   See, for example, Moore (1995, 2014) and Rhodes and Wanna's critique of the public value paradigm in Rhodes and Wanna (2009).
6   See, for example, Bovaird and Quirk (2016).

Wanna's aforementioned challenge to the role that the prevalent public value paradigm accords public servants (Rhodes and Wanna 2009) illustrates how these are matters of robust contestation and debate, not just technical transmission in a lecture theatre. However, if the provision of support for ministers in the future will require renewed value to be ascribed to traditional craft skills like counselling, stewardship, practical wisdom and political nous, and requires public servants to negotiate values, meanings and relationships (Rhodes 2016), these skills and the training to acquire them need to be grounded in the broader narratives, paradigms and discourses of public service.

2. Part of this re-engagement with public sector values and norms should include an engagement with public service history.

This point deepens the previous point's focus on the idea of the public service as an institution with its own trajectories and sources of equilibrium and change.

Wanna has consistently argued that the retrospective study of public administration has value, warning 'we should not be so focused on the issues of the day that we lose the capacity to contextualise those issues or to imagine alternative approaches' (Scott and Wanna 2005). Examples of such engagement in Wanna's case include his review of the traditions of Australian governance, and the role they have played in 'establishing and adapting the public sector' (Wanna and Weller 2003); and, a couple of years later, his review of Australian administrative history, responding to a concern from practitioners that the literature 'merely documents yesteryear and records where we have been, rather than giving us future insights' (Scott and Wanna 2005).

High rates of interorganisational mobility, porous organisational structures, regular organisational restructuring, the loss of traditional record-keeping practices and increasing co-design and delivery with the private and non-profit sectors make it difficult for public servants themselves to become the custodians of institutional memory.[7] At risk, therefore, is an understanding of what worked and what didn't; how and why the norms and values I mentioned earlier have developed

---

7   As an empirical example of the argument put here, Stark's recent comparison of institutional memory loss in public sector organisations in Australia, Canada, New Zealand and the UK emphasises the 'formal-institutional, the agential, and the contextual dimensions of memory' (2019).

over time; how these norms and values are reflected in organisations and institutions; why institutional cultures of policy design and delivery have evolved and why they might be different.

One potential role for academics in that environment is to work with practitioners to supply them with the tools (narratives, discourses, ideas), and the actual venues and practices, in which such memory work might be operationalised. Such work could differentiate between the administrative and policy histories of particular kinds of public sector work, such as regulation or network management; or follow the particular policy trajectories of, say, environmental policy, fiscal policy, social policy and so on.

3. Academics should engage with practitioners to help frame questions, problems and issues.

As I interviewed a very senior public servant in a state Department of the Premier and Cabinet for my research, I noticed that he had made notes against the questions I'd sent him in advance. When I thanked him, with some embarrassment, for taking the time to do that, out of what must have been a horrendous schedule, he graciously responded by saying that he should thank me for giving him the opportunity to step back and reflect on his work; something he thought all public servants should do, from time to time.

As 'the interpreters of interpretations' (Sullivan 2016), academics play a critical role in uncovering, and making such frames and discourses explicit and available for scrutiny by practitioners, particularly where there is a multiplicity of roles and discourses at play with little formal acknowledgement of their impact. Again, such interpretation can apply to broad fields in public administration or more specific policy issues and their history. As practitioners become aware of such frames, they also become aware of alternative ways of framing their practice. They become aware of the values and norms that their work has prioritised, and those that have been given less importance, or left out altogether (Schön 1983). An interesting example of such work can be found in Podger and Wanna's introduction to the collected valedictories of Australian departmental secretaries, in which they emphasise the variety of views these mandarins express on 'how the public service looks to them, on its performance and on the challenges confronting public administration into the future' (Wanna, Vincent and Podger 2012).

Such framing also helps practitioners understand the systemic linkages and connections that characterise their policy fields or programs, together with the consequences and effects generated by such linkages.

Public servants are working in a policy environment characterised by multiple and overlapping complex problems, a high degree of uncertainty about means and ends, few expert actors to whom practitioners can turn for technical solutions and weakened traditional hierarchical models of public sector organisation (Dunlop and Radaelli 2018). Responding to that environment involves a high level of competence in what White and McSwain call 'the structuralist attitude' (McSwite 2001, 113): understanding systemic and localised links, patterns, causes, norms, and being able to 'discern (or be schooled to discern) the basic shape and direction, that is, the tendencies of the specific situations in which they [find] themselves' (White and McSwain 1990, 9). As these authors point out, such competence is at least one aim of the case study method adopted in the US and by ANZSOG here, and needs to be accompanied by academic guidance and mentoring. A return to, or at least buttressing, the craft skills alluded to earlier would equally require the kinds of 'theory competency' academics might help practitioners acquire.

4. Academics need to collaborate with practitioners to help fit public sector organisational cultures to new tasks and roles.

In one of his articles on the debate over public sector regeneration, Wanna argues his role, and the role academics should perform more generally, is to be 'a bit iconoclastic'; to ask 'what rationales, reasons, precepts and assumptions are hidden behind the debate about regeneration?' (Wanna 2005).

Politicians, academics and senior public servants have been drawing attention to the increasing 'scope, pace and nature of change' in the public sector ever since Wilson's classic nineteenth-century essay noted that 'the functions of government are every day becoming more complex and difficult, they are also vastly multiplying in number' (1887).[8] Few APS leaders in recent years have failed to call for greater innovation and risk-taking in the public service.[9]

---

8   More recently, cf. Reid (1983). Encel, Wilenski and Schaffer (1981) describe public administration becoming 'more complex, difficult and messier' because of expanding areas of government activity and citizens' reluctance to passively accept government decisions.

9   Other paradigms, such as 'collaboration' and 'joined up government' in all its forms, have similarly been around since the early 2000s (Halligan, Buick and Flynn 2011).

As head of PM&C, Peter Shergold frequently remarked on the difficulty of changing cultures, compared with changing organisational structures and processes. This is where, it seems to me, an important academic contribution can be made.

The exercise of agency, within formal and normative frameworks for accountability and performance, is a critical ingredient in equipping public sector organisations and their employees to deal with the challenges their current and future environments present.

Yet for all that, the question of how innovation should be balanced and shaped by its public sector context is seldom raised, let alone detailed, in the frequent exhortations by prime ministers and senior public service managers to be more innovative and less risk-averse. For example, it is important to appreciate that a fundamental role of the public sector is to provide the formal, legal certainty of the rule of law and administration that allows individuals and businesses to operate with confidence. As Podger argues, innovation in the public sector is not the same as innovation in the private sector (Podger 2015).

Apart from the obvious conditions and resources required for organisational autonomy and the exercise of discretion, when we talk about 'innovation' we are really talking about the reframing vital as a precondition for ensuring public sector organisations are innovative, including framework goals and performance measures; providing sufficient autonomy to lower-level units to implement these goals as they see fit, and to propose changes to them; regular performance reporting and peer review; and periodic revision of the goals, metrics and methods (Sabel and Zeitlin 2008).

Consequently, agency involves a temporal orientation: understanding the routines and traditions of the past and their constraining, taken-for-granted schemas of action; the imaginative, idealistic projection of strategies into the future; and the capacity of actors to make practical and normative judgements about the demands, dilemmas, and ambiguities of presently evolving situations (Emirbayer and Mische 1998). All these are matters that I have suggested should form a focus for the way academics and practitioners collaborate.

In conclusion, as the inaugural Sir John Bunting Chair of Public Administration at ANZSOG and The Australian National University, Wanna's name is indelibly linked to that consummate public servant, under whose leadership:

governments [were] effectively supported in a period of transition from a small, rule-bound and administratively-oriented service to a large, professionally and policy-focused agency capable of responding to a whole new order of demands from ministers and governments. (Bailey 1995)

Professor Wanna's contribution has shown us the importance of the academic–practitioner interface in effecting the next stage of that transition.

References

Ahamed, S. and G. Davis. 2009. 'Public policy and administration'. In R. A. W. Rhodes (ed.) *The Australian Study of Politics*. Basingstoke: Palgrave MacMillan. doi.org/10.1057/9780230296848_16.

Australian Government. 2018. *Independent Review of the Australian Public Service*. Available at: www.apsreview.gov.au/.

Bailey, P. 1995. 'Sir John Bunting, AC, KBE, 1918–95'. *Canberra Bulletin of Public Administration* 78: 29–31.

Bartunek, J. M. and S. L. Rynes. 2014. 'Academics and practitioners are alike and unlike: The paradoxes of academic–practitioner relationships'. *Journal of Management* 40(5): 1181–1201. doi.org/10.1177/0149206314529160.

Bovaird, T. and B. Quirk. 2016. 'Resilience in public administration: Moving from risk avoidance to assuring public policy outcomes'. In T. Klassen, D. Cepiku and T. Lah (eds) *The Routledge Handbook of Global Public Policy and Administration*. London: Routledge.

Davis, G. and J. Wanna. 1997. 'Does the teaching of public administration have a future?' *Australian Journal of Public Administration* 56(4): 3–4. doi.org/10.1111/j.1467-8500.1997.tb02482.x.

Dunleavy, P., H. Margetts, S. Bastow and J. Tinkler. 2006. 'New public management is dead—Long live digital-era governance'. *Journal of Public Administration Research and Theory* 16(3): 467–494. doi.org/10.1093/jopart/mui057.

Dunlop, C. A. and C. M. Radaelli. 2018. 'The lessons of policy learning: Types, triggers, hindrances and pathologies'. *Policy & Politics* 46(2): 255–272. doi.org/10.1332/030557318X15230059735521.

Emirbayer, M. and A. Mische. 1998. 'What is agency?' *American Journal of Sociology* 103(4): 962–1023. doi.org/10.1086/231294.

Encel, S., P. Wilenski and B. Schaffer. 1981. 'Introduction'. In S. Encel, P. Wilenski and B. Schaffer (eds) *Decisions: Case Studies in Australian Public Policy*. Melbourne: Longman Cheshire.

Goldstein, E. 2018. 'What follows the end of history? Identity politics'. *The Chronicle of Higher Education*, 27 August. Available at: www.chronicle. com/article/What-Follows-the-End-of/244369.

Halligan, J., F. Buick and J. O'Flynn. 2011. 'Experiments with joined-up, horizontal and whole-of-government in Anglophone countries'. In A. Massey (ed.) *International Handbook on Civil Service Systems*. Cheltenham, UK: Edward Elgar Publishing.

Hood, C. and M. Lodge. 2006. *The Politics of Public Service Bargains: Reward, Competency, Loyalty – and Blame*. Oxford: Oxford University Press. doi.org/10.1093/019926967X.001.0001.

Kelly, J. and J. Wanna. 2004. 'Crashing through with accrual-output price budgeting in Australia: Technical adjustment or a new way of doing business?' *American Review of Public Administration* 34(1): 94–111. doi.org/10.1177/0275074003253315.

Kettl, D. F. 2000. 'Public administration at the millennium: The state of the field'. *Journal of Public Administration Research and Theory* 10(1): 7–34. doi.org/10.1093/oxfordjournals.jpart.a024267.

Legrand, T. 2016. 'Elite, exclusive and elusive: Transgovernmental policy networks and iterative policy transfer in the Anglosphere'. *Policy Studies* 37(5): 440–455. doi.org/10.1080/01442872.2016.1188912.

Lindquist, E., S. Vincent and J. Wanna (eds). 2013. *Putting Citizens First: Engagement in Policy and Service Delivery for the 21st Century*. Canberra: ANU Press. doi.org/10.22459/PCF.08.2013.

Martin, R. C. 1952. 'Political science and public administration: A note on the state of the union'. *The American Political Science Review* 46(3): 660–676. doi.org/10.2307/1952277.

McSwite, O. C. 2001. 'Theory competency for MPA-educated practitioners'. *Public Administration Review* 61(1): 111–115. doi.org/10.1111/0033-3352.00010.

Moore, M. H. 1995. *Creating Public Value: Strategic Management in Government*. Boston: Harvard University Press.

Moore, M. H. 2014. 'Public value accounting: Establishing the philosophical basis'. *Public Administration Review* 74(4): 465–477. doi.org/10.1111/puar.12198.

Moran, T. and Department of the Prime Minister and Cabinet, Advisory Group on Reform of Australian Government Administration. 2010. *Ahead of the Game: Blueprint for the Reform of Australian Government Administration*. Canberra: Australian Government.

Podger, A. 2015. 'Innovation in the public sector: Beyond the rhetoric to a genuine "learning culture"'. In J. Wanna, H.-A. Lee and S. Yates (eds) *Managing Under Austerity, Delivering Under Pressure: Performance and Productivity in Public Service*. Canberra: ANU Press. doi.org/10.22459/MUADUP.10.2015.07.

Pollitt, C. 2015. 'Towards a new world: some inconvenient truths for Anglosphere public administration: The IIAS Braibant Lecture 2014'. *International Review of Administrative Sciences* 81(1): 3–17. doi.org/10.1177/0020852314544069.

Pollitt, C. and G. Bouckaert. 2011. *Public Management Reform: A Comparative Analysis – New Public Management, Governance, and the Neo-Weberian State*. Oxford: Oxford University Press.

Posner, P. L. 2009. 'The pracademic: An agenda for re-engaging practitioners and academics'. *Public Budgeting and Finance* 29(1): 12–26. doi.org/10.1111/j.1540-5850.2009.00921.x.

Reid, J. 1983. *Review of Commonwealth Administration: Report*. Canberra: Australian Government.

Rhodes, R. A. W. 2016. 'Recovering the craft of public administration'. *Public Administration Review* 76(4): 638–647. doi.org/10.1111/puar.12504.

Rhodes, R. A. W. and J. Wanna. 2007. 'The limits to public value, or rescuing responsible government from the platonic guardians'. *Australian Journal of Public Administration* 66(4): 406–421. doi.org/10.1111/j.1467-8500.2007.00553.x.

Rhodes, R. A. W. and J. Wanna. 2009. 'Bringing the politics back in: Public value in Westminster parliamentary government'. *Public Administration* 87(2): 161–183. doi.org/10.1111/j.1467-9299.2009.01763.x.

Rhodes, R. A. W., J. Wanna and P. Weller. 2008. 'Reinventing Westminster: How public executives reframe their world'. *Policy & Politics* 36(4): 461–479. doi.org/10.1332/030557308X313705.

Rowse, T. 2002. '"The responsive public servant": Coombs the man, Coombs the report'. *Australian Journal of Public Administration* 61(1): 99–102. doi.org/10.1111/1467-8500.00263.

Sabel, C. F. and J. Zeitlin. 2008. 'Learning from difference: The new architecture of experimentalist governance in the EU'. *European Law Journal* 14(3): 18–45. doi.org/10.1111/j.1468-0386.2008.00415.x.

Schön, D. 1983. *The Reflective Practitioner: How Professionals Think in Action.* New York: Basic Books.

Scott, J. and J. Wanna. 2005. 'Trajectories of public administration and administrative history in Australia: Rectifying "a curious blight"?' *Australian Journal of Public Administration* 64(March): 11–24. doi.org/10.1111/j.1467-8500.2005.00412.x.

Scott, R. 2003. 'Political science and public administration: The saga of a difficult relationship'. *Australian Journal of Public Administration* 62(2): 113–120. doi.org/10.1111/1467-8497.00330.

Shergold, P. 2015. *Learning from Failure: Why Large Government Policy Initiatives have gone so Badly Wrong in the Past and how the Chances of Success in the Future can be Improved: An Independent Review of Government Processes for Implementing Large Programs and Projects.* Canberra: Australian Government.

Shergold, P. 2016. 'Three sectors, one public purpose'. In D. Gilchrist and J. Butcher (eds) *The Three Sector Solution: Delivering Public Policy in Collaboration with Not-For-Profits and Business.* Canberra: ANU Press. doi.org/10.22459/TSS.07. 2016.02.

Stark, A. 2019. 'Explaining institutional amnesia in government'. *Governance* 32(1): 143–158. doi.org/10.1111/gove.12364.

Sullivan, H. 2016. 'Interpretivism and public policy research'. In N. Turnbull (ed.) *Interpreting Governance, High Politics and Public Policy: Essays Commemorating Interpreting British Governance.* New York: Routledge.

Ventriss, C., J. L. Perry, T. Nabatchi, H. B. Milward and J. M. Johnston. 2019. 'Democracy, public administration, and public values in an era of estrangement'. *Perspectives on Public Management and Governance* 2(4): 275–282. doi.org/10.1093/ppmgov/gvz013.

Walker, D. 1993. 'Critics fail to quell rage at rationalism'. *The Age*, 15 February.

Wanna, J. 2003. 'Public policy and public administration'. In I. McAllister, S. Dowrick and R. Hassan (eds) *The Cambridge Handbook of Social Sciences in Australia.* Cambridge: Cambridge University Press.

Wanna, J. 2005. 'Prospects for regeneration in government – What we talk about is more important than what we do or how we do it'. *Australian Journal of Public Administration* 64(2): 20–26. doi.org/10.1111/j.1467-8500.2005. 00432.x.

Wanna, J. 2006. *Improving Implementation: Organisational Change and Project Management.* Canberra: ANU E Press. doi.org/10.22459/II.02.2007.

Wanna, J. 2008. 'Independence and responsiveness – Re-tying the gordian knot: IPAA roundtable'. *Australian Journal of Public Administration* 67(3): 340–344. doi.org/10.1111/j.1467-8500.2008.00591.x.

Wanna J., J. Butcher and B. Freyens. 2010. *Policy in Action: The Challenge of Service Delivery.* Sydney: UNSW Press.

Wanna, J., J. Forster and J. Kelly. 2000. *Managing Public Expenditure in Australia.* St Leonards: Allen & Unwin.

Wanna, J., L. Jensen and J. de Vries. 2003. *Controlling Public Expenditure: The Changing Roles of Central Budget Agencies – Better Guardians?* Cheltenham, UK: Edward Elgar.

Wanna, J., E. Lindquist and P. Marshall (eds). 2015. *New Accountabilities, New Challenges.* Canberra: ANU Press. doi.org/10.22459/NANC.04.2015.

Wanna, J. and C. Ryan. 2003. 'An impeditive administrative culture? The legacy of Australia's first Auditor-General on the Australian Audit Office'. *Australian Journal of Politics and History* 49(4): 469–480. doi.org/10.1111/j.1467-8497. 2003.00309.x.

Wanna, J. and S. Vincent (eds). 2018. *Opening Government: Transparency and Engagement in the Information Age.* Canberra: ANU Press. doi.org/10.22459/ OG.04.2018.

Wanna, J., S. Vincent and A. Podger. 2012. *With the Benefit of Hindsight: Valedictory Reflections from Departmental Secretaries, 2004–2011.* Canberra: ANU E Press. doi.org/10.22459/WBH.04.2012.

Wanna, J. and P. Weller. 2003. 'Traditions of Australian governance'. *Public Administration* 81(1): 63–94. doi.org/10.1111/1467-9299.00337.

Wanna, J., P. Weller and C. O'Faircheallaigh. 1992. *Australian Public Sector Management in Australia.* South Melbourne: Macmillan.

Weller, P. and J. Wanna. 1997. 'Departmental Secretaries: Appointment, termination and their impact'. *Australian Journal of Public Administration* 56(4): 13–25. doi.org/10.1111/j.1467-8500.1997.tb02485.x.

White, O. and C. McSwain. 1990. 'The phoenix project: Raising a new image of public administration from the ashes of the past'. *Administration & Society* 22(1): 3–38. doi.org/10.1177/009539979002200101.

Wilson, W. 1887. 'The study of administration'. *Political Science Quarterly* 2(2): 197–222. doi.org/10.2307/2139277.

Appendix 1: John Wanna's main publications

Authored or co-authored books

Wanna, J. 1981. *Defence Not Defiance: The Development of Organised Labour in South Australia*. Adelaide: Adelaide CAE, Government Printer.

Davis, G., J. Wanna, J. Warhurst and P. Weller. (1988) 1993. *Public Policy in Australia*. Second Edition. Sydney: Allen & Unwin.

Wanna, J., C. O'Faircheallaigh and P. Weller. (1992) 1999. *Public Sector Management in Australia: New Challenges, New Directions*. Second Edition. Melbourne.

Wanna, J., J. Forster and J. Kelly. 2000. *Managing Public Expenditure in Australia*. Sydney: Allen & Unwin.

Wanna, J., C. Ryan and C. Ng. 2001. *From Accounting to Accountability: A Centenary History of the Australian National Audit Office*. Sydney: Allen & Unwin.

Rhodes, R. A. W., J. Wanna and P. Weller. 2009. *Comparing Westminster*. Oxford: Oxford University Press. doi.org/10.1093/acprof:oso/9780199563494.001.0001.

Wanna, J., J. Phillimore and A. Fenna. 2009. *Common Cause: Strengthening Australia's Cooperative Federalism*. Melbourne: Council for the Australian Federation.

Butcher, J., B. Freyens and J. Wanna. 2010. *Policy in Action: The Challenge of Service Delivery*. Sydney: UNSW Press.

Wanna, J. and T. Arklay. 2010. *The Ayes Have It: The History of the Queensland Parliament, 1957–1989*. ANZSOG Series. Canberra: ANU E Press. doi.org/10.22459/AH.07.2010.

Edited or co-edited books

Forster, J. and J. Wanna (eds). 1990. *Budgetary Management and Control: The Public Sector in Australasia.* Melbourne: Macmillan.

Bell, S. and J. Wanna (eds). 1992. *Business–Government Relations in Australia.* Sydney: Harcourt Brace Jovanovich.

Stevens, B. and J. Wanna (eds). 1993. *The Goss Government: Promise and Performance of Labor in Queensland.* Melbourne: Macmillan.

Caulfield, J. and J. Wanna (eds). 1995. *Power and Politics in the City: Brisbane in Transition.* Melbourne: Macmillan.

Forster, J., P. Graham and J. Wanna (eds). 1996. *Entrepreneurial Management in the Public Sector.* Melbourne: Macmillan.

Keating, M., J. Wanna and P. Weller (eds). 2000. *Institutions on the Edge? Capacity for Governance.* Sydney: Allen & Unwin.

Jensen, L., J. de Vries and J. Wanna (eds). 2003. *Controlling Public Expenditure: The Changing Roles of Central Budgetary Agencies – Better Guardians?* Cheltenham, UK: Edward Elgar.

Patapan, H., J. Wanna and P. Weller (eds). 2005. *Westminster Legacies: Democracy and Responsible Government in Asia and the Pacific.* Sydney: UNSW Press.

Wanna, J. and P. Williams (eds). 2005. *Yes Premier: Labor Leadership in Australia's States and Territories.* Sydney: UNSW Press.

Arklay, T., J. Nethercote and J. Wanna (eds). 2006. *Australian Political Lives: Chronicling Political Careers and Administrative Histories.* ANZSOG Series. Canberra: ANU E Press. doi.org/10.22459/APL.10.2006.

Wanna, J. (ed.) 2007. *Improving Implementation: Organisational Change and Project Management.* ANZSOG Series. Canberra: ANU E Press. doi.org/10.22459/II.02.2007.

Wanna, J. (ed.). 2007. *A Passion for Policy: Essays in Public Sector Reform.* ANZSOG Series. Canberra: ANU E Press. doi.org/10.22459/PFP.2007.

O'Flynn, J. and J. Wanna (eds). 2008. *Collaborative Governance: A New Era of Public Policy in Australia?* ANZSOG Series. Canberra: ANU E Press. doi.org/10.22459/CG.12.2008.

Wanna, J. (ed.). 2009. *Critical Reflections on Australian Public Policy: Selected Essays*. ANZSOG Series. Canberra: ANU E Press. doi.org/10.22459/CRAPP. 05.2009.

Jensen, L., J. de Vries and J. Wanna (eds). 2010. *The Reality of Budgetary Reform in OECD Nations: Trajectories and Consequences*. Cheltenham, UK: Edward Elgar Publishing.

Chalmers, R. 2011. *Inside the Canberra Press Gallery: Life in the Wedding Cake of Old Parliament House*. Edited by S. Vincent and J. Wanna. ANZSOG Series. Canberra: ANU E Press. doi.org/10.22459/ICPG.10.2011.

Lindquist, E. A., S. Vincent and J. Wanna (eds). 2011. *Delivering Policy Reform: Anchoring Significant Reforms in Turbulent Times*. ANZSOG Series. Canberra: ANU E Press. doi.org/10.22459/DPR.04.2011.

Podger, A., S. Vincent and J. Wanna (eds). 2012. *With the Benefit of Hindsight: Valedictory Reflections from Departmental Secretaries, 2004–2011*. ANZSOG Series. Canberra: ANU E Press. doi.org/10.22459/WBH.04.2012.

Simms, M. and J. Wanna (eds). 2012. *Julia 2010: The Caretaker Election*. Canberra: ANU E Press. doi.org/10.22459/J2010.02.2012.

Lindquist, E. A., S. Vincent and J. Wanna (eds). 2013. *Putting Citizens First: Engagement in Policy and Service Delivery for the 21st Century*. ANZSOG Series. Canberra: ANU E Press. doi.org/10.22459/PCF.08.2013.

Podger, A., D. Trewin, J. Wanna and P. White (eds). 2013. *Towards a Stronger, More Equitable and Efficient Tax-Social Security System*. Canberra: Academy of Social Sciences in Australia.

Boston, J., J. Wanna, V. Lipski and J. Pritchard (eds). 2014. *Future-Proofing the State: Managing Risks, Responding to Crises and Building Resilience*. Canberra: ANU Press. doi.org/10.22459/FPS.05.2014.

Baume, P. 2015. *A Dissident Liberal: the Political Writings of Peter Baume*. Edited by J. Wanna and M. Taflaga. Canberra: ANU Press. doi.org/10.22459/DL.09. 2015.

Johnson, C., J. Wanna and H.-A. Lee (eds). 2015. *Abbott's Gambit: The 2013 Australian Federal Election*. Canberra: ANU Press. doi.org/10.22459/AG. 01.2015.

Wanna, J., H. Lee and S. Yates (eds). 2015. *Managing Under Austerity, Delivering Under Pressure: Performance and Productivity in Public Service*. ANZSOG Series. Canberra: ANU Press. doi.org/10.22459/MUADUP.10.2015.

Wanna, J., E. A. Lindquist and P. Marshall (eds). 2015. *New Accountabilities, New Challenges*. ANZSOG Series. Canberra: ANU Press. doi.org/10.22459/NANC.04.2015.

Wanna, J., E. A. Lindquist and J. de Vries (eds). 2015. *The Global Financial Crisis and its Budget Impacts in OECD Nations: Fiscal Responses and Future Challenges*. Cheltenham, UK: Edward Elgar. doi.org/10.4337/9781784718961.

Podger, A. and J. Wanna (eds). 2016. *Sharpening the Sword of State: Building Executive Capacities in the Public Services of the Asia-Pacific*. ANZSOG Series. Canberra: ANU Press. doi.org/10.22459/SSS.11.2016.

de Percy, M. and J. Wanna (eds). 2018. *Road Pricing and Provision: Changed Traffic Conditions Ahead*. ANZSOG Series. Canberra: ANU Press. doi.org/10.22459/RPP.07.2018.

Podger, A., T.-T. Su, H. Chan, J. Wanna and M. Niu (eds). 2018. *Value for Money: Budget and Financial Management Reform in the People's Republic of China, Taiwan and Australia*. ANZSOG Series. Canberra: ANU Press. doi.org/10.22459/VM.01.2018.

Podger, A., T.-T. Su, J. Wanna, H. Chan and M. Niu (eds). 2020. *Designing Governance Structures for Performance and Accountability: Developments in Australia and Greater China*. ANZSOG Series. Canberra: ANU Press. doi.org/10.22459/DGSPA.2020.

Mercer, T., R. Ayers, B. Head and J. Wanna (eds). 2021. *Learning Policy, Doing Policy: Interactions Between Public Policy Theory, Practice and Teaching*. ANZSOG Series. Canberra: ANU Press. doi.org/10.22459/LPDP.2021.

Book chapters

Wanna, J. 1981. 'The economy of South Australia'. In Constitutional Museum of Adelaide (ed.) *South Australia 1855: Historical Essays and Teachers' Handbook*. Adelaide: Constitutional Museum of South Australia.

Wanna, J. 1981. 'A paradigm of consent: The origins of the South Australian trade union movement'. In Constitutional Museum of Adelaide (ed.) *South Australia 1855: Historical Essays and Teachers' Handbook*. Adelaide: Constitutional Museum of South Australia.

Wanna, J. 1984. 'The sixties and beyond, 1960–1984'. In C. Vevers (ed.) *To Unite More Closely: A History of the United Trades and Labor Council of South Australia*. Adelaide: United Trades and Labor Council.

Wanna, J. 1986. 'The state and industrial relations in South Australia'. In K. Sheridan (ed.) *The State as Developer: Public Enterprise in South Australia.* Adelaide: Royal Australian Institute of Public Administration in association with Wakefield Press.

Coaldrake, P. and J. Wanna. 1988. 'The budgetary process'. In B. Galligan (ed.) *Comparative State Policies.* Melbourne: Longman Cheshire.

Head, B. and J. Wanna. 1991. 'Fiscal federalism: Commonwealth conditional funding and state responses'. In J. Forster and J. Wanna (eds) *Budgetary Management and Control: The Public Sector in Australasia.* Melbourne: Macmillan.

Forster, J., B. Head and J. Wanna. 1991. 'The effectiveness of the business regulation review unit'. In B. Head and E. McCoy (eds) *Deregulation or Better Regulation: Issues for the Public Sector.* Melbourne: Macmillan.

Forster, J. and J. Wanna. 1991. 'Issues in contemporary budgetary management and control'. In J. Forster and J. Wanna (eds) *Budgetary Management and Control: The Public Sector in Australasia.* Melbourne: Macmillan.

Wanna, J. 1991. 'Intergovernmental relations in selected policy areas – business'. In B. Galligan, O. Hughes and C. Walsh (eds) *Intergovernmental Relations and Public Policy.* Sydney: Allen & Unwin.

Wanna, J. 1991. 'Parliamentary commissions of review: The Criminal Justice Commission and the Electoral and Administrative Review Commission'. In C. Hughes and R. Whip (eds) *Political Crossroads: The 1989 Queensland Election.* St Lucia: University of Queensland Press.

Wanna, J. 1993. 'Managing the politics: the Party, factions, parliament and parliamentary committees'. In B. Stevens and J. Wanna (eds) *The Goss Government: Promise and Performance of Labor in Queensland.* Melbourne: Macmillan.

Wanna, J. 1993. 'Spitting images? Political parties and the policy process'. In A. Hede and S. Prasser (eds) *Policy-Making in Volatile Times.* Sydney: Hale & Iremonger.

Wanna, J. and B. Stevens. 1993. 'The Goss government: An agenda for reform'. In B. Stevens and J. Wanna (eds) *The Goss Government: Promise and Performance of Labor in Queensland.* Melbourne: Macmillan.

Wanna, J. 1994. 'Can the state "manage" the macro-economy?' In S. Bell and B. Head (eds) *State, Economy and Public Policy.* Melbourne: Oxford University Press.

Wanna, J. 1994. 'EARC: An evaluation of its achievement'. In S. Prasser (ed.) *Was EARC Worth It?* Brisbane: Royal Institute of Public Administration Australia (Queensland Division).

Wanna, J. 1994. 'Public sector management'. In A. Parkin, J. Summers and D. Woodward (eds) *Government, Politics, Power and Policy in Australia.* Fifth edition. Melbourne: Longman Cheshire.

Caulfield, J. and J. Wanna. 1995. 'Policy provisions and urban planning in an Australian city: Dilemmas of city governance'. In J. Walter, H. Hinsley and P. Spearritt (eds) *Changing Cities: Reflections on Britain and Australia.* London and Melbourne: Sir Robert Menzies Centre for Australian Studies, London University, and Monash University.

Wanna, J. 1997. 'Managing budgets'. In H. Bakvis, R. A. W. Rhodes and P. Weller (eds) *The Hollow Crown: Countervailing Trends in Core Executives.* London: Macmillan.

Wanna, J. 1997. 'Public sector management'. In A. Parkin, J. Summers and D. Woodward (eds) *Government, Politics, Power and Policy in Australia.* Sixth edition. Melbourne: Longman Cheshire.

Wanna, J. 1999. 'Administrative reform in the Australian public sector'. In H. S. Chan and H. Ng (eds) *Handbook of Comparative Public Administration in the Asia-Pacific Basin.* New York: Marcel Dekker.

Keating, M. and J. Wanna. 2000. 'Remaking federalism?' In M. Keating, J. Wanna and P. Weller (eds) *Institutions on the Edge? Capacity for Governance.* Sydney: Allen & Unwin.

Wanna, J. 2000. 'Conclusion: Institutional adaptability and coherence'. In M. Keating, J. Wanna and P. Weller (eds) *Institutions on the Edge? Capacity for Governance.* Sydney: Allen & Unwin.

Wanna, J. 2000. 'Queensland: Consociational factionalism or ignoble cabal?' In A. Parkin and J. Warhurst (eds) *The Machine: Labor Confronts the Future.* Sydney: Allen & Unwin.

Wanna, J. and G. Withers. 2000. 'Creating capability: Combining economic and political rationalities in industry and regional policy'. In G. Davis and M. Keating (eds) *The Future of Governance.* Sydney: Allen & Unwin.

Uhr, J. and J. Wanna. 2000. 'The future roles of parliament'. In M. Keating, J. Wanna and P. Weller (eds) *Institutions on the Edge? Capacity for Governance.* Sydney: Allen & Unwin.

Gash, A. and J. Wanna. 2001. 'The role of the Auditor-General in scrutinizing ministerial ethics'. In J. Fleming and I. Holland (eds) *Motivating Ministers to Morality*. Aldershot: Ashgate.

Kelly, J. and J. Wanna. 2001. 'Are Wildavsky's guardians and spenders still relevant? New public management and the politics of government budgeting'. In R. L. Jones, J. Guthrie and P. Steane (eds) *Learning from International Public Management Reform*. Amsterdam: JAI Elsevier Science.

McAllister, I. and J. Wanna. 2001. 'Citizens' expectations and perceptions of governance'. In G. Davis and P. Weller (eds) *Are You Being Served? State, Citizens and Governance*. Sydney: Allen & Unwin.

Wanna, J. 2001. 'Trade unions'. In W. Prest (ed.) *The Wakefield Companion to South Australian History*. Adelaide: Wakefield Press.

Bishop, P. and J. Wanna. 2002. 'Reforming government: Outsourcing, privatisation and commercialisation'. In E. van Acker and G. Curran (eds) *Business, Government and Globalisation*. Frenchs Forest: Pearson Longman.

Conley, T. and J. Wanna. 2002. 'Impacts of globalisation and Australian policy'. In E. van Acker and G. Curran (eds) *Business, Government and Globalisation*. Frenchs Forest: Pearson Longman.

Wanna, J. 2002. 'A handmaiden to the market? The treasury and economic governance'. In S. Bell (ed.) *Economic Governance and Institutional Dynamics*. Melbourne: Oxford University Press.

Bartos, S. and J. Wanna. 2003. 'Good practice: Does it work in theory? Australia's quest for better outcomes'. In L. Jensen, J. de Vries and J. Wanna (eds) *Controlling Public Expenditure: The Changing Roles of Central Budgetary Agencies – Better Guardians?* Cheltenham, UK: Edward Elgar.

Jensen, L. and J. Wanna. 2003. 'Conclusion: Better Guardians?' In L. Jensen, J. de Vries and J. Wanna (eds) *Controlling Public Expenditure: The Changing Roles of Central Budgetary Agencies – Better Guardians?* Cheltenham, UK: Edward Elgar.

Wanna, J. 2003. 'Introduction: The changing role of central budget agencies'. In L. Jensen, J. de Vries and J. Wanna (eds) *Controlling Public Expenditure: The Changing Roles of Central Budgetary Agencies – Better Guardians?* Cheltenham, UK: Edward Elgar.

Wanna, J. 2003. 'Public policy and public administration'. In I. McAllister, S. Dowrick and R. Hassan (eds) *The Cambridge Handbook of Social Sciences in Australia*. Melbourne: Cambridge University Press.

Wanna, J. 2003. 'Queensland'. In J. Moon and C. Sharman (eds) *Australian Politics and Government: The Commonwealth, the States and Territories*. Melbourne: Cambridge University Press. doi.org/10.1017/CBO9780511756061.004.

Wanna, J. 2003. 'Wayne Keith Goss: The rise and fall of a meticulous controller'. In D. Murphy, R. Joyce, M. Cribb and R. Wear (eds) *The Premiers of Queensland*. Third edition. St Lucia: University of Queensland Press.

Bishop, P. and J. Wanna. 2004. 'Public sector reform'. In E. van Acker and G. Curran (eds) *Governing, Business and Globalisation*. Second edition. Sydney: Pearson Longman.

Conley, T. and J. Wanna. 2004. 'Australian responses to globalisation'. In E. van Acker and G. Curran (eds) *Governing, Business and Globalisation*. Second edition. Sydney: Pearson Longman.

Eccleston, R. and J. Wanna. 2004. 'Business and the politics of taxation'. In E. van Acker and G. Curran (eds) *Governing, Business and Globalisation*. Second edition. Sydney: Pearson Longman.

Head, B., J. Wanna and P. Williams. 2005. 'Leaders and the leadership challenge'. In J. Wanna and P. D. Williams (eds) *Yes Premier: Labor Leadership in Australia's States and Territories*. Sydney: UNSW Press.

Patapan, H. and J. Wanna. 2005. 'The Westminster legacy: Conclusion'. In H. Patapan, J. Wanna and P. Weller (eds) *Westminster Legacies: Democracy and Responsible Government in Asia and the Pacific*. Sydney: UNSW Press.

Wanna, J. 2005. 'New Zealand's Westminster trajectory: Archetypal transplant to maverick outlier'. In H. Patapan, J. Wanna and P. Weller (eds) *Westminster Legacies: Democracy and Responsible Government in Asia and the Pacific*. Sydney: UNSW Press.

Wanna, J., B. Head and P. Williams. 2005. 'Leaders and the leadership challenge'. In J. Wanna and P. Williams (eds) *Yes Premier: Labor Leadership in Australia's States and Territories*. Sydney: UNSW Press.

Wanna, J. and P. Williams. 2005. 'Peter Beattie: The "boy from Atherton" made good'. In J. Wanna and P. Williams (eds) *Yes Premier: Labor Leadership in Australia's States and Territories*. Sydney: UNSW Press.

Wanna, J. and P. Williams. 2005. 'The twilight zone of state leaders'. In J. Wanna and P. Williams (eds) *Yes Premier: Labor Leadership in Australia's States and Territories*. Sydney: UNSW Press.

Wanna, J. 2007. 'Budget process'. In B. Galligan and W. Roberts (eds) *The Oxford Companion to Australian Politics*. Melbourne: Oxford University Press.

Wanna, J. 2007. 'Introduction: Improving implementation – the challenge ahead'. In J. Wanna (ed.) *Improving Implementation: Organisational Change and Project Management*. ANZSOG Series. Canberra: ANU E Press. doi.org/10.22459/II.02.2007.01.

Wanna, J. 2007. 'Policy studies'. In B. Galligan and W. Roberts (eds) *The Oxford Companion to Australian Politics*. Melbourne: Oxford University Press.

Althaus, C. and J. Wanna. 2008. 'The institutionalisation of leadership in the Australian Public Service'. In P. 't Hart and J. Uhr (eds) *Public Leadership: Perspectives and Practices*. Canberra: ANU Press. doi.org/10.22459/PL.11.2008.10.

Wanna, J. 2008. 'Collaborative government: Meanings, dimensions, drivers and outcomes'. In J. O'Flynn and J. Wanna (eds) *Collaborative Governance: A New Era of Public Policy in Australia?* ANZSOG Series. Canberra: ANU E Press. doi.org/10.22459/CG.12.2008.01.

Wanna, J. 2008. 'Nation-building in Australia: A discourse, iconic project or tradition of resonance?' In J. Butcher (ed.) *Australia Under Construction: Nation-building Past, Present and Future*. ANZSOG Series. Canberra: ANU E Press. doi.org/10.22459/AUC.04.2008.01.

Wanna, J. and R. A. W. Rhodes. 2009. 'The executives'. In R. A. W. Rhodes (ed.) *The Australian Study of Politics*. London: Palgrave MacMillan.

Craik, J. and J. Wanna. 2010. 'Committed cities and the problems of governance: Micromanaging the unmanageable'. In S. Kallidaikurichi and B. Yuen (eds) *Developing Living Cities: From Analysis to Action*. Singapore: World Scientific Publishing Company.

Hawke, L. and J. Wanna. 2010. 'Australia after budgetary reform: A lapsed pioneer or decorative architect?' In L. Jensen, J. de Vries and J. Wanna (eds) *The Reality of Budgetary Reform in OECD Nations: Trajectories and Consequences*. Cheltenham, UK: Edward Elgar Publishing. doi.org/10.4337/9781849805636.00010.

Wanna, J. 2010. 'Investigating the reality of reform in modern budgeting'. In L. Jensen, J. de Vries and J. Wanna (eds) *The Reality of Budgetary Reform in OECD Nations: Trajectories and Consequences*. Cheltenham, UK: Edward Elgar Publishing. doi.org/10.4337/9781849805636.00007.

Wanna, J. 2010. 'Issues and agendas for the term. In C. Aulich and M. Evans (eds) *The Rudd Government: Australian Commonwealth Administration 2007–2010*. ANZSOG Series. Canberra: ANU E Press. doi.org/10.22459/RG.12.2010.02.

Wanna, J. 2010. 'The work-in-progress of budgetary reform'. In L. Jensen, J. de Vries and J. Wanna (eds) *The Reality of Budgetary Reform in OECD Nations: Trajectories and Consequences*. Cheltenham, UK: Edward Elgar Publishing. doi.org/10.4337/9781849805636.00019.

Lindquist, E. A. and J. Wanna. 2011. 'Delivering policy reform: Making it happen, making it stick'. In E. A. Lindquist, S. Vincent and J. Wanna (eds) *Delivering Policy Reform: Anchoring Significant Reforms in Turbulent Times*. ANZSOG Series. Canberra: ANU E Press. doi.org/10.22459/DPR.04.2011.01.

Mulgan, R. and J. Wanna. 2011. 'Developing cultures of integrity in the public and private sectors'. In A. Graycar and R. Smith (eds) *Handbook of Global Research and Practice in Corruption*. Cheltenham, UK: Edward Elgar Publishing.

Podger, A. and J. Wanna. 2012. 'Introduction'. In A. Podger, S. Vincent and J. Wanna (eds) *With the Benefit of Hindsight: Valedictory Reflections from Departmental Secretaries, 2004–2011*. ANZSOG Series. Canberra: ANU E Press. doi.org/10.22459/WBH.04.2012.

Simms, M. and J. Wanna. 2012. 'The caretaker election of 2010: "Julia 10" versus "Tony 10" and the onset of minority government'. In M. Simms and J. Wanna (eds) *Julia 2010: The Caretaker Election*. Canberra: ANU E Press. doi.org/10.22459/J2010.02.2012.01.

Wanna, J. 2012. 'The influence of unions and business in the 2010 federal election: Claims of "slash and burn" and still "no response and no answers"'. In M. Simms and J. Wanna (eds) *Julia 2010: The Caretaker Election*. Canberra: ANU E Press. doi.org/10.22459/J2010.02.2012.23.

Wanna, J. 2012. 'Ministers as ministries and the logic of their collective action'. In K. Dowding and C. Lewis (eds) *Ministerial Careers and Accountability in the Australian Commonwealth Government*. ANZSOG Series. Canberra: ANU E Press. doi.org/10.22459/MCAACG.09.2012.02.

Fels, A. and J. Wanna. 2014. 'Foreword'. In J. Boston, J. Wanna, V. Lipski and J. Pritchard (eds) *Future-Proofing the State: Managing Risks, Responding to Crises and Building Resilience*. Canberra: ANU Press. doi.org/10.22459/FPS.05.2014.

Wanna, J. 2014. 'Administrative history as biography'. In G. Davis and R. A. W. Rhodes (eds) *The Craft of Governing: The Contribution of Patrick Weller to Australian Political Science*. Sydney: Allen & Unwin.

Wanna, J. 2014. 'Governance and public policy'. In K. Barnes and P. Spearritt (eds) *Drivers of Change for the Australian Labour Market to 2030*. Canberra: Academy of the Social Sciences.

Wanna, J. 2014. 'Regional political leadership'. In R. A. W. Rhodes and P. 't Hart (eds) *Oxford Handbook of Political Leadership*. Oxford: Oxford University Press. doi.org/10.1093/oxfordhb/9780199653881.013.038.

Johnson, C. and J. Wanna. 2015. 'Conclusion: Reflections on *Abbott's Gambit* – mantras, manipulation and mandates', In C. Johnson, J. Wanna and H.-A. Lee (eds) *Abbott's Gambit: The 2013 Australian Federal Election*. Canberra: ANU Press. doi.org/10.22459/AG.01.2015.25.

Johnson, C., J. Wanna and H.-A. Lee. 2015. 'Introduction: Analysing the 2013 Australian federal election'. In C. Johnson, J. Wanna and H.-A. Lee (eds) *Abbott's Gambit: The 2013 Australian Federal Election*. Canberra: ANU Press. (Extracts republished in *Inside Story*, February 2015.) doi.org/10.22459/AG.01.2015.

Lindquist, E. A., J. de Vries and J. Wanna. 2015. 'Meeting the challenge of the global financial crisis in OECD nations: Fiscal responses and future challenges'. In J. Wanna, E. A. Lindquist and J. de Vries (eds) *The Global Financial Crisis and its Budget Impacts in OECD Nations: Fiscal Responses and Future Challenges*. Cheltenham, UK: Edward Elgar.

Lindquist, E. A., J. de Vries and J. Wanna. 2015. 'Readiness, resilience, reform and persistence of budget systems after the GFC: Conclusions and implications'. In J. Wanna, E. A. Lindquist and J. de Vries (eds) *The Global Financial Crisis and its Budget Impacts in OECD Nations: Fiscal Responses and Future Challenges*. Cheltenham, UK: Edward Elgar.

Lindquist, E. A. and J. Wanna. 2015. 'Is implementation only about policy execution? Advice for public sector leaders from the literature'. In J. Wanna, E. A. Lindquist and P. Marshall (eds) *New Accountabilities, New Challenges*. ANZSOG Series. Canberra: ANU Press. doi.org/10.22459/NANC.04.2015.07.

Rayner, J. and J. Wanna. 2015. 'An overview of the 2013 federal election campaign: Ruinous politics, cynical advertising and contending agendas'. In C. Johnson, J. Wanna and H.-A. Lee (eds) *Abbott's Gambit: The 2013 Australian Federal Election*. Canberra: ANU Press. doi.org/10.22459/AG.01.2015.01.

Wanna, J. 2015. 'Australia and New Zealand responses to the "fiscal tsunami" of the global financial crisis: Preparation and precipitous action with the promise of consolidation'. In J. Wanna, E. A. Lindquist and J. de Vries (eds) *The Global Financial Crisis and its Budget Impacts in OECD Nations: Fiscal Responses and Future Challenges*. Cheltenham, UK: Edward Elgar.

Wanna, J. 2015. 'Delivering under pressure: Public service, productivity and performance'. In J. Wanna, H. Lee and S. Yates (eds) *Managing Under Austerity, Delivering Under Pressure: Performance and Productivity in Public Service.* ANZSOG Series. Canberra: ANU Press. doi.org/10.22459/MUADUP.10. 2015.01.

Wanna, J. 2015. 'Policy analysis at the federal government level'. In B. Head and K. Crowley (eds) *Policy Analysis in Australia.* Bristol: Policy Press. doi.org/ 10.1332/policypress/9781447310273.003.0005.

Wanna, J. 2015. 'An impecunious election: The significance of fiscal and economic issues'. In C. Johnson, J. Wanna and H.-A. Lee (eds) *Abbott's Gambit: The 2013 Australian Federal Election.* Canberra: ANU Press. doi.org/ 10.22459/AG.01.2015.18.

Wanna, J. 2015. 'Introduction: Embracing new accountabilities, confronting new challenges – canvassing options for next generation improvements'. In J. Wanna, E. A. Lindquist and P. Marshall (eds) *New Accountabilities, New Challenges.* ANZSOG Series. Canberra: ANU Press. doi.org/10.22459/ NANC.04.2015.01.

Wanna, J. 2015. 'Through a glass darkly: The vicissitudes of budgetary reform in Australia'. In J. Wanna, E. A. Lindquist and P. Marshall (eds) *New Accountabilities, New Challenges.* ANZSOG Series. Canberra: ANU Press. (Originally presented as the Certified Practicing Accountants Annual Research Lecture.) doi.org/10.22459/NANC.04.2015.05.

Wanna, J. and M. Taflaga. 2015. 'Introduction: A dissident liberal – a principled political career'. In P. Baume, *A Dissident Liberal: The Political Writings of Peter Baume.* Edited by J. Wanna and M. Taflaga. Canberra: ANU Press. doi.org/10.22459/DL.09.2015.

Allen, P. and J. Wanna. 2016. 'Developing leadership and building executive capacity in the Australian public services for better governance'. In A. Podger et al. (eds) *Sharpening the Sword of State: Building Executive Capacities in the Public Services of the Asia-Pacific.* Canberra: ANU Press. doi.org/10.22459/ SSS.11.2016.02.

Wanna, J. 2018. 'Assessing the likelihood of proposed reform pathways to road pricing in Australia: Do they necessarily involve "diabolical politics"?' In M. de Percy and J. Wanna (eds) *Road Pricing and Provision: Changed Traffic Conditions Ahead.* ANZSOG Series. Canberra: ANU Press. doi.org/ 10.22459/RPP.07.2018.10.

Wanna, J. 2018. 'Government budgeting and the quest for value-for-money outcomes in Australia'. In A. Podger, T.-T. Su, H. Chan and J. Wanna (eds). 2018. *Value for Money: Budget and Financial Management Reform in the People's Republic of China, Taiwan and Australia.* ANZSOG Series. Canberra: ANU Press. doi.org/10.22459/VM.01.2018.02.

Wanna, J. and M. Taflaga. 2018. '"I'm not expecting to lose" ... the election overview and campaign narrative'. In A. Gauja, P. Chen, J. Curtin and J. Pietsch (eds) *Double Disillusion: The 2016 Australian Federal Election.* Canberra: ANU Press. doi.org/10.22459/DD.04.2018.02.

Wanna, J. 2020. 'Business'. In A. Gauja, M. Sawer and M. Simms (eds) *Morrison's Miracle: The 2019 Australian Federal Election.* Canberra: ANU Press. doi.org/10.22459/MM.2020.19.

Podger, A., H. S. Chan and J. Wanna. 2020. 'Designing governance structures for performance and accountability: Developments in Australia and greater China'. In A. Pdoger, T-t. Su, J. Wanna, H. S. Chan and M. Niu *Designing Governance Structures for Performance and Accountability: Developments in Australia and Greater China.* ANZSOG Series. Canberra, ACT: ANU Press. doi.org/10.22459/DGSPA.2020.01.

Wanna, J. 2020. 'Theorising public bureaucracies: Comparing organisational purpose, function and form, while counter-posing political control versus bureaucratic autonomy'. In A. Pdoger, T-t. Su, J. Wanna, H. S. Chan and M. Niu *Designing Governance Structures for Performance and Accountability: Developments in Australia and Greater China.* ANZSOG Series. Canberra, ACT: ANU Press. doi.org/10.22459/DGSPA.2020.02.

Wanna, J. 2021. 'Delivering public policy programs to senior executives in government—the Australia and New Zealand School of Government 2002–18'. In T. Mercer, R. Ayers, B. Head and J. Wanna (eds) *Learning Policy, Doing Policy: Interactions Between Public Policy Theory, Practice and Teaching.* ANZSOG Series. Canberra: ANU Press. doi.org/10.22459/LPDP.2021.04.

Journal articles

Wanna, J. 1980. 'The economic development of South Australia: A Marxist analysis'. *Journal of Australian Political Economy* 9(November): 3–24.

Wanna, J. 1982. 'Urban planning under social democracy – The case of Monarto, South Australia'. *Australian Quarterly* 54(3): 260–270. doi.org/10.2307/20635178.

Wanna, J. 1983. 'Groups in contention: Industrial relations theory'. *Arena* 64(September): 100–109.

Wanna, J. 1984. 'Regional development and economic restructuring in South Australia'. *Australian and New Zealand Journal of Sociology* 20(3): 350–364. doi.org/10.1177/144078338402000304.

Wanna, J. 1985. 'The motor vehicle industry in South Australia to 1945'. *Journal of the Historical Society of South Australia* 13: 139–144.

Wanna, J. 1987. 'A paradigm of consent: Explanations of working class moderation in South Australia'. *Labour History* 53(November): 54–72. doi.org/10.2307/27508860.

Coaldrake, P. and J. Wanna. 1988. '"Not like the good old days": The political impact of the Fitzgerald Inquiry into police corruption in Queensland'. *Australian Quarterly* 60(4): 404–414. doi.org/10.2307/20635502.

Davis, G. and J. Wanna. 1988. 'The Fitzgerald commission: The politics of inquiries'. *Canberra Bulletin of Public Administration* 55(June): 78–83.

Wanna, J. 1988. 'Industrialisation in South Australia: A reply to Stutchbury'. *Australian Economic History Review* 28(2): 75–84. doi.org/10.1111/aehr. 282005.

Wanna, J. 1989. 'Centralisation without corporatism: The politics of New Zealand business in the recession'. *New Zealand Journal of Industrial Relations* 14(1): 1–15. doi.org/10.26686/nzjir.v14i1.3772.

Wanna, J. 1989. 'A purchase on corruption: The Fitzgerald Inquiry into police corruption in Queensland'. *Australian Left Review* 3(July/August): 26–31.

Wanna, J. 1989. 'Ross Fitzgerald and Harold Thornton; *Labor in Queensland: From the 1880s to 1988*'. Book review. *Imago* 1(2): 64–65.

McCoy, E. and J. Wanna. 1991. 'The Queensland Nationals in opposition: The 1990 Cribb Report into the future directions of the party'. *Australian Quarterly* 63(2): 178–186. doi.org/10.2307/20635626.

Wanna, J. 1991. 'Community power debates: Themes, issues and remaining dilemmas'. *Urban Policy and Research* 9(4): 193–208. doi.org/10.1080/08111149108551470.

Wanna, J. 1991. 'The Hawke–Keating leadership challenge – June 1991'. *Policy, Organisation and Society* 3(Winter): 85–87. doi.org/10.1080/10349952.1991. 11876762.

Wanna, J. 1991. 'The politics of public budgeting'. *Australian Journal of Public Administration* 50(4): 572–573. doi.org/10.2307/977083.

Wanna, J. 1992. 'No Minister – Michael Pusey; *Economic Rationalism in Canberra – a Nation-Building State Changes its Mind*'. Book review. *Australian Left Review* 136(February): 43–44.

Wanna, J. 1992. 'Trust, distrust and public sector reform: Labor's managerialism in Queensland'. *Policy, Organisation and Society* 5(Winter): 74–82. doi.org/10.1080/10349952.1992.11876781.

Wanna, J. 1994. 'Awaiting better times: A faltering recovery'. *Australian Journal of Politics and History* 40(3): 391–396.

Wanna, J. 1994. '*Lobbying Canberra in the Nineties*, Peter Sekuless and *No is Not an Answer: Lobbying for Success*, Peter Cullen'. Book review. *Economic Analysis and Policy* 23(2): 200–201. doi.org/10.1016/S0313-5926(93)50040-1.

Caulfield, J. and J. Wanna. 1996. 'How do we manage our cities? Problems and prospects for urban policy in the 1990s'. *Policy, Organisation and Society* 12(Winter): 156–172. doi.org/10.1080/10349952.1996.11876656.

Forster, J., J. Kelly and J. Wanna. 1996. 'The rise and rise of the Department of Finance'. *Canberra Bulletin of Public Administration* 82(December).

Wanna, J. 1996. 'British public management: Achievements, problems and prospects'. *Australian Journal of Public Administration* 55(1): 127–129. doi.org/10.1111/j.1467-8500.1996.tb01191.x.

Wanna, J. and P. Weller. 1997. 'Departmental secretaries: Appointment, termination and their impact'. *Australian Journal of Public Administration* 56(4): 13–25. doi.org/10.1111/j.1467-8500.1997.tb02485.x.

Kelly, J. and J. Wanna. 1998. 'Same means, different ends? Expenditure management in Australia and Canada'. *Financial Management Institute Journal* 9(3): 18–25. Also appears in the French version of the same volume, with the title 'Même approche, résultats différents? La gestion des depenses en Australie et au Canada'.

Wanna, J. and P. Weller. 1998. 'When winners are losers: The stalemate of Australian politics'. *Asia-Pacific Review* 5(3): 87–104. doi.org/10.1080/13439009808719992.

Wanna, J. 1999. 'The international move to accrual methods of accounting and budgeting in the public sector: An Australian perspective'. *Financial Management Institute Journal* 10(3): 29–31. Also appears in the French version of the same volume, with the title 'Partout dans le monde, de plus en plus de pays adoptent la comptabilité d'exercise pour leur secteur public: le point de vue australien'.

Wanna, J. 1999. 'Once more into surplus: Reforming expenditure management in Australia and Canada'. *International Public Management Journal* 2(1): 127–146. doi.org/10.1016/S1096-7494(00)87435-8.

Kelly, J. and J. Wanna. 2000. 'New public management and the politics of government budgeting'. *International Public Management Review* 1(1): 33–55.

Wanna, J. 2001. 'A conservative debacle: The electoral rout in Queensland 2001'. *Australasian Parliamentary Review* 16(1): 34–44.

Wanna, J. 2001. 'A Nova Gestão Pública e as Politicas de Programaçao Orcamentária do Governo' ['New public management and the politics of government budgeting']. *Revista do Serviço Público* 52(3): 53–82.

Ryan, C. and J. Wanna. 2003. 'An impeditive administrative culture? The legacy of Australia's first Auditor-General on the Australian Audit Office'. *Australian Journal of Politics and History* 49(4): 469–480. doi.org/10.1111/j.1467-8497.2003.00309.x.

Wanna, J. 2003. 'Politics as a new vocation: The future of political science'. *Australian Journal of Political Science* 38(1): 141–148. doi.org/10.1080/1036 114032000056297.

Wanna, J. 2003, 'Whither the New Zealand experiment: Thermidorean reaction or rediscovering the importance of capacity – some views from New Zealand'. *Australian Journal of Public Administration* 62(4): 3–6. doi.org/10.1111/j..2003.00344.x.

Wanna, J. and P. Weller. 2003. 'Traditions of Australian governance'. *Public Administration: an International Quarterly* 81(1): 63–94. doi.org/10.1111/1467-9299.00337.

Arklay, T. and J. Wanna. 2004. 'The Queensland elections of 2004: The art of "non-campaigning"'. *Australasian Parliamentary Review* 19(1): 3–17.

Casey, J. and J. Wanna. 2004. 'Report on the national conference of the Institute of Public Administration of Australia, Brisbane 27–28 November 2003'. *Australian Journal of Public Administration* 63(4): 104–106. doi.org/10.1111/j.1467-8500.2004.00364.x.

Kelly, J. and J. Wanna. 2004. 'Crashing through with accrual-output price budgeting in Australia: Technical adjustment or a new way of doing business?' *American Review of Public Administration* 34(1): 94–111. doi.org/10.1177/0275074003253315.

Wanna, J. 2004. 'The 2004 federal election – Party platforms toward the public service'. *Australian Journal of Public Administration* 63(4): 119–122. doi.org/10.1111/j.1467-8500.2004.00408.x.

Scott, J. and J. Wanna. 2005. 'Trajectories of public administration and administrative history in Australia: Rectifying a "curious blight"'. *Australian Journal of Public Administration* 64(1): 11–24. doi.org/10.1111/j.1467-8500.2005.00412.x.

Sharma, B. and J. Wanna. 2005. 'Performance measures, measurement and reporting in government organisations'. *International Journal of Business Performance Management* 7(3): 320–333. doi.org/10.1504/IJBPM.2005.006723.

Wanna, J. 2005. 'The Australian federal election 2004: Howard's scare campaign prompted Labor's train-wreck'. *Representation* 41(4): 291–299. doi.org/10.1080/00344890508523324.

Wanna, J. 2005. 'Mapping research agendas with government: Surveys, priorities and future needs'. *Australian Journal of Public Administration* 64(1): 8–10. doi.org/10.1111/j.1467-8500.2005.00411.x.

Wanna, J. 2005. 'Prospects for regeneration in government – What we talk about is more important than what we do or how we do it'. *Australian Journal of Public Administration* 64(2): 20–26. doi.org/10.1111/j.1467-8500.2005.00432.x.

Wanna, J. 2006. 'From afterthought to afterburner: Australia's cabinet implementation unit'. *Journal of Comparative Policy Analysis* 8(4): 347–369. doi.org/10.1080/13876980600971334.

Wanna, J. 2006. 'Innovative state strategies in the Antipodes: Enhancing the ability of government to govern in the global context'. *Australian Journal of Political Science* 41(2): 161–176. doi.org/10.1080/10361140600672410.

Wanna, J. 2006. 'Insisting on traditional ministerial responsibility and the constitutional independence of the public service: the Gomery Inquiry and the Canadian sponsorship scandal'. *Australian Journal of Public Administration* 65(3): 15–21. doi.org/10.1111/j.1467-8500.2006.00490a.x.

Rhodes, R. A. W. and J. Wanna. 2007. 'The limits to public value, or rescuing responsible government from the platonic guardians'. *Australian Journal of Public Administration* 66(4): 406–421. doi.org/10.1111/j.1467-8500.2007.00553.x.

Wanna, J. 2007. 'Australian federalism: A polity of shared responsibilities and divided accountabilities'. *Journal of Comparative Government and European Policy* 5(2): 263–284. doi.org/10.1515/ZSE.2007.014.

Wanna, J. 2007. 'Improving federalism: Drivers of change, repair options and reform scenarios'. *Australian Journal of Public Administration* 66(3): 275–279. Reprinted in Brown, A. J. and A. Podger (eds). 2008. Australian Federalism – Rescue and Reform: Proceedings of the IPAA National Roundtable, Tenterfield, N.S.W., 23–25 October 2008, *Public Administration Today* 16(July–Sept): 36–41. doi.org/10.1111/j.1467-8500.2007.00541.x.

Rhodes, R. A. W. and J. Wanna. 2008. 'Stairways to Heaven: A reply to Alford'. *Australian Journal of Public Administration* 67(3): 367–370. doi.org/10.1111/j.1467-8500.2008.00594.x.

Rhodes, R. A. W., J. Wanna and P. Weller. 2008. 'Reinventing Westminster: How public executives frame their world'. *Policy & Politics* 36(4): 461–479. doi.org/10.1332/030557308X313705.

Wanna, J. 2008. 'Australia's national election 2007 – The triumph of semblance over substance'. *Representation – Journal of Representative Democracy* 44(1): 79–86. doi.org/10.1080/00344890801931709.

Wanna, J. 2008. 'Independence and responsiveness – Re-tying the Gordian Knot'. *Australian Journal of Public Administration* 67(3): 340–344. doi.org/10.1111/j.1467-8500.2008.00591.x.

Wanna, J. 2009. 'Bringing the politics back in: Public value in Westminster parliamentary government'. *Public Administration* 87(2): 161–183. doi.org/10.1111/j.1467-9299.2009.01763.x.

Wanna, J. 2009. 'Health governance – Redesigning the structure of Australia's national health system'. *Public Administration Today* 18(January–March): 22–25.

Wanna, J. 2010. 'Business and unions'. In 'Kevin '07 – The 2007 Australian election, part 2', special issue. *Australian Cultural History: The Journal of the History of Culture in Australia* 28(1): 15–22. doi.org/10.1080/07288430903165287.

Wanna, J. 2010. 'The changing climate for public sector governance'. *Public Administration Today* 21(January–March): 9–10.

Wanna, J. 2010. 'The global financial crisis of 2008–2009: Learning how not to repeat the mistakes'. *Public Administration Today* 21(January–March): 16–19.

Wanna, J. 2011. 'To collaborate means to share responsibilities – IPAA's 2010 national conference report'. *Public Administration Today* 25(January–March): 9–10.

Wanna, J. 2011. 'Treasury and economic policy – Beyond the dismal science'. *Australian Journal of Public Administration* 70(4): 347–364. doi.org/10.1111/j.1467-8500.2011.00747.x.

Wanna, J. and P. Weller. 2011. 'The irrepressible Rod Rhodes: Contesting traditions and blurring genres'. *Public Administration* 89(1): 1–14. doi.org/10.1111/j.1467-9299.2011.01902.x.

Chan, M., J. Ma, A. Podger, T.-T. Su and J. Wanna. 2012. 'Putting the citizens at the centre: Making government more responsive'. *Australian Journal of Public Administration* 71(2): 101–110. doi.org/10.1111/j.1467-8500.2012.00773.x.

Podger, A., J. Ma, H. Chan, T.-T. Su and J. Wanna. 2013. 'Recalibrating a dynamic balance: Local autonomy within national policy frameworks able to adjust to changing circumstances'. *Australian Journal of Public Administration* 72(3): 189–200. doi.org/10.1111/1467-8500.12022.

Wanna, J. 2013. 'Critiquing performance management regimes and their links to budgetary decision-making and resource allocation'. *Public Administration and Policy* 16(2): 5–16.

Wanna, J. 2014. 'Australia's future as a "Westminster democracy" – threats to combat, stark choices to make …'. *Australian Journal of Public Administration* 73(1): 19–28. doi.org/10.1111/1467-8500.12068.

Wanna, J. 2014. 'A most peculiar implosion – the Australian federal election September 2013: A case of a fractured government that inflicted defeat upon itself'. *Representation* 50(2): 271–281. doi.org/10.1080/00344893.2014.934506.

In addition to these articles, John Wanna wrote a regular series of 'Political Chronicles' for the *Australian Journal of History and Politics* with 26 consecutive six-monthly chronicles on Queensland politics from 1990 to 2004, and 35 chronicles on federal politics from 2005 to 2020 (each published in the June and December issues of the journal).

Important occasional papers and conference papers

Wanna, J. 1989. 'Australian intergovernmental relations and business policy'. In Centre for Australian Public Sector Management (ed.) Managing Intergovernmental Relations in Australia: Two Case Studies. Research Paper No. 7. Brisbane: Griffith University.

Head, B., J. Wanna and J. Warburton. 1990. Implications of 'Fiscal Centralisation' for Public Sector Management in Australia. Research Paper No. 11. Brisbane: Centre for Australian Public Sector Management, Griffith University.

Caulfield, J. and J. Wanna. 1994. 'Federalism and the problem of coordination in planning policy and policy-centric versus urban-centric approaches to the city'. In *Metropolis Now: Getting It Right City Image Conference, Brisbane, Australia, March 14–18 – Handbook and Proceedings*. Brisbane Development Association.

Forster, J. and J. Wanna. 1995. 'The implementation of devolved resource management in the Commonwealth budget sector under the running costs arrangements'. Major review of Devolution of Running Cost Flexibilities, prepared as issues paper for Commonwealth Parliament. House of Representatives Standing Committee on Banking, Finance and Public Administration: ss. 188–205.

Wanna, J. 2000. 'Negotiating the boundaries between electoral and political inquiry'. In J. Peace and J. Taylor (eds) *Electoral Research – The Core and the Boundaries*. Adelaide: South Australia State Electoral Office Research Series.

Wanna, J. 2001. 'One step forward – Two steps back? Do governments spend our money better?' Public Lecture Series 2001, Griffith University, Nathan, Queensland, 25 October.

Wanna, J. 2002. 'Is the house underestimated?' *About the House: House of Representatives Magazine* 14(November–December): 31–32.

Ryan, C. and Wanna, J. 2003. 'Research report on review of budgetary processes in six sub-national jurisdictions: Participatory budgeting in the ACT'. Report to the Scottish Parliament, under International Team Leader and Convenor Professor Colin Talbot (UK).

Wanna, J. 2004. 'Democratic and electoral shifts in Queensland: Back to first past the post voting'. Democratic Audit of Australia, The Australian National University, Canberra. Available at: apo.org.au/sites/default/files/resource-files/2004-03/apo-nid8397.pdf.

Wanna, J. 2005. 'Public service, public values: The implementation of a charter of values in the Australian Public Service'. Paper presented at the Australasian Political Studies Association Conference, Otago University, Dunedin, New Zealand, 28–30 September.

Wanna, J. 2006. 'Between a rock and a hard place: The nonsense of Australia's Charter of Budget Honesty Act 1998'. Paper presented at the Australasian Political Studies Association Conference, Newcastle, 25–27 September.

Wanna, J. 2013. 'Towards a stronger, more equitable and efficient tax-social security system: Report on the proceedings of the Castles Tax and Social Security Roundtable'. Academy of the Social Sciences in Australia – Academy Papers 1/2013: 10–27.

Teaching cases (researched and written for the Australia and New Zealand School of Government [ANZSOG])

2010. *Institution-building at the Department of Climate Change: Administrative Leadership of a Roller-Coaster Ride* (A) 2010–117.1, (B) 2010–117.2 and (C) 2010–117.3. With Paul 't Hart.

2011. *Treasury and the Global Financial Crisis* (A) 2011–119.1 and (B) 2011–119.2. With Paul 't Hart.

2012. *Improving Decision Making in Government Service Delivery.* (i) The Federal Government's response to the Global Financial Crisis; and (ii) to the Northern Territory Emergency Response (NT Intervention). ANZSOG Case Program/ Department of Prime Minister and Cabinet.

Other professional writing

Wanna, J. 1982. 'Trade unions in South Australia'. Curatorial text. Adelaide: Constitutional Museum.

Wanna, J. 1983. 'The Labour movements and the Labor Party in the 1890s'. *South Australia in the 1890s.* Adelaide: Constitutional Museum.

Wanna, J. 1994. 'Factional influence in the Queensland Government'. In Caxton Legal Centre, *Heal Street News No. 917,* (December): 1–14.

Wanna, J. 1996. 'The changing conditions of appointment and termination of department secretaries in the APS'. Mimeograph. Institute of Public Administration Australia, December.

Wanna, J. 2003. 'ASAP corporate services review and the shared services initiatives: Problems with aligning services and priorities'. *Public Interest* (newsletter of Institute of Public Administration Australia Queensland) April: 12–14.

Appendix 2: Higher degree students supervised by John Wanna 1983–2020

Year	Student	Higher degree research program	Main topic
Higher degree students (Masters) at Canterbury and Griffith Universities			
1984	Phillip Cheyne	Univ Cant MPhil	Administrative policies in New Zealand
1988	Yvonne Bain	Griffith Univ MPhil	Postwar compulsory education policy in Australia
1989	Alan Forbes	Griffith Univ MAdmin	Industrial planning for the cement industry
1991	Peter Graham	Griffith Univ MPhil	The Australia Card – A case study
1991	Chris Case	Griffith Univ MAdmin	Deductible gift recipient funding for health services
1991	Annette P Hogan	Griffith Univ MAdmin	Devolved public management in public rehabilitation services
1993	Judith Robb	Griffith Univ MAdmin	Program management in health
1994	Michael Lord	Griffith Univ MAdmin	Agricultural research funding policy in government
1994	Deidre Baker	Griffith Univ MAdmin	Implementing vocational education policies
1994	Mark McDonnell	Griffith Univ MBA	Funding government nursing homes
1994	Geoffrey Murphy	Griffith Univ MBA	A more productive detective in policing
1995	Rochelle Jesser	Griffith Univ MAdmin	Industrial regional development in Queensland

Year	Student	Higher degree research program	Main topic
1996	Karalise Goodwin	Griffith Univ MAdmin	Equity and accountability policies in the Queensland Public Service
1996	Daniel Baldwin	Griffith Univ MAdmin	Prison policies towards sex offenders
1997	Patricia Roche	Griffith Univ MAdmin	Parliamentary ethics policies and practices (pecuniary interests)
1997	Geoffrey Carpenter	Griffith Univ MAdmin	Performance benchmarking in public agencies
1997	Paul Woodward	Griffith Univ MAdmin	Regionalisation in the Queensland public sector
1999	Tony Wade	Griffith Univ MAdmin	Accountability in Meals on Wheels
1999	Bob Shead	Griffith Univ MBA	Implementing accrual budgeting in Australia
2001	Brett Schimming	Griffith Univ MAdmin	Strategic leadership in organisations
2002	Karen Struthers	Griffith Univ MAdmin	Public–private partnerships in state government schools
Higher degree students (PhD) Griffith University			
1991	Stephen Bell	Griffith Univ PhD	Manufacturing and the state
1991	Brian Roper	Griffith Univ PhD	Political economy of New Zealand
1993	Neal Ryan	Griffith Univ PhD	Implementation of technology
1995	Christine Ryan	Griffith Univ PhD	Accrual accounting in government
1995	Peter Backhouse	Griffith/Adelaide Univs PhD	Doctors and governments in delivering health policy
1996	Debra Harker	Griffith Univ PhD	Self-regulation in advertising
1998	John Pragasam	Griffith Univ PhD	Accountancy issues and efficacy in the public sector
2000	Xandra Flach	Griffith Univ PhD	Labor's factions in Queensland
2001	Kai-Chee Cheung	Griffith Univ PhD	Budgeting in Chinese governments
2001	Joanne Kelly	Griffith Univ PhD	Comparative budgeting and expenditure control
2002	Geoff Allen	Griffith Univ PhD	History of public service efficiency drives
2002	Edward Cruz	Griffith Univ PhD	Economic policy

Year	Student	Higher degree research program	Main topic
2003	Ashley Lavelle	Griffith Univ PhD	Federal Labor in opposition
2004	Scott Prasser	Griffith Univ PhD	Royal commissions
2004	Geoff Edwards	Griffith Univ PhD	Public policy and leadership
2005	Alex Gash	Griffith Univ PhD	Comparative state pensions schemes and rationing
2006	Brian Stephenson	Griffith Univ PhD	Vince Gair as Queensland Premier and senator
2010	Tracey Arklay	Griffith Univ PhD	Arthur Fadden as PM
2011	Suzanne Lawson	Griffith Univ PhD	Place management and spatial targeting in service delivery
2013	Mary-Ann McQuestin	Griffith Univ PhD	Federal financial arrangements under Rudd
Higher degree students (PhD) at The Australian National University (ANU)			
2006	James Matthews	ANU PhD	Executive management and Senate scrutiny of legislation
2007	Chris Beer	ANU PhD	Urban planning for communities
2008	Stewart Ashe	ANU PhD	Defence policies
2010	Alison Procter (Oakleigh)	ANU PhD	Not-for-profits working for governments
2011	Robyn Hardy	ANU PhD	Cost-shifting in Australia
2012	Karen Tindall	ANU PhD	Consular services overseas
2012	Christopher Vas	ANU PhD	Public service adaptability
2012	Michael de Percy	ANU PhD	Introduction of broadband
2013	Harvey Whiteford	ANU PhD	Shaping national mental health strategies
2013	John Butcher	ANU PhD	Government compacts with NGO sector
2014	Adam Masters	ANU PhD	International partnerships: NGOs and policymaking
2014	James Low	ANU PhD	Singaporean public service executive training
2015	Marija Taflaga	ANU PhD	Opposition policymaking
2016	Tanja Porter	ANU PhD	Social media impacts on policy
2017	John Hawkins	ANU PhD	Treasurers and Treasury
2017	Tom King	ANU MPhil	Lifespans of minor political parties
2017	Ram Ghimire	ANU PhD	Nepalese public sector reform

Year	Student	Higher degree research program	Main topic
2019	Val Barnett	ANU PhD	Deficiencies in the management of parliaments
2019	Isi Unikowski	ANU PhD	Intergovernmental administrative relations
2020	Stephen Darlington	ANU PhD	The outcomes of e-health initiatives in Australia, USA and UK
2020	Mansur Chisni	ANU PhD	Medium-term expenditure frameworks in East Asia
2020	Grant Douglas	ANU PhD	ICT fiascos in government payroll systems
Current higher degree students (PhD)			
In progress	Michael O'Toole	ANU PhD	Shared services models
In progress	Robert McMahon	ANU PhD	Adaptive leadership in the public service
In progress	Andrew Morgan	ANU PhD	Cost-benefits and rate of returns on public investments
In progress	Joy Yabo Yan	ANU PhD	Primary care health policies
In progress	Warren Thomson	Bond Univ PhD	Major party responses to minor parties
In progress	Ann Hogan	Griffith Univ PhD	Biography of Tom Burns – Labor politician